REVISE
GEOGRAPHY

A COMPLETE REVISION COURSE FOR
GCSE

Clifford Lines MSc (Econ)
Formerly Assistant Director,
E. Sussex College of Higher Education

Laurie Bolwell MA, DPhil, FColl P
Head of Department of In-Service Development
University of Brighton

BPP Letts Educational Ltd

First published 1979

Revised 1981, 1983, 1989, 1992

Illustrations: Tek-Art, Ian Foulis Ltd

© C. J. Lines and L. H. Bolwell 1979, 1981, 1983, 1987, 1989, 1992
© Illustrations: BPP (Letts Educational) Ltd 1979, 1981, 1983, 1987, 1989, 1992

All our Rights Reserved. No part of this
publication may be reproduced, stored in
a retrieval system, or transmitted, in any
form or by any means, electronic, mechanical,
photocopying, recording or otherwise, without
the prior permission of BPP (Letts Educational) Ltd

British Library Cataloguing in Publication Data
Lines, C. J.
 Revise geography: a complete revision
 course for GCSE. –4th ed. –(Letts
 study aids)
 1. Geography – Examinations, questions, etc
 I. title   II. Bolwell, L. H.
 910´.76 G131

ISBN 1 85758 008 7

Printed in Great Britain by BPCC Wheatons Ltd, Exeter

 Acknowledgements

The authors and publishers are grateful to the following organizations for permission to reprint material to which they hold copyright:

Text and artwork
Examining groups: London East Anglian Group pp.143, 149; Midland Examining Group pp 140, 145, 146; Northern Examining Association pp. 151, 153; Northern Ireland Schools Examinations and Assessment Council p.142; Scottish Examination Board p.149; Southern Examining Group p.151; Welsh Joint Education Committee p.139. *Others:* BAA plc, p. 138; Cambridge University Press, *South American Development: a Geographical Introduction* by R & R Bromley, p.103; Macmillan, 'Learning through Fieldwork' from *The Geography Teacher's Guide to the Classroom* by Laws, p.163 and *Ordnance Survey Mapwork–a course for first examinations* by Worthington and Gant, pp.161 and 162; *Punch*, p.49; *The Times*, p.137.

Photographs
Aerofilms, pp. 2, 10, 11, 16, 47, 59, 136; Associated Press, pp. 19, 110; Barnaby's p. 137; J. Allan Cash, pp. 82; Newcastle City Council, p. 31; Oxfam, p. 105; Presse- und Informationsamt der Bundersregierung, p.77; Spectrum, pp.102, 107; USDA Soil Conservation Service, p.117; Dr A.C. Waltham, p.13.

CONTENTS

Preface	v
Introduction	vii
Analysis Table of Examination Syllabuses	x
The GCSE	xii

1 Map work and physical geography

1.1	Interpretation of OS Map 1:50 000	1
1.2	Interpretation of OS Map 1:25 000	3
1.3	Interpretation of weather maps and meteorological information	4
1.4	The hydrological cycle: river valleys	7
1.5	Glaciation	9
1.6	Coastal environments	11
1.7	Desert environments	13
1.8	Limestone and chalk environments	15
1.9	Granite environments	16
1.10	Volcanoes and earthquakes	17

2 The British Isles

2.1	Climate and weather	20
2.2	Farming as a system	20
2.3	Farming contrasts	22
2.4	Energy resources	24
2.5	Location of industry	27
2.6	Manufacturing industries	29
2.7	Industrial growth and decline	31
2.8	Service industries	33
2.9	Transport networks	35
2.10	Ports	36
2.11	Population distribution and movement	38
2.12	New towns and expanded towns	40
2.13	Urban land use	42
2.14	The functions of settlements	44
2.15	Urban planning	47
2.16	Regional contrasts–Industries of the London Basin	50
2.17	Regional contrasts–South Wales	52
2.18	Regional contrasts–The Scottish Highlands and Islands	54
2.19	National Parks	56
2.20	The holiday industry	59

3 Western Europe

3.1	Population distribution in Norway and Sweden	61
3.2	Agricultural problems in the EC	62
3.3	Farming in Denmark	65
3.4	Land reclamation in the Netherlands	66
3.5	Energy resources	68
3.6	An old-established industrial region	70
3.7	Movements of population	72

3.8	Service industries in Switzerland	74
3.9	Inland waterways	75
3.10	Rotterdam	77
3.11	Urban development–Paris	78
3.12	Regional contrasts–Ranstad	80
3.13	Regional contrasts–Southern Italy	80
3.14	Regional contrasts–Norwegian fjords	82
3.15	Mediterranean tourism	83

4 The developing world

4.1	The development gap	85
4.2	Hunger and poverty	86
4.3	The savanna lands	88
4.4	Farming in the monsoon lands	89
4.5	The tropical rain forest ecosystem	92
4.6	Exporting food crops and forest products	94
4.7	Opening up empty regions	96
4.8	The Green Revolution	98
4.9	Developing transport networks	99
4.10	Establishing new industries	101
4.11	Multi-purpose development schemes	103
4.12	Urbanization and the growth of shanty towns	104
4.13	A developing world city–Mexico City	106
4.14	Tourism in the developing world–Tanzania	108
4.15	Aid from the developed world	109

5 Social and environmental issues

5.1	The growth of world population	112
5.2	Exhaustion of natural resources	113
5.3	Hostile environments	114
5.4	Land use and ownership conflicts	115
5.5	Soil erosion and conservation	117
5.6	Irrigation	118
5.7	The greenhouse effect	119
5.8	Air pollution	121
5.9	Water pollution	122
5.10	Traffic in cities	123

6 Self-test unit

6.1	Map work and physical geography	125
6.2	The British Isles	126
6.3	Western Europe	127
6.4	The less developed world	128
6.5	Social and environmental issues	129

7	**An analysis of examination questions**	132
8	**Practice in answering questions**	139
9	**Coursework and fieldwork**	160
10	**The Examination**	165
	Skills	167
	Glossary	168
	Index	174

PREFACE

Many people regard examinations in the same way as a visit to the dentist—an unpleasant necessity which causes much anxiety beforehand, but which can give great relief once the event is over. The analogy is not perfect, since before an examination a great deal of preparation is possible which can reduce or eliminate anxiety in the examination room, whereas no similar preparation is possible before a visit to the dentist.

This book is designed to give you a greater understanding of the GCSE course in Geography, and what will be expected of you in the examination. It is not, however, an examination 'crammer', nor does it contain model answers which can be learned parrot-fashion, only to be promptly forgotten once the examination is over.

We have attempted to retain in this new edition the best of the original material, while recognizing that the subject is constantly evolving, and that new techniques and new approaches have replaced out-moded topics and ideas. Examples of questions set by the seven Examination Groups have been included. They have been selected from the most recent examination papers that are available and advice is given as to how they should be answered.

The core units have been selected to cover the major topics and issues which may occur in the examinations, but this book is not intended to be a guide to 'spotting' questions. Any attempt at 'spotting' is your own responsibility, since it is you who will benefit or suffer from the consequences.

The production of this book has been very much a team effort, the support for our writing from other members of the team, which we have greatly appreciated. In addition to the help and encouragement of the staff at Letts Educational, we have received detailed advice and criticisms from three specialist advisers whose experience of the teaching and examining of Geography has been of the utmost value. We should like to express our special thanks to these advisers: Graham Browne, a secondary school teacher closely involved with GCSE Geography planning in his own school in Hertfordshire; John Graham, Adviser in Social Subjects, Renfrew Division, and a member of the Joint Working Party in Geography set up to design the courses and examinations for Foundation, General and Credit levels in Scotland; and Norman law, Head of Geography and Assistant Head of Upper School, Waingel's Copse School near Reading.

Although many people have helped us in a variety of ways, any shortcomings which this book may possess are entirely our responsibility.

C.J. Lines
L.H. Bolwell
August 1992

INTRODUCTION

Guide to using this book

This book has been designed to meet the needs of students taking the GCSE, or the Standard Grade of the Scottish Certificate of Education examination. Its main object is to help you to acquire the knowledge, understanding, skills and values which will enable you to give your best performance in the Geography examination. It contains core material which is central to the syllabuses, a self-test unit, an analysis of examination questions, and guidelines as to how they should be answered, as well as advice on coursework and the written examination.

We know that these examinations are a demanding challenge and that your school or college will have provided some preparation. Nevertheless, during our many years as examiners, we have found that a significant number of candidates, through inexperience and inadequate preparation, lack confidence when faced by an examination paper, and consequently fail, or obtain low marks. Many candidates who are expected to obtain good results could do even better if they knew how to make the most of the opportunities which the examination situation provides.

This book is not intended as a substitute for the many excellent textbooks available. It has been written to complement them by providing advice based on experience, which will enable you to approach the examination with understanding and confidence.

To get the best from the study scheme in this book you are advised to follow the procedure outlined below.

1 USING THE ANALYSIS TABLE OF EXAMINATION SYLLABUSES

The analysis table on pages x–xi shows how the core material in units 1–5 relates to the specific syllabuses set by the Examination Groups. Many syllabuses contain options, so that candidates have a choice of topics, but in drawing up this chart we have included all the options. Consequently you should check what options your school expects you to take, and then select only those topics in the columns which are relevant to your programme.

Syllabuses change from time to time, so that information provided may be out of date. If in doubt, consult your teacher — the table is intended only to be a useful guide. A list of Examination Groups and the Boards which make up each group has also been included (page xv), since many teachers, as well as candidates, may want to know where to write for details of the syllabuses and further information.

2 THE GCSE EXAMINATION

The GCSE is a national examination, and the important questions you might want to ask about the examination have been identified and answered in some detail.

3 REVISING AND TESTING YOURSELF

Before you begin to work through the core material, turn to 'Planning a revision programme' on page viii, where you are told how to plan your revision so that the actual examination is the final stage of many weeks of preparation.

Units 1–5 contain the core material of the book. These units consist of five main topics which have been broken down further into a number of sub-units. The units have been carefully chosen because we know that may candidates do not have the time to revise the whole syllabus and a selection must, therefore, be made. Our choice of units is based on careful analysis of the syllabuses prepared by the GCSE Examination Groups. You will also need to make a personal selection, based on the particular requirements of your Examination Group. Some of the units are case studies drawn from a particular region or continent. They can be used to answer questions of a more general nature, or as a basis for similar studies in other parts of the world. This core material is followed by a self-test unit which provides an opportunity for revision of the information in the core units.

4 DIFFERENT KINDS OF QUESTION

In unit 7 there is a careful analysis of the various types of examination question which are set and the particular problems associated with each. A study of this section will help you to understand how each type of question should be tackled.

5 PRACTICE IN ANSWERING QUESTIONS

Unit 8 contains a selection of examples of examination questions for you to work through. Guidance on what should be included in your answers is given at the end of the questions in the answer section.

ADVICE ON COURSEWORK AND FIELDWORK

Now that coursework and fieldwork are a compulsory part of the examination and worth at least 20 per cent of the final examination marks, it is essential for you to know how to plan your work and how to present it to achieve maximum effect. Unit 9 shows you the stages you should follow when carrying out a project or piece of fieldwork, and suggests ways in which your findings should be presented.

LAST MINUTE ADVICE

Unit 10 gives advice on what you should do during the period immediately before the examination and how you can make the best use of your time during the examination itself.

Learning and understanding

A proportion of the marks in the GCSE examination will be allocated for factual information which you should have learned. Geography is a subject which deals with an extensive variety of facts and these need to be learned and understood.

There are a number of ways in which this can be done. Some people prefer reading about something several times, before testing themselves to see how much they can remember. Others write notes and draw sketch maps as they read, and use the notes for revision purposes. Another means of learning is to write down only key words or sentences and to learn these by heart. In this method sketch maps and diagrams are simplified and treated in the same way as key words. Whatever method you decide is best for you, and it may not be one of the three already described, use it consistently and do not worry if your friends have adopted a totally different approach.

Do not fall into the trap of believing that you are learning a great deal just because you are spending many hours reading books or writing notes. The only real test of whether you know and understand what you have read is by writing out from memory the main points and then checking them against the material you have read.

Although knowledge of facts is essential, the emphasis in the examination is towards the application of these facts, and you must be able to show that you understand how significant they are in a particular situation. For example, the types of aid given by developed countries to countries of the developing world can be learned as a list. What is more significant is being able to recognize which forms of aid are needed by developing countries. This requires an understanding of their physical, historical, cultural and economic backgrounds. Egypt's problems are different from those of the Sudan, its neighbour to the south, and the types of aid needed are consequently different.

The emphasis in the examination towards questions which require you to interpret information, give opinions and form judgements means that you cannot base your learning solely on your ability to remember facts. It is essential that you understand what you have learned and can apply your knowledge to dif-ferent situations. One of the best ways of doing this is to practise answering questions which pose problems or ask you to use data in the form of statistics, maps, photographs or charts. A range of these questions is to be found in Section 8, and your school may have other examples.

It is essential to know the basic ideas which underly the various topics on which you may be examined. In this book, the basic ideas associated with each unit have been listed at the end of the unit.

The GCSE will test your knowledge of, and ability to use skills such as interpretation of maps and photographs, and the drawing of graphs and charts. Understanding of skills is very important, as in many cases twice as many marks are allocated for skills as for recall of facts. One way you should prepare for the examination is by checking to see how many of these skills and ideas you understand thoroughly. The self-test exercises in Section 6 will help you to identify your strengths and weaknesses.

Finally, you must also be aware of values and attitudes as they can be applied to specific situations and environments. Reference to these values is made in a number of the core units.

Planning a revision programme

DIFFERING VIEWPOINTS ON EXAMINATIONS

You may find that your friends and teachers have differing views about examinations. Some people dismiss examinations as an evil which should not disturb the normal pattern of life any more than is necessary. In other words, they do not consider that there should be detailed preparation before an examination and they often suggest that people who spend long hours revising are doing themselves more harm than good.

At the other extreme, some people you know may take examinations very seriously. They believe in revising for many weeks before the exam and think it necessary to burn the midnight oil until the day of the examination. Total dedication to revision is the only means, they consider, by which the best results can be achieved.

Between these two extremes there are many viewpoints and there is no doubt that the method which best suits one candidate may not suit another. You may have friends whom you envy because of the apparent ease and speed with which they can complete their homework and examination revision. Indeed, you may be such a person yourself, but for the majority of people a sensibly planned programme of work before an examination is of immeasurable value.

GETTING THE TIMING RIGHT

An examination is similar in many ways to a track event in athletics or an important match on the games field. The performer needs to reach peak condition just as the event is about to take place. Good athletes have a carefully designed training schedule which tunes them both physically and mentally for the event. A training programme for an examination may seem like taking the matter too seriously, but there is much to be said for having a systematic revision programme which will allow you to produce your best performance at the time of the examination. The emphasis must be on planning the work and keeping to a timetable, so that the revision is not done as an indigestible lump just before the written papers are taken.

A REVISION SCHEDULE

Geography is only one of perhaps six or more subjects which you will be examined in at GCSE, and it is important, therefore, to work out a revision schedule which gives sufficient time to each of the subjects which will be examined. Bearing this in mind, the following timetable has been drawn up for examinations which it is assumed will take place in mid-June. A similar time-scale would apply to a November or January examination. For Scottish students with the Standard Grade SCE in mid-May, the time-scale below should be put back by one month.

1 Last week in March

(a) Review performance in mock examination, if one was held. Identify weaknesses for particular attention.

(b) Draw up revision schedule, selecting the necessary material in this book and in any other.

(c) Plan a weekly programme for the months of April and May. As part of April is likely to include the Easter vacation, increase the work-load for this period accordingly.

(d) Plan to complete the revision schedule about two weeks before the examination takes place, *i.e.* by the beginning of June. This should allow time to look at the main revision points in the days before the examination.

2 April and May

Follow your revision schedule, allocating a number of hours at different times of the week for Geography. It is difficult to be precise about the number of hours you should spend, since this will depend partly on the other subjects and your school timetable. Five hours per week in one-hour sessions is a rough estimate of the amount of time you should spend.

3 The two weeks before the examination

Spend this time refreshing your memory of the most important revision points. Use the self-test questions (Section 6) in this book if you have not already done so.

By this time, given a heading such as 'The Savanna Lands', you should be able to make brief notes about the climate, physical features, soils, vegetation, natural resources, agriculture and problems of this region. You should also be able to mark savanna regions on a map of the world and to recognize temperature and rainfall charts for these regions, whether they are north or south of the Equator.

Analysis Table of Examination Syllabuses 1993

		LEAG			MEG					NEA					NISEAC	SEB	SEG				WJEC
Syllabus		A	B	D	A	B	C	D	E§	A	B	C	D	E			A 1163	A (Ex) 1165	B 1166	M* 1183	0118
Number of papers		3	2	2	1	1	1–2	1	2	2	1–2	2	2	2	1–2	1–2	2	3	2	1	2
Method of differentiation C=Common papers D=Different papers S=Stepped papers		C	C	D	D	D	D	D	S	S	S	S	S	S	D	D	S	S	C	C	D/S
Objective test		•								•											
OS or similar map question ?=may be set					• ?	•		•	• ?		•		• ?	• ?	• ?	• ?	•	•			
Value of coursework % of Total		30	40	25	25	28	20-50	50	40	25	25-60	30	50	20	20	50	25	0	40	80	20
Mapwork and physical geography																					
1.1	1:50 000 OS map			•	•	•		•				•	•	•	•	•	•				
1.2	1:25 000 OS map			•	•			•			•		•	•	•	•	•	•			
1.3	Interpretation of weather maps	•		•									•		•	•	•	•			•
1.4	The hydrological cycle: river valleys	•	•	•	•	•	•	•	•	•	•	•	•	•	•	•	•	•	•	•	•
1.5	Glaciation				•	•		•	•			•				•	•	•	•		•
1.6	Coastal environments		•	•	•	•		•	•		•	•				•	•	•	•		•
1.7	Dessert environments					•		•	•		•						•	•			
1.8	Limestone and chalk environments				•	•		•	•			•				•		•	•		
1.9	Granite environments				•	•		•	•			•			•		•	•			•
1.10	Volcanoes and earthquakes				•	•	•	•		•		•				•	•	•	•	•	•
The British Isles																					
2.1	Climate and weather	•			•							•	•	•	•	•	•	•			•
2.2	Farming as a system	•	•	•	•	•	•	•	•	•	•	•	•	•	•	•	•	•	•	•	•
2.3	Farming contrasts	•	•	•	•	•	•	•		•	•	•	•	•		•	•	•	•		•
2.4	Energy resources	•	•	•	•	•	•	•	•	•	•	•	•	•	•	•	•	•	•	•	•
2.5	Location of industry	•	•	•	•	•	•	•	•	•	•	•	•	•	•	•	•	•	•	•	•
2.6	Manufacturing industry	•	•	•	•	•	•	•	•	•	•	•	•	•	•	•	•	•	•	•	•
2.7	Industrial growth and decline	•	•	•	•	•	•	•	•	•	•	•	•	•	•	•	•	•	•	•	•
2.8	Service industries	•	•	•	•	•	•	•	•			•	•	•	•	•	•	•	•	•	•
2.9	Transport networks	•	•	•		•	•	•		•	•	•				•	•	•	•		•
2.10	Ports	•		•		•				•	•	•						•	•		•
2.11	Population distribution and movement	•	•	•	•	•	•	•	•	•	•	•	•	•	•	•	•	•	•	•	•
2.12	New and expanded towns	•	•	•		•	•	•	•	•	•	•		•		•	•	•	•		•
2.13	Urban land use	•	•	•	•	•	•	•	•	•	•	•	•	•	•	•	•	•	•	•	•
2.14	Settlement functions	•	•	•	•	•	•	•	•	•	•	•	•	•	•	•	•	•	•	•	•
2.15	Urban planning	•	•	•	•	•	•	•	•		•	•	•	•	•	•	•	•	•		•
2.16	Regional contrasts: the London Basin		•					•				•		•		•	•	•			
2.17	Regional contrasts: South Wales		•			•		•								•		•	•		•
2.18	Regional contrasts: Scottish Highlands/Isles		•					•								•		•	•		•
2.19	National Parks	•	•	•				•		•		•					•	•	•	•	
2.20	Holiday centres	•	•	•		•	•	•		•	•	•				•	•	•	•	•	
Western Europe																					
3.1	Population distribution in Norway and Sweden	•				•	•														
3.2	Agricultural problems in the EC	•	•			•	•	•			•		•	•	•						
3.3	Farming in Denmark	•		•		•		•			•			•							•
3.4	Land reclamation in the Netherlands	•			•			•									•	•			
3.5	Energy resources	•	•					•				•			•	•					•

Analysis Table of Examination Syllabuses 1993

		LEAG			MEG					NEA					NISEAC	SEB	SEG				WJEC
	Syllabus	A	B	D	A	B	C	D	E §	A	B	C	D	E			A 1163	A (Ex) 1165	B 1166	M * 1183	0118
	Number of papers	3	2	2	1	1	1–2	1	2	2	1–2	2	2	2	1–2	1–2	2	3	2	1	2
	Method of differentiation C=Common papers D=Different papers S=Stepped papers	C	C	D	D	D	D	D	S	S	S	S	S	S	D	D	S	S	C	C	D/S
	Objective test	•								•											
	OS or similar map question ?=may be set				•?	•		•	•?		•		•?	•?	•?	•?	•	•			
	Value of coursework % of Total	30	40	25	25	28	20-50	50	40	25	25-60	30	50	20	20	50	25	0	40	80	20
3.6	An old-established industrial region	•	•		•	•	•	•		•	•		•			•	•	•	•	•	•
3.7	Movements of population	•	•		•	•	•	•	•	•	•	•	•			•	•	•	•	•	•
3.8	Service industries in Switzerland	•	•		•	•		•	•		•	•								•	•
3.9	Inland waterways	•	•			•	•	•			•						•	•	•		•
3.10	Rotterdam	•				•					•										
3.11	Urban development: Paris	•	•		•	•	•	•	•	•	•	•	•			•		•	•		•
3.12	Regional contrasts: Randstad	•	•		•	•	•	•		•	•	•	•					•	•	•	
3.13	Regional contrasts: Southern Italy	•				•	•	•		•	•		•					•	•	•	
3.14	Regional contrasts: Norwegian fjords									•	•		•	•							
3.15	Mediterranean tourism	•	•	•	•	•	•	•	•	•	•		•			•	•	•	•	•	•
	The less developed world																				
4.1	The development gap	•	•				•	•	•		•	•	•	•	•	•	•	•	•	•	•
4.2	Hunger and poverty	•	•			•		•	•	•	•	•	•	•		•	•	•	•	•	•
4.3	The savanna lands	•	•	•	•		•		•	•	•		•	•		•	•	•	•	•	•
4.4	Farming in the monsoon lands	•	•		•	•	•		•	•	•	•	•			•	•	•	•	•	•
4.5	The tropical rain forest ecosystem	•	•		•		•		•	•	•	•	•	•		•	•	•	•	•	•
4.6	Exporting food crops and forest products	•	•	•	•	•			•	•	•					•	•	•			•
4.7	Opening up empty regions	•			•		•	•	•	•	•		•			•	•	•	•		•
4.8	The Green Revolution	•	•				•		•	•	•	•	•			•	•	•	•		•
4.9	Developing transport networks	•		•	•		•		•	•	•	•	•			•		•	•		•
4.10	Establishing new industries	•	•		•	•	•		•	•	•	•	•			•	•	•	•		•
4.11	Multi-purpose schemes	•	•	•			•	•	•		•	•	•	•		•	•	•	•		•
4.12	Urbanisation and the growth of shanty towns	•	•	•	•	•	•	•	•	•	•	•	•	•		•	•	•	•	•	•
4.13	A Third-World city	•	•	•	•	•	•	•	•	•	•	•	•			•	•	•	•		•
4.14	Developing tourism	•	•	•	•	•	•	•	•	•	•		•			•	•	•	•		
4.15	Aid from the developed world	•	•				•		•		•		•			•	•	•	•		•
	Social and environmental issues																				
5.1	Growth of world population		•		•	•	•		•	•		•	•	•		•	•	•	•	•	•
5.2	Exhaustion of natural resources	•			•		•	•	•	•	•	•	•			•	•	•	•		
5.3	Hostile environments					•	•		•							•	•	•	•		
5.4	Land use and ownership conflicts	•				•	•		•		•		•			•	•	•	•		
5.5	Soil erosion and conservation	•	•		•		•	•	•	•	•	•	•			•	•	•	0	•	
5.6	Irrigation	•	•				•	•	•	•	•	•	•			•	•	•	•		•
5.7	The Greenhouse effect	•	•				•	•	•	•	•		•			•	•	•	•		
5.8	Air pollution	•	•				•	•	•	•	•		•			•	•	•	•		•
5.9	Water pollution	•	•				•	•	•	•	•	•	•			•	•	•	•		
5.10	Traffic in cities	•	•			•	•	•	•		•					•	•	•	•		•

Key: §   MEG/WJEC
       (Ex)   External
       *   For more mature candidates

THE GCSE

As a future examination candidate you need to know as much as possible about the GCSE examination and how it will affect you. Here are some of the questions and answers that were given during a briefing session with a group of secondary students.

What does the Geography examination test?

The GCSE is designed to test your knowledge and understanding of Geography, as well as your ability to use a range of skills, demonstrate your awareness of environmental problems, and make value judgments on geographical issues.

The emphasis is on your ability to understand Geography rather than your skill in memorizing pages of facts. The examination will test your grasp of facts and generalizations by asking questions which are designed to make you think. For example, a question may test your knowledge of the factors which help to determine where a new supermarket should be located, by asking you to choose a site for one on a map of a particular area, giving reasons for the site you have chosen. In other words you will be asked to apply your knowledge rather than to write down all you know in the form of an essay.

In addition, the GCSE will take into consideration course work, which must include field work and may, in some cases, also include other work done at school during the course and marked by your teachers. This coursework will be worth at least 20 per cent of the final marks. As a result performance in the written examination will only partly account for the grade obtained.

In what ways will the examination test knowledge, understanding and skills?

There are a great many specific facts you must know when you study Geography. These range from the names of places to the reasons why the rate of population growth varies from place to place. Armed with a battery of factual information you are better equipped to understand key geographical ideas, such as the idea that the earth's crust is unstable and is composed of different rock types. Knowledge is therefore an essential first step towards understanding, and there is no escaping from the need to build up a substantial body of knowledge to help you form general ideas which you can the apply in different situations.

To succeed in Geography you must know and be able to use a wide range of skills. Some of these skills, such as the interpretation of aerial photographs, are distinctive to Geography. Other skills, for example calculating and classifying, are shared with other subjects such as Mathematics and Biology. Many of these skills are best developed through practical activities and fieldwork, since they also give you the opportunity to observe and record information and then to interpret and analyse it.

What is meant by examining issues, values or problems?

Teaching values is a relatively new development in Geography. The values which are of particular concern to geographers are those which help us to understand the behaviour of people in relation to their environment, for example, the attitudes and arguments which arise in an area through which a new section of motorway is to be built. The more we are aware of environmental issues and problems, the greater will be our ability to find suitable solutions and avoid similar problems in the future.

In the past, Geography teachers avoided teaching values, because they wanted to be seen to be neutral and not pushing a particular point of view. If, for example, a teacher argued a particular political party line over the establishment of nuclear power stations, parents with other political views could rightly complain that their children were being indoctrinated with a particular viewpoint. But as geographers continue to study the environment it has become increasingly clear that if we are to understand fully the character of places, we have to take into account the motives, values and emotions of the people who live there. This does not mean, however, that in future Geography lessons will be biased. The general criteria laid down for the GCSE examination by the Secondary Examination Council state that 'every possible effort must be made to ensure that syllabuses and examinations are free of political, ethnic, gender and other forms of bias'. Do not, therefore, answer GCSE questions on values by giving a biased point of view. Your practical work and discussions in class should help you to become more aware of the different values which operate in particular geographical situations.

Why should we bother with values in Geography? There are three main reasons.

1 We need to understand the values which influence how people behave in relation to their environment. For example, many adults prefer to remain living in economically depressed regions where there are few job opportunities, because staying in their own community and 'belonging' to the place where they were born is the most desirable thing as far as they are concerned.

2 We need to be able to examine evidence logically and to discuss it thoughtfully in order to analyse the issues which arise from the conflicting values which may exist in a particular situation. For example, the possibility of locating London's third airport at Stansted in Essex aroused opposition from those who wanted to preserve a beautiful country area, from those who feared that house prices would fall, from those who were opposed to the rapid growth of air transport, and from those in other parts of the country, particularly the north, who wanted expansion of airport facilities in their own areas. It was supported, however, by those who believed Gatwick and Heathrow to be overcrowded, by those who thought it would create new jobs in Essex, and by people who believed it to be a more accessible location than either Heathrow or Gatwick.

3 By examining issues of this nature we begin to realize where we stand, that is, we become more aware of our own values and how they affect our own behaviour. We also being to realize that we are members of social and environmental systems which influence our attitudes to issues and problems. For example, what is our attitude to Britain giving aid to the developing world? By analysing and discussing environmental issues and by becoming more proficient at identifying and investigating the values which underly different points of view, we become more skilled at making our own decisions.

It is very important that during your GCSE course you have many and varied opportunities to explore values in Geography. It is also important that you show your ability to do this in your written work as well as in discussion. The broad areas which the examiners are likely to assess are:

1 a sensitive awareness of the environment;

2 an appreciation of the significance of values and attitudes in the making of decisions about how the environment should be managed;

3 understanding of changes in physical and human environments, and the need for conservation;

4 awareness of social and spatial inequalities;

5 attempts to reduce and eliminate inequalities based on racism, sexism or social structure;

6 awareness of the contrasting opportunities and constraints facing people who live in different places and under different physical and human conditions.

Are more marks given for knowledge than for understanding, skills and values?

No. You cannot expect to find questions on the examination paper which solely test knowledge. The examiners allocate a proportion of the marks to skills, values and understanding as well as to knowledge and the questions are often divided into sections so that each of these objectives can be awarded marks. The examiners follow a set plan in the way they award marks. For example, the Southern Examining Group, Syllabus A, allocates marks in the following manner:

You will see that in Papers 1 and 2, the written question papers, only 20 per cent of the marks are given for recall of facts. Other syllabuses may have slightly different proportions but no Geography syllabus gives more than 40 per cent of the marks to the ability to remember facts. This is well worth considering when you are testing your friends or reading through your notes as part of revision for the GCSE. The examination is not a kind of 'Mastermind' quiz where your score depends on the number of correct factual answers you can give. Notice how important skills are and that understanding and application follow closely behind.

Will the same examination be taken by candidates all over the country?

No, there is not one set of examination papers for all candidates. Schools decide which of a number of Examination Groups they wish to work with. As a national examination, the GCSE is set and marked by seven Examining Groups, four in England and one each in Wales, Northern Ireland and Scotland. These Examining Groups have to work within a framework of National Criteria. These National Criteria are guidelines about what should be examined, how it should be examined and how marks should be awarded. Although you will be taking an examination which will be different from that taken in schools and colleges linked to other Examination Groups, there will be similarity between the way the papers are set and marked.

I am not good at Geography, will I stand a chance of passing this new examination?

There is no reason why students who find Geography a difficult subject should not achieve a grade in the GCSE. The examination has been designed to reward candidates of differing abilities for what they know, understand and can do, and they will be rewarded for their positive achievements.

Candidates who pass the examination will be given grades according to the level of their performance. There is a single, seven-point scale using the grades A,B,C,D,E,F and G. In Scotland the numbers 1 to 7 are being used instead of letters, and awards made at three levels: Foundation Level for grades 6 and 7, General Level for grades 3, 4 and 5 and Credit Level for grades 1 and 2. The certificate you are awarded will show what grade you have achieved for each subject that you take.

	%			
	Paper 1	*Paper 2*	*Paper 3 (Geographical enquiry)*	*Total*
Recall of specific facts	4	16	0	20
Understanding and application	2	20	8	30
Skills	17	7	4	38
Values, attitudes and judgements	2	7	3	12
Component mark allocation (%)	25	50	25	100

In a survey of the results of the 1991 GCSE examination in Geography, 47.9 per cent of the candidates achieved A, B or C grades and only 2.4 per cent were ungraded.

How will the examination give students who are good at Geography the chance to show their ability?

Some parents and students have expressed their concern that, because this examination is taken by all students, the questions must be very easy to give those with less ability the opportunity to pass. The Examining Groups have overcome this problem in a number of ways. In some cases there are different papers, so that high-flying students take a paper targeted for grades A. B, C or D, while less able students take an alternative for grades D, E, F or G.

Another way is to offer the same question paper to all candidates but to design the questions so that they are 'stepped'. This means that each question is divided into a number of parts. The first parts are the easier and then they become progressively more difficult. Less able students should be able to answer the early parts of a stepped question, whereas the more able should successfully answer the later parts as well. Coursework can also include exercises of differing degrees of difficulty.

How will the marks be given fairly, not varying from one examiner to another?

The marking of the GCSE is strictly controlled by the Examination Groups. In addition, a body known as the Secondary Examinations Council will monitor the syllabuses, the gradings and the marking systems. Coursework will be marked by your teacher following precise guidelines given by the Examination Group. These marks will be checked by a specially chosen examiner who will either visit your school and look at the coursework or receive samples by post to see that the marks have been awarded fairly.

Examination Boards: Addresses

Northern Examining Association

JMB	Joint Matriculation Board
	Devas Street, Manchester M15 6EU
ALSEB	Associated Lancashire Schools Examining Board
	12 Harter Street, Manchester M1 6HL
NREB	Northern Regional Examinations Board
	Wheatfield Road, Westerhope, Newcastle upon Tyne NE5 5JZ
NWREB	North-West Regional Examinations Board
	Orbit House, Albert Street, Eccles, Manchester M30 0WL
YHREB	Yorkshire and Humberside Regional Examinations Board
	Harrogate Office – 31-33 Springfield Avenue, Harrogate HG1 2HW
	Sheffield Office – Scarsdale House, 136 Derbyshire Lane, Sheffield S8 8SE

Midland Examining Group

Cambridge	University of Cambridge Local Examinations Syndicate
	Syndicate Buildings, 1 Hills Road, Cambridge CB1 2EU
O & C	Oxford and Cambridge Schools Examination Board
	10 Trumpington Street, Cambridge CB2 1QB *and*
	Elsfield Way, Oxford OX2 8EP
SUJB	Southern Universities' Joint Board for School Examinations
	Cotham Road, Bristol BS6 6DD
WMEB	West Midlands Examinations Board
	Norfolk House, Smallbrook Queensway, Birmingham B5 4NJ
EMREB	East Midlands Regional Examinations Board
	Robins Wood House, Robins Wood Road, Aspley, Nottingham NG8 3NH

London East Anglian Group

London	University of London School Examinations Board
	Stewart House, 32 Russell Square, London WC1B 5DN
LREB	London Regional Examining Board
	Lyon House, 104 Wandsworth High Street, London SW18 4LF
EAEB	East Anglian Examinations Board
	The Lindens, Lexden Road, Colchester CO3 3RL

Southern Examining Group

AEB	The Associated Examining Board
	Stag Hill House, Guildford GU2 5XJ
Oxford	Oxford Delegacy of Local Examinations
	Ewert Place, Summertown, Oxford OX2 7BZ
SREB	Southern Regional Examinations Board
	Eastleigh House, Market Street, Eastleigh, Southampton SO5 4SW
SEREB	South-East Regional Examinations Board
	Beloe House, 2-10 Mount Ephraim Road, Tunbridge Wells TN1 1EU
SWEB	South-Western Examinations Board
	23-29 Marsh Street, Bristol BS1 4BP

Wales

WJEC	Welsh Joint Education Committee
	245 Western Avenue, Cardiff CF5 2YX

Northern Ireland

NISEC	Northern Ireland Schools Examinations Council
	Beechill House, 42 Beechill Road, Belfast BT8 4RS

Scotland

SEB	Scottish Examination Board
	Ironmills Road, Dalkeith, Midlothian EH22 1BR

1 MAPWORK AND PHYSICAL GEOGRAPHY

1.1 Interpretation of OS map 1:50 000

The mapwork question, which is sometimes a compulsory part of the Geography examination, is set either as a separate paper or as part of a paper which may also contain questions relating to the British Isles or general world Geography.

Maps used are usually on the 1:50 000 or 1:25 000 scales, but maps of other scales may also be used, and may be of areas outside the UK.

Some Examination Groups allow additional time, which can be used for looking at the map and question paper but not for writing the answer. Many candidates find that the time allowed for the map question is barely sufficient, so it is essential to use all the time effectively, including any time allowed for reading.

When you are told to start the examination, and before you read the questions, examine the map, using the stages set out below. To illustrate the sequence the 1:50 000 map of the Rhondda Valley at the back of this book will be used as an example.

1 Think of the map as part of a larger picture and try to relate the extract to its region. The Rhondda and Taff Valleys, for example, are part of the drainage pattern of South Wales. The land is generally higher in the north and lower in the south, with steep-sided ridges between the valleys. The extract covers part of the South Wales coalfield and this gives some clues as to the human and economic backgrounds.

2 Do not, at this stage, look at the details on the map but notice the patterns made by such things as the routeways, the settlements and other land-use features such as the forest areas. Often these patterns emerge more clearly if you half close your eyes or look at the map from a distance of a metre or more. On the Rhondda map the manner in which the roads and railways follow the river valleys is clearly seen and the distinction between the hillsides with forests and those without provides another kind of pattern.

3 Finally, before you start to write the answers to the questions spend a minute or so looking at some of the detailed information which the map extract provides. Note the scale, which series of the 1:50 000 it is part of and the contour interval which is used. Look at some of the symbols which recur frequently. For example on the Rhondda map the signs used to indicate tip heaps or mounds are widespread.

TYPES OF QUESTIONS WHICH MAY BE ASKED

Map references and Ordnance Survey symbols using the six-figure code
For example:
Name the features at 048970 and 019959.
Give the map references for Treforest College and Porth railway station.
Remember that the eastings (horizontal) numbers precede the northings (vertical) numbers.

Compass directions
In which direction is Porth (024918) from Ystrad (985953)?
What direction is Pentre (970962) from Mountain Ash (047995)?
Know the 16 compass points (*e.g.* N, NNE, NE, NE by E, E, *etc.*) to give an accurate answer.

Distances
To measure distances it is best to use either the straight edge of a piece of paper or a length of thick cotton. The length should be measured against the scale at the bottom of the map. Pocket map-measures can also be bought.
What is the shortest distance, to the nearest kilometre, from Pentre Church (969963) to the chapel at Ferndale (999969)?
What is the shortest distance by road?
Why is one distance greater than the other?

Drawing cross-sections
For this you will need a straight edge of paper along which to mark the contours and their heights. When drawing the diagram remember not to exaggerate the vertical interval, or low hills will look like the Alps. The Rhondda map extract is a particularly difficult one to use as an example for making cross-sections because there are many contours which are close together, making it necessary to be very precise to achieve an accurate cross-section.
Draw a cross-section from the railway station at Pontypridd (072898) to the post office at Gilfach Goch (982892). Mark on the cross section the A4119 road, a footpath and an electricity transmission line. A suitable vertical interval for this cross-section would be 1 mm on your diagram equals 10 metres on the map.

Identification from a viewpoint
Sometimes you are asked to imagine you are standing at a certain viewpoint and to identify certain features which might be seen from the viewpoint. For example:
You are standing on the golf course (004933) at 327 metres above sea level. What are the names of the two valleys, one to the east and the other to the west?
What is the map reference for the nearest coal mine?
Would it be possible to see the settlement at Gilfach Goch?

Communications
Questions usually relate to the ways road or rail routes are influenced by relief and other physical features. On the Rhondda map the major roads and railways follow the river valleys closely, except the A4119 between Tonyrefail (0088) and Trealaw (9992) which crosses a col between the valleys of two streams.
Why do the routes follow the river valleys so closely?
How could coal from the mine at Ynysybwl (0694) reach the main railway line?
Give the map reference for one location where there is evidence of a railway which no longer operates.

2 Mapwork and physical geography

Fig. 1.1 Aerial view of Pontypridd

Settlement

Questions on settlement may be concerned with:

Distribution

For example, on the Rhondda map, settlement is almost entirely confined to the valley bottoms and sides. Only isolated farms or small settlements are to be found on the higher ground.

Site and position

Where, particularly, towns or villages are located.
Pontypridd for example, is located at the meeting point of two rivers on the lower ground at a natural route focus.

Function

Map evidence to show the reasons for the growth of a settlement.
Abercynon, like Pontypridd, is a route centre. In addition there is a mine located in the valley to the south of the town. Maerdy (9798) appears to have no other function than as a mining settlement.

Shape

Whether the settlement is nucleated, linear, in bead-like clusters, or has some other distinctive shape for which a reason may be apparent.
Many of the valley settlements in South Wales are linear in shape as a result of the limitations on building imposed by the steep valley sides.
Mountain Ash in the north-east of the map extract has this characteristic linear shape.
In the Rhondda valleys the settlement is almost continuous, forming a series of linear clusters with their own centres, usually at bridging points.

Sketch map on a smaller scale

Sometimes you are asked to reproduce certain features of the map or part of the map on a sketch map which is a scaled-down, simplified version of the map extract.

A drawing of the outline area covered by the Rhondda map, one quarter the size of the original is a square with sides of 13 cm. To mark features such as the Rivers Taff and Rhondda Fawr, or the largest single area of forest on this outline you need to add some grid lines, if they have not been provided by the examiners. These will help you to locate accurately the features which you have been asked to mark. Do not spend too much time attempting to achieve a perfect sketch, since only a few marks are likely to be allocated to this task.

You should note that, although the size of the sketch map is a quarter of the size of the map extract, the linear scale used is *half* the scale used on the original extract, *i.e.* 1 cm to 1 km instead of 2 cm to 1 km. Therefore, if you were asked to draw a sketch map of the Rhondda extract at half the scale of the original you would draw it 13 cm × 13 cm.

Descriptions of physical features and land use

You may be asked to describe the physical features of part of the map. For example, compare the physical features of the valleys of the River Taff from Abercynon to Pontypridd with those of its tributary the Nant Clydach.

It may also be necessary to explain how a physical feature was formed. Thus an answer describing the meanders of the River Taff four kilometres north of Pontypridd may require sketches and notes explaining how meanders form in a river valley.

Land use descriptions based on a detailed knowledge of the Ordnance Survey conventional signs are also frequently set. Compare the land use in square 0499 with that in 0691. So long as you know the signs and can estimate their significance in the area selected for examination, you should have no difficulties in answering this type of question.

Interpretation of an aerial photograph

An oblique aerial photograph relating to part of the map may be used as part of the map question, or as a separate optional question elsewhere in the examination paper.

The photograph is normally used to test your skills in:

Relating places and objects in the photograph with their counterparts on the map.

Orientating the photograph to compass directions given on the map and explaining features.

Identifying facts shown on the photograph which are not evident on the map or vice versa.

See if you can answer the following questions about the photograph (fig. 1.1) which relates to the Rhondda extract.

Give the map reference for the viaduct which can be seen near the bottom left of the photograph.

What is the name of the river which the viaduct crosses?

What is the map reference for the two bridges which are close together and cross the river to the right of centre in the photograph?

In which direction was the camera pointing when the photograph was taken?

List three features which are to be seen in the photograph but not on the map.

Why do you think many of the streets and rows of houses are built parallel to the river?

Summary

Basic ideas

The map is an important tool for geographers, and the ability to understand and use maps is an essential element of this subject.

Information on the map can often be enhanced by a good oblique aerial photograph.

Key terms

Scale; cross-section; communications; settlement distribution; nuclear and linear settlement; land use; oblique aerial photo.

1.2 Interpretation of OS map 1 : 25 000

Practically everything written about the interpretation of the OS map 1 : 50 000 of the Rhondda Valley applies to the 1 : 25 000 York extract which is located at the back of this book.

Most Examination Groups expect candidates to be able to interpret maps of either scale, so it is important for you to be equally familiar with both. The questions which follow about the York sheet should help you to check whether you have understood and can answer the types of question which were discussed in the previous pages with reference to the Rhondda map.

When you first look at the York sheet can you imagine the part of England covered by this extract? For what is York well known historically, culturally and as an industrial city? Having set the scene in your own mind you are ready to look at the map for distribution patterns.

What pattern is made by the main roads and railways leading into York? What shape are many of the fields, are they square, long and narrow or irregular?

What differences are there in the patterns formed by the roads and houses in the outer residential areas of York such as Osbaldwick, 6351, and the inner part of the city, 6051?

Approximately how much of the map is taken up by the city of York and neighbouring built-up areas? (Each grid square is 1 km^2.)

Now that you have tried to put the extract into its regional setting and also looked at the broad patterns to be found on the sheet, try to answer the following questions and then check your answers with a friend.

1 Give six-figure map references for:
York Castle; the Church with a spire at Stockton on the Forest; the sewage works at Osbaldwick.

2 What features are to be found at:
642513; 602546; 622508?

3 What is the distance, to the nearest kilometre, from Pigeoncote Farm (6255) to Novia Scotia Farm (6554):
(a) in a straight line?
(b) by the shortest road route?

4 What direction is York Castle from Stockton in the Forest? What direction is the University of York from the Castle?

5 Draw a sketch-map on half the scale of the original and mark on it the Rivers Ouse and Foss; the multiple track railway; the A1079(T) from the city wall eastwards to the edge of the map; the largest area of woodland.

6 Describe the location of the large factory in 6053. Suggest advantages which this site has for a factory.

7 Describe briefly the types of land use to be found in squares 6150 and 6255.

8 What evidence is there that livestock is probably kept on the farms?

9 Comment on the drainage pattern in the area east of grid line 63 and north of grid line 52.

The photograph of York (fig. 7.4, page 136) which shows part of the city is discussed in unit 7. Look at both the photograph and the map and list four advantages of the site for the development of a town.

Mapwork and physical geography

1.3 Interpretation of weather maps and meteorological information

WEATHER SYMBOLS

Make sure you know the weather symbols used on meteorological maps — fig. 1.3A will help you. Remember that cloudiness is measured in oktas (eighths) and that fog or mist may make it impossible to see the sky, so there is a 'sky obscured' sign.

The most difficult symbols to remember are those for wind speed. The number of feathers and half feathers indicates the speed, which is measured in knots.

Look at the symbols used on the weather map (fig. 1.3B). For each weather station the information shown relates to temperature, cloud cover, wind speed and direction, and precipitation.

1 Find the warm, cold and occluded fronts.
2 Describe the weather conditions at stations A, B and C.
3 Was the pressure at D high or low?

UNDERSTANDING THE WEATHER

The weather map shows a low pressure system passing over southern England, with higher pressure over the North Sea. Lows, like the one shown, are very common over Britain and can occur at any time of the year. They usually swing from west to east and the weather

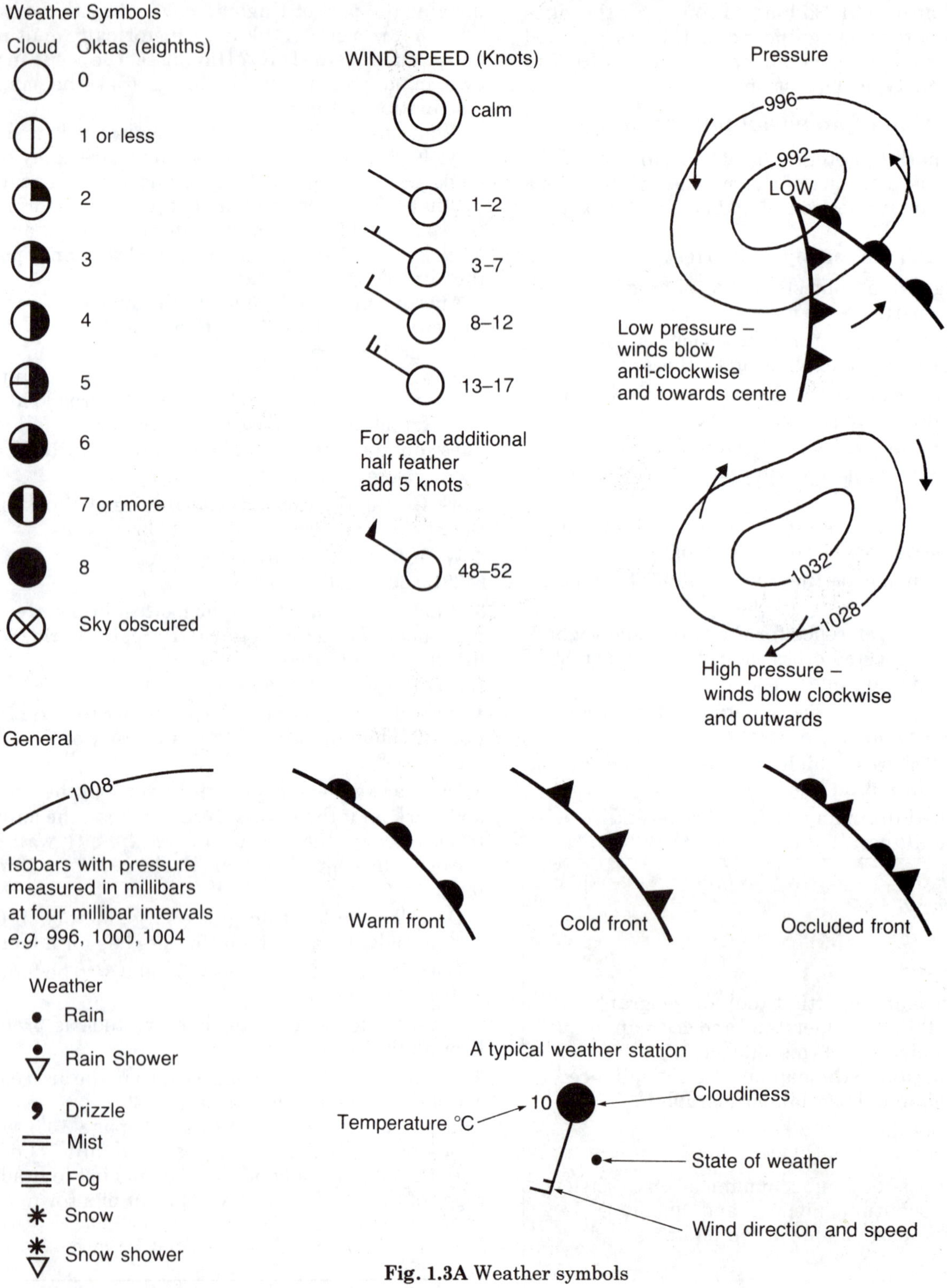

Fig. 1.3A Weather symbols

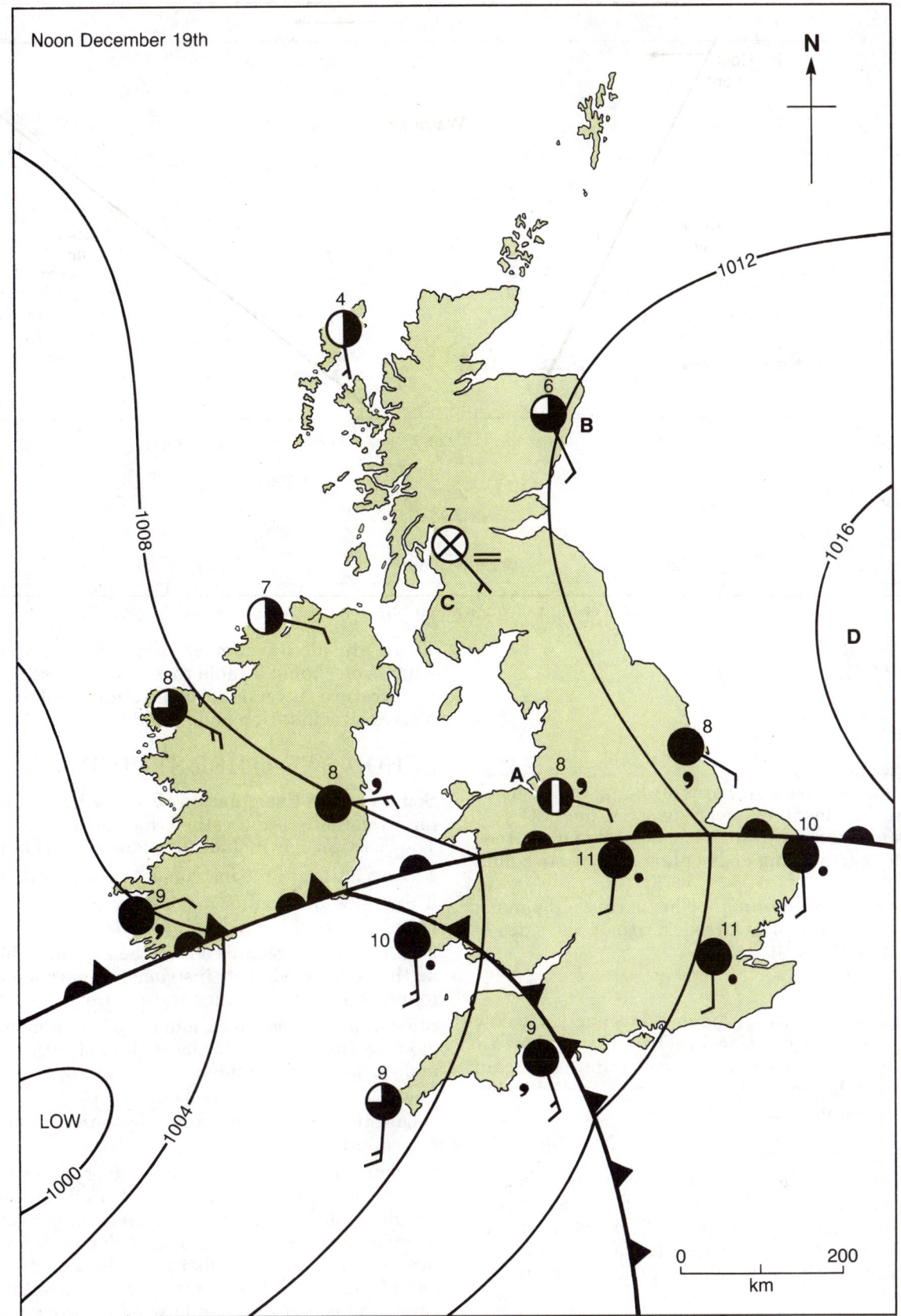

Fig. 1.3B Weather map of Britain

experienced as the low passes usually follows a distinctive pattern, as shown in fig. 1.3C.

High pressure, sometimes called an anti-cyclone, brings a different weather pattern with little or no wind and clear skies. In winter fog and frost may occur, whereas in summer a persistent 'high' with much sunshine may result in a heat-wave and drought.

On the weather map (fig. 1.3B) the warm and cold fronts are moving northwards towards Scotland.

1 What weather forecast would you give for northern England and southern Scotland for the remainder of December 19th?

2 What would you expect to happen to the temperature in London as the depression moves northwards?

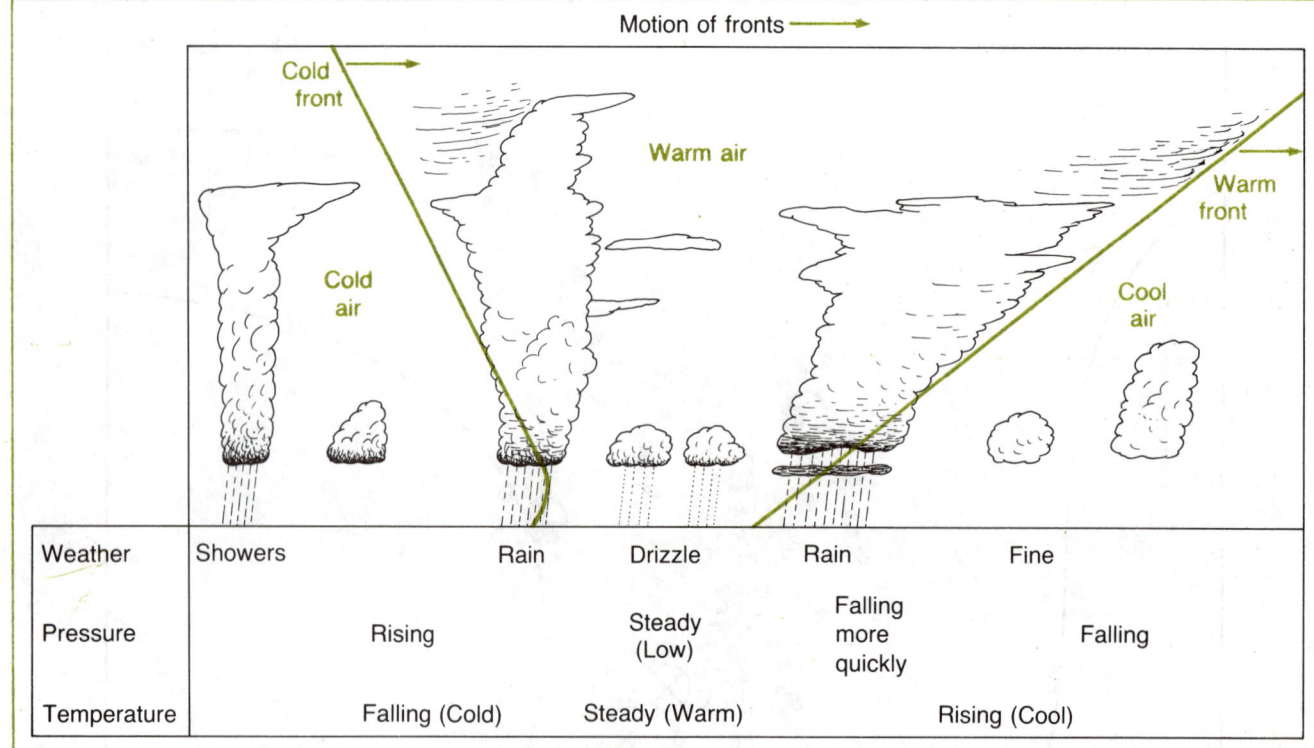

Fig. 1.3C Cross-section through the fronts of a low pressure system

WEATHER CONDITIONS AND THEIR CAUSES

Rainfall

There are three types:
Cyclonic rain caused by warm air being undercut by colder air in a low pressure system. See fig. 1.3C.
Convectional rainfall, which is caused by air warmed by the hot earth rising and cooling as it meets colder layers.
Relief or orographic rainfall. This is caused by moist air being cooled as it is forced to rise up the sides of hills or mountains.

Hail

Raindrops which pass through a layer of air below freezing point may freeze to form hail. In turbulent air the hail may be tossed about, collecting more rain droplets and becoming larger. Finally, the hail may fall as large stones, damaging crops.

Frost

On a clear calm night in winter the earth's surface cools by radiation and the air close to the earth also cools. Any moisture it contains will condense on cold surfaces and freeze to give a white frost. Valleys can become frost pockets, as cold air tends to sink to the valley bottom.

Fog

If air containing water vapour is cooled the point may be reached where the water vapour is condensed into tiny drops of water which remain suspended in the air to form a fog. Dust, smoke or other pollutants in the air may cling to the water droplets to form 'smog'. Frost and fog often occur in high pressure conditions.

Apart from the four types of weather described above you should also know what causes such things as thunderstorms, gales, and land and sea breezes.

There are also a number of technical expressions which you should be able to explain. These include: temperature inversion, convection, radiation, air masses, precipitation and humidity.

SCHOOL WEATHER STATION

Sometimes an Examination Group will set a question on a weather station rather than on a weather map. The question may include all or some of the following:

1 Descriptions of the instruments and how they work.

2 Suitable location for a school weather station and the positions of the individual instruments.

3 How weather records should be kept and the information displayed. The instruments most commonly found at a school weather station are:

Stevenson screen, maximum and minimum thermometer, hygrometer (measures humidity), rain gauge and measuring cylinder, wind vane, anemometer (measures wind speed), sunshine recorder.

4 Questions on modern aids to weather forecasting, e.g. satellites, computers.

You should be able to draw meteorological instruments, know how they work and also know where they should be placed to be most effective. Daily readings of maximum and minimum temperatures can be averaged over a month but remember that the rainfall for each day of the month is added to give the month's total. Line graphs, bar charts and wind roses provide suitable means of displaying the information. Recordings made over a period of time may form part of your coursework for the GCSE examination.

WEATHER AND PEOPLE

You should know how the weather affects the lives and work of people, for example the importance of weather forecasts for farmers, airline pilots, climbers, fishermen and the officials at Wimbledon and other sporting events.

Mapwork and physical geography 7

> **Summary**
>
> *Basic ideas*
>
> Weather maps not only indicate the prevailing weather but also suggest possible changes in the immediate future.
>
> There are a number of physical explanations for weather phenomena such as rainfall and frost.
>
> Practical weather observations can be carried out using the instruments of a school weather station.
>
> *Key terms*
>
> High and low pressure; fronts; cyclonic; convectional and relief rainfall; smog; Stevenson screen.

1.4 The hydrological cycle: river valleys

THE HYDROLOGICAL CYCLE

The movement of water between the atmosphere, the land and the sea is known as the hydrological cycle (hydrology is the study of water on the earth). It is called a cycle because it is a continuous process. Water circulates from the oceans to the atmosphere and to the land, over and over again. The processes involved are shown in fig. 1.4A, and because these processes are linked to one another in a distinct relationship, the hydrological cycle can also be called a system (see unit 2.2). The system requires a supply of energy to keep it going and this energy is provided by the sun.

Here are some explanations of the processes and other terms used on fig. 1.4A.

Evaporation — Water molecules from the sea, lakes and other sources are transferred into water vapour in the air by the sun's energy (heat). This water vapour rises and cools until it condenses.

Condensation — As the air is cooled, water vapour is transformed into water droplets which form clouds. The droplets increase in size until they fall as precipitation.

Precipitation — Rain, hail or snow falls to the earth and some soaks into the soil, percolates into the underlying rocks and moves slowly downwards through the rocks towards the lower ground and the sea. Some reaches the surface as spring water and then flows as run-off in streams and rivers.

Transpiration — Water from the soil is drawn up into plants by their root systems. Some of this water is released from the plants' leaves into the atmosphere. This process is called transpiration. When the water passes into the air as water vapour, the process is called evapotranspiration.

Water table — The boundary, normally below the ground's surface, which marks the upper limit of water saturation.

RIVER VALLEYS

Surface run-off in the hydrological cycle takes the form of streams and rivers. The area drained by a single river system is called a drainage basin and is an example of an 'open' system. This means that there are inputs from outside the system, such as precipitation, and outputs from the system, such as the flow of water and the material it carries into a sea or lake. There are also throughputs within the system of such things as the flow of water in the drainage basin and infiltration from the surface into the water table. Within the river basin water erosion, deposition and weathering processes (chemical and mechanical) create distinctive channel and valley landforms.

Erosion

Erosion occurs where a stream has an excess of energy; this is likely to be the case in the upper course (fig. 1.4B). There are three main forms of erosion:

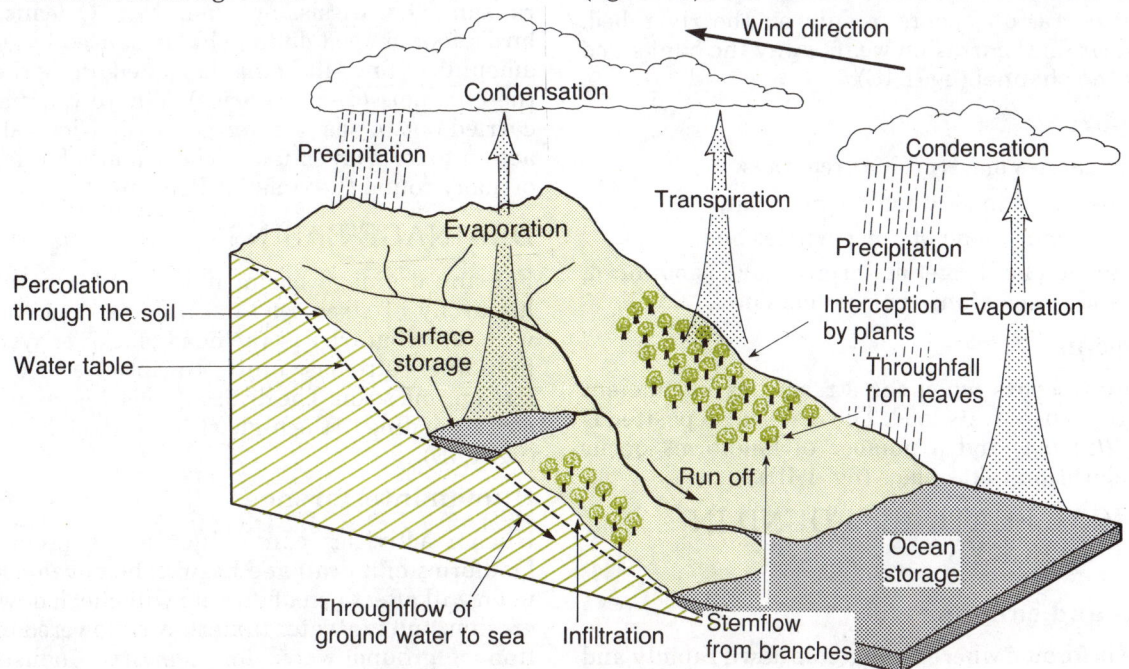

Fig. 1.4A The hydrological cycle

8 Mapwork and physical geography

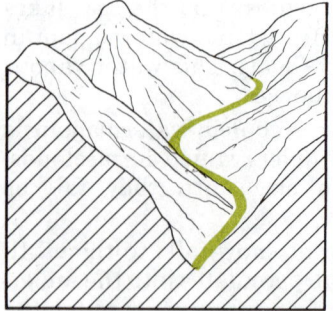

Fig. 1.4B Upper course — stream flowing between interlocking spurs

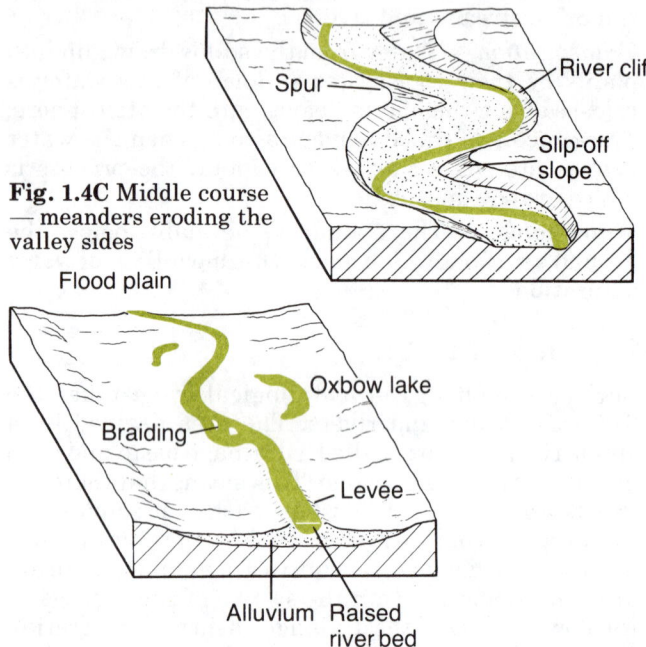

Fig. 1.4C Middle course — meanders eroding the valley sides

Fig. 1.4D Lower course — wide flood plain and raised river bed

hydraulic action — the dragging effect of the flow of water, which erodes poorly consolidated material; corrosion, which is the solution of rocks such as chalk and limestone in the flowing water; and the main form of erosion, which is corrasion — the bombardment of the river bed and sides by debris carried by the stream. Vertical corrasion occurs mainly on the river bed, while horizontal corrasion wears away the banks and sides of the channel (fig. 1.4C).

Transport

A stream carries material in three ways:

(a) the dissolved load of soluble material,

(b) the suspended load of fine particles and

(c) the bed load of larger material, which is bounced, pushed and rolled along the channel floor.

Deposition

Deposition occurs when the stream has insufficient energy to transport its load. The material deposited is called *alluvium*, and a number of landforms occur when deposition takes place (fig. 1.4D).

PHYSICAL FEATURES FOUND IN RIVER VALLEYS

Gorges and canyons

A gorge is formed where a river cuts down rapidly and the other forces of weathering 'open up' the valley sides very slowly. This happens in dry climates, such as Arizona where the Grand Canyon of the Colorado River cuts down for more than a mile. Gorges are known as canyons in America.

When a river cuts down through hard, resistant rock a gorge can be formed. This happens below the Niagara Falls in North America.

Waterfalls

These can be found where a hard bar of rock crosses a river valley. The Kaieteur Falls in Guyana occur where the Potaro River flows over a ledge of conglomerate.

Waterfalls may form at the edge of a plateau. The Livingstone Falls on the Congo are an example.

Waterfalls may be caused by faults. In Britain, Gordale Scar was formed by the mid-Craven fault.

In glaciated regions the steep valley sides and hanging valleys result in spectacular falls, for example, the Bridal Falls in the Yosemite Valley, California.

Cataracts and rapids

When a river passes over hard rocks which are dipping gently downstream, a series of rapids may result, *e.g.* the cataracts on the Nile in southern Egypt.

River terraces

If the base level of a river is lowered, for example, by a fall in sea level or by an earth movement, then the river begins to down-cut more vigorously and the old flood plain is left as river terraces on either side of the valley. Gravel and alluvium are left on the terraces, several sets of which may be formed with successive changes of base level. Much of the central area of London is built above the present flood plain of the Thames. 'Knick points' are formed at the point in the river's long profile where the river begins to cut down more rapidly.

Deltas and estuaries

Deltas are formed at the mouth of a river if there are no strong tidal currents to scour and remove the alluvium deposits. The delta of the River Nile is fan shaped where the river enters the nearly tideless Mediterranean. The Mississippi near New Orleans forms a bird's foot shaped delta. This is caused by enormous amounts of fine silt being deposited along the edge of the channels (distributaries). Where the material is carried out to sea, a river mouth is widened by tidal action to form an estuary. The Thames Estuary is one of many round the coast of Britain.

DRAINAGE BASINS

For any drainage basin, it is possible to identify a hierarchy of streams. First-order streams are those without tributaries at the head of a river system. Two first-order streams unite to form a second-order stream, and so on. The drainage basin is given an order corresponding to the highest-order stream in the basin (fig. 1.4E).

Human interference

Human activities can influence the processes and landforms of a drainage basin. The development of a town will affect run off, a dam will check downstream erosion, and the water table may be lowered by extraction of ground water for domestic, industrial and agricultural use.

Mapwork and physical geography

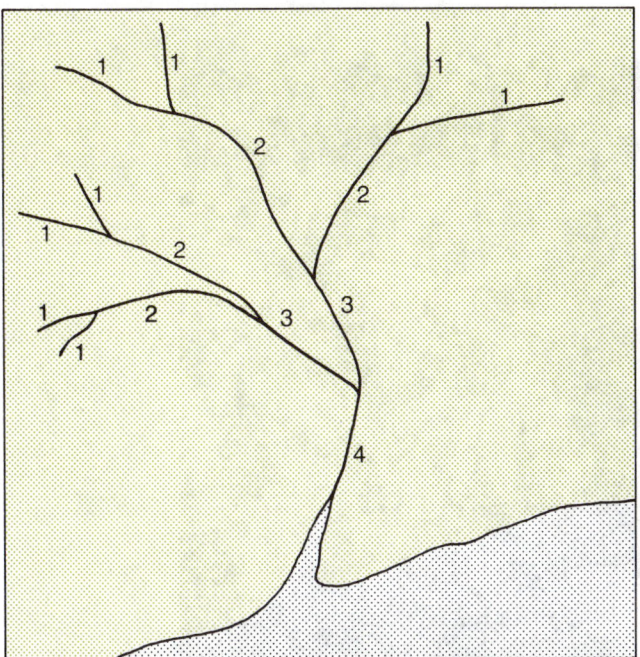

Fig. 1.4E A fourth-order drainage basin

The quality of the water can be influenced by pollution from industrial waste, agricultural fertilizers and pesticides, sewage and other pollutants.

Conflicts for water resources may occur, for example the demand for water from Welsh rivers and lakes by the water-deficient areas of the Midlands and North-West.

Summary

Basic ideas

Water circulates from the oceans to the atmosphere and to the land over and over again.

The hydrological cycle is an example of a system.

Distinctive physical features result from erosion and deposition by rivers.

The drainage basin is an example of an open system.

Drainage basins contain a hierarchy of streams.

Human interference can influence the processes, landforms and quality of the water in a drainage basin.

Key terms

System; evaporation; condensation; transpiration; infiltration; water table; hydraulic action; corrosion; corrasion; deposition; hierarchy; pollution.

1.5 Glaciation

In high latitudes or altitudes where there is less heat from the sun the hydrological cycle involves precipitation in the form of snow and rivers of ice instead of water. Glaciers operate within the system like rivers and produce distinctive landforms, which in highland regions, are mainly the result of erosion and in lowland regions consist mainly of deposition features.

HIGHLAND GLACIATION

The aerial photograph (fig. 1.5A) shows many of the features which are associated with glaciation in a highland region. Erosion by ice has made the valleys U-shaped, while ice erosion and the breaking up of rocks by frost action have carved the landscape into ridges, hollows and peaks. In the photograph, two glaciers can be seen. The larger one which ends in a lake is much darker in colour than the one near **E**, because it is loaded with rock material, called moraine, which has either fallen on to the glacier or has been torn from the valley sides by the ice. The features marked by letters are:

A A ribbon lake formed from meltwater from the glacier. The lake has filled a part of the valley which was deepened and widened when the glacier was much longer than it is now.

B A corrie (sometimes known as a cirque or cwm), an armchair-like hollow which was formed by ice and frost action.

C A waterfall leading from a hanging valley.

D The dark stripe is a medial moraine formed when two glaciers join. Lateral moraine is the name given to the debris on the sides of the glacier, while a terminal moraine is formed where the glacier melts.

E A glacier snout with terminal moraine. Streams flow away from the base of the ice sheet.

F The peaks in the distance are pyramid-like in shape with their sides steepened by ice and frost-thaw action.

G The mountain ridges are steepened in the same way to form arêtes or knife-like ridges.

In an examination you may be asked to:

1 Identify these features on a map or a diagram.

2 Draw sketches of them and, where possible, give named examples.

3 Explain how these features were formed.

4 Describe the human uses to which the highland areas are put.

LOWLAND GLACIATION

Low-lying areas which have emerged from underneath glaciers contain distinctive features, different from those to be found in glaciated mountain regions. Glaciers passing over lowland regions form an ice sheet which is capable of eroding hollows in the bedrock and reshaping rock outcrops over which it passes. Most features of lowland glaciation are, however, the result of deposition under ice or by meltwater. About ten per cent of the earth's land area is covered by material left behind by Ice Age glaciers and ice sheets. This material is called glacial drift and consists of clay (fine rock dust), sand, gravel and boulders. As the ice melts this drift is deposited to form distinctive landforms.

The features shown in fig. 1.5B were formed as follows:

Roches moutonnées — Outcrops of rock eroded by a glacier to form a steep slope on the downstream side and a gentle slope upstream. They are also a feature of valleys in regions of highland glaciation.

Irregularly-shaped lakes — Hollows gouged from the bedrock by glaciers, in which lakes have formed. Northern Canada has many such lakes.

10 Mapwork and physical geography

Fig. 1.5A Grimsel ober Unteraargletscher

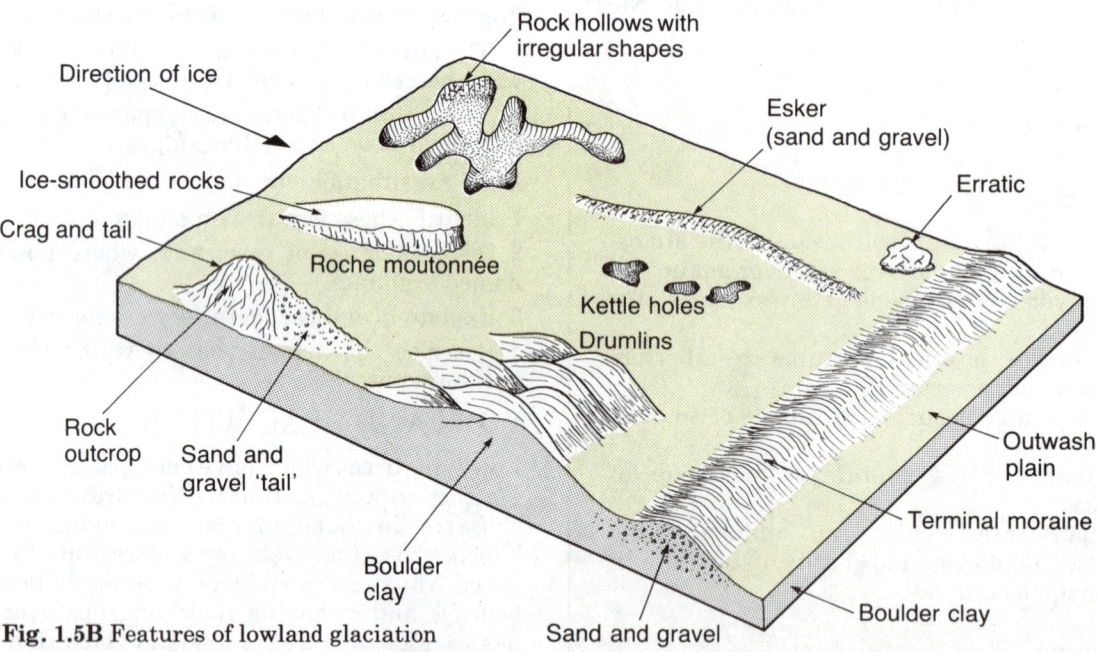

Fig. 1.5B Features of lowland glaciation

Esker — A snake-like winding ridge of sand and gravel. An esker usually follows the direction of ice flow. Eskers were formed by meltwater streams flowing in or on the ice. Eskers are common in Finland.

Kettle hole — A hollow in the ground, formed by lumps of ice melting within glacial material. There are many in central Ireland.

Drumlin — A smooth mound of boulder clay with a rock core, which is egg-shaped. Drumlins occur in 'swarms', making the landscape look like a 'basket of eggs'. It is not certain how they were formed. The central part of Glasgow is built on drumlins.

Erratic — A boulder carried some distance by a glacier, before being deposited when the glacier melted. Erratics in East Anglia originated in Norway.

Terminal moraine — The final melting point of a glacier or ice-sheet. The moraine often forms low hills of sand and gravel. The Holt-Cromer ridge in Norfolk is the remnants of a terminal moraine.

Boulder clay — A clay formed from rock flour which sometimes contains larger pieces of rock. Much of East Anglia is covered by boulder clay.

Outwash plain — A plain covered by material washed away from a glacier or ice sheet. The material consists of sand, gravel and clay which have been sorted into layers by meltwater. Areas of the Midwest in the USA are part of a huge outwash plain.

HUMAN ACTIVITY IN GLACIATED REGIONS

The spectacular scenery of glaciated highland regions attracts many tourists, and some regions, such as Yosemite in California, have been made into National Parks. Winter sports, hiking, camping and water sports on the lakes are tourist activities. U-shaped valleys are often suitable sites for HEP schemes. Glaciated lowlands are sometimes covered with boulder clay, e.g. East Anglia, and are fertile. Sandy areas form heath land.

Summary

Basic ideas

Glaciers are part of the hydrological cycle. Ice can carry material and use it to erode a landscape and form distinctive features.

Glaciated highland regions attract tourists and winter sports enthusiasts.

Low-lying areas where ice sheets melted contain a variety of glacial features.

Key terms

Moraine; corrie; pyramidal peak; glacial drift; boulder clay; roche moutonnée; esker; kettle hole; drumlin; erratic; outwash plain.

1.6 Coastal environments

COASTAL DEPOSITION

The aerial photograph of Northam Burrows (fig. 1.6A) shows many of the features which are associated with the building-up of a section of coastline by deposition of material. Waves are responsible for carrying much sand and shingle along a beach. When winds strike the beach at an angle, waves carry the material along the beach causing what is known as longshore drift. Groynes are built to check this movement and it may also be stopped by a headland or a river mouth. Currents are also important carrying agents, particularly in estuaries where tidal currents may clear away deposits, depositing them further along the coast or out to sea.

Figure 1.6B shows a stretch of coastline with the prevailing winds blowing from the south-west. Beach material builds up to the west of the groynes and where there is an opening in the coast a spit develops with marshland behind. Parts of the south coast of England are being shaped in this way with longshore drift up the English Channel from west to east. Figure 1.6C shows in detail how material such as pebbles moves along a small section of the beach shown in fig. 1.6B as a result of waves breaking at an oblique angle along the shoreline. The swash (forward movement) of the waves moves the material diagonally up the beach. The retreating water, or backwash, of the waves washes some of the material towards the sea and at right angles to the beach.

Fig. 1.6A Aerial view of Northam Burrows

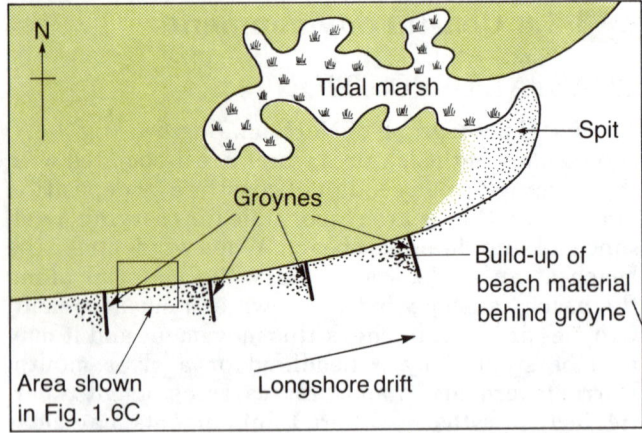

Fig. 1.6B Longshore drift

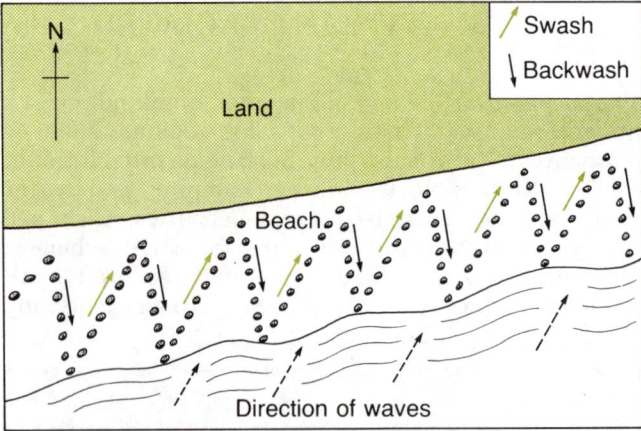

Fig. 1.6C Movement of pebbles along a beach

SPITS

Spits occur where material carried along a coast is deposited as a result of the coast changing direction inwards at a bay or river mouth. The material is piled up on the sea bed and eventually forms a ridge which continues to grow at its tip. New material is added until a spit is formed such as at Orfordness in Suffolk or Spurn Head at the mouth of the Humber.

Material is deposited on the sheltered side during storms and marshes develop linking the spit with the previous coastline.

Waves and cross-currents can form a hook of material at the end of the spit and in time more hooks may be added as the spit grows.

Make a sketch the same size as the photograph, fig. 1.6A, marking clearly the following: (a) tip of spit, (b) hooked section, (c) sand dunes, (d) direction of prevailing wind, (e) former cliff line, (f) marshland, (g) reclaimed farmland, (h) direction of movement of material.

BARS

A spit which grows across a bay, completely sealing it, is called a bar. Lagoons and marshes fill the space between the bar and the mainland. Chesil Beach in Dorset has linked the Isle of Portland to the mainland, forming a special kind of connecting bar, called a tombolo.

COASTAL EROSION

The sea erodes in four different ways:

(a) By hydraulic action, that is the pressure of the waves carrying material crashing against the shore and cliff face.

(b) By corrasion (abrasion), with waves dragging pieces of rock up and down the beach and acting like a giant piece of glass paper.

(c) By attrition, when the pieces of rock being carried are themselves worn down.

(d) By corrosion, especially on coasts made of chalk or limestone where the rock is dissolved in the sea water.

When a stretch of coastline is made up of rocks of differing degrees of hardness, a series of headlands and bays is formed.

At Lulworth Cove in Dorset the sea has broken through a layer of hard limestone parallel with the coast and has scooped out the softer rocks behind to form a curved bay.

Erosion of a shoreline by the sea results in the cutting back of the land, which, if it is hilly, will end in a sea cliff. At low tide a wave-cut platform marks the area where the cliffs once stood.

Undercutting of the cliffs by wave action may result in caves. Where the rocks are strongly jointed, compressed air caused by waves may force a channel up through the joints to the ground above. This results in a blow hole, which is most active during storms when waves surge through the cave below.

A natural arch is formed when two caves on either side of a headland join. Durdle Door in Dorset and the Needle Eye near Wick in Scotland are arches joined to the mainland. In time the arch is weakened by further erosion and collapses, leaving a stack. The Needles off the Isle of Wight are probably the best known stacks in this country.

TYPES OF COASTLINE

Rias

The increase in sea level at the end of the Ice Age resulted in the submergence of some sections of coast-

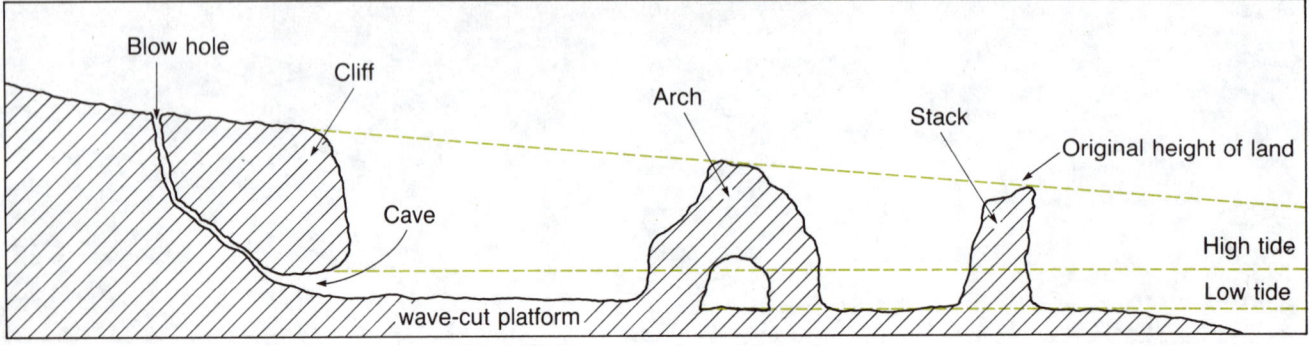

Fig. 1.6D Features of coastal erosion

line and the lower parts of the river valleys. In hilly areas the drowned valleys form a ria. A ria is funnel shaped and becomes more shallow inland. Surrounding hills rise from the edge of the river as the water has covered the original flood plain. Rias are common in southwest Ireland, Brittany and the south coast of Devon and Cornwall. Plymouth Sound is a ria with deep water, making a suitable anchorage for large ships.

Fjords

These occur in such regions as western Norway, British Columbia, Alaska and New Zealand. They are the result of the drowning of deep glacial valleys which have all the characteristics of glaciation — a U shape, truncated spurs, hanging valleys and waterfalls.

The Sogne Fjord in Norway is 100 miles long. Parallel to the mainland of fjord coasts there is often a series of islands, known in Norway as 'skerries'. They protect shipping from the worst of the storms, but harbours are rare because the fjords are usually too steep-sided for large ports to develop.

Longitudinal coastlines

These are sometimes known as Dalmatian coastlines, because one of the best examples is the Dalmatian coast of Yugoslavia. The mountains lie in bands parallel to the coast and submergence has flooded the lower ground, forming long off-shore islands with straight coastlines.

HUMAN ACTIVITIES

Where the climate is suitable, coastal regions attract tourists in large numbers (see unit 3.15). They are also residential areas. Fishing and fish processing are important industries and where there are suitable harbours other industries have developed, e.g. iron and steel, shipbuilding, oil refineries.

ADDITIONAL INFORMATION REQUIRED

1 Sections of coastline frequently form the 1 : 50 000 or 1 : 25 000 map extract and you should try to look at previous map questions or photographs which were based on coastal scenery.

2 Learn the location and names of all the coastal features described in this section.

3 Find out what is meant by, and examples where appropriate of: a cuspate foreland; a raised beach, fetch of the wind; strandflat; offshore bar.

Summary

Basic ideas

Waves are responsible for carrying sand and shingle along a coastline.

Currents are also important carrying agents, particularly in estuaries.

Some sections of coastline are being eroded, whereas others are being built up.

The most important industry connected with coastlines is tourism.

Key terms

Longshore drift; swash; backwash; hydraulic action; corrasion; attrition; corrosion; tourism.

1.7 Desert environments

WIND EROSION

In dry climates, where there is little moisture in the ground, wind erosion can be very powerful. The wind blows away fine material and lowers the surface level; this is called deflation. Depressions such as the huge Qattara depression in the Egyptian desert were caused by deflation. Sometimes oases or salt lakes are found on the floor of such hollows, where the water table reaches the surface.

Hard grains of quartz and other rock particles carried by the wind have a sand-blasting effect on rocks or any other obstacles they hit. This action is called

Fig. 1.7A A group of mesas in the Arizona desert

abrasion. Where layers of rocks are of different hardness, fantastically carved rocks known as yardangs can be formed. The removal of fine particles can leave behind bare rock or a pebble-covered surface, called desert pavement.

Constant movement and abrasion of sand particles rounds them until they become like millet seeds. This process is called attrition and explains the fine sand which forms the dunes and sand seas of hot deserts.

WATER EROSION

Rainfall in desert regions is rare, but the few storms can be very severe, causing short-lived torrents. Steep-sided ravines or wadis are formed by these floods. Downwash on mountain sides can help to form a pediment, a sloping surface of material with channels cut by the occasional run-off from cloudbursts.

The results of erosion by previous river systems may be found in deserts in the form of mesas, or as buttes if they are fairly small. These are the remnants of horizontally-bedded layers, most of which have been removed in the past by water erosion. A cap of harder rock preserves part of the original surface.

WIND DEPOSITION

Sand-bearing winds may be checked by obstacles in their path. A rock, a bush or even a dead donkey can check the sand particles and start the formation of a dune. Wind currents form different shaped dunes, the most common being the crescent-shaped barchan and the ridge-shaped seif dune.

Dunes are constantly moving as sand is blown up the slope of the dune and rolls over the crest. Oases and other obstacles can be smothered by the advancing sand.

DESERT LANDSCAPES

There are three main types:

Erg — sand desert consisting of a sea of dunes.

Reg — stoney desert with a surface of gravel.

Hamada — rock desert, with bare rock and patches of rubble and sand.

HUMAN ACTIVITIES

Considerable sums of money are being spent in some desert regions to irrigate the land and produce crops,

Fig. 1.7B Features produced by wind erosion in arid climates

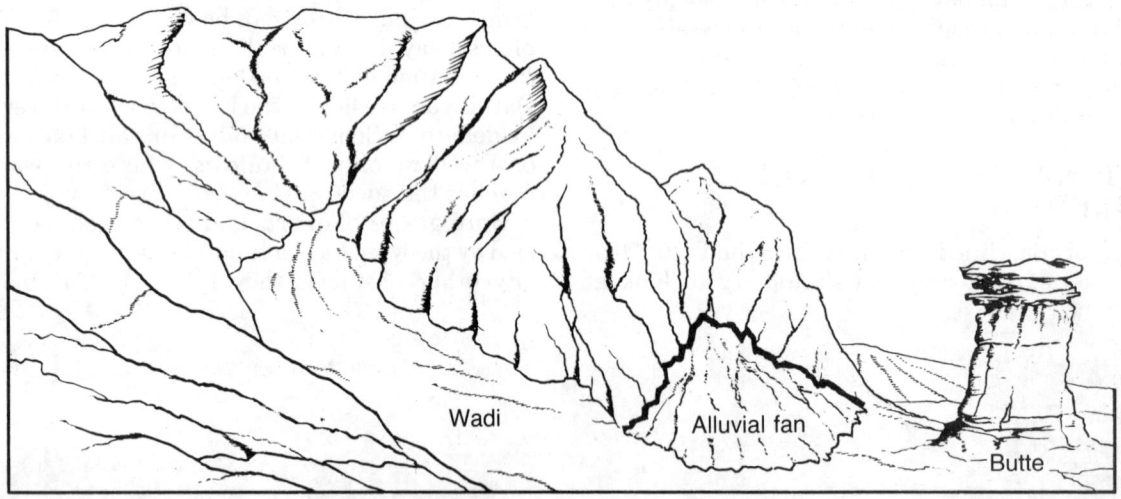

Fig. 1.7C Features produced by water erosion

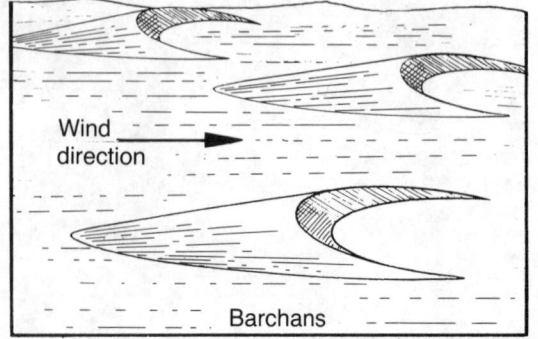
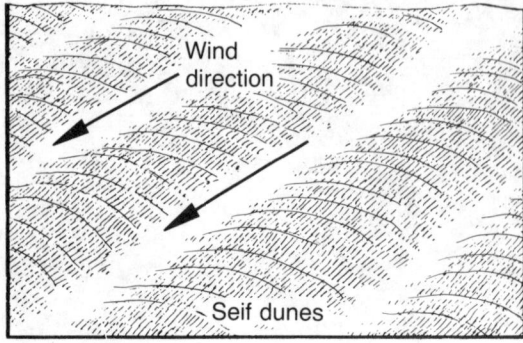

Fig. 1.7D Features of wind deposition

Mapwork and physical geography

e.g. Negev in Israel. Minerals such as oil (Saudi Arabia), iron ore (Mauritania and West Australia) and copper (Queensland) are exploited in desert areas.

Summary

Basic ideas

Erosion in arid landscapes is caused by both wind and water.

Desert landscapes contain a number of physical features which result from erosion and deposition.

Irrigation can completely change the scenery of a desert region.

Key terms

Abrasion; attrition; wadi; mesa; butte; alluvial fan; deflation hollow; yardang; desert pavement; barchan; seif dune; erg; reg; hamada.

1.8 Limestone and chalk environments

Figure 1.8A shows most of the features you would expect to find in limestone districts. The scenery and underground caves are caused by the reaction of limestone to rainwater.

LIMESTONE

Limestone is a form of calcium carbonate, which is usually deposited in thick layers. The horizontal divisions are known as bedding planes, and joints are the vertical divisions that form after deposition.

Rain water, which is slightly acidic, dissolves limestone (chemical weathering) and works its way down the joints and along the bedding planes until it reaches an impervious layer. On the surface a 'pavement' may occur where the bare limestone is exposed in blocks.

Swallow holes are found where the water disappears underground. The scenery of limestone areas is sometimes known as karst topography.

UNDERGROUND FEATURES

The dissolving of the limestone results in the development of underground tunnels and caves, which are explored by pot-holers. Water rich in calcium drips from the ceilings of these caves to form deposits known as stalactites (which hang down), and stalagmites (which grow up from the floor). They sometimes join to form pillars and other weird shapes, examples of which may be seen at Kent's Cave near Torquay, Ingleborough Cave in Yorkshire, and at Cheddar. Underground lakes may occur, with the water reaching the surface many miles from the point where it disappears below ground.

NATURAL ARCHES AND GORGES

Sometimes the roof of a limestone cave collapses, forming a steep-sided gorge. If part of the roof survives it forms a natural arch. Gordale Scar near Malham and Trow Ghyll gorge, also in Yorkshire, are both examples formed by the collapse of caves. Cheddar Gorge was most likely formed by river action when the water-table was higher.

CHALK SCENERY

Chalk, a softer rock than limestone, is soluble in rainwater but does not usually produce underground caves. When the rocks are tilted, scarp and dip slopes are formed. The dip slope ending in a scarp is called a cuesta. Springs appear where the chalk meets clays or similar impervious layers. Water soaks underground so there are no streams, except where rivers cross chalk areas, such as in the Mole valley at Dorking or the river Ouse at Lewes. The scenery produces rolling hills, like Salisbury Plain, with dry valleys where streams used to flow when the water table was higher.

Water held in the chalk saturates the lower layers. The upper surface of this zone of saturated rock is called the water table. The water table will come closer to the surface in wet weather and fall during dry spells. Its level is also affected by water being pumped out of the chalk to provide the water supply for neighbouring regions.

HUMAN USE OF LIMESTONE AND CHALK

Limestone is an important building stone. Many cathedrals and well-known buildings such as the

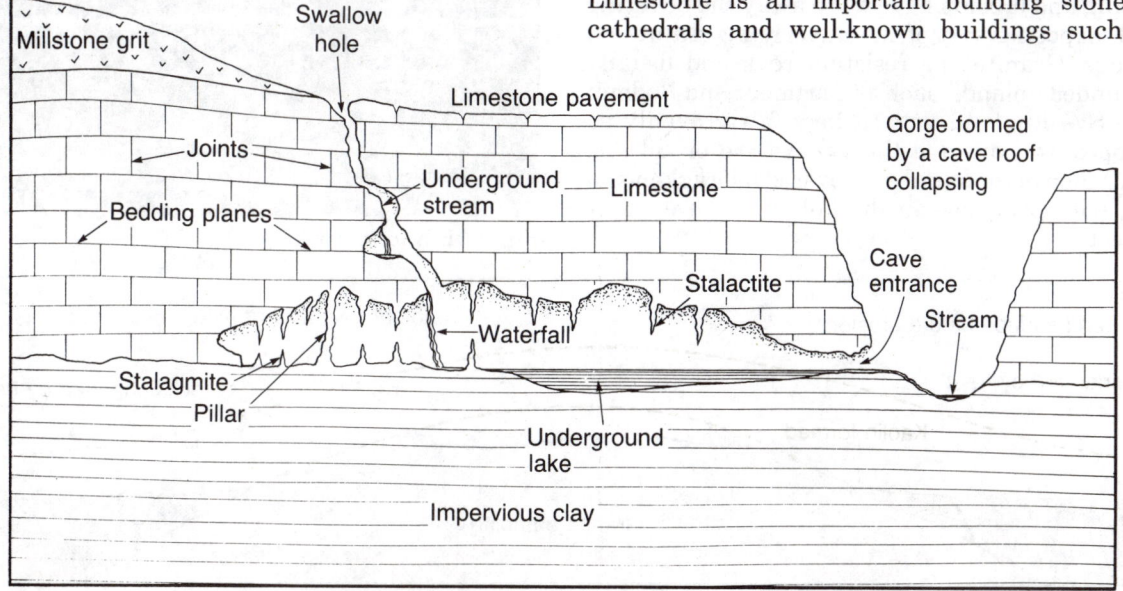

Fig. 1.8A Cross-section of a limestone area

Mapwork and physical geography

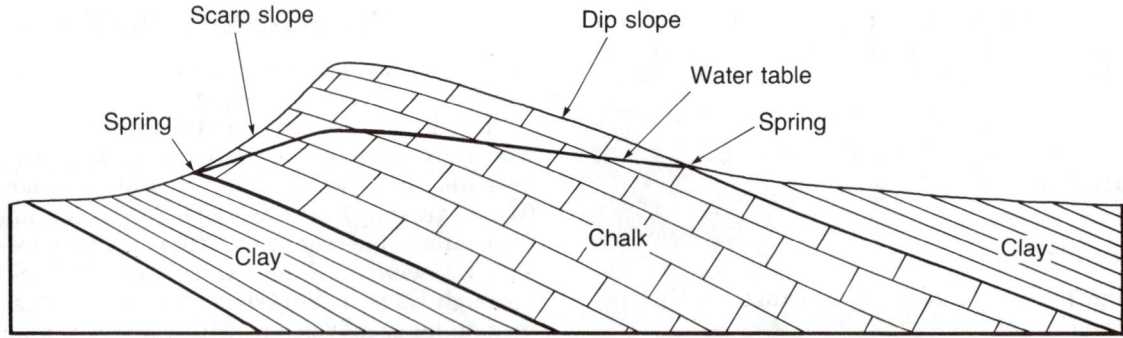

Fig. 1.8B Cross-section of a chalk cuesta

Houses of Parliament are built of this rock. In some areas it is also used to build dry-stone walls around fields. Both limestone and chalk are sources of lime, which is used in making mortar and cement. It is also used as a fertilizer, particularly on acid soils.

Larger underground caves such as Wookey Hole near Cheddar are visited by tourists, while less accessible cave-systems attract pot-holers.

> **Summary**
>
> *Basic ideas*
>
> Limestone is soluble in rain water, which is slightly acidic, and a number of surface and underground features are the result.
>
> Chalk scenery may include scarp and dip slopes and other characteristic features.
>
> *Key terms*
>
> Bedding planes; joints; swallow holes; stalagmites; stalactites; limestone pavement; gorge; cuesta; scarp and dip; dry valley; water table.

1.9 Granite environments

HOW GRANITE WAS FORMED

Granite is an igneous rock formed underground from molten material which cooled slowly. It usually developed as large dome-shaped masses which are called batholiths. In many regions, including Britain, weathering and erosion have worn away the covering material, exposing part of the underlying granite on the surface. Granite is a resistant rock and usually forms rounded uplands, such as Dartmoor and Bodmin Moor in SW England. It weathers fairly evenly so steep slopes are rare and the valleys are broad and shallow. Much of the surface is covered in bracken and heather, with peat bogs in the hollows where water can collect.

TORS

Granite moorland sometimes contains large blocks of rock which stand up above the surrounding region in a variety of strange shapes. These blocks are called tors and were probably formed by deep chemical weathering in well-jointed rock. Granite contains many joints and these can be seen very clearly in the tors where weathering has opened them up to form blocks of different shapes and sizes. Freeze-thaw mechanical weathering during the Ice Age shattered some of the rock and the slopes below many tors are strewn with boulders.

CHINA CLAY

Around the edges of granite batholiths, other rocks were changed by the heat to become metamorphic rocks. Gases and water broke down felspar crystals in the granite and a fine white clay called kaolin, or

Fig. 1.9B Kaolin workings

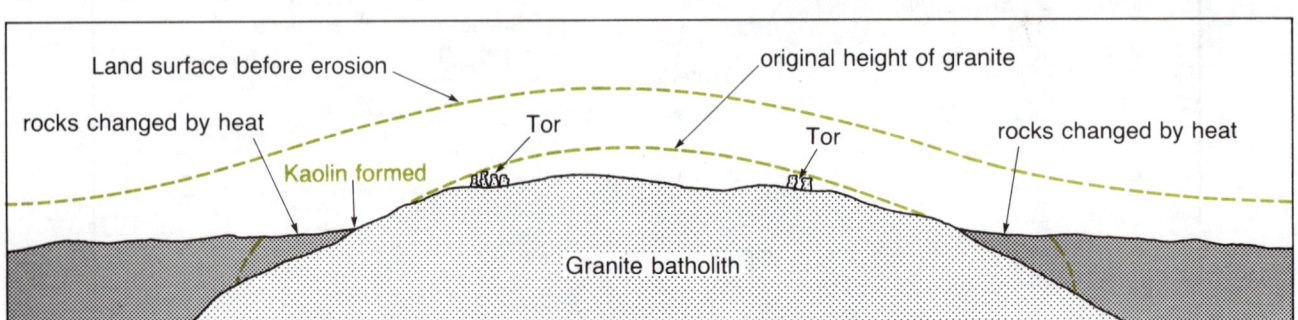

Fig. 1.9A Cross-section of a granite upland region

china clay, was formed. It is used in the manufacture of chinaware and porcelain and as a filler in the manufacture of paper, rubber and paint. Mining is extensive north of St. Austell in Cornwall and the area is sometimes known as the 'Cornish Alps' (see fig. 1.9B). Granite is also in demand as a building stone and for road making.

Summary
Basic ideas

Granite is a hard, resistant rock which usually forms areas of upland.
These uplands may contain granite tors and have kaolin deposits on their margins.

Key terms

Igneous; batholith; tor; kaolin; china clay.

1.10 Volcanoes and earthquakes

PLATES

The earth we live on has a very thin shell of rock, called the crust. This crust is made up of several pieces, called plates. Beneath these plates are partially molten layers which make up the mantle. These layers are heated from the earth's core by convection currents which cause the molten rock to flow towards the crust, where it is cooled and spreads before sinking back to be heated again.

The plates shown on fig. 1.10A move slowly over the mantle in the directions shown by the arrows. This means that in some mid-ocean areas the plates are moving apart. Molten rock rises to form a ridge where the plates are separating. Elsewhere, as around the edge of the Pacific Ocean, plates move past each other or collide. When two plates collide, one rides over the other, and rocks on or near the earth's surface are folded and pushed up to form mountain chains, such as

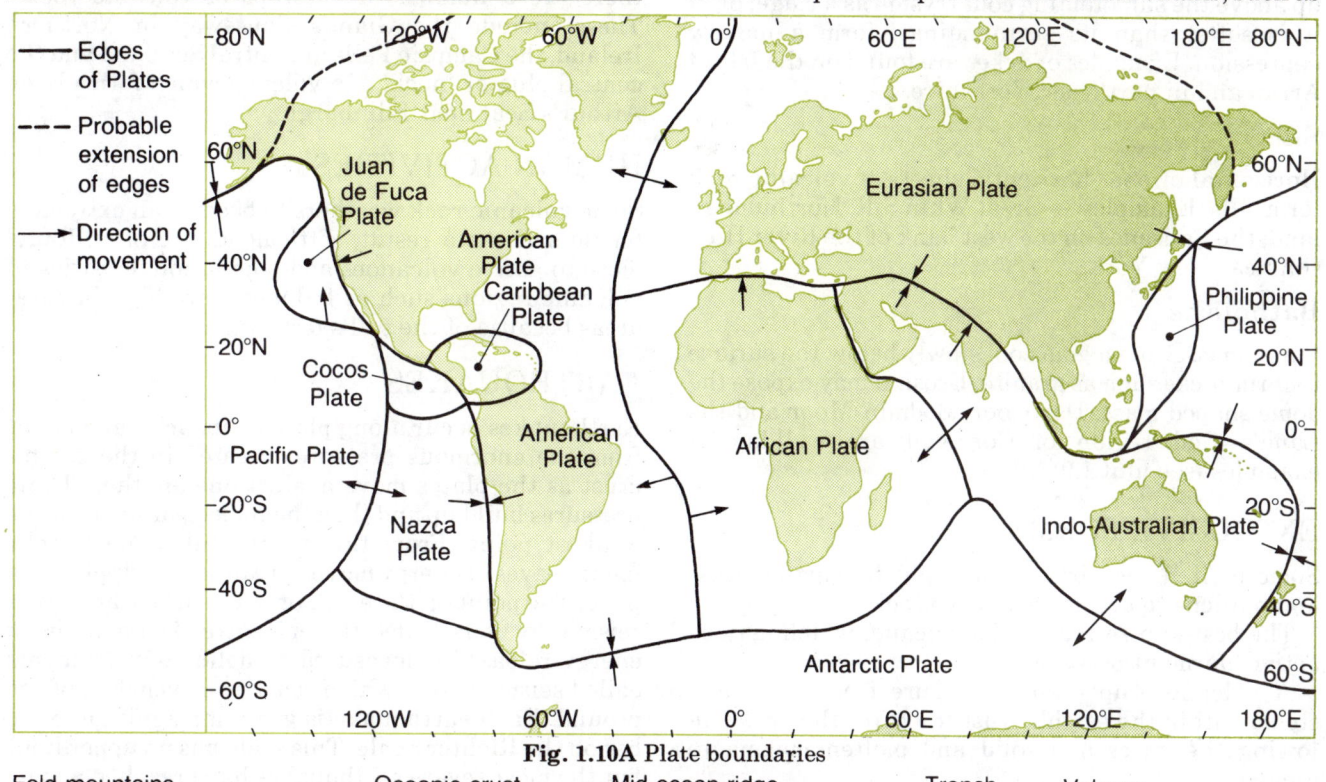

Fig. 1.10A Plate boundaries

Fig. 1.10B Converging and diverging plates

the Alps and Andes. Plates which are moving together are called converging plates, while plates moving apart are diverging.

VULCANICITY

The boundaries of plates, or plate margins, are zones of weakness in the earth's crust and it is here that volcanoes and earthquakes occur. Through these weaknesses molten rock, called magma, oozes up to form intrusive or extrusive rock forms. Intrusive rock, like granite, is formed under the surface but may be exposed after a period of time as a result of weathering or earth movements.

INTRUSIVE FORMS

Dykes

Magma which seeps upwards along vertical cracks hardens to form dykes. After erosion a dyke may stand up above the surrounding countryside as a ridge, or, if it is softer than its surroundings, form a narrow depression. Examples of dykes are found on the Isle of Arran and in north-east Yorkshire.

Sills

Horizontal or near-horizontal sheets of volcanic rock form sills. Examples — Great Whin Sill, Northumberland; the Palisades on the west bank of the River Hudson near New York.

Batholiths

Large masses of magma cool slowly below the surface to form rocks such as granite. Erosion may expose the dome-shaped mass. Dartmoor, Bodmin Moor and the Land's End region of Cornwall are well-known examples (see unit 1.9).

EXTRUSIVE FORMS

Some molten rock breaks through the earth's crust and hardens to become extrusive rock.

The best-known type is the volcano, which may be active, dormant or extinct.

A volcano erupts when pressure from gases and steam within the earth's crust fractures the crust, allowing the gases and solid and molten magma to escape.

Lava is molten magma which hardens when it has been cooled at the surface. If the lava is acidic it contains much silica and it hardens quickly, building steep-sided volcanoes, which are likely to erupt explosively because the vents are sealed by the hardened lava. If it is basic lava (rich in iron and other minerals) it cools slowly and may spread out to form a shield volcano. The eruption may be quiet, as the vent is not sealed. Fine powdered lava may also be ejected. This falls as ash and makes an ash cone.

Composite cones are made up of layers of ash and lava flows. Some of the lava may flow from secondary vents. Mount Etna in Sicily has many such vents.

Some volcanoes have lost the main part of the cone by eruptions or earth movements, leaving a huge rounded basin which is called a caldera. Lakes may fill the bottom of the basin with the steep crater sides giving a saucer-like shape. Crater Lake in Oregon, USA fills an ancient caldera.

Although there are no active volcanoes in Britain there are a number of outcrops of volcanic rocks. These include the Giant's Causeway in Northern Ireland, the Campsie Fells in Central Scotland and the central plug or 'neck' of a volcano which forms King Arthur's Seat near Edinburgh.

HUMAN ACTIVITIES

Some volcanic rock weathers to become an extremely fertile soil. As a result, settlements are often found close to active volcanoes and population densities in volcanic regions such as Indonesia are high in rural areas because of the soil's fertility.

EARTHQUAKES

Earthquakes occur along plate boundaries and result from the enormous pressures created in the earth's crust as the plates move against one another. These pressures build up and then the rocks tear apart at the weakest point. From this point, called the seismic focus, waves of energy move outwards like ripples on a pond. The point on the earth or sea's surface above the seismic focus is called the epicentre. The amount of energy released is measured by delicate instruments called seismometers which react to movements of the ground. Each earthquake is given a magnitude number on the Richter Scale. This scale has no upper limit but the most severe earthquakes have reached a mag-

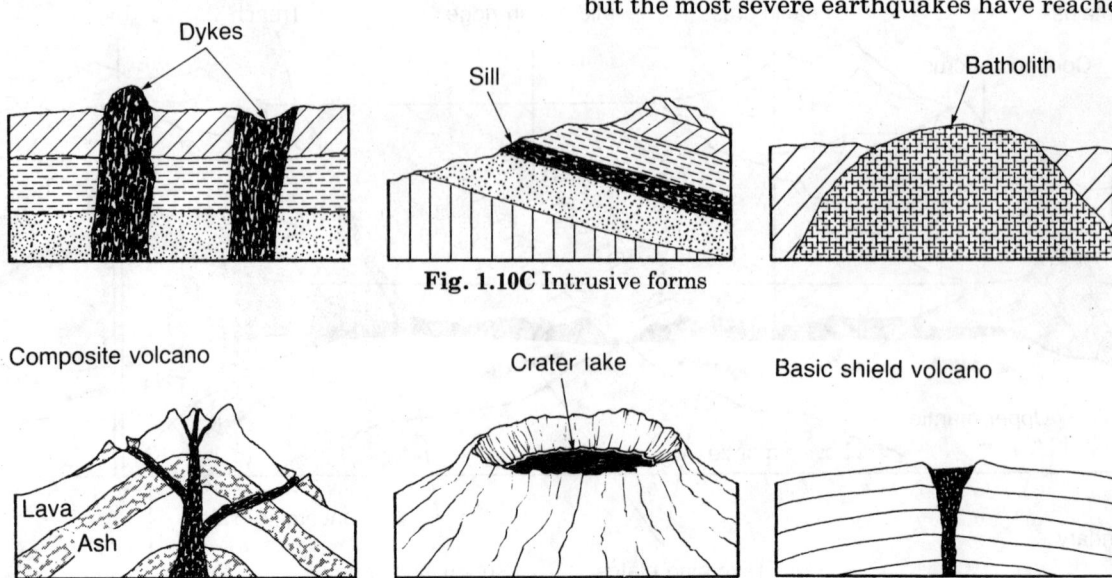

Fig. 1.10C Intrusive forms

Fig. 1.10D Extrusive forms

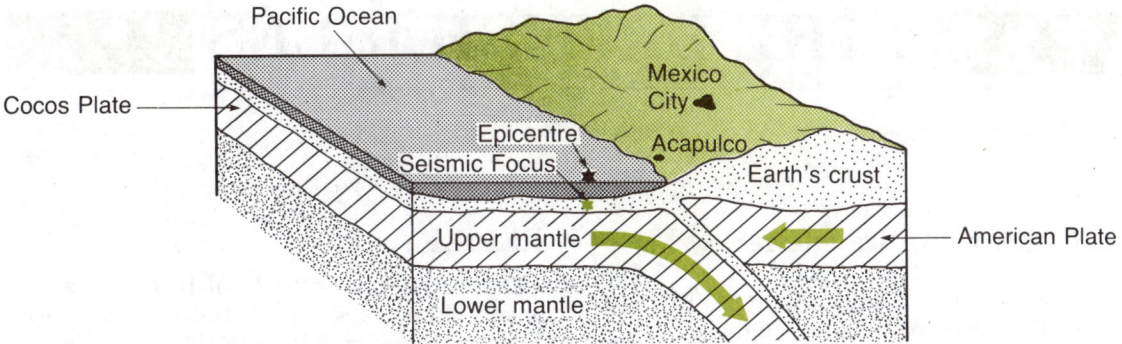

Fig. 1.10E The cause of the 1985 earthquake in Mexico City

nitude of 8.9. Earthquakes with a magnitude of 6 and upwards are capable of causing widespread damage.

Figure 1.10E shows the reasons for the severe earthquake which destroyed many buildings in the centre of Mexico City in September 1985. It measured 7.8 on the Richter Scale and caused considerable loss of life. Find this region in your atlas.

TSUNAMIS

Earthquakes which occur on or under the sea bed can cause tidal waves, which increase in magnitude in shallow waters near a coast. The Mexican earthquake did not produce a large tidal wave, but in 1983 over 50 people were killed by tidal waves which struck the north-west coast of Japan. *Tsunami*, the Japanese word for tidal wave, is given to these phenomena.

Summary

Basic ideas

The earth's crust is unstable and is formed of a number of moving plates.
Plate margins are zones of weakness where volcanoes and earthquakes occur.
Vulcanicity results in intrusive and extrusive rock formations.
Volcanic soils can be very fertile.

Key terms

Plate; converging; diverging; magma; intrusive; extrusive; seismic focus; epicentre; Richter Scale; tsunami.

Fig. 1.10F The Mexico City earthquake

2 THE BRITISH ISLES

2.1 Climate and weather

Climate may be thought of as the average state of the weather. The British climate is so changeable that many people say we have no climate, only weather. The main factors influencing the climate are as follows:

LATITUDE

Since the country lies between 50°N and 60°N the climate is 'cool temperate' and extremes of heat and cold are not maintained for long. The average (mean) annual range of temperature is small with the greatest range in the south-east, for example, 14.4°C in the London area.

THE NORTH ATLANTIC DRIFT

This is a warm ocean current, also called the Gulf Stream, which crosses the Atlantic and spreads around the coast of Britain. Its greatest effect is felt in winter when it keeps the western part of the country warmer than the eastern half. Because of its influence the north-west of Scotland has a higher average temperature in January than does the south-east of England.

PREVAILING WINDS

Westerly winds prevail over the British Isles. They blow between the Icelandic low pressure and the Azores high. Since these winds blow across the North Atlantic Drift they are warm and moisture-laden. They carry maritime influences up long estuaries such as the Severn and across the western peninsulas.

RELIEF

Most of the upland areas of Britain are found in the west. When the moisture-laden westerlies reach Britain, they are forced to rise over these highlands, and heavy relief rain falls thoughout the year. The western half of the country is therefore generally wetter than the eastern half.

AIR MASSES

Day-to-day variations of the weather are caused by the fact that different air masses influence the weather at different times. Maritime air masses from the tropics or from the polar area meet continental air masses along 'fronts' (see unit 1.3). As these fronts cross the country there are rapid and marked changes in wind direction, temperature and weather conditions. When continental air masses are in control we may have very cold winters or fine, hot summers. Oceanic air masses bring less extreme, more moist conditions.

Summary

Basic ideas

Climate is the average state of the weather.
The British climate is influenced by a number of interacting factors.
Day-to-day variations in weather are the result of the presence of different air masses over the country.

Key terms

Climate; prevailing winds; cool temperate; air mass; annual range of temperature; maritime influences.

2.2 Farming as a system

DEFINITION OF A SYSTEM

A system is a set of objects or parts which are linked together in a way we can recognize. The system has one or more functions to perform, i.e. it has a purpose or job to do. Systems in Geography are open systems, that is, they need a supply of energy to keep them going. By adjusting to changing conditions the system is kept in a condition of stability which is known as a 'steady state'.

A farm satisfies this definition of a system:

1 It is made up of a set of parts — the farm buildings, the fields, the silage bins or grain stores, the machinery and workshops. These parts are interrelated; for example, the grass cut from the fields may be stored as

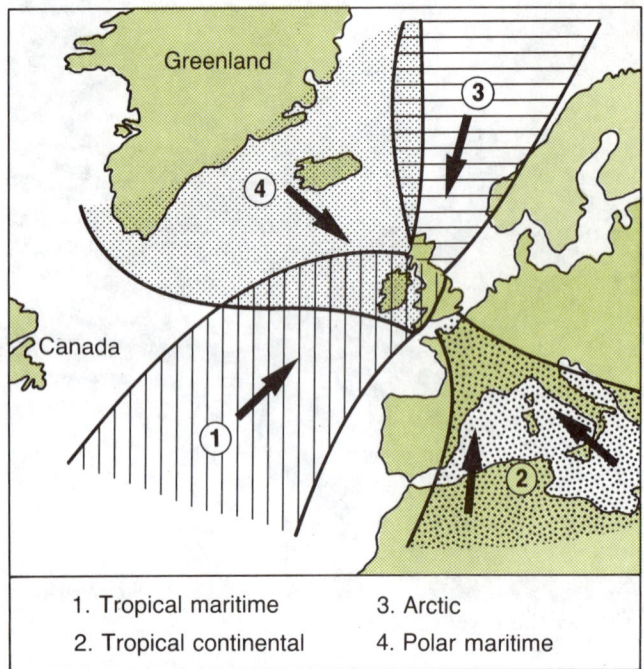

1. Tropical maritime   3. Arctic
2. Tropical continental   4. Polar maritime

Fig. 2.1 Air masses which influence the British climate

silage until it is fed in winter to the animals in the cowsheds.

2 The system has a purpose — the production of food and other valuable crops.

3 The farm needs supplies of energy to keep it going. The basic form of energy is the sunshine, which causes plant growth. The labour of the farmer and his workers is another essential form of energy upon which the system depends.

4 The farmers of Britain also have to adjust regularly the ways in which they manage and run their farms and the products upon which they concentrate. These adjustments are the result of new farming techniques, the availability of new equipment and machinery, and changes in government or European Community (EC) regulations which affect the profitability of different farming activities.

PHYSICAL ENVIRONMENT FACTOR

The physical environment influences considerably the nature of farming practised in different parts of the country. For example, the mild winters and substantial rainfall make grass the most suitable crop to be grown in the western part of Britain. Conversely the sunny summers, lower rainfall totals and flat land of eastern England are physical factors which are much more favourable to arable farming.

Relief and geology also have their effects. In Scotland, for example, 70 per cent of the land area is unsuitable for farming. Even on a single farm, variations in geology and slope can produce different land uses. Cattle rearing for milk production may be concentrated on the rich wet meadows found on the low-lying fields with heavy clay soil, while cereal crops are grown on the lighter, better drained and more fertile soils of the hillside of a downland farm in southern England.

THE FARMER AS DECISION-MAKER

Farming is one of the most important industries in Britain. At present, in most parts of the country it is a highly successful and profitable industry.

The success of British farming is dependent largely upon the ability of farmers to make the right decisions. The farmer must decide how best to use the land at his disposal; how much money and other resources he can risk investing, and which are the products that are likely to bring the greatest rewards. The farmer also has many day-to-day decisions to make, such as when to start harvesting, when to time the lambing season or when to sell his animals.

When the farmer makes the right decisions the farm is successful. Profit is the income that is obtained in excess of the cost of production. The farmer who makes a profit then has to decide what proportion should be reinvested in the farm (new machinery, modernization of buildings) and how much he can save or spend on his family.

THE FARM AS A SYSTEM

Figure 2.2 illustrates the way in which we can look at the farm as an open system. The two key factors which determine how the system operates are:

(a) the physical environment in which the farm is located;
(b) the decisions made by the farmer.

INPUTS AND OUTPUTS

Inputs are the raw materials of farming. They include physical inputs such as soil quality, climate, animal breeds and seeds, together with human inputs, especially the labour needed to work the land. Another very important input to British farms is the money (capital) invested in the farm to maintain and improve it.

Inputs

(a) Physical
 e.g. soil
  climate
  seeds

(b) Human
 e.g. capital
  labour
  EC regulations
  technology
  expert advice
  training for workers

PARTS OF THE FARM

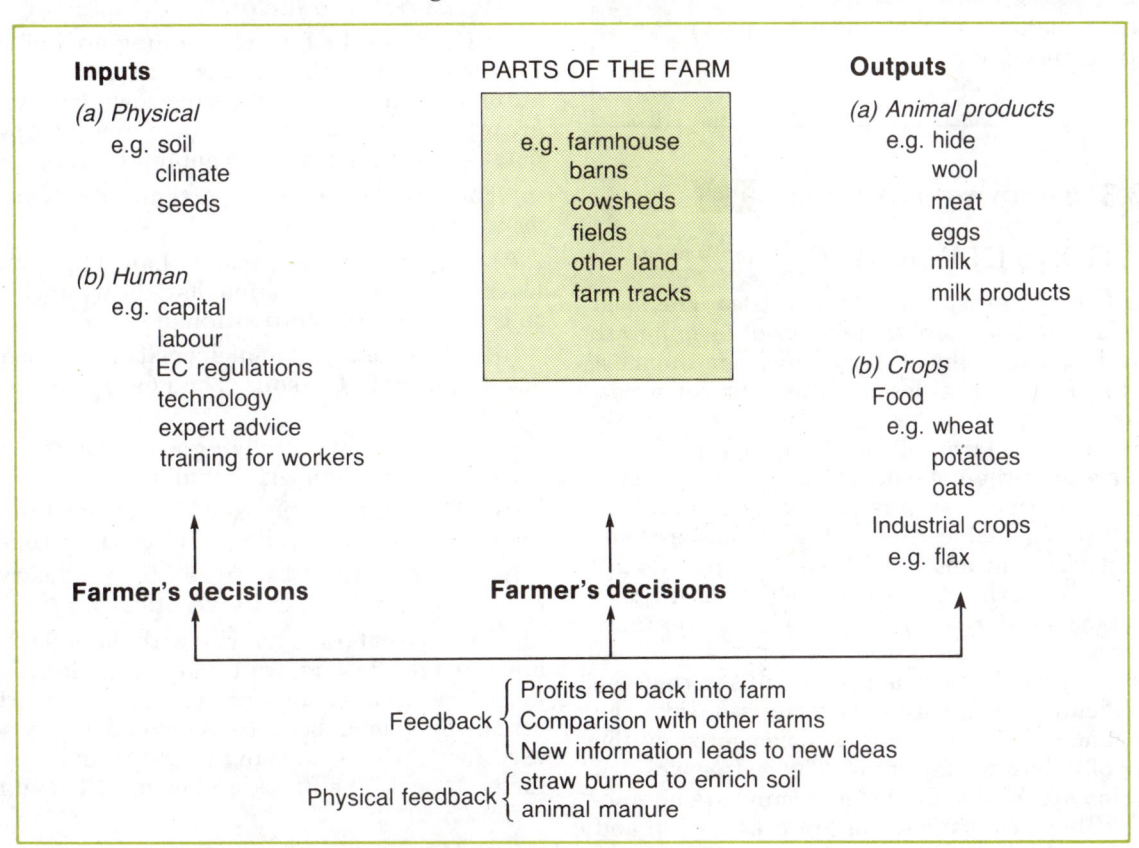

e.g. farmhouse
 barns
 cowsheds
 fields
 other land
 farm tracks

Outputs

(a) Animal products
 e.g. hide
  wool
  meat
  eggs
  milk
  milk products

(b) Crops
 Food
 e.g. wheat
  potatoes
  oats

 Industrial crops
 e.g. flax

Farmer's decisions ← → **Farmer's decisions**

Feedback { Profits fed back into farm
 Comparison with other farms
 New information leads to new ideas

Physical feedback { straw burned to enrich soil
 animal manure

Fig. 2.2 The farm as a system

Outputs are the products of the farm, which may be animals, animal products, or crops.

Inputs and outputs are not totally separate, for example the animal manure which is part of the farm production may also be a key input, as fertilizer for a field in which the farmer is growing carrots organically, for sale to health shops.

FEEDBACK

Farmers have to ask themselves constantly how well their farm is operating. Evidence to answer the question comes partly from how high or low profits are. A farmer will also compare what he produces with the operations of other farmers, and get expert advice from the agricultural advisory services (ADAS) and farming journals. From experience and new knowledge, the farmer may change his decisions and practice from time to time, to try to make his farm system operate more effectively and profitably.

Summary

Basic ideas

Farming is a primary industry whose major concern is the production of food and commercial crops.
The farmer is a decision maker who has to decide how best to use his land and invest his money (capital) and labour to obtain good results.
Farming may be seen as an open system which regulates itself in response to changing conditions.

Key terms

Decision making; system; input; output; interrelationships; profit.

2.3 Farming contrasts

VARIATIONS IN FARMING

Farming is very varied in the British Isles. The least commercial and least profitable types of farming are found in the parts of the country which are the most difficult to farm — the coolest and the mountain areas. The most profitable farms are the large, highly mechanized arable farms of eastern England.

Large areas of the uplands are moorlands — open hills covered with coarse grass, heather and bracken. As far as farming is concerned, the moorlands are marginal lands. This means that the land is just fertile enough to give farmers a reasonable living in good years, but in bad years even the most able farmers may make a loss.

In very general terms it is possible to say that the most difficult areas are characterized by the predominance of sheep-rearing, supplemented by the breeding of calves for fattening. The wetter western areas which are most suitable for farming are characterized by the predominance of grass as a crop and dairy cows as the most important animals. The most fertile eastern and southern areas concentrate on the growing of cereals.

TYPES OF FARMING

1 Pastoral farming is the rearing of animals that feed on grass and other vegetation. In countries like Britain, this type of farming may also be called *commercial grazing* because the wool, hides and meat are produced for profit.

2 Arable farming is the ploughing and cultivation of land for the production of crops. This may be *intensive*, where the land is virtually gardened by the use of many workers, or *extensive*, where large areas of land are cultivated by a small labour force using modern machinery.

3 Mixed farming, where crops are grown and livestock is also kept, is the most common type of farming in Britain.

TWO CONTRASTING FARMING REGIONS

Below are two examples of quite different farming regions in the British Isles.

1 Agriculture in East Anglia
Physical background

East Anglia is a low plateau. The plateau dips eastwards and is bordered in the west by a chalk scarp called the East Anglian Heights, which rises to just over 100 metres. The scarp is broken by the Breckland, a low-lying sand and gravel area covered by heath. The plateau is plastered with glacial deposits, boulder clays, sands and gravels. Two distinctive areas are the Fens, which are made up of silt and peat deposits, and the Broads, shallow lakes formed by the drowning of peat workings from medieval times.

Agriculture: main factors

(a) This is the chief arable farming area of England. Fifty per cent of the land is used to produce grain, autumn-sown wheat and spring-sown barley. Cereals are grown in rotation with valuable cash crops such as potatoes, sugar beet and vegetables.

(b) The reasons for the importance of arable farming are:

(i) The climate. The eastern half of the country has less rain and more sunshine than the western half, and so is better for the cultivation of cereals.

(ii) Many of the glacial deposits have been broken down to form fertile soils. The Fens are a very fertile area.

(iii) The flat and low lying areas allow farmers to use efficient mechanized techniques.

(iv) There is easy access to London and the towns of the industrial East Midlands, to market crops.

(v) The growth of the frozen food industry means there is a ready market for vegetables.

(c) The type of farming varies with the soils. The Fens are noted for flowers, fruit and vegetables. The chalk and richer glacial soils are especially important for cereals and sugar beet. Heavy boulder clay soils are used for cattle — dairying (milk) near London, beef further north. The Breckland is infertile and remains mainly heath.

(continued on page 24)

An East Anglian System

INPUTS

Physical
e.g.
Relief
Climate
Soils

Human
e.g.
Skilled labour force
Business expertise
Modern technology

(Stores)

Seeds
Fertilizers

EC subsidies
Capital investment

(Throughputs)

PROCESSES

Farming Activities
e.g.
Cultivation
Adding fertilizers
Grain harvesting
Cash crop picking
Drying grain
Transporting cash crops to factory

OUTPUTS

Farm Products
e.g.
Sugar beet
Vegetables for freezing
Grain (wheat, barley)
Fruit

PROFIT?

LOSS?

£
↓

FARMER'S DECISIONS   FARMER'S DECISIONS

Feedback on success of business

A Hill Farm System

INPUTS

Physical
e.g.
Relief
Climate
Soils

Human
e.g.
Family labour
Traditional practices

(Stores)

Animal feed
Food supplements

Hill farm subsidies
EC subsidies
Advice on diversification

(Throughputs)

PROCESSES

Farming Activities
e.g.
Lambing
Shearing
Calving
Hay-making
Transporting animals to market

OUTPUTS

Farm Products
e.g.
Wool
Fat lambs
Breeding ewes
Cattle for fattening
Bull calves

PROFIT?

LOSS?

£
↓

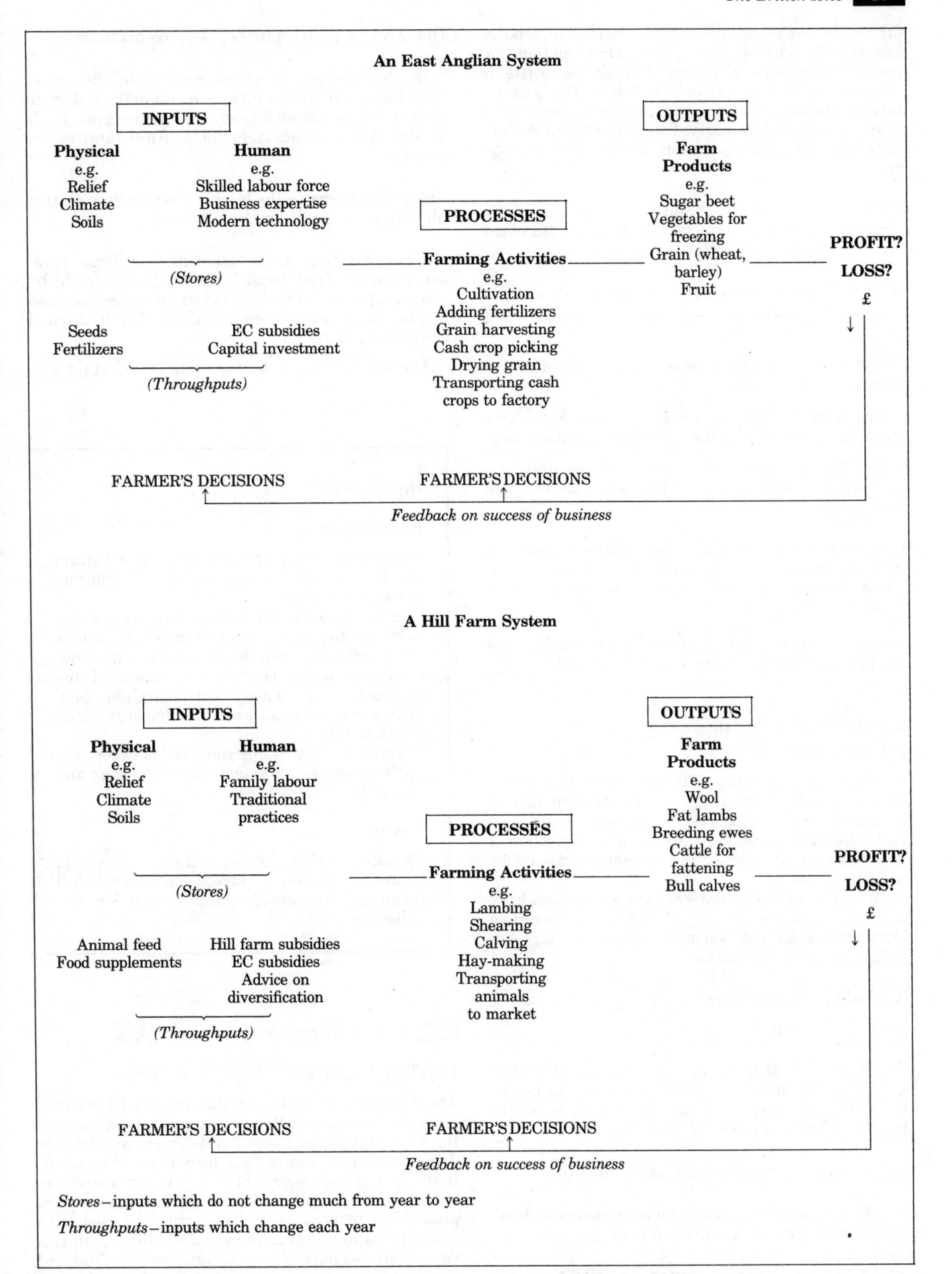

FARMER'S DECISIONS   FARMER'S DECISIONS

Feedback on success of business

Stores – inputs which do not change much from year to year
Throughputs – inputs which change each year

Fig. 2.3 Two contrasting farming systems

(d) Sugar beet is a very profitable crop but its production is limited by the Government. One hundred tonnes of beet produce 20 tonnes of sugar; the 'waste' is returned to the farms as animal fodder. The beet are lifted in the autumn and the processing factories work from September to January. This fits well into the 'off-peak' period for work with cereals and other rotation crops.

(e) The farms are large, highly mechanized, and use efficient, modern techniques. They have benefited greatly from EC agricultural policies.

(f) The farms have to face a number of problems:

(i) Cold north-east winds and late springs affect yields.

(ii) Large mechanized farms require a great deal of capital.

(iii) Although few labourers are needed, farms have to compete with the high wages offered in the towns.

(iv) To maintain efficiency and profitability, farmers have to keep up with new research and techniques.

(g) Industries are related to agriculture — brewing, milling, mustard and shoemaking at Norwich, fertilizer manufacture and agricultural equipment at Ipswich.

Typical farming activities in East Anglia are summarized in the system shown in fig. 2.3.

2 Hill farming in Mid Wales
Physical background

Mid Wales is essentially an upland plateau area with thin acid soils. Since it lies in the western half of Britain the region is exposed to oceanic influences and has a substantial rainfall – an annual precipitation of 1500mm (approx 60 ins) is not uncommon. Some falls as snow in winter.

Hill farms lie more than 300 metres above sea level and summers are cool, e.g. 13.5°C as the average temperature for the warmest month. Winters are mild, e.g. December 4.5°C.

Agriculture: main factors

(a) The main crop is grass.

(b) Since much of the land is exposed moorland the most suitable animal economy is sheep rearing. In more sheltered parts cattle are also reared, usually to be sold to lowland farms for fattening.

(c) Farms are generally small and family run.

(d) Many of the farms would be uneconomic without Government grants and EC subsidies.

(e) There are very limited possibilities for diversifying activities. Many farmers try to add to their income by offering camping and caravan sites to tourists.

Hill farmers have a number of problems to face:

(i) The increase in sheep rearing in the richer farming regions of Britain may result in the reduction of EC subsidies for all farmers. On the marginal lands of Mid Wales a reduction could prove fatal to the industry.

(ii) Bad weather in the lambing season may destroy all hopes of a profit for the year's work.

(iii) Hill farming areas are suffering from rural depopulation. Traditional farms are being bought by townspeople who offer high prices for retirement and holiday homes and for smallholdings. The traditional economy is in decline.

The hill farming system is summarized in fig 2.3.

Summary

Basic ideas

There is a variety of farming types in Britain which are largely the result of differing physical conditions.

In the better farming areas farmers are able to choose to practice a wide range of activities, but in difficult regions farmers have to work out a system which reflects the nature of the physical environment. On marginal land grants and subsidies are vital elements of the farming income.

There is a striking contrast between the predominant farming features of the west and east of the British Isles.

Key terms

Physical environment; arable farming; pastoral farming; mixed farming; hill farming; marginal land; cash crops; subsidies.

2.4 Energy resources

BRITISH ENERGY RESOURCES

The development of Britain into the chief industrial power in the world in Victorian times was based upon the vast quantities of power which were available to drive machinery and to heat furnaces and kilns. At that time the basic source of energy in Britain was an abundance of cheap coal. During the 19th century, production of coal in this country increased from about 10 million tonnes to over 200 million tonnes a year. Coal was burned to heat water, which produced steam power for ships, trains and factory machinery. Coal was also used as coke in furnaces to produce iron and steel. It later became the main fuel for the generation of electricity.

The British Isles 25

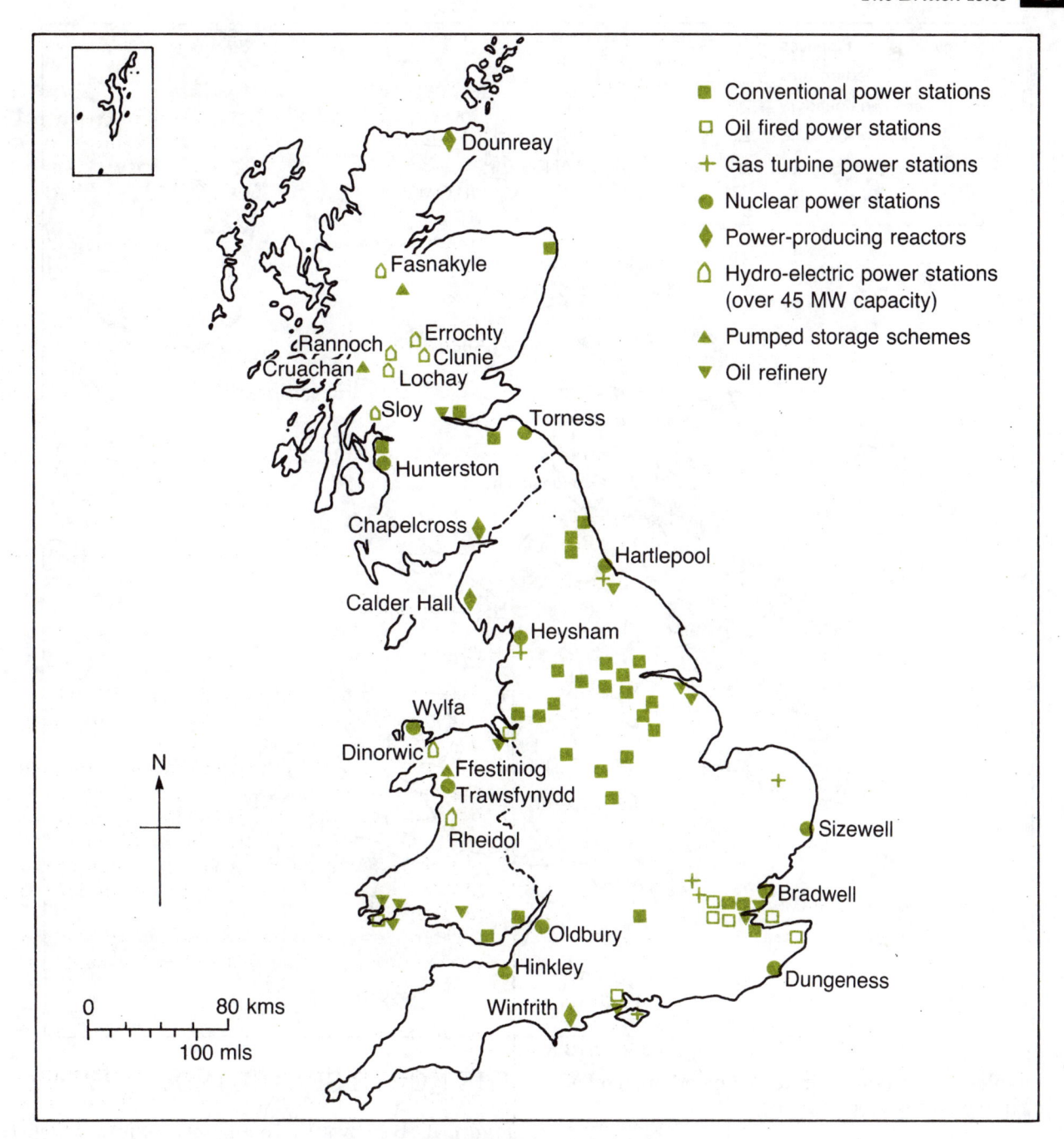

Fig. 2.4A Energy resources

Legend:
- ■ Conventional power stations
- □ Oil fired power stations
- + Gas turbine power stations
- ● Nuclear power stations
- ♦ Power-producing reactors
- ⌂ Hydro-electric power stations (over 45 MW capacity)
- ▲ Pumped storage schemes
- ▼ Oil refinery

We have become less dependent on coal mining because of the discovery of other sources of energy — petroleum, natural gas, atomic energy and hydro-electricity.

ENERGY SUPPLIES: MAIN FACTORS INVOLVED

1 Coal-fired power stations are still the most common. The two chief clusters are along the lower Thames and along the Trent valley. The River Trent runs along the edge of the chief coalfield of Britain — the Yorkshire, Nottinghamshire and Derbyshire field. Large quantities of water are required for generating electricity and this is obtained from the river. The coal required by the Thames-side stations is shipped from the north.

2 Nuclear power stations have been developed since 1955. Britain is a major nuclear power producer, with France, the USA and USSR. You can see from the map (fig. 2.4A) that the stations are located on the coast or near other large areas of water (Trawsfynydd is alongside a lake). They have also been built in remote areas such as North Wales, the Lake District and Dungeness, away from large cities. Nuclear Electric, the company operating the nuclear power stations, generates one-fifth of all the UK's electricity.

3 Oil-fired stations are situated close to oil refineries so that the fuel can be fed to them directly from the storage tanks. Since much of our oil is imported, the refineries are near the coast, so water is readily available. Examples of such stations are Pembroke (on Milford Haven) and Fawley (on Southampton Water). The discovery of the North Sea oilfields

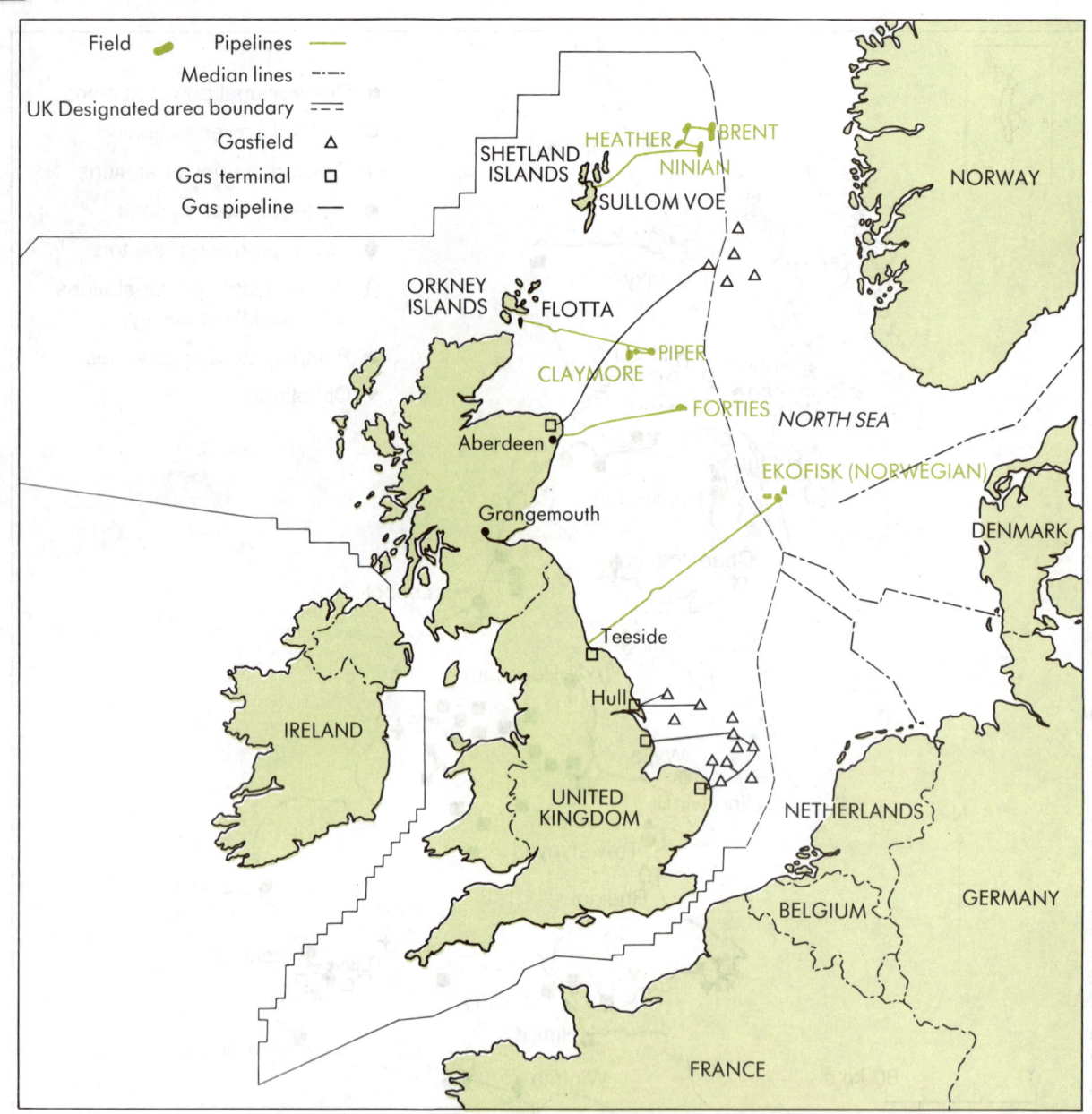

Fig. 2.4B North Sea oil

and enabled Britain to continue to depend upon oil as a very important source of energy.

4 Hydroelectric power stations are found in highland areas with heavy rainfall — the Scottish Highlands and North Wales. This is not a major source of energy in Britain at present.

5 Natural gas from the North Sea is increasingly being used for electricity production. A number of combined cycle gas turbine (CCET) stations have been built and more are planned. These plants produce less than half the carbon dioxide produced on a coalfield station and they are more efficient, so the environment benefits.

6 The National Grid: power generated along the coast and estuaries and in the upland areas is transmitted to cities and industries by means of the National Grid. Cables capable of carrying 400 kilovolts have been built to form a 'supergrid' so that power is available in any part of the country when it is needed. We can even borrow from France if necessary. Since 1961 a cable under the English Channel has provided a direct link with the power stations in the Alps.

THE NORTH SEA OIL INDUSTRY

Figure 2.4B shows the main sectors into which the North Sea has been divided. The governments which control each sector allocate exploitation and drilling rights to various oil companies. The extraction of oil in the British sector began in 1970–71, in the Forties field. Since then a number of fields have been discovered and developed by the building of pipelines to line them with Britain.

The main fields are in three clusters:

1 To the east of the Shetlands

(a) Ninian and Heather fields, which are linked by pipeline with the oil terminal at Sullom Voe.

(b) Brent and other small fields, which are also linked with Sullom Voe.

2 To east of the Orkneys

Piper and claymore fields, which are lined by pipeline with Flotta and Scapa Flow.

3 To the east of mainland Scotland

(a) the Forties field, with a pipeline to the coast which runs on to the refinery at Grangemouth.
(b) Ekofisk, which is a Norwegian field. It has a pipeline to Teesside.

IMPACT OF THE OILFIELDS

Jobs were created in the industrial estuaries of Teesside and Clydeside and in the Firth of Forth, Moray Firth and NW Scotland as production platforms, drilling rigs and pipes were needed. Shore-based jobs were also created at the ends of the pipelines; Sullom Voe, for example, became one of the most important oil ports in the world.

Land and house prices have risen rapidly in areas connected with the oil industry, because of the high wages paid in the industry, and Aberdeen has become an important oil marketing centre. In the last 15 years the city has changed dramatically and has become the oil capital of the north, with strong American connections. New airport services have developed, especially at Dyce (Aberdeen).

It is planned to build new petrochemical areas at Peterhead and in the Moray Firth and Firth of Forth. The recent fall in oil prices, however, has stopped further exploration in the North Sea.

THE SIGNIFICANCE OF NORTH SEA OIL TO BRITAIN

Britain has become an oil-exporting nation and earns vast amounts of money from the oil trade. Commercial production of North Sea oil coincided with economic epression and a serious decline of manufacturing industries in Britain. Britain's prosperity partly depends on the revenues from oil, which were large in the late 1970s when there was a shortage of supplies, but fell greatly in the mid 1980s when there was a glut in supplies. The fall i prices led to a decline of shore-based oil-related industries. Sullom Voe and other centres have declined in importance.

Summary

Basic ideas

Britain is now less dependent upon coal as a source of energy than at any other time in its modern industrial history.

The use of particular sources of energy has led to a distinctive pattern of electricity generating stations and refineries.

The North Sea oil industry has led to considerable industrial growth in parts of Scotland.

Key terms

Energy; National Grid; power; hydroelectricity; oilfields; nuclear power.

2.5 Location of industry

The location of industry is the spatial distribution of industrial activity, that is, where manufacturing plants and other industries are sited.

Industrialists wish to make the maximum profit. To do this they seek to produce their goods at the lowest cost, to sell as widely as possible and to distribute their goods as efficiently as possible. Whenever possible, industries are located at the most advantageous place to achieve these goals.

The three main factors which influence where industries are located are therefore:

1 the availability of raw materials;
2 the location of markets;
3 the availability of a transport system to link the two.

FACTORS IN INDUSTRIAL LOCATION

1 Raw materials

One way of reducing transport costs is to locate industry near the source of its raw materials (i.e. the materials used in the manufacturing process). This is the key consideration in the case of industries which use vast amounts of bulky raw materials.

2 Fuel and power

Industries need a form of energy which will drive the machinery. When industries were dependent upon coal as a source of power, the main manufacturing regions in Britain grew up on the chief coalfields. Today there is much greater freedom of location for many industries, because they depend upon electricity which is distributed almost everywhere by the National Grid.

3 Markets

The markets are the places where there is a demand for an industry's products. Manufacturing industries are drawn towards their major markets because this reduces transport costs. The advantages of a market location include:

(a) reducing the problem of packaging and transporting goods which are bulky and therefore expensive to transport;
(b) the location of a factory in a large centre of population which is an important market means that a labour supply (work force) is available;
(c) the presence of a large works in an area which forms an important market gives the product good publicity.

4 Labour

The location of industry is influenced both by the availability of a suitably-sized labour force and also by the quality of labour available. At one time, most factory workers were skilled, but today many workers are only semi-skilled and carry out routine assembling jobs or simple machine processes. New industries based on modern technology, however, still require highly-skilled workers, who need special training.

Some industries are based upon the availability of cheap labour. Because we have reasonably good wages in Britain, some industries have moved away to Third-World countries to exploit cheap labour. Other industries seek well-disciplined workers who are unlikely to interrupt production through strikes.

So labour is a very complex factor of location.

5 Capital

Large amounts of money are needed to buy raw materials and to run and promote an industry. Fixed

28 The British Isles

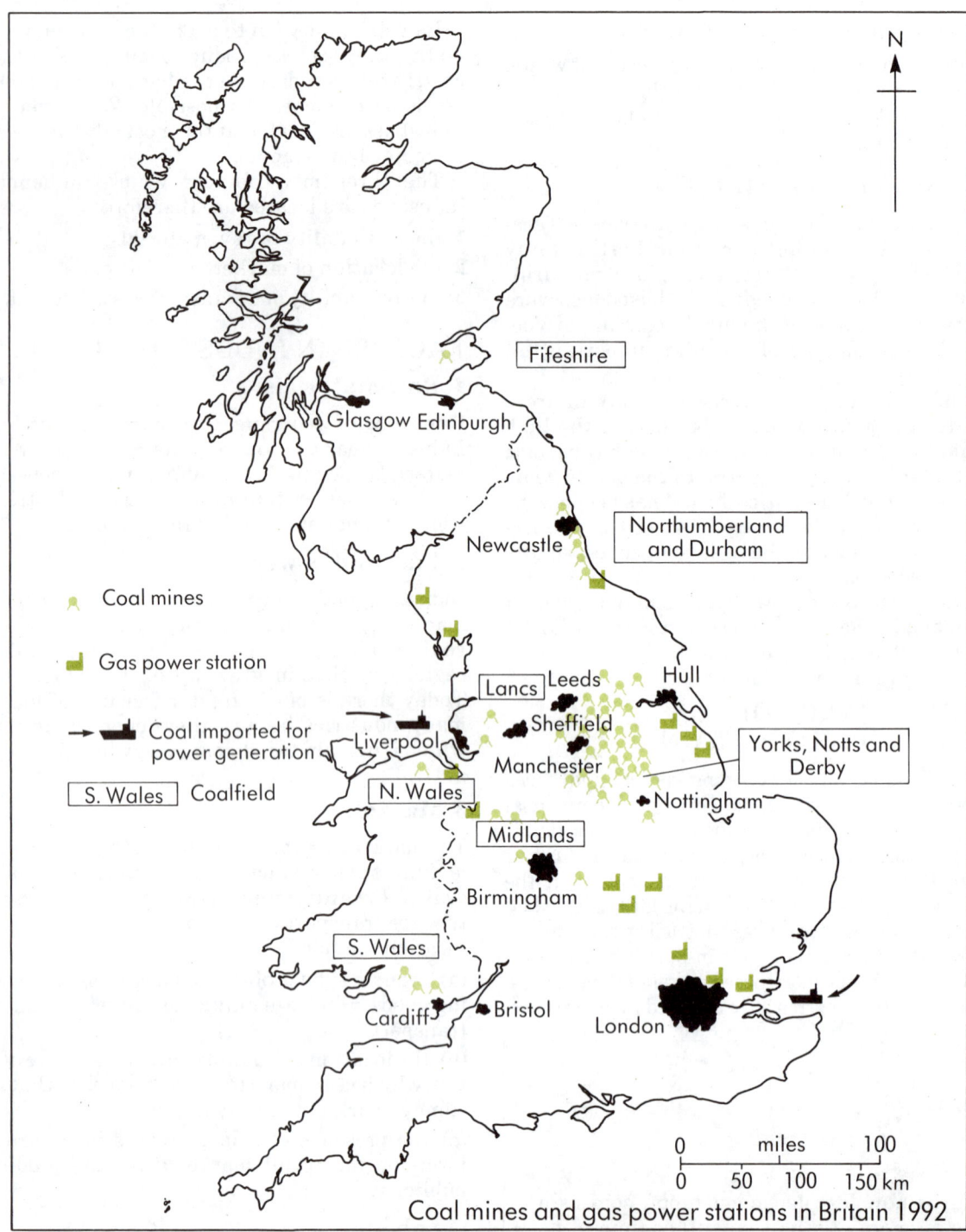

Fig. 2.5 Great Britain: coalfields

Coal mines and gas power stations in Britain 1992

capital is money invested in buildings and machinery. Circulating capital is money which is tied up in stocks of raw materials and half-finished goods.

Developed countries like Britain have sufficient wealth to invest in manufacturing industries, but in developing countries such as Tanzania industrial expansion may be hindered by the lack of capital.

6 Site requirements

Some modern industries require particular types of site. For example, an integrated steelworks needs a large area of flat land, while a chemical plant may need a site where it is possible to dispose easily of dangerous waste.

7 Perception

When a new industry is being established, a decision has to be made to develop a particular site in preference to other ones. The decision is the result of judgements made by those with the power and authority to make such decisions, and is based upon the advantages the chosen site is perceived to have.

LOCATION OF TRADITIONAL INDUSTRIES

Since coal was the dominant form of fuel and power, it was essential in the past for large industries to be located at coalfields or at a location to which coal could be transported easily. Industries which developed in London depended upon coal shipped from north-east England.

Many traditional industries were located originally

in response to conditions that no longer apply. In the past a location was often chosen because an industrialist lived at a particular place, and the transport system and distribution network that the industry needed were established. Because it is usually very expensive to relocate elsewhere, many old industries have tended to stay in the locality where they were first established. This is called *industrial inertia*.

LOCATION OF MODERN INDUSTRIES

The industries which have grown during this century have been mainly consumer industries, such as radio and other electrical goods. These industries depend upon small components which can be moved easily. Since electricity is distributed by National Grid, and gas by pipeline, industries do not have to locate at the source of their energy supplies. Many modern industries are market orientated.

The location of some industries is not dependent upon any particular factor of industrial location. These are called *footloose* industries. Some new hi-tech industries are examples of footloose industries.

THE INFLUENCE OF PUBLIC POLICY

As a result of the decline of traditional industries, the older industrial regions of Britain have declined dramatically in prosperity. Various governments have attempted to revive these areas by encouraging new industries to locate in them to replace the traditional ones. Industries have been given grants and subsidies to locate new works in economic problem areas. Today the EC allocates money for the revival of the poorest areas of Western Europe, such as Northern Ireland.

Governments have also interfered in negative ways. Controls have been used to check the concentration of manufacturing industries in the most popular areas, such as London. One of the purposes of building new and extended towns around London was to disperse industries away from the capital.

PROBLEMS CREATED BY INDUSTRIAL DEVELOPMENT

Major industrial development can create environmental problems such as traffic congestion, pollution and waste disposal. Changes in industrial activity have also caused considerable unemployment problems in older industrial regions.

> **Summary**
>
> *Basic ideas*
>
> The location of industry is determined by a number of factors.
>
> Significant differences exist between the factors which determined the location of traditional manufacturing industries and the industries which have been established in recent years.
>
> The location of industry in Britain has been significantly influenced by public policy decisions made by the government.
>
> *Key terms*
>
> Raw materials; market; labour; transport; footloose industry; industrial inertia; development areas.

2.6 Manufacturing industries

DEFINITION

Manufacturing industries are those industries which process or assemble components to make finished products. Unlike service industries, manufacturing industries have an end product for sale.

BROAD CATEGORIES OF MANUFACTURING INDUSTRIES

1 Raw materials-orientated industries

For some manufacturing industries, the vital factor of location is proximity to the source of key raw materials. Usually this is because the manufacturing process involves a great loss of bulk, but it may also be because the raw materials are difficult to transport.

2 Market-orientated industries

At one time only a few major industries, principally the food processing industry, were found near their markets. Today industries often locate near their markets, in order to cut down on transport costs. Usually, market-orientated industries use small quantities of raw materials, and produce fragile or bulky products which are not easy to transport.

3 Port industries

These are mainly industries which depend upon imported raw materials. These are essentially *break of bulk* industries; oil refining belongs to this category, for port location means there is no need to transport bulky crude oil from the ports. Newer light industries which assemble or package commodities for export may be located at suitable ports.

Two distinctive port industries which could not easily be located elsewhere are shipbuilding and ship repair.

STEEL MAKING

Figure 2.6A summarizes the main steps in the production of steel goods. In unit 2.2 you were given the definition of a system. An integrated steelworks may be regarded as a system and fig. 2.6B illustrates this. Additional inputs have been added to the raw materials shown in fig. 2.6A.

The British Isles

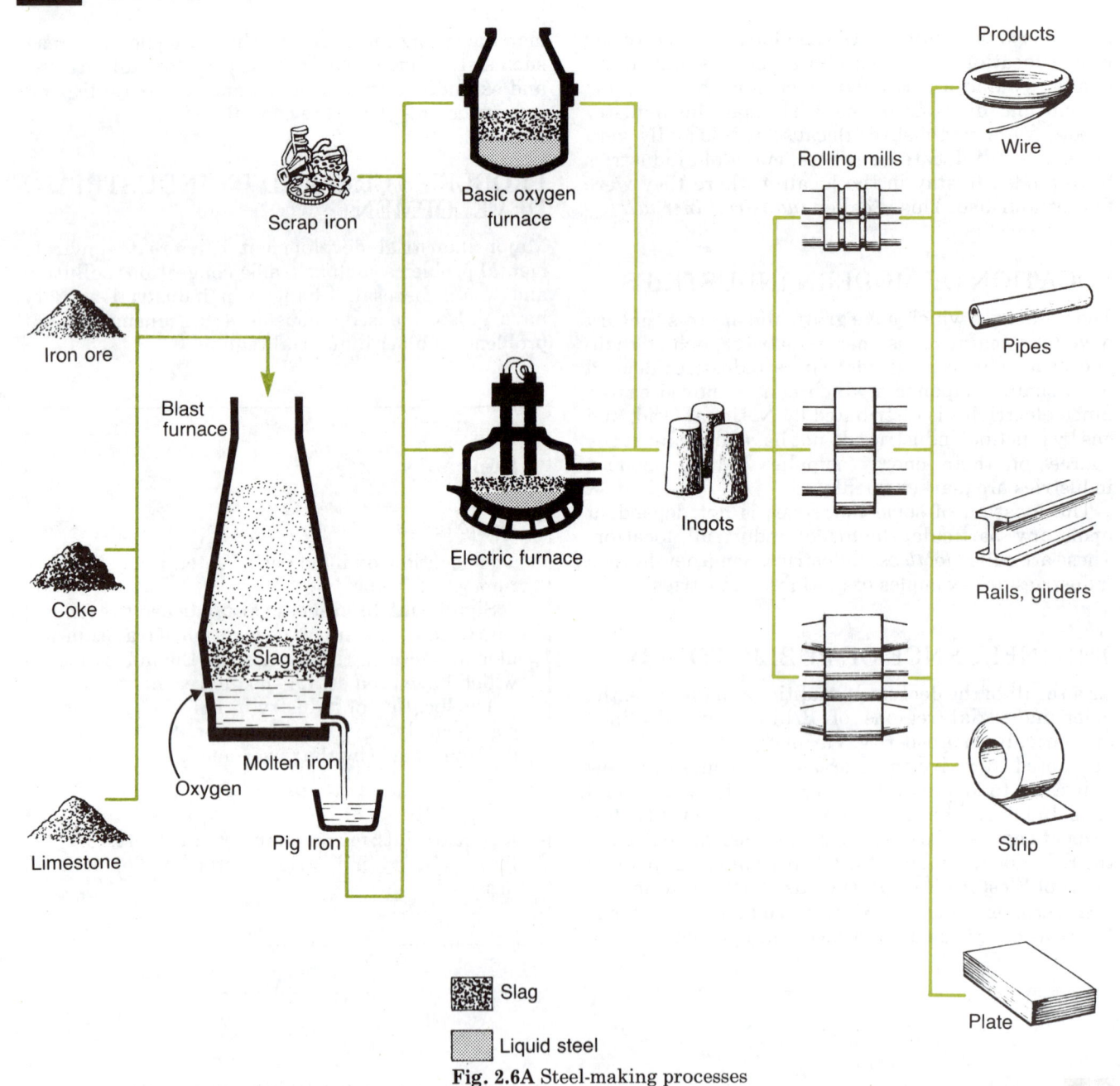

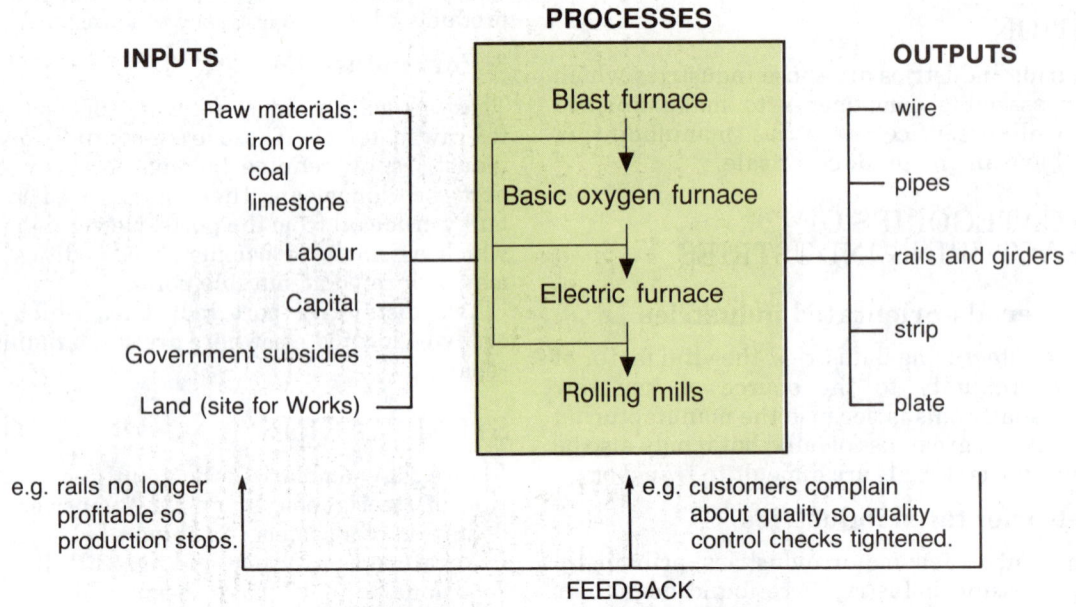

Fig. 2.6A Steel-making processes

Fig. 2.6B A systems diagram of steel-making

INPUTS
- Raw materials: iron ore, coal, limestone
- Labour
- Capital
- Government subsidies
- Land (site for Works)

PROCESSES
- Blast furnace
- Basic oxygen furnace
- Electric furnace
- Rolling mills

OUTPUTS
- wire
- pipes
- rails and girders
- strip
- plate

e.g. rails no longer profitable so production stops.

e.g. customers complain about quality so quality control checks tightened.

FEEDBACK

The British Isles 31

> **Summary**
>
> *Basic ideas*
>
> Manufacturing can be seen as a system. Different industries place different emphases upon specific factors of location.
>
> The steel industry of Britain has contracted significantly as a result of competition from overseas.
>
> *Key terms*
>
> Raw materials-orientated; market-orientated; break of bulk; system; nationalization; contraction.

2.7 Industrial growth and decline

In the course of the Industrial Revolution, major new industrial regions grew up. The industries which expanded rapidly were largely heavy industries, producing goods which were heavy and bulky compared with other products. The most important industry was the manufacture of iron and steel, upon which other industries such as shipbuilding, locomotive engineering and boiler-making depended. The coal and iron-mining industries are classed as *primary industries*, because they make available natural resources suitably processed for other industries. Iron and steel manufacturing, shipbuilding and other types of heavy engineering are *secondary industries*, because they are concerned with processing raw materials to produce goods.

It is the coalfield-based heavy industrial regions that have now declined in Britain.

AN EXAMPLE OF A FORMER HEAVY INDUSTRIAL REGION IN WHICH TRADITIONAL INDUSTRIES HAVE DECLINED – NORTH-EAST ENGLAND

The industrial strength of North-east England was originally based upon the coal obtained from the Northumberland and Durham coalfield. The chief industries were coal mining and exporting, shipbuilding, iron and steel making, engineering and chemicals. Apart from the chemical industry the traditional industries have now declined.

The chemical industry centres on Billingham (ICI). It uses coal by-products, chemicals from the Tees saltfield and by-products from the oil refineries on Teesmouth. Major products are paints, fertilizers, explosives, plastics and Terylene (at Wilton).

As in South Wales (unit 2.17) some of the basic industries have been in decline for more than 50 years, but their demise has accelerated in the last ten.

Reasons for the decline of regions such as the North-east include:

1 The disappearance of traditional markets — coal is far less important a fuel than once it was; there is a surplus of shipping in the world, so shipbuilding has declined.

2 Inability to compete with new industrial regions which have significantly lower production costs e.g. the steel industry of Brazil, the Japanese shipbuilding industry.

3 Failure to invest in modern machinery and production techniques.

4 Inability to attract new industries to the old regions because of the unattractive appearance of the old industrial landscapes, with sub-standard housing, a polluted environment, and large areas of derelict land.

Many efforts have been made to revitalize the region. Obsolete housing has been removed and replaced by new estates. Planned new towns such as Washington have been built to provide more attractive environments to which industries from other parts of Britain and from overseas have been attracted, e.g. the Nissan works at Washington.

Fig. 2.7A Redevelopment in the North-east: the Newcastle Metro system

Urban re-development

Much of the urban redevelopment has focused upon Newcastle, the economic capital of the region, and upon Gateshead, which lies immediately south of the River Tyne. In 1977 the Newcastle and Gateshead inner City Partnership was set up. It was intended to tackle the economic, social and environmental difficulties faced by the two inner city areas. The inner city areas suffered from:

(a) Poor housing conditions.

(b) A declining and ageing population.

(c) High unemployment.

(d) Many families have very low incomes.

(e) A higher crime rate than in other parts of the region.

The aim of the partnership was to make inner city areas places where people would want to live and work.

In Newcastle itself there had been major redevelopment of the Central Business District and new housing estates built nearby even before the partnership began. City transport has now greatly improved with the building of the Metro system. Economic development has focused upon the creation of enterprise workshops, offices built for new and expanding industries, and the fostering of tourism. The inner city partnership has an action programme to attract new industries and jobs into the inner cities. Run down industrial areas have been improved, new access roads built and grants made available to improve factories. The heart of the old industrial region was the River Tyne, and the old riverside wharf has been cleaned up and landscaped. Moorings have also been provided for leisure and residential uses.

Similar efforts are being made throughout the region. The closure of the steelworks at Consett took away the entire economic base of the town but new enterprises are now attempting to provide new job opportunities. Industrial museums have been opened where old industries once existed as part of a drive to obtain new income for the region from tourism.

AN EXAMPLE OF A GROWING INDUSTRIAL REGION

One of the few rapidly growing industrial regions of Britain lies to the west of London, along the M4 motorway. It is not a completely built-up urban region as the old industrial regions were. The new region is a corridor within which new industries are clustered in and around the main towns, such as Swindon and Reading.

The M4 motorway was opened in December 1971, having cost £140 million and taken 12 years to build. The M4 links London with South Wales and the West Country, making journeys between London and Cardiff, Newport and Bristol much quicker, but it does more than this. Patterns of travel have changed significantly and it is now possible to live in the countryside near Swindon and to commute to London daily.

The motorway has been a magnet for new industries. This is because:

1 Modern footloose industries are not bound to specific locations.
2 Industries located near the M4 have easy access to the chief British market, London.
3 The motorways with which the M4 links give easy access to other parts of Britain.
4 London's two main airports are conveniently close to the M4, so business journeys to the USA, Europe and other major markets are easy.
5 There is little industrial blight from the 19th century, so managers and workers can live in attractive environments close to clean, modern factories.
6 New industries such as microelectronics need to attract highly-skilled scientific staff, who can be recruited from the universities and polytechnics of London and the south-east.
7 It is an attractive region in which to live for American, Japanese and German managers of factories owned by foreign firms.

As a result the M4 corridor is a developing and prosperous industrial region.

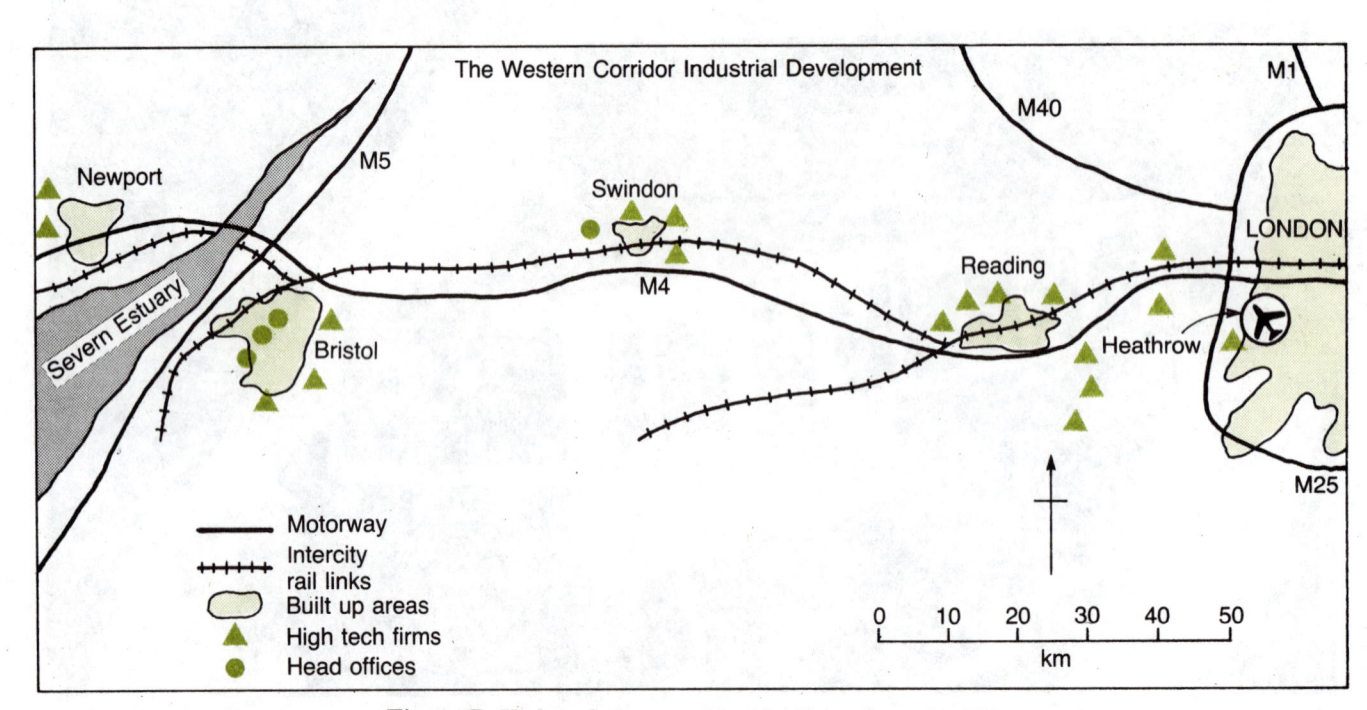

Fig. 2.7B High tech firms and head offices along the M4

> **Summary**
>
> *Basic ideas*
>
> Industries operate in an environment in which change is continuous.
>
> This change results in the growth of new industries and the decline of others.
>
> The most recent changes have produced a decline of traditional manufacturing industries and the growth of new 'sunrise' and service industries.
>
> *Key terms*
>
> Heavy industry; primary industry; secondary industry; footloose industries; environment; industrial blight.

2.8 Service industries

A service industry is an industry that provides a facility or service, instead of manufacturing goods. Service industries belong to the category of *tertiary industry*, which is now the chief source of employment in Britain.

Important categories of service industries are:

1 Government, national security and defence. Workers in many sections of this group tend to be concentrated in London.

2 Transport services: the provision of transport — road, rail, air and sea both for manufactured goods and for people.

3 Wholesale distribution: when goods are produced in a factory, or food on a farm, the products are often taken in bulk to a wholesaler. The wholesaler breaks down the quantities into small lots and sorts and packs the goods. He then distributes them to retailers who sell the goods.

4 Retailing: the selling of products to the consumer. Some large firms such as Sainsbury and Tesco now act both as wholesalers and as retailers, having large regional warehouses from which goods are sent to individual shops.

5 Communications: this category is concerned with the transmitting and receiving of information and messages. The chief form today is telecommunication.

6 Banking and finance: this is a very broad category which includes local bank and building society offices, found in every small town, as well as international finance houses in the City of London and in the centres of other major cities. Associated with the financial institutions are commodity markets where stocks and bonds for commodities such as grain, tea and metals are bought and sold.

7 Entertainment and leisure.

8 Tourism: this is an increasingly important industry in Britain and is an important source of foreign earnings for the country.

9 Personal service: the occupations in which customers are served directly — the hairdresser or dentist for example.

FACTORS AFFECTING THE DISTRIBUTION OF SERVICE INDUSTRIES

The distribution of population does not determine the distribution of service industries, not even personal service, which might be expected to be needed equally by people. In the private sector, personal services are distributed according to the population's ability to pay for them. In the public sector, unequal distribution is the result of another factor — some places are more attractive to work in than others. The people of the South Wales valleys have fewer doctors than do parts of the south-east of England, because fewer doctors wish to live in an old industrial region.

Uneven distribution is also the result of the fact that many service industries are concentrated in the capital city and other major urban areas. Government is concentrated in London, and so are theatres and concert halls, hotels and major sporting facilities such as Wembley, Lord's, Wimbledon and Twickenham. Large, prosperous cities and towns can support many facilities profitably because of their own large populations and also because they act as magnets to people who travel to the city to use these facilities. Cities 'pull' people, while the lack of facilities in other areas 'pushes' people to the large centres.

Concentration in particular centres is also the result of the economic benefits which can be gained from clustering or *agglomeration*. For example, trading in commodities in London is closely linked with the work of the international banks and the Stock Exchange. These allied activities are made more efficient and more economic by their nearness to each other, which makes cooperation easy. Similarly, the clustering of hotels, restaurants and theatres in London cuts down travel costs for the tourist and makes London more attractive.

DECENTRALIZATION

The concentration of service industries in a few major urban centres may cause considerable problems:

1 The additional traffic generated by workers travelling to the city centre creates traffic congestion.

2 Insurance offices, banks, hotels etc. can pay much more for building land than the private housebuilder or local authority. This may result in people being pushed out of residential areas, which are then used for commercial activities.

3 The whole character of the city centre changes when high-rise commercial blocks replace traditional buildings.

4 High buildings need deep roots, and sinking foundations deeply in cities such as London has meant the destruction of valuable archaeological evidence of past ages.

As a result there have been some attempts to push service industries out of London and the major city centres. The government has dispersed national government offices away from London, for example: the Royal Mint is now in Llantrisant and the Motor Vehicle Licensing Department is in Swansea — both in a region of high unemployment.

AN EXAMPLE OF CENTRALIZATION

In 1969 the Development of Tourism Act passed by Parliament provided for a grant to be paid for every bedroom built in new hotels by March 1973. As a result, the number of requests for planning permission for new hotels in London went up by 1000 per cent. The first applications were to develop sites in the West End, especially the Mayfair/Piccadilly area. Later

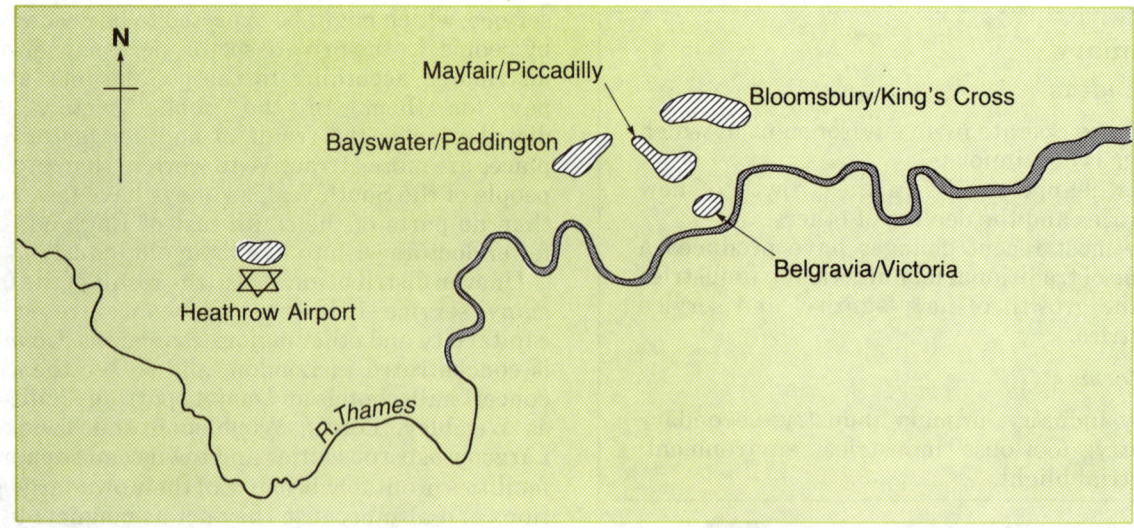

Fig. 2.8A Chief hotel development areas

developers looked westwards to suitable sites near Heathrow airport, and in Knightsbridge and other areas which lie between Heathrow and the West End of London. The effect has been to change the appearance of London's skyline dramatically, and also to make tourism a more important service industry in the capital.

Reasons for the encouragement of hotel building were:

1 If London was to remain one of the chief business cities of the world, it had to have modern hotels as good as those available in rival business centres such as New York, Tokyo and Frankfurt.

2 The expansion of tourism would contribute to the prosperity of the country.

3 Property developers could make huge profits by investing in hotel building in such an important business and tourist centre.

4 Hotel development provided work for the building trade and for companies which provided materials for the builders.

AN EXAMPLE OF DECENTRALIZATION

One example of a development which has taken activities away from centres such as Earl's Court or Wembley in London is the building, with government approval, of the National Exhibition Centre on the edge of Birmingham. It has been built on a 125 hectare site between Birmingham and Coventry. The advantages of this location are shown in fig. 2.8B.

The building of the National Exhibition Centre has stimulated other industries in the region. Shops, offices, banks, motels and hotel accommodation were needed near the Centre. Hotels in Birmingham and Coventry have expanded and new ones have been built to meet the needs of foreign visitors. A new railway station has also been built on the London-Birmingham-Manchester-Liverpool line. The airport has also become busier.

Birmingham has become a centre for national and international events.

Summary

Basic ideas

'Service industry' is a very broad but important industrial category. 'Push' and 'pull' factors affect the distribution of services, and processes of centralization and decentralization can be recognized. Service industries are not evenly distributed in relation to the distribution of population.

Key terms

Personal services, distribution, concentration, decentralization, tourism, agglomeration.

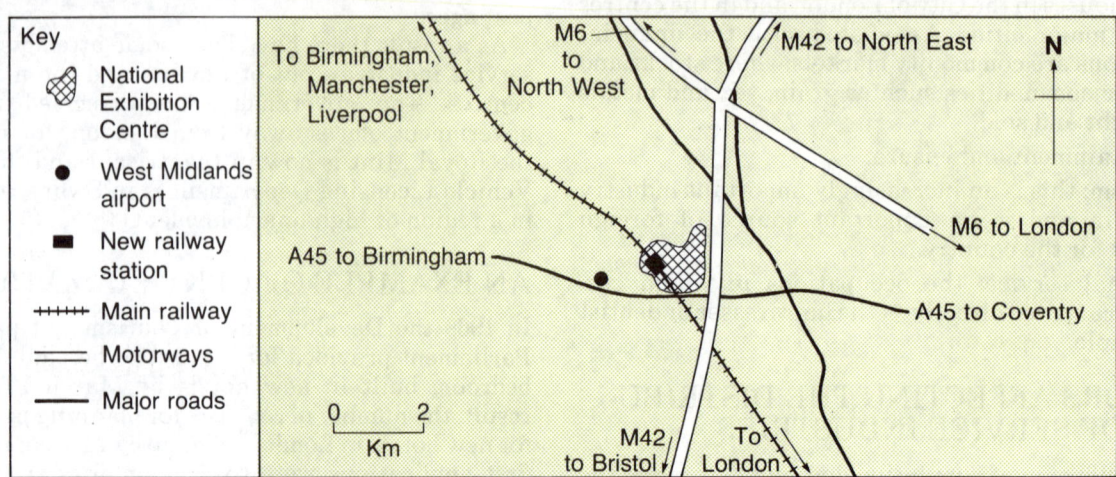

Fig. 2.8B Location of the national exhibition centre

2.9 Transport networks

The movement of raw materials, goods and people results in the creation of transport networks. A network is a set of routes which connects junctions and termini. There are road, rail and air transport networks as well as sea-going and inland waterway networks.

PURPOSES OF NETWORKS

Transport networks are built:

1 To make possible the flow of goods and services between existing settlements.

2 To open up a region, or to give access to a resource which is economically valuable.

3 For strategic reasons — governments need a good network of railways, roads and air routes to transport troops and supplies quickly.

THE PATTERN OF NETWORKS

The patterns formed by different networks are influenced by a number of factors. The most important are:

1 Shape

The shape of the area to be covered influences the pattern that will be established. For example, the road network in Chile, which is a very long but narrow country, will be different from that of a country shaped like Spain.

2 Relief

Mountains and rivers may be obstacles to the building of roads and railways, so the network pattern which evolves in a region will tend to reflect the chief relief features of that region.

3 Size

In a small country a dense road network may be established relatively quickly and easily, whereas in a much larger country the overall density of roads or railways may be less.

4 Population

In general, countries which are densely populated have denser transportation networks than equally rich countries which have more sparsely distributed populations.

5 State of development

The density of the transportation networks depends upon the level of development of the country or region. For example a rich nation such as the USA has a much denser air traffic network than an underdeveloped country with few airports and a small demand for air travel.

6 Other factors

The network pattern may also be influenced by factors such as the alignment of international borders, and historical factors.

CHARACTERISTICS OF A NETWORK

Networks are said to have the following components:

1 Edge

(also called arc or link): a direct route which connects two *nodes* such as railway stations.

2 Vertex

(plural vertices): a location or node on a network, for example a road junction or terminus.

3 Connectivity

This is the degree to which vertices are linked together. The degree of connectivity may be compared from one network to another, and used as a measure of change in a single network over a period of time.

MAPPING A NETWORK

Networks are often simplified as maps or graphs. These are called *topological* maps or graphs. On topological maps the edges and vertices (routes and junctions) are shown accurately, but distances and directions may be altered to make the diagram simpler to read. The route maps in London underground trains are topological maps and so are British Rail maps of inter-city services.

TYPES OF NETWORK

1 A minimally connected network

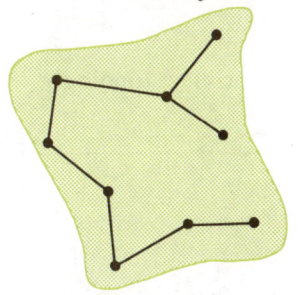

Fig. 2.9A A minimally connected network

Look at fig. 2.9A. There are eight edges and nine vertices. This is a minimally connected network, because the number of edges is one less than the number of vertices. This can be expressed as a formula:

$$e = (v - 1)$$

If one edge is removed from a minimally connected network, one part of the network will become disconnected from the rest.

2 A complex network

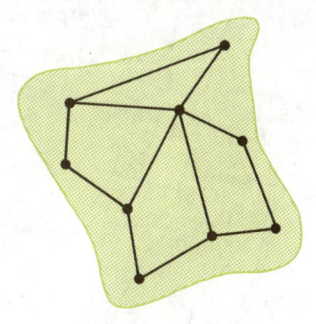

Fig. 2.9B A complex network

In a complex network, most vertices are connected to more than one other vertex (fig. 2.9B). In the figure there are twelve edges and nine vertices, so the formula above does not apply to this network. If one edge is removed the network will still be connected.

THE BETA (β) INDEX

The beta index is a simple way of measuring the connectivity of networks. The index is calculated by dividing the total number of edges by the total number of vertices. The formula is therefore:

$$\beta = \frac{e}{v}$$

The beta index for the network in fig. 2.9A is $\frac{8}{9} = 0.89$

The beta index for the network in fig. 2.9B is $\frac{12}{9} = 1.33$

For a given number of vertices, the more edges there are to connect them, the greater the degree of connectivity and the higher the beta index.

Summary
Basic ideas

The movement of goods, materials and people results in the creation of transport networks.

The pattern of networks is influenced by the interplay of a number of factors.

The connectivity of a network can be indicated by the beta index.

Key terms

Network; edge; vertex; connectivity; topological maps; beta index.

2.10 Ports

GENERAL FEATURES

Britain's industrial wealth was built upon overseas trade. Industrial raw materials such as rubber and food were imported into Britain and finished manufactured goods, such as textiles, were exported. The gateways which linked Britain with the rest of the world were the major ports which developed on river estuaries: Southampton, Liverpool, Bristol, Clydeside and London.

In recent years the ways in which goods are handled at ports have changed fundamentally. Traditionally, every item of cargo carried by a ship had to be handled separately, unless it could be transferred to the shore by pipeline. Many goods were lifted off in nets. Dockers worked in the ships' holds to load the nets, loads were lifted by crane and another team of dockers was needed to empty the nets on shore. The place at which goods were transferred in this way was known as the *break of bulk point*.

Traditional techniques have been replaced by container trade. Containers are weatherproof boxes of a standard size, 2.5 metres wide, 2.5 metres high and up to 13 metres long. This size has been agreed internationally, so the same equipment can handle containers from any country in the world. Lorries, trains and cranes can also handle containers easily all over the world. The containers are packed at the point of production and can then be shifted rapidly to the destination equally easily by river, rail or road.

A TRADITIONAL PORT — LIVERPOOL

The chief town of the Mersey estuary is Liverpool. The growth of the port of Liverpool and of the Merseyside industrial region occurred over the last 200 years because the Mersey estuary is the natural outlet for Lancashire and the north-west Midlands.

Main factors

1 In the past the chief port for the region was Chester,

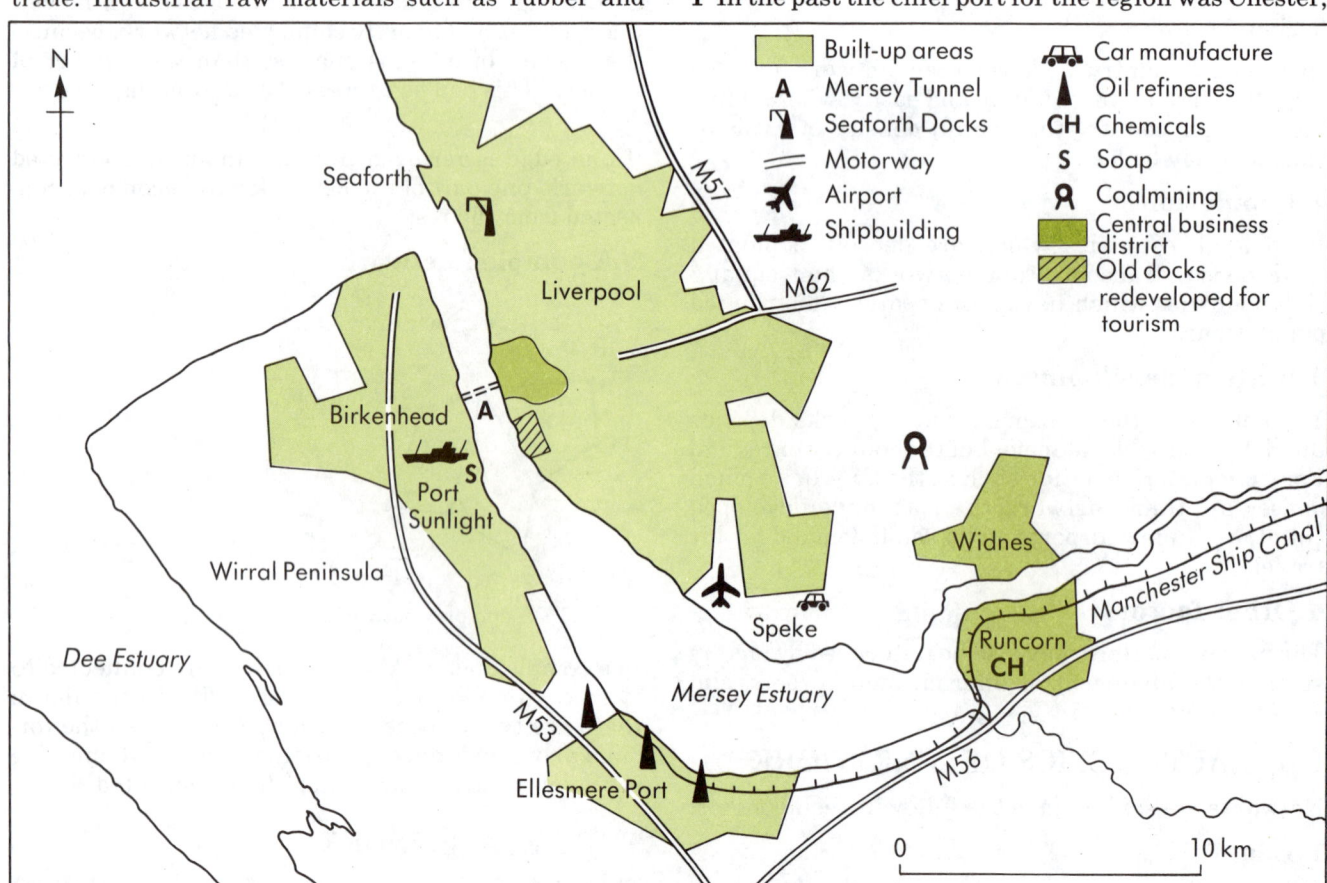

Fig. 2.10A The Mersey estuary

on the Dee estuary. The Dee gradually silted up but, because of its shape, the mouth of the River Mersey was kept silt-free by the tides. The development of the triangular trade between England, Africa and America made Liverpool an important port.

2 As the modern cotton textile industry grew on the Lancashire coalfield, Liverpool handled the import of raw materials and the export of finished goods, especially to the USA. Since the Mersey lies at the north-western end of the Midland gate it also became the chief port for Birmingham, the West Midlands and the Potteries.

3 The expansion of the cotton industry led to the development of other industries on Merseyside. Coal from the North Wales and Lancashire coalfields and salt from the Cheshire field provided raw materials for a chemical industry supplying heavy chemicals (Runcorn), and soap (Port Sunlight) for the textile industry.

4 The development of overseas trade encouraged the establishment of a shipbuilding industry (Birkenhead) and 'port industries'—sugar refining and flour milling at Liverpool.

5 When Britain became less dependent on coal and more dependent upon imported oil, oil refineries were established on the estuary (Ellesmere Port).

6 The old docks of Liverpool have now been made obsolete by the building of Seaforth Docks. There are grain stores, timber yards, a frozen-meat terminal and three container terminal berths at the new docks. Goods can be transported by rail from the new marshalling yards or along the M62 and M6 motorways.

7 The decline of the traditional textile, coal and engineering industries in the north-west led to much unemployment. Merseyside was made a 'development area' and firms were encouraged to build new factories along Merseyside. The new factories have not proved very successful and some are being closed.

8 To provide better housing and attractive sites for new factories, new towns have been developed at Kirby, north of Liverpool, and Runcorn.

9 Liverpool is now less important than Southampton for cargo tonnage and ranks fifth in the country.

A NEW CONTAINER PORT— FELIXSTOWE

Traditionally our chief ports have traded mainly with other continents. This has changed in recent years as a result of the following factors:

1 When Britain joined the EC our trading links with New Zealand, Australia and other Commonwealth countries became less important, while trade with European countries increased.

2 The importance of Rotterdam as the chief port of Europe, from whence goods are re-exported to Britain.

3 The decline in manufacturing in Britain has resulted in the rapid growth of imports from the continent: machine tools, car parts for assembling, consumer goods.

These factors have given the ports of the east coast, which had been small and insignificant, a tremendous advantage over traditional ports which do not face Europe. In 1964 Felixstowe in Suffolk was a small port with a limited amount of trade, but it is now large and busy. In its first four years as a container port, Felixstowe's trade increased by more than 400 per cent and it is now the sixth port for goods tonnage in the country.

Reasons for Felixstowe's success include:

1 Its position. It faces Europe and had existing links with Zeebrugge (Belgium) and Rotterdam (Holland).

2 It was redeveloped as a container port before traditional ports accepted the new technology, and so was able to built up new trading links swiftly and with very little competition.

3 It is a privately owned port which ignored the conditions of work and wages which operated in the traditional ports. This enabled Felixstowe to trade more cheaply and to turn ships around more quickly. Felixstowe was thus able to attract American as well as European trade.

4 The improvements to the A45 road and the completion of the M11 and M25 motorways have made the transfer of goods from Felixstowe to major cities and industrial regions in Britain more efficient.

MODEL OF A PORT

Figure 2.10B shows the chief conditions that favour the expansion of modern ports. Since chips have increased in size tremendously in recent years, deep-water approaches are needed in which there is no great range between high and low tides to force ships to wait for the tide. Dock fees are high and modern ships are very expensive to run, so rapid turn-around is vital.

The dock itself needs basins large enough to take the ships or terminal jetties at which they can tie up. They also need to provide repair and maintenance docks. In addition to the usual warehouses and sheds, modern ports require space for the storage of bulk cargoes and containerized general cargoes.

Since industries develop where raw materials are landed, and industrial area is needed near the docks which is large enough to allow for the expansion of industry. Two other important factors are also shown on the model. One is the need for efficient, rapid transport to distribute the imports and to bring cargoes to the docks for export. The other is the advantage of having an industrial hinterland so that return cargoes are available to keep ships working profitably.

GREENOCK

Port activities have moved downstream on the River Clyde in recent years. The fastest growing section is at Greenock. This fact may be explained by asking how well Greenock fits the model.

1 The estuary is wide and deep (nearly 11 metres) at Greenock. The approach is easy and there is a sheltered anchorage offshore.

2 There is no need for ships to wait for the tide.

3 The infilling of old dockland has provided room for expansion.

4 It has a modern container terminal.

5 There are sugar and oil-seed refineries near the docks.

6 It has a large modern ship repair dock (graving dock).

7 It has a direct freightliner link with Glasgow.

8 The M8 links it with Glasgow and the Central Lowlands.

9 It is able to export the machinery, metal goods, whisky and other products of its hinterland.

If you compare this with the results you get from

The British Isles

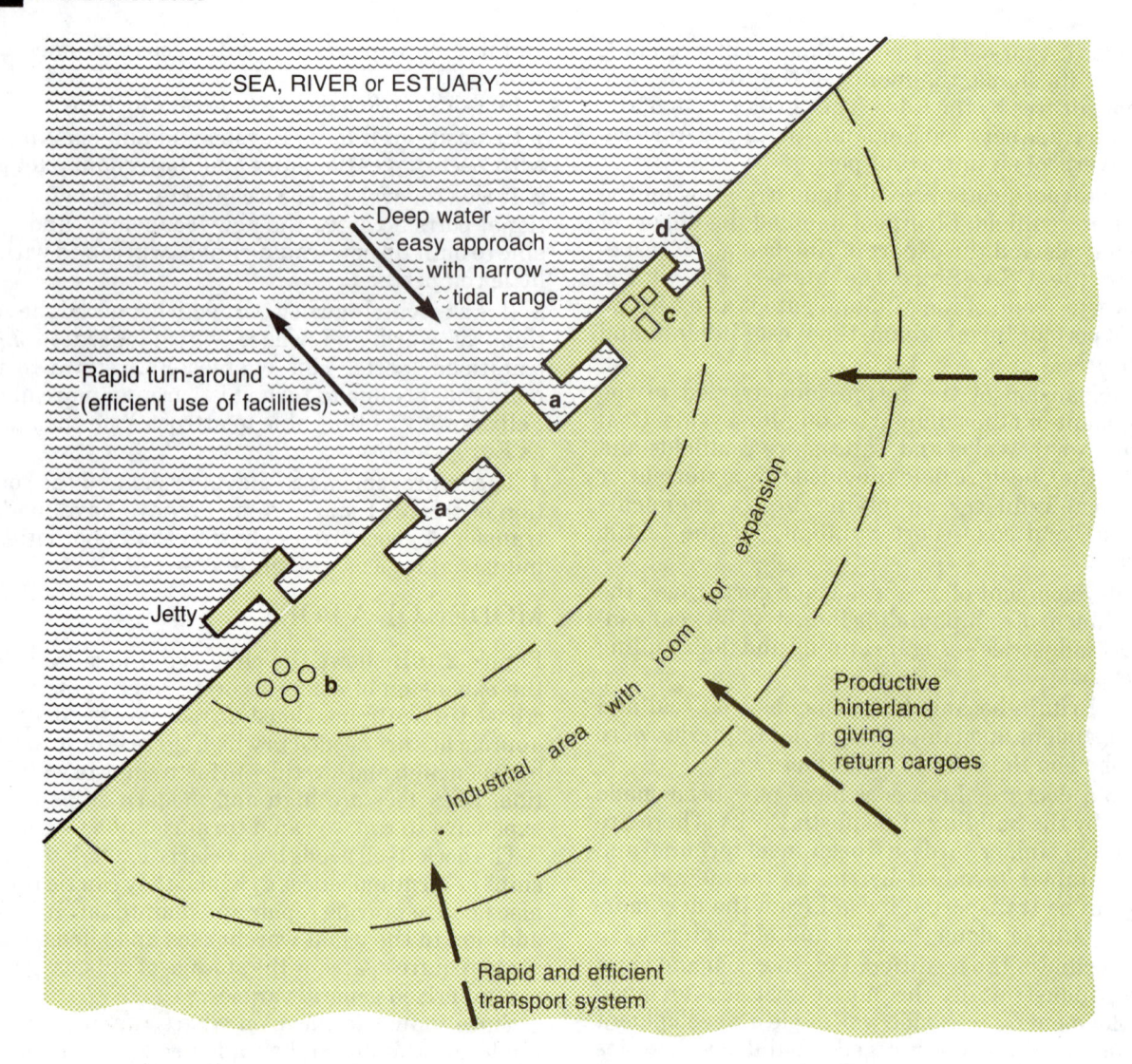

[Figure: A model of a port, showing labels: SEA, RIVER or ESTUARY; Deep water easy approach with narrow tidal range; Rapid turn-around (efficient use of facilities); Jetty; Industrial area with room for expansion; Productive hinterland giving return cargoes; Rapid and efficient transport system]

a Large, well-equipped dock basins
b Facilities for handling bulk cargoes (*e.g.* oil)
c Facilities for handling containers
d Repair and maintenance docks

Fig. 2.10B A model of a port

applying the model to ports further up the Clyde, you will see why Greenock has expanded at their expense.

> **Summary**
>
> *Basic ideas*
> Britain was once the most important trading nation in the world and dependent upon its ports for exporting and importing goods.
> The sites for major ports were provided mainly by river estuaries.
> Old important ports have declined and new onces developed as changes have occurred in transportation and in response to Britain's closer linke with Europe.
>
> *Key terms*
> Imports; exports; break of bulk point; containers; hinterland; port industries.

2.11 Population distribution and movement

THE BASIC PATTERN

Figure 2.11 shows the distribution of population in the British Isles. Although the average density for the whole country is 229 persons per square km, there are great differences in density between various parts of the country.

REASONS FOR THE PRESENT DISTRIBUTION

1 The physical character of the country

The parts of the United Kingdom with the sparsest populations are found in north and west — the

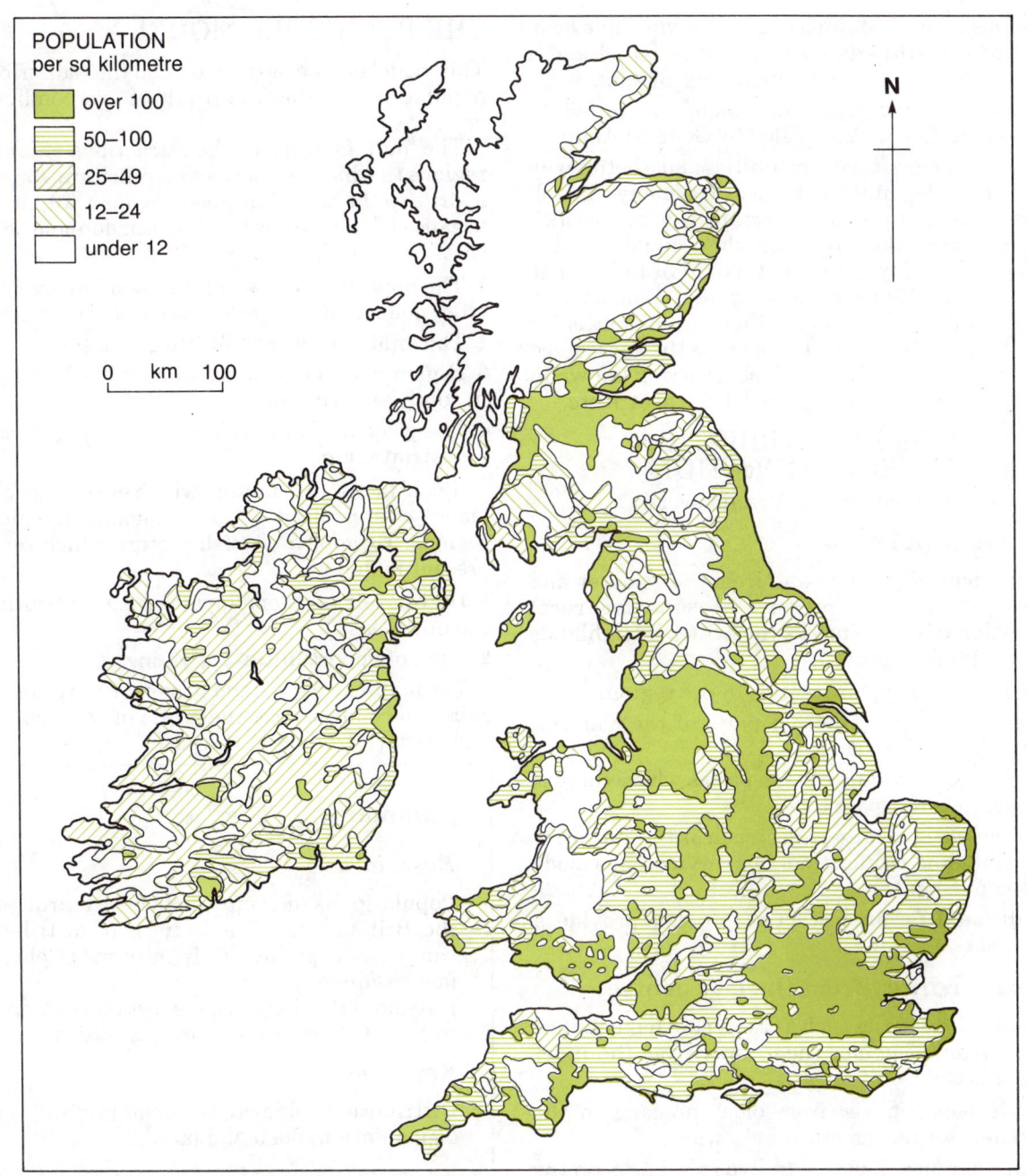

Fig. 2.11 Distribution of population in the British Isles

Highland zones of Britain. These are the poorest farming regions and have sparser populations than the richer agricultural regions such as East Anglia, the Vale of York and the lowlands of the south-west of England.

2 The early pattern of industrialization

This concentrated new towns and cities on and near coalfields.

3 The dominance of London

London has always acted as a magnet to people. Although it was not on a coalfield, London became the financial and international marketing centre for British industry. As the largest and richest domestic (home) market, it also developed industries of its own. The London region therefore became the major region of dense population not related to a coalfield during the Industrial Revolution.

4 Recent changes

These have weakened the traditional distributional influence of the coalfields. Areas of dense population have developed along the south coast, with major centres such as Brighton. In the last thirty years new industrial activities have been attracted to regions such as East Anglia and as a result the Norwich region is becoming increasingly densely populated.

THE MOVEMENT OF POPULATION — MIGRATION

Migration is the permanent or long-term movement of an individual or group of people to a new place. Migration therefore causes a redistribution of population.

Important reasons for migration include:

1 Differing economic prosperity between regions.

2 The difference in economic prosperity between countries: this causes international migration movements. Unemployed British steel workers and shipbuilders have moved to Germany to get work. Ethnic minority groups such as West Indians have moved to Britain because of high unemployment in their home islands.

3 Religious reasons: Jewish emigrants who have been allowed to leave Russia have settled in Israel and a number of western countries including Britain.

4 Political reasons: Ugandan Asians emigrated to Britain when they were expelled by General Amin.

5 Perception of greater opportunities and a better way of life: since the nineteenth century many British families have emigrated to certain Commonwealth countries where they believed they could build a better life and enjoy a higher standard of living. The favourite destinations were Australia, Canada and New Zealand. At the same time, Commonwealth citizens have made for London because they perceived it to be a place where they could become well known in their chosen field — music, television, theatre etc.

PATTERNS OF REDISTRIBUTION RESULTING FROM MIGRATION

Three significant patterns in Britain are:

1 Rural depopulation

The movement of people away from the remoter and less prosperous rural regions. Reasons for rural depopulation of areas such as the Scottish Highlands (see unit 2.18) include:

(a) The lack of job opportunities in the region.

(b) Wages are higher in other parts of the country, especially the major cities.

(c) Young people want to live in places where there is more to do in their spare time.

(d) The decline of local services, such as the closure of railway lines and reduction of bus services, has made life less convenient.

(e) Traditional farming practices do not provide a high income.

2 Migration away from the city centre

The population of cities such as Liverpool has declined in recent years. The movement away from the inner city areas is the result of:

(a) People being moved from older housing in the cities to new towns and estates elsewhere.

(b) The preference of people to live in suburbs on the edges of cities or in surrounding small towns and villages. This has been made possible by the building of motorways and ring roads which have made longer journeys quicker. This process is known as suburbanization.

(c) The decline of traditional industries in the cities, which has encouraged workers to move away.

(d) The suburbanization of industry, the building of modern factories and offices on the edges of cities, has encouraged people to move out of cities to live nearer the places where jobs are now located.

3 Immigration into the inner city

As the indigenous city populations have moved away from their old homes in some cities, they have been replaced by groups of immigrants. The immigrants were attracted to this country to take up low-paid and semi-skilled work at a time when there were labour shortages in key industries and services. As a result, some inner cities now have large ethnic minority communities — Pakistani communities in Bradford, Indians and Sikhs in Southall, West Indians in Nottingham and so on.

THE PUSH/PULL MODEL

This model depicts migration and the redistribution of population as being the result of two conflicting forces:

The 'pull' factors are the attractions offered by the regions to which people move. In Britain, for example, a 'drift to the south' has been evident for many years because of the pull exerted by London and the southeast. This pull is due to:

1 The opportunities which the London area seems to offer, compared with other parts of the country.

2 The mild and sunny climate of the south.

3 Higher average housing standards which are found in south-eastern areas.

4 The growth of new industries, away from the older industrial regions.

'Push' factors are factors which encourage people to leave over-populated or economically depressed regions. Examples of push factors which operate at present include:

1 High levels of unemployment, e.g. in Scotland and the north-east.

2 Lack of opportunities for young people.

3 The inability of the land to support large families on subsistence farms, e.g. the crofts of western Scotland and western Ireland in the past.

Summary

Basic ideas

Population is unevenly distributed throughout the British Isles. The pattern of distribution cannot be explained fully in terms of physical factors alone.

Remote rural areas have lost population, but so have the centres of our large cities.

Key terms

Distribution; migration; immigration; rural depopulation; push and pull.

2.12 New towns and expanded towns

BACKGROUND

Before the Second World War there was a severe housing shortage in many parts of Britain. In addition, many of the houses which did exist in cities and industrial regions were out of date and lacked modern facilities such as hot running water, bathrooms and indoor lavatories. The housing situation was worsened by the destruction of houses by German bombing during the war. After 1945 a major national effort was made to solve severe housing problems.

Some definitions:

New town: an urban settlement planned and built to ease the housing pressure in existing towns and cities. The new towns provide work as well as homes for the families who live in them. In Britain the new towns are towns which were built as the result of Parliament passing the New Towns Act in 1946.

Expanded town: a town where planned growth has occurred according to the Town Development Act

(1952). This Act of Parliament encouraged the rapid development of towns in country areas, to ease congestion and housing problems in the cities. Andover and Basingstoke are examples of expanded towns.

Overspill: an excess of population which leaves the city because of overcrowding or as a result of urban renewal programmes (see unit 2.15). Overspill estates were set up in towns such as Luton to receive families from London.

THE DEVELOPMENT OF NEW TOWNS

After the Second World War a series of new towns was built. These towns now number over 30 and have a population of about two million.

Towns like Stevenage, Harlow and Crawley were planned to provide new homes and jobs and better surroundings for people living in London. Peterlee, Country Durham, was planned to rehouse people from local mining villages and Corby was designed to serve the iron and steel industry of the area. Altogether 14 new towns were developed in areas of high unemployment to attract manufacturing investment. They include Skelmersdale and Warrington in the north-west and East Kilbride and Glenrothes in Scotland.

The first towns which were built such as Corby and Crawley are known as Mark 1 new towns. Later the planning goals were changed and in particular, traffic-free shopping precincts and larger population targets were built into plans for the next set of towns. The final phase of new town development was the planning of new cities at Telford in Shropshire, at Central Lancashire and at Milton Keynes, Buckinghamshire. The target populations for these cities were about 250,000 but only Milton Keynes is likely to achieve anything like this size.

AIMS OF THE NEW TOWN PLANNERS

The new towns were originally intended to be:

1 Of limited size

They were expected to grow to about 60 000 population so that they would be similar in size and character to the old country towns. The planners envisaged an *optimum population size* for them. The advantages of keeping the new towns reasonably small were seen to be as follows:

(a) People would live in walking or cycling distance of their work.
(b) Everyone would be able to live close to the surrounding countryside.
(c) It would be possible for a community spirit to develop quickly in the new towns.
(d) Small towns could be built quickly.

2 Comprehensively planned

To provide a markedly better living environment.

3 Socially balanced

All the towns were to have a mixture of age, income and social groups.

4 Separate from the parent city

So that the new towns did not become just suburbs.

5 Self-contained

This meant that:
(a) the towns developed their own identities;
(b) shopping and entertainment facilities needed by the people would be provided locally;
(c) new towns had industries which provided work for the inhabitants, so that they would not become commuter or dormitory towns.

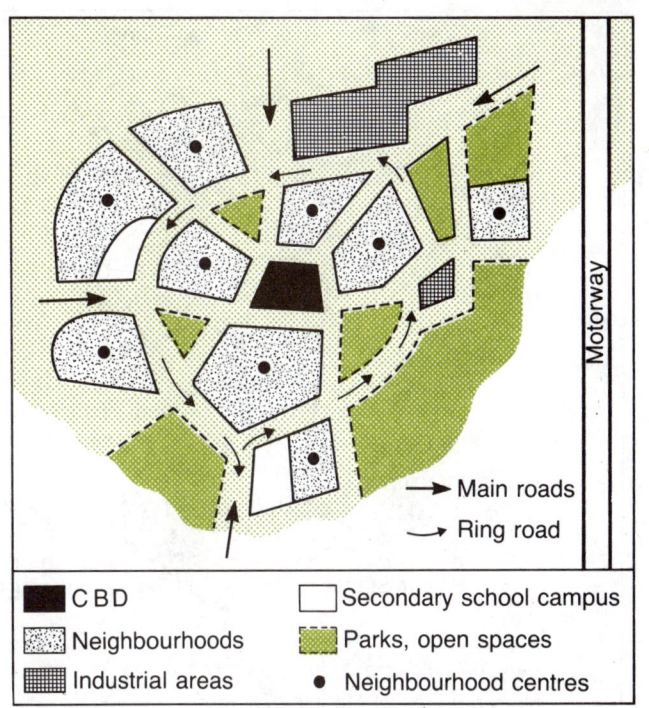

Fig. 2.12A A new town model

A NEW TOWN MODEL

Apply the criteria listed above to the model shown in fig. 2.12A.

AN EXAMPLE — TELFORD NEW TOWN

Telford was built on the rim of the West Midlands conurbation. It is only 35 km west of the city boundary of Birmingham.

Small towns such as Oakengates, and villages like Madeley already existed in the area. Around the existing settlements there was much uneven land because there had been quarrying and shallow mining in the past.

It was planned to develop a series of communities. A single community would consist of about 8000 homes (existing and new ones). Each community was to be provided with a primary school and local facilities such as a doctor's surgery, library, coffee bar, a pub and some shops. Three communities were grouped to form one district and each district had a secondary school and a larger shopping centre.

Factories which already existed within the new town boundary were allowed to expand and new industrial estates were built to attract additional industries from Birmingham and the West Midlands generally. A high-speed ring road and the M54 link were planned to provide the industries with an efficient transport system and to link Telford with the older urban centres. The M54 connects with the M6, M5 and M1 networks.

Originally Telford was planned to grow to a population of 225 000 by 1991, but for a number of reasons this will not be achieved. At present the population has grown beyond the 100 000 mark and the new target is a population of 150 000.

CRITICISMS OF NEW TOWNS AND EXPANDED TOWNS

Planners have revised their ideas about how housing and population problems should be solved. They have

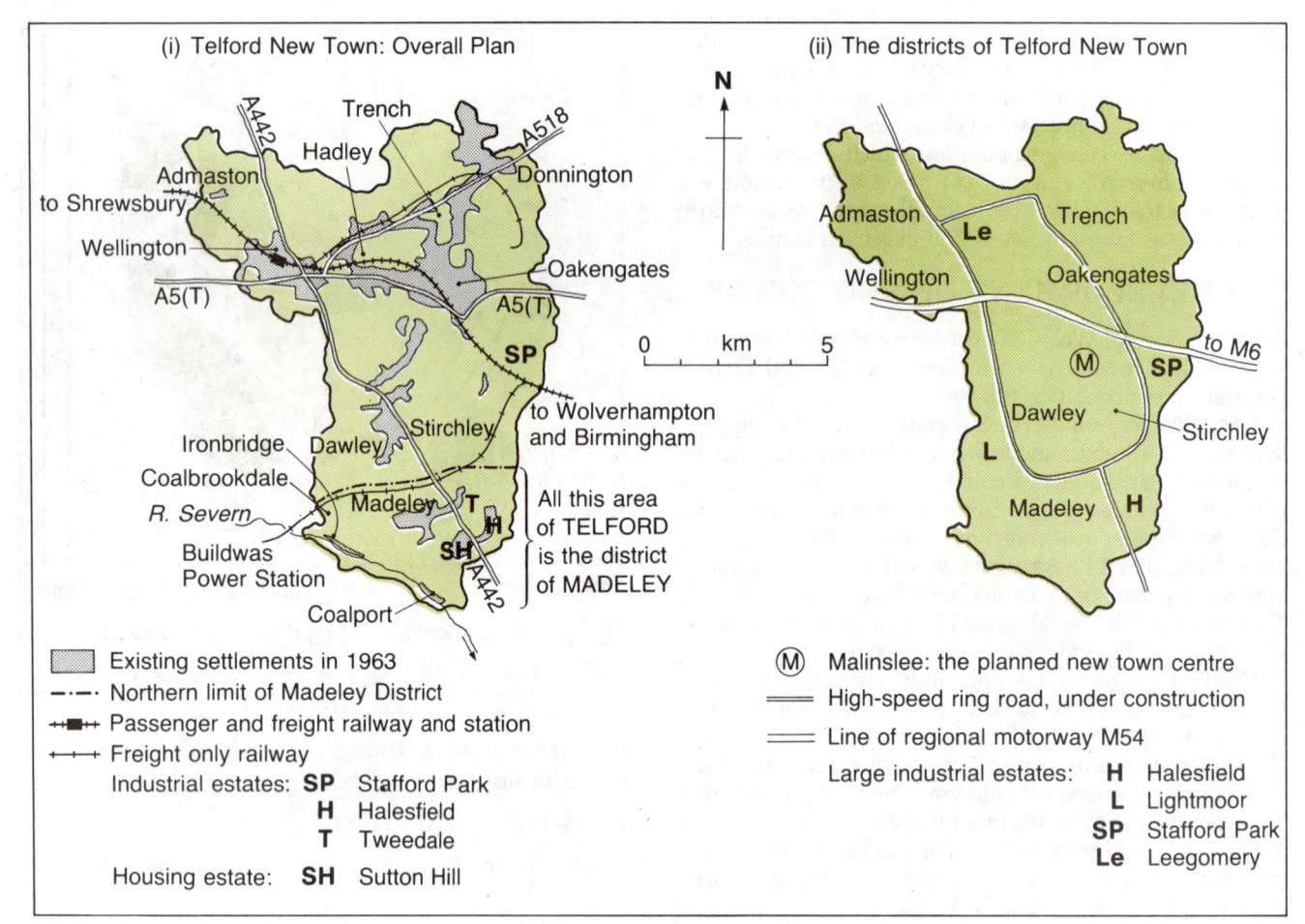

Fig. 2.12B Telford new town

realized that:

1 The decline in birthrate has meant that there is less need for new settlements in Britain.

2 The movement of industries to the new industrial estates in expanded and new towns has drained the economic life of the inner city areas and has taken jobs away from older towns.

3 The mass movement of people away from the inner cities to new towns has further accelerated the decline of inner city areas.

4 Young married couples have found that the cost of living in new towns, especially rents and house prices, is much higher than in the areas from which they moved.

Summary

Basic ideas

New towns have been planned in Britain as an important way of solving the housing and economic problems of cities.

The new town building programme has been supplemented by the creation of expanded towns and overspill estates.

New towns were designed as independent, self-contained, socially balanced communities.

Key terms

New town; expanded town; overspill; self-contained; social balance; optimum size.

2.13 Urban land use

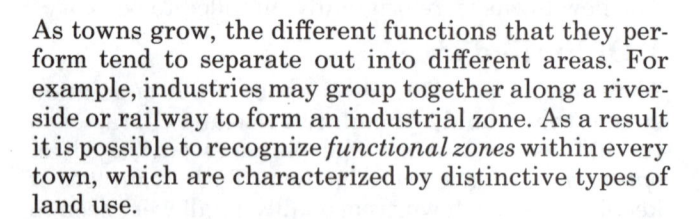

As towns grow, the different functions that they perform tend to separate out into different areas. For example, industries may group together along a riverside or railway to form an industrial zone. As a result it is possible to recognize *functional zones* within every town, which are characterized by distinctive types of land use.

A CITY MODEL

Towns and cities may be divided into different 'functional regions'. Each type of region has its own character and its own functions to perform. Figure 2.13A is a model of the functional regions of an older town or city.

CHIEF FUNCTIONAL ZONES

1 Central Business District (CBD)

The heart of the city, which contains the chief commercial, shopping and social facilities of the town or city. In the USA it is known as 'downtown', but in Britain we speak of the city or town centre.

2 The zone in transition, or the twilight zone

This zone borders the CBD. It is a very mixed area. It usually contains small industries e.g. printing works and warehouses. The houses are old and low-cost, often small terraces or tenements. Larger houses in the zone have been converted into offices, e.g. estate agents and insurance companies, or into flats. There is

The British Isles 43

1 Central business district
2a ⎫ Other business
2b ⎭ districts in the city

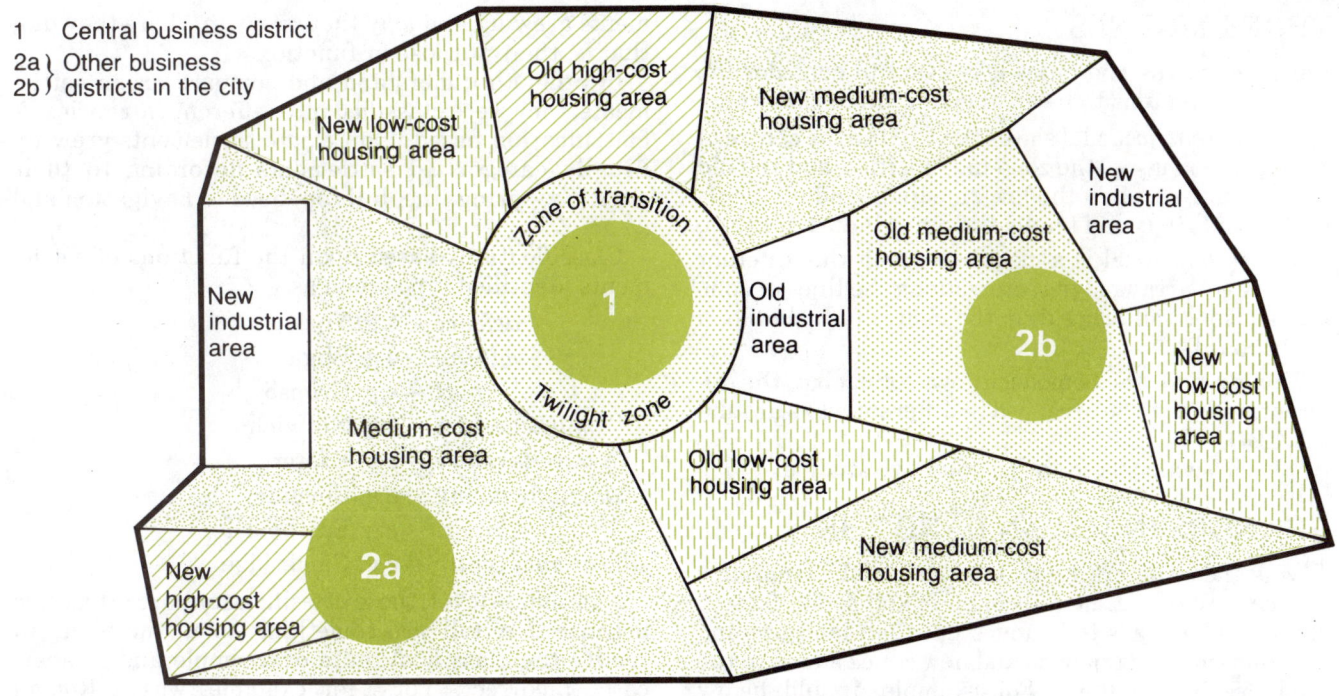

Fig. 2.13A Model of land-use pattern in an old industrial city

an air of decay and deterioration, which is increased by the presence of demolition sites and rebuilding.

3 Old industrial areas

These were developed near the town centres. They were established at a time when the convergence of roads and railways made the town centre the most accessible place for industry. Old industrial areas are often found close to railways. Today these areas may also be decaying because the new industries have been located on the edges of the town or city.

4 New industrial areas

These are the result of the suburbanization of industry. As city centres became congested with traffic, and old industrial premises became out of date, industry began to move to the edge of the city. Modern planned industrial estates provide better premises. They are often located on ring roads or near motorways and so are very accessible. Since managers and workers may also have moved to new estates in the suburbs, it is easy for them to get to work.

5 Residential areas

These are shown in the model divided in two ways: (a) into regions of high-, medium- and low-cost housing; and (b) into new and old areas. The old areas tend to be near the city centre. The grouping of people according to income into different types of residential areas is called *residential segregation*.

6 Suburban shopping centres

These are also shown in the model. They are smaller versions of the CBD and serve a particular part of the town. They are shown by the smaller green circles.

7 Commuters' zone

This zone is not part of the built-up area of the city, but belongs to the city as a whole because it is the region from which workers who live outside the city are drawn to work in the city. Most commuters in Western cities are professional and white-collar workers who choose to live away from their work. In Eastern-bloc cities, many skilled and semi-skilled workers travel long distances each day to work in the city.

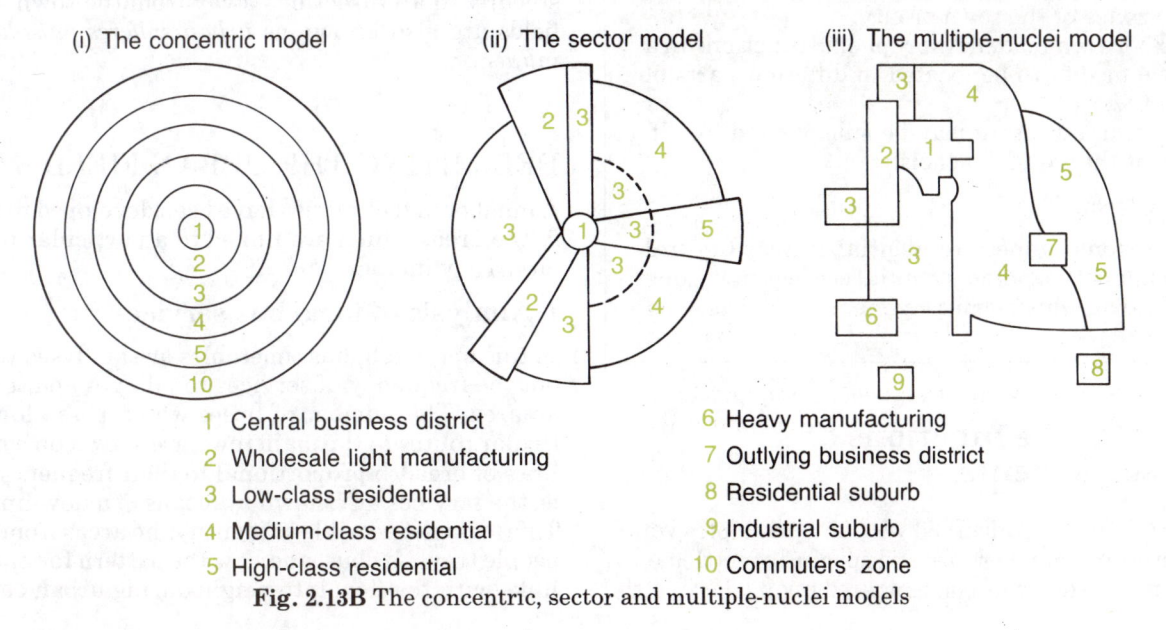

(i) The concentric model   (ii) The sector model   (iii) The multiple-nuclei model

1 Central business district
2 Wholesale light manufacturing
3 Low-class residential
4 Medium-class residential
5 High-class residential
6 Heavy manufacturing
7 Outlying business district
8 Residential suburb
9 Industrial suburb
10 Commuters' zone

Fig. 2.13B The concentric, sector and multiple-nuclei models

THREE MODELS

For older towns and cities it is usual to consider the functional regions to be arranged in three patterns:

1 The *concentric* model shows the CBD as the centre of concentric rings — the zone in transition and the old industrial area, then the low-, medium- and high-cost residential rings and finally the outer industrial area.
2 The *sector* model is a model in which the different regions are arranged in sectors along the lines of communications radiating from the centre (a little like a darts board).
3 The *multiple nuclei* model allows for each of the different regions to be arranged in different ways around the CBD.

Apply these models to towns you have studied.

CHANGES IN URBAN LAND USE

Towns and cities are dynamic aspects of the landscape and change over time as economic and social factors change. This leads to changes in urban land use and old zones may be replaced and new zones added to the land use of the town. For example, in old heavy industrial regions the sites of mines and factories have been flattened and turned into sites for council housing estates or for new light industrial development.

Urban renewal, the replacement of out-of-date housing and industrial regions with new commercial buildings and housing, has involved the clearing of obsolete buildings and the redevelopment of areas to meet the needs of today. Narrow congested roads can be replaced by urban motorways. People can be rehoused in better accommodation. The cleared land can also be redeveloped to provide the greatest possible income for its owners, e.g. by building high-rise blocks of prestige offices.

Renewal, however, causes problems for inner-city people. Cheap housing is demolished and communities are broken up.

Summary

Basic ideas

Urban structure is the result of the spatial relationships that exist between the chief land-use zones of the town or city.

There is a tendency for specific functions in a town or city to be located in different parts of the town.

Urban structure may be summarized by different theoretical models.

Key terms

Functional zones; residential zones; Central Business District; residential segregation; zone in transition; commuter zone.

2.14 The functions of settlements

Geographers are concerned with the principles which determine the number, size and spacing of settlements. In the past, study was concentrated upon *where* settlements grew up and *why* they grew up where they did, that is, their purpose or function.

In order to understand and compare urban settlements, they were classified into different categories. A classification based upon *where* settlements grew up usually categorized settlements according to their sites, e.g. spring line, hill top, head of navigation and so on.

Classifications based upon the functions of settlements identified types such as:

defence — e.g. York
mining — e.g. Wigan
port — e.g. Grimsby
market centre — e.g. Norwich
route centre — e.g. Exeter
manufacturing — e.g. Coventry
resort — e.g. Eastbourne
educational centre — e.g. Cambridge

At a simple level, these classifications are attractive because they tell you something about the town. In reality the classification is over-simple and in some cases incorrect. York, for example, was a Roman fortress, but for centuries it has been an important religious centre. It was also an important market centre, manufacturing town, a centre of the railway industry and is now a tourist centre and university city. So this type of classification is inadequate because most towns have a range of functions for their inhabitants and for the people who live in the surrounding areas, and the relative importance of the different functions may change significantly over time.

URBAN FIELD OR URBAN SPHERE

The recognition of the fact that towns and cities provide services for the areas that surround them (their hinterlands) led to the emergence of the concept of the *urban field* or *sphere*.

The urban field is the area that is economically and socially linked with a town or city. The use of the word *field* is significant. As in Physics, in 'magnetic field', the term suggests that the degree of attraction of the town or city is greatest close to it and decreases steadily in all directions away from the town. Urban fields are also known as *urban spheres* or *spheres of influence*.

DELIMITING THE URBAN FIELD

A number of techniques have been developed to identify the areas which are linked to a particular town or city. They include:

1 Analysis of local bus services

In this approach, bus timetables are analysed to work out the frequency of services to villages and towns in an area. The number of buses which pass along particular routes to the main town are shown on a map by lines of breadth proportional to their frequency. That is, the services are shown by means of a flow-line map. This makes it possible to identify the areas from which people travel by bus, and how the pattern for one town links with the flow into neighbouring urban centres.

2 Analysis of the local newspaper

The number of mentions that different villages or smaller towns receive in a local newspaper published in a larger town can be totalled up over a period of time. Isolines can be drawn to show points of equal value on a map of the region served by the newspaper (its circulation area), all the villages with the same number of mentions lying on the same isoline. Usually the more isolated and more distant villages are the ones which are mentioned least.

3 Mapping the delivery and service areas of town centre shops and offices

The areas to which deliveries are made by furniture shops, electrical goods shops etc. and the areas served by insurance offices, the catchment area of the secondary school or college of further education, and similar services, are mapped to show the extent of the surrounding area which is regularly served by the town or city.

When this technique is used, the lines drawn for each service plotted do not coincide; there is no definite boundary to the urban field.

Usually these zones are identified in the field:

(a) *Zone of dominance* — this zone is enclosed by all the services mapped.

(b) *Zone of competition* — the area covered by some of the services but not by others.

(c) *Zone of indifference or marginal influence* — outside the boundaries shown on the map and so an area where the town has little or no influence.

4 The use of desire line maps

This technique is based upon a survey of people who live in the hinterland, to find out where they choose to go to buy the goods or get the services they need. Lines

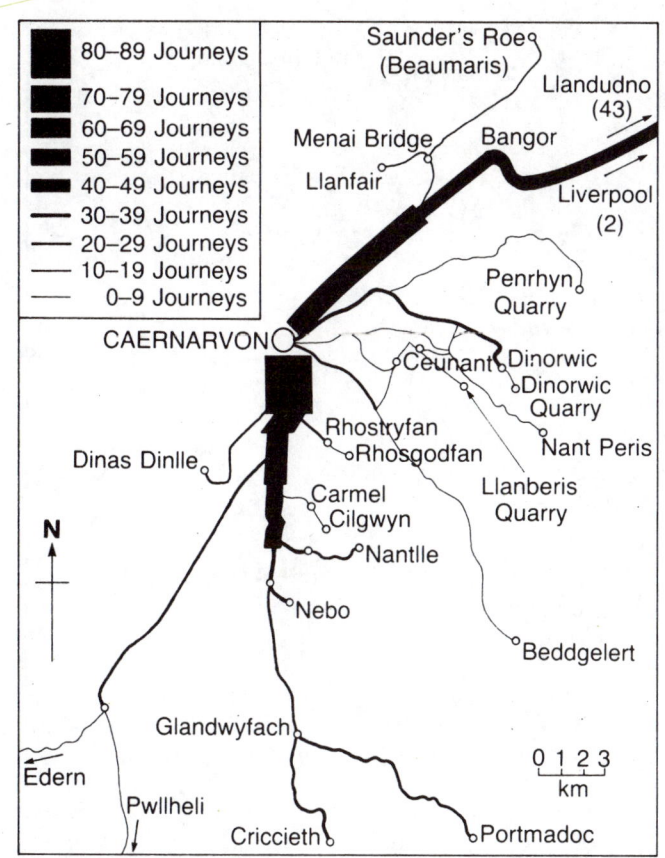

Fig. 2.14A The urban field of Caernarvon as delimited by local bus services

Increased car ownership and the decline in country bus services have made this method much less useful than it was when first used 40 years ago. Figure 2.14A, for example, was drawn before the decline of rural services.

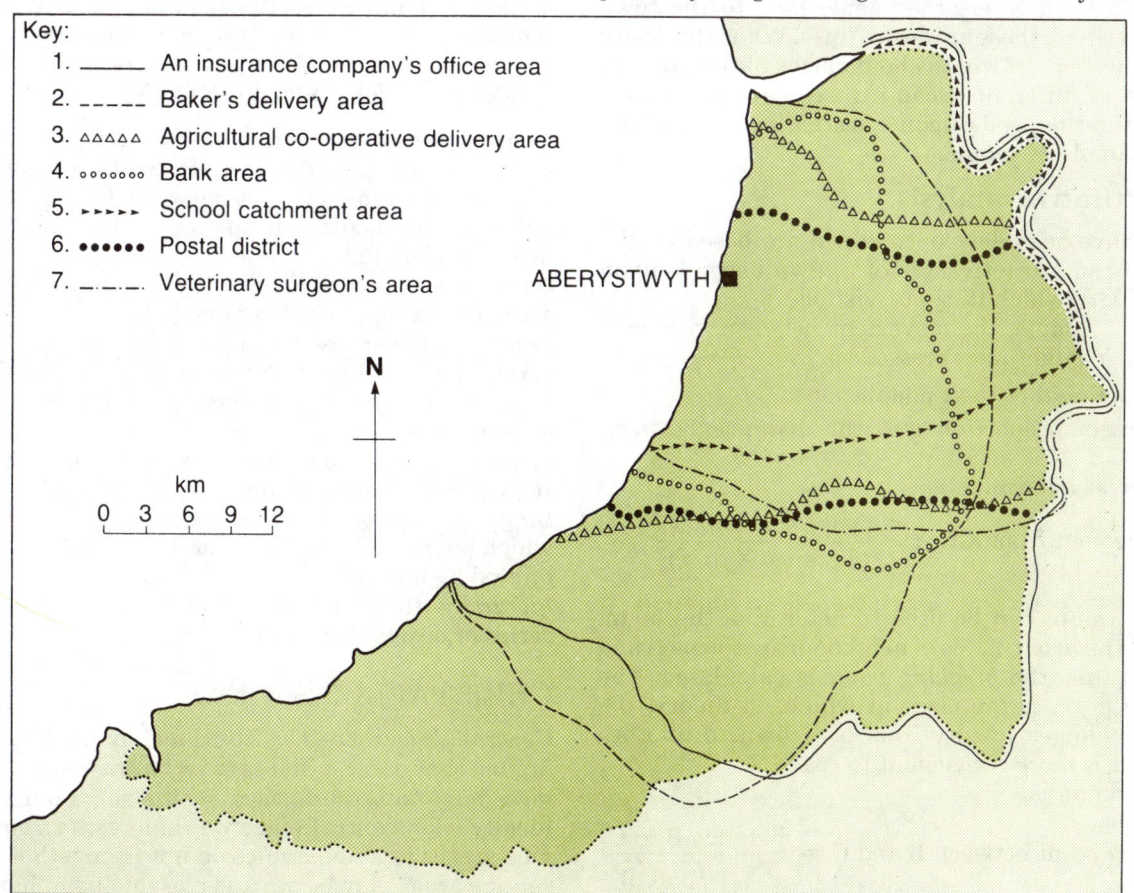

Fig. 2.14B The urban field of Aberystwyth

46 The British Isles

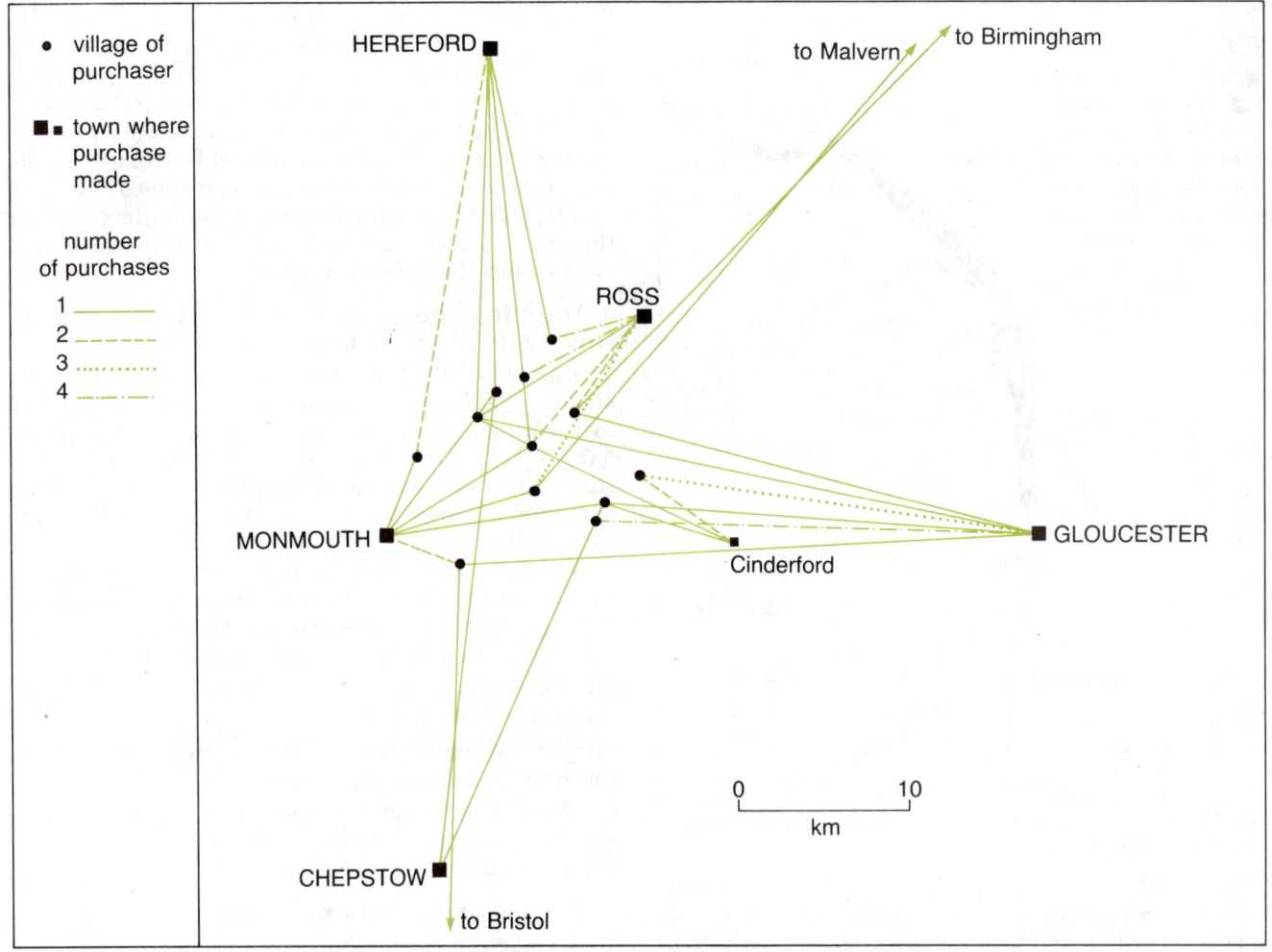

Fig. 2.14C A desire-line diagram related to the purchase of furniture

are drawn from where the people live, to the town which is visited; these are desire lines. When the desire lines have been drawn, the boundaries of the areas of influence of different urban centres can be mapped. This method depends upon questioning a carefully chosen sample of people.

5 Quantitative analysis

Models have been developed which are based on the idea that the attractiveness of a town depends upon the ease with which it can be visited.

So, for example, the movement between village X and town Y might be expressed as:

(a) proportional to their populations;
(b) inversely proportional to the distance between them.

This gives a formula:

$$\text{Movement from X to Y} = \frac{\text{pop. X} \times \text{pop. Y}}{(\text{distance X to Y})^2}$$

This formula can be used to determine the boundaries of the urban fields of neighbouring towns B and C. To do this, the *breaking point* is calculated. The breaking point is the place at which, in theory, the shopper changes loyalty from one town to another because it is more convenient to reach.

The formula is:

$$\text{Breaking point between B and C} = \frac{\text{distance B to C}}{1 + \sqrt{\frac{\text{pop. B}}{\text{pop. C}}}}$$

This formula gives the distance of the breaking point from the smaller of the two towns.

CENTRAL PLACE THEORY

Central place theory is a theory which seeks to explain the relationship of urban settlements to each other. This theory provides a framework for the study of urban settlements throughout the world. Key definitions include:

central place: a settlement which provides one or more services for people living outside it;

functions: lower order functions include the kinds of service provided by a corner shop; higher order functions are the types of service provided by a departmental store;

threshold population: the minimum number of people required to support a function economically;

range of goods or service: the maximum distance over which people will travel to purchase goods or services offered by a central place;

hierarchy: the organization of central places into a series of orders or grades.

CHRISTALLER'S IDEAS

Central place theory was outlined by Christaller. He argued that central places exist because essential services have to be performed for the surrounding area. Ideally each central place would have a circular service area, but since circles do not fit together neatly, service areas may be seen as closely-fitting hexagons. Central places compete with each other and the suc-

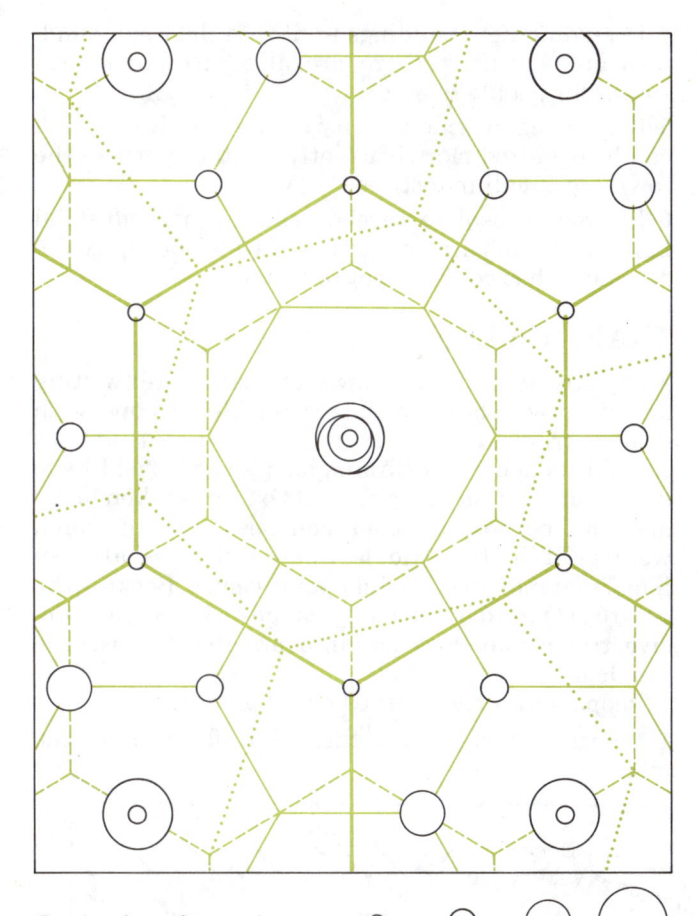

Grade of service centre ○ ◯ ◯ ◯
Associated zone of influence —— – – – ····· ——

Fig. 2.14D Christaller's theoretical landscape

cessful centres acquire new functions and so operate at a higher level in the hierarchy. Christaller identified seven levels in the urban hierarchy. The theory is designed to provide an explanation of the size and spacing of settlements as well as of the relationships between the central place and the area it serves.

> **Summary**
>
> *Basic ideas*
>
> Towns and cities serve surrounding areas which may be termed their urban fields.
> Urban fields can be delimited in a number of ways.
> Central place theory provides a framework for understanding the pattern of relationships between settlements.
>
> *Key terms*
>
> Urban field; urban sphere; desire lines; breakpoint; urban hierarchy; central place theory.

2.15 Urban planning

The building of new towns in Britain has been an important part of urban planning since the Second World War (see unit 2.12). Planners have been faced with a number of urgent problems, of which the provision of more modern homes is only one.

Chief problems which have had to be faced are:

1 The congestion caused by the growth of road transport in town and city centres.

2 The existence of obsolete housing and redundant buildings in the zone of transition in the inner cities (unit 2.13).

3 The out-of-date character of many residential areas.

4 The disappearance of the countryside as towns and cities expand.

URBAN RENEWAL (see also unit 2.13)

The modernization and renewal of urban areas is known as urban renewal. Much of the renewal work is

Fig. 2.15A Aerial photograph of central Birmingham showing Bull Ring

concerned today with keeping people and jobs in the inner city areas. Some urban renewal is *spontaneous*, i.e. it is carried out by private developers who can get higher rents and land prices for new buildings. *Comprehensive* renewal is the large-scale rebuilding of large sections of the inner city.

Since the Second World War, the whole of Birmingham's city centre has been renewed. Old houses, shops, obsolete warehouses, old factories and narrow inadequate roads have been removed from the urban landscape. They have been replaced by modern roads and by the Bull Ring centre. A more recent example of comprehensive urban renewal is the redevelopment of London's disused docklands, such as the St. Katherine's dock area.

The aims of central redevelopment of this type are:

1 To ease traffic congestion in the city centre by building roads which can cope with modern traffic needs.

2 Separating people and traffic, by the building of pedestrian precincts and walkways. This makes the pedestrian safer and can speed up traffic flow.

3 Conserving the environmental quality of an area by keeping and repairing valuable old buildings and districts within the town.

4 Designing new buildings to fit into their surroundings and ensuring there are also attractive open spaces for people to enjoy.

5 Relocating outside the city centre activities which can be operated more efficiently in other parts of the town, e.g. small industries.

6 Removing obsolete warehouses and other industrial buildings which are unsightly and which occupy valuable land that could be put to better use.

TRAFFIC PLANS

Many streets in British towns and cities are twisting and narrow. These roads are unable to cope with modern traffic, but not every town or city is able to rebuild its centre as Birmingham and Sheffield have done. For example the centre of Oxford is taken up by ancient and world-famous colleges, some of which were built in the Middle Ages. Oxford is also an important industrial and shopping centre. Because the centre of Oxford became very congested, a comprehensive traffic plan was put into practice to ease the problem.

People now driving into Oxford find:

1 By-passes which take through-traffic around the city.

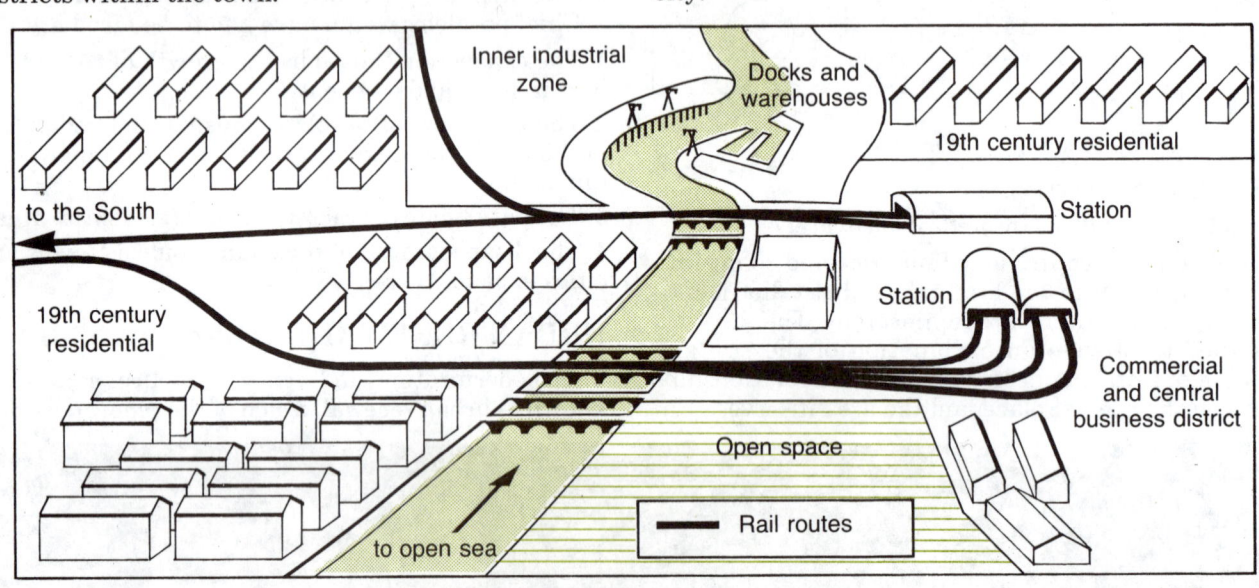

Fig. 2.15B An old industrial landscape

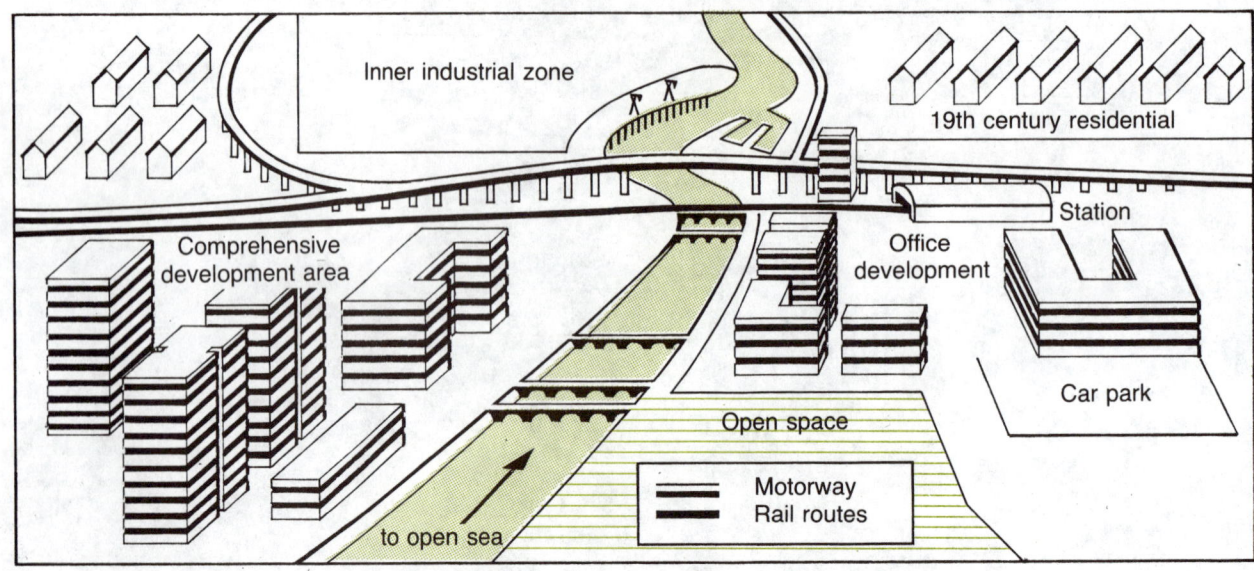

Fig. 2.15C The landscape after urban renewal

2 Areas of the town are marked off as controlled- or disc-parking zones. In the controlled zone, parking is free but in the disc zone cars cannot be parked for more than two hours and must display a disc showing the time at which they were parked.

3 Some streets are traffic free.

4 A 'park and ride' system, whereby cars can be left on the outskirts of the city and motorists get to the city centre by bus. In ways like these, our older cities have tried to at least reduce the problems caused by increasing traffic.

OLD AND NEW INDUSTRIAL LANDSCAPES

Some zones in towns were built before the development of modern road transport. In the early years of industrialization the new factories and works were built alongside canals and railways. Workmen's houses were built nearby, since in those days people walked to work. As a result, a mixed land-use pattern developed, as shown in the diagram of the old industrial landscape in figure 2.15B. The best urban renewal plans for such areas are able to combine the old with new developments to produce a cleaner, more attractive, better planned urban landscape, but problems have occurred.

Fig. 2.15D 'Wave Bye Bye to Gran'; a satirical view of urban renewal

GREEN BELTS

One way in which the unplanned expansion of towns and cities (urban sprawl) was controlled by planners

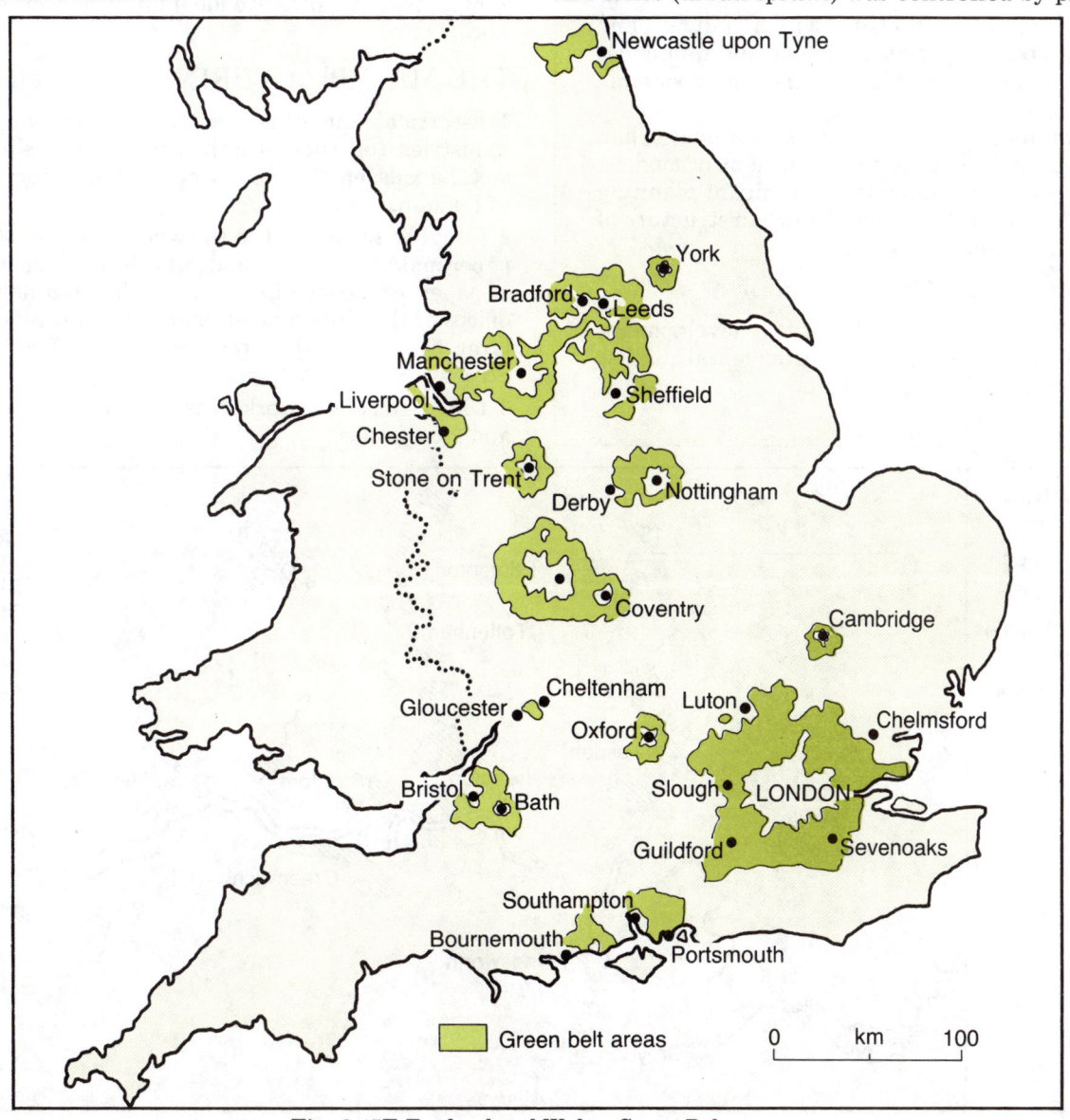

Fig. 2.15E England and Wales: Green Belt areas

was by the establishment of green belts around our chief towns and cities.

Definition:
A belt of countryside surrounding cities and conurbations, in which new developments are severely restricted so that the area will remain rural and undeveloped.

Examples
Outer London is bounded by the metropolitan green belt, 10–15 kilometres wide. This belt has prevented London spreading over areas in the Home Counties and developments have consequently taken place beyond the green belt, in areas such as mid-Sussex and north Essex where good train services enable people to commute to work in London.

The functions of a green belt can be summed up as:
1 To check the growth of a large built-up area.
2 To prevent neighbouring towns from merging.
3 To preserve the special character of a town.
4 To provide amenities for the city dwellers.

Summary
Basic ideas

Planning is a process which guides and stimulates the growth of towns and influences how towns adapt to new social and economic conditions.

Planning is necessary to improve urban living conditions. The development of modern road transport has caused significant planning problems and changes in the urban structure of our towns and cities.

Key terms

Urban renewal; comprehensive redevelopment; old industrial landscape; environmental quality; traffic congestion; green belts.

2.16 Regional contrasts — industries of the London Basin

WHY INDUSTRIES HAVE DEVELOPED

1 As London is an important port, it is easy to bring raw materials and fuels into the region. Coal and oil are brought to Thames-side and used in power stations to generate electricity for the factories.

2 Because it is so large a city, it has a huge labour force. Special skills have been developed over a long period in crafts and industries which grew up in the wealthy capital — for example, in the fashion trade.

3 The City of London provides finance and insurance for industries.

4 The people of London provide a market for much of what is manufactured there. Because of the wealth concentrated in the capital city, many luxury industries exist. Large quantities of foods, clothing, vehicles etc. are also needed.

5 As London is the centre of communications in this country, manufactured goods can be distributed easily throughout the country and can also be exported from the port of London.

6 Some industries such as paper-milling require large quantities of water.

7 Flat riverside sites are ideal for large works such as Ford.

THE MANUFACTURING INDUSTRIES

1 Electrical and other forms of engineering. These industries, together with the making of cars and other metal goods, employ nearly half of the factory workers of London.

2 Roughly 13 per cent of the workers are in paper and paper-making, printing and publishing. Vast quantities of paper are needed in a city which contains the head offices of the Government, banks, insurance and other large firms as well as the newspaper offices in Fleet Street.

3 One in ten of the workers is employed in the clothing and food trades.

Industrial Areas
1 West London
2 Lea Valley
3 Lower Thames Valley
4 Inner London
5 Wandle Valley

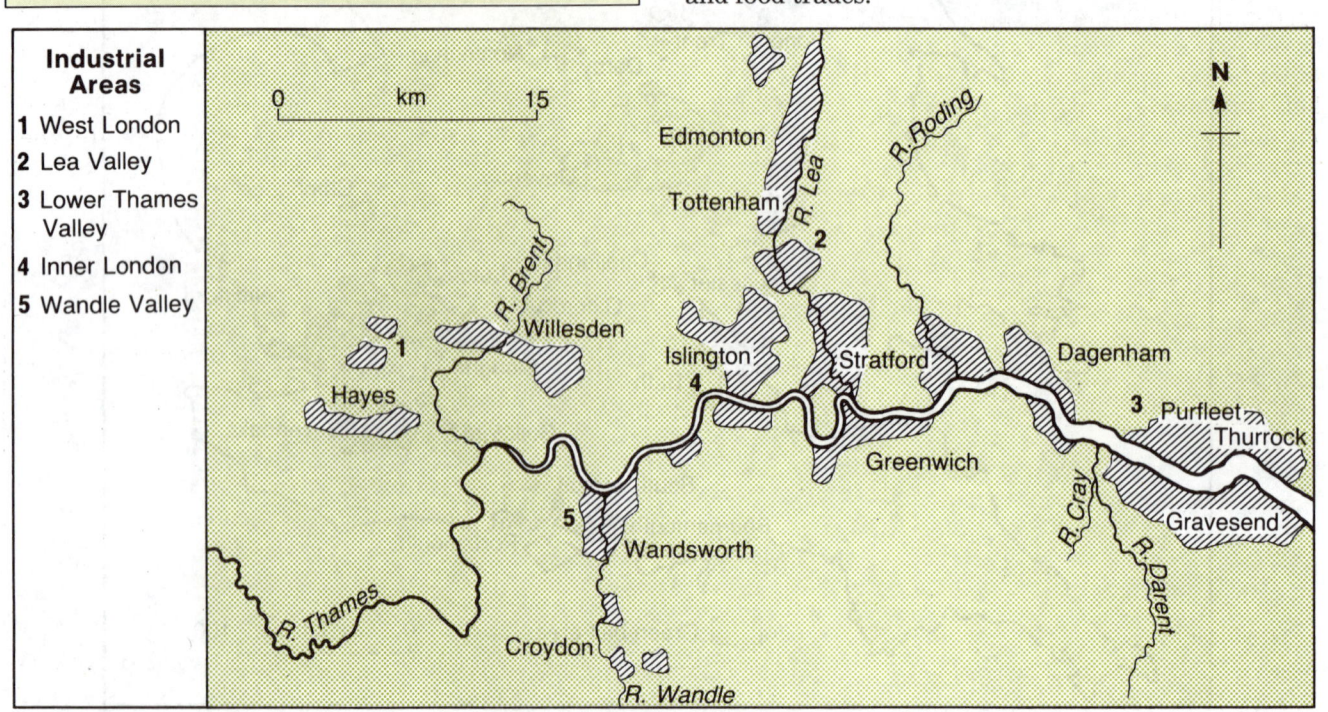

Fig. 2.16A London: industrial areas

THE MAIN INDUSTRIAL AREAS

(Numbers refer to areas in fig. 2.16A)

The West (1)

Factories line the Great West Road (A4), Western Avenue (A40), the North Circular Road and the Kingston by-pass. The factories depend on road transport and make 'consumer goods' such as domestic equipment (e.g. Hoover at Perivale), office equipment, food and drink, plastic goods.

The Lea valley (2)

Factories are linked by the Cambridge road (A11) and the old Navigation canal. The most distinctive industry is the manufacture of furniture, but there are also metal and engineering works.

Lower Thames valley (3)

This region extends eastwards from central London as far as Purfleet and Thurrock on the north bank of the river and to Gravesend on the south bank. Large cement works use chalk quarried locally. There are also gas works (Beckton), power stations (Barking), engineering (Ford at Dagenham), and important paper and board mills (Purfleet). At the mouth of the Thames there are large oil refineries at Thames Haven and Canvey Island (north bank) and on the Isle of Grain (south bank).

Inner London (4)

This is the oldest industrial area which grew up in the West End and east of the City. Many of the industries are located in small workshops — clothing, footwear and furniture for example.

The Wandle valley (5)

This is one of the valleys along which industries have spread from the centre. These include electrical engineering and consumer goods.

THE DEVELOPMENT OF LONDON'S DOCKLAND

During the 1960s and 1970s the trade which once passed through London's docks moved away to Rotterdam or smaller ports such as Felixstowe with their up-to-date container terminals and efficient working practices.

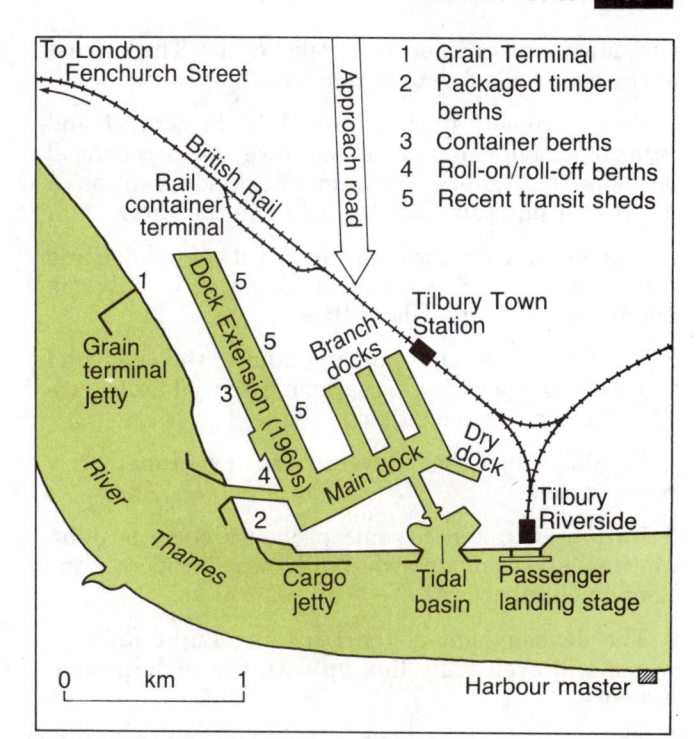

Fig. 2.16C Tilbury Docks

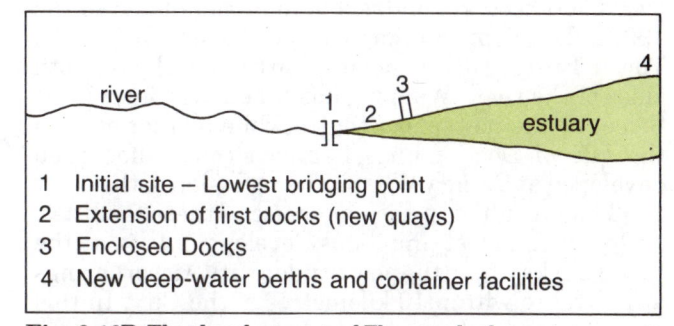

1. Initial site – Lowest bridging point
2. Extension of first docks (new quays)
3. Enclosed Docks
4. New deep-water berths and container facilities

Fig. 2.16D The development of Thames docks

The London docks from Tower Bridge to Woolwich became a derelict area until 1981 when the London Docklands Urban Development Corporation was set up to attract investors to spend large sums of money on the region, backed up by Government funds for roads and other facilities. The aim was to develop commercial and residential buildings in attractive settings close to the City of London. Instead of looking westwards, the developers were encouraged to look east, despite the

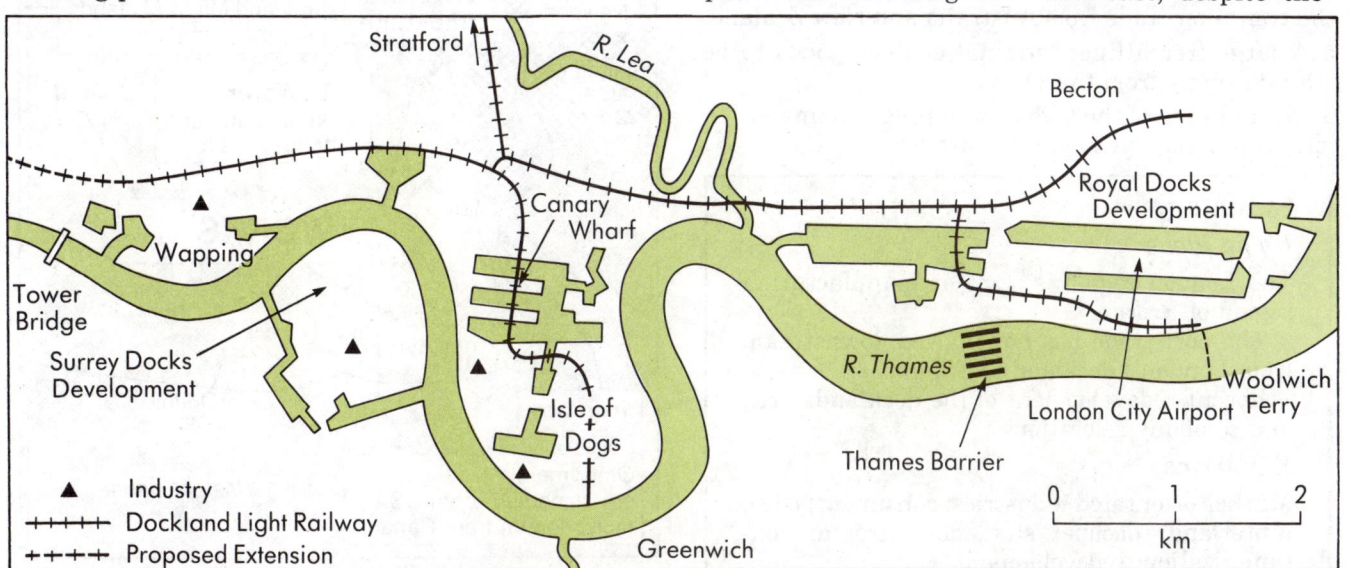

Fig. 2.16B The development of London's dockland

run-down landscape of the derelict docks. The success of the scheme is due to a number of factors:

1 The extremely high price of land in central and suburban London for new office or residential development. Office rents in docklands can be a quarter or one third what is asked in the City.

2 The proximity of the docks to the City of London and the West End. The Bank of England is only six kilometres from the Isle of Dogs.

3 The juxtaposition of building land to the river and the dock basins with considerable potential for leisure activities and scenic views.

4 Funding by the Government for inner city regeneration.

5 Initiatives taken by entrepreneurs such as John Mowlem and Company who built, own and operate the London City Airport.

6 The development of the Dockland Light Railway which will eventually link up with the underground network.

7 The setting up of the Isle of Dogs Enterprise Zone to attract industry. The dockland development extends over 2000 hectares and is due to be completed in the 1990s. Development has extended eastwards from Tower Bridge with residential areas nearby on both sides of the river. Wapping has taken over from Fleet Street as the newspaper centre while further east on the Isle of Dogs a huge financial centre has been developed at Canary Wharf. The recession of the early 1992 has resulted in the under-use of these facilities.

One of the most ambitious developments is at the Royal Docks where the new London City Airport brings air travel to within 10 kilometres of the City. In this region houses, shops, hotels, a science park and an exhibition centre are planned.

REASONS FOR TILBURY'S GROWTH

1 It is the nearest dock to the sea, and since they do not have to travel up-river, the ships can turn around quickly and keep down costs.

2 The water is 13 metres deep at Tilbury, so it can take bigger ships than the old London docks.

3 Tilbury has roll-on/roll-off services.

4 Tilbury is a container port and handles, for example, the container trade from Australia and New Zealand.

5 A large freightliner terminal enables goods to be moved rapidly from the docks.

6 The building of the M25 orbital road has linked Tilbury into London's motorway network.

Summary

Basic ideas

The London region is a major manufacturing region of Britain.

The port trade has now moved downstream from London's dockland to Tilbury.

Recent redevelopment of the docklands area and company relocation.

Key terms

Market-orientated industries; consumer goods; hinterland; decline; shift downstream; containerization; redevelopment.

2.17 Regional contrasts — South Wales

South Wales contains most of the population of Wales, because of the industries which developed on the coalfield.

THE TRADITIONAL INDUSTRIES OF WALES

In the past the industrial areas of Wales depended upon two major industries: coal mining and steel production. Rural areas were dependent upon farming, especially hill sheep farming.

The coal industry began to decline after the First World War (1914–18) when ships became oil-burning instead of coal-burning. In recent years the number of mines has decreased rapidly and famous coal mining areas such as the Rhondda valleys have lost their industrial base completely.

Between the two World Wars trading estates were built to ease serious unemployment. The recent decline in British manufacturing industry led to closure of factories which had originally intended to revive the Welsh economy.

There are still two modern integrated steel works in Wales: at Margam near Port Talbot and Llanwern near Newport. In both plants the workforces have been drastically reduced recently. Fig. 2.17A shows the factors which led to the establishment of the Llanwern works.

INFRASTRUCTURE

Since the 1950s major efforts have been made to improve the infrastructure of the region to make South Wales a more attractive location to industrialists and financiers. The infrastructure is the basic framework upon which industry operates. The Severn Bridge and the M4 motorway made South Wales more accessible from London and its two chief airports, Heathrow and Gatwick. Within South Wales the Heads of the Valleys road links

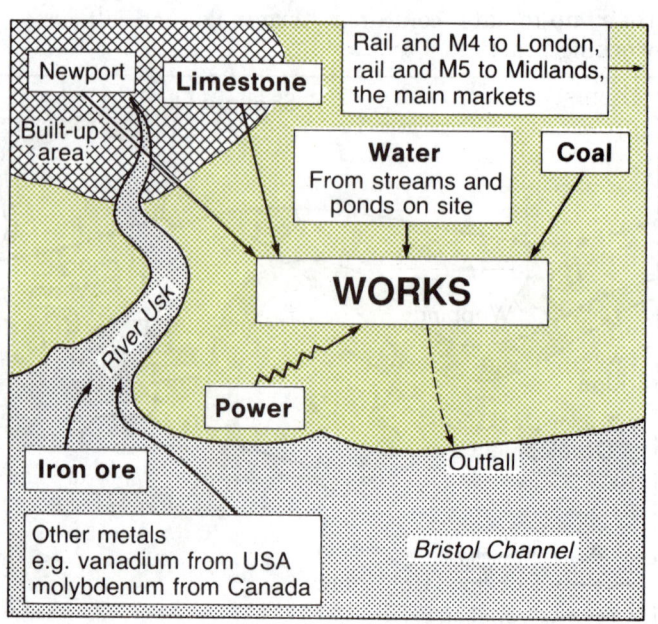

Fig. 2.17A Llanwern steelworks, Newport

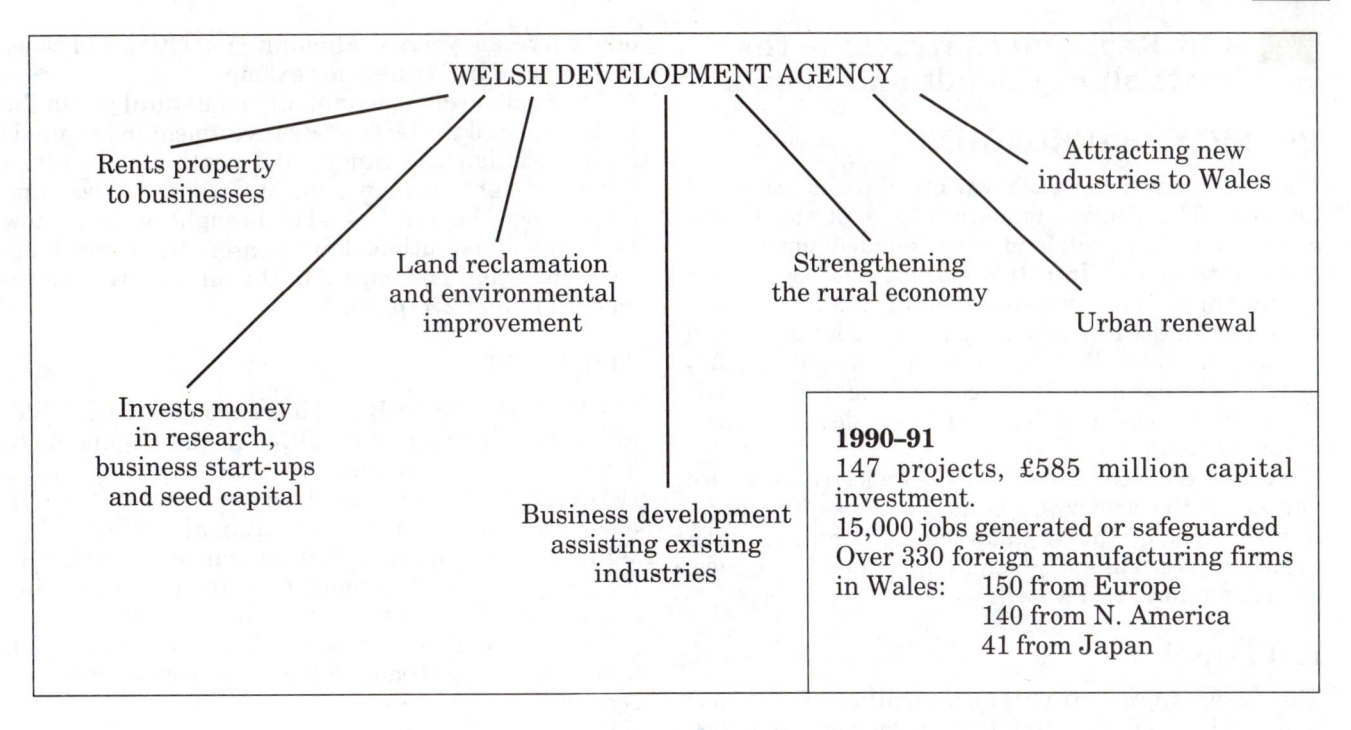

```
                    WELSH DEVELOPMENT AGENCY

   Rents property                                    Attracting new
   to businesses                                     industries to Wales

              Land reclamation        Strengthening
              and environmental       the rural economy
              improvement                            Urban renewal

   Invests money
   in research,                       ┌─────────────────────────────────────┐
   business start-ups                 │ 1990-91                             │
   and seed capital                   │ 147 projects, £585 million capital  │
                                      │ investment.                         │
                                      │ 15,000 jobs generated or safeguarded│
                   Business development│ Over 330 foreign manufacturing firms│
                   assisting existing  │ in Wales:   150 from Europe        │
                   industries          │             140 from N. America    │
                                      │             41 from Japan           │
                                      └─────────────────────────────────────┘
```

Fig. 2.17B Chief activities of the WDA

South Wales with the M50 and M5 to give access to the Midlands.

THE WELSH DEVELOPMENT AGENCY (WDA)

The WDA was set up in 1976 to:

1 Further the economic development of Wales.

2 Promote industrial efficiency in Wales.

3 Encourage the improvement of the environment.

The WDA also decided to encourage managers to create job opportunities for the disabled.
Fig. 2.17B shows the chief activities of the WDA.
It concentrates on helping small and medium sized industries because they are now the driving force of the economy. The industrial sector in which most money has been invested by the WDA is the manufacture of office and data processing equipment.

The WDA encourages communities to help themselves. Rural Enterprise groups have been set up to provide programmes for rural areas. The programmes are agreed by Local Authorities, industrialists and the local people.

Environmental improvement

Setting up new industries proceeds alongside environmental improvement schemes, especially land reclamation and urban renewal. Old coal tips which are ugly and often health hazards and other old industrial sites contaminated by poisonous wastes have been removed. The reclaimed land has been put to new uses—better housing, modern factory sites and so on.

The WDA has an Urban Renewal Unit which supports the renewal of the centres of old industrial towns such as Rhyl, Merthyr Tydfil, Ebbw Vale and Llanelli. In North Wales renewal has included the building of a new shopping and leisure centre on Deeside and a tunnel under the river Conwy to divert holiday traffic from the centre of Conwy town.

HOW SUCCESSFUL ARE THESE EFFORTS?

The Welsh economy is now one of the fastest growing of all the regions of the United Kingdom. Cardiff is attracting a number of new financial and business firms and over 40 new Japanese owned plants have been located in Wales. One new problem is the result of that success: there is now a shortage of good industrial property, especially in south-east Wales.

Summary

Basic ideas

South Wales was once a typical, traditional heavy industrial region with its economy based on coal mining and iron and steel.

It is now the chief centre of the British steel industry. New developments have been developed with a view to making the region more attractive to new industries to create a different employment pattern. The Welsh Development Agency has played a key part in this initiative in South Wales and the rest of the country. An improved infrastructure, environmental improvement, and determined efforts to attract new industry has made South Wales more diversified economically and more prosperous.

Key terms

Coal mining; iron and steel; trading estates; infrastructure; WDA; urban renewal; land reclamation.

2.18 Regional contrasts — the Scottish Highlands and Islands

PHYSICAL BACKGROUND

The Highlands consist of a variety of rocks and relief features. The central mountain area of the Cairngorms is a high tableland with rounded summits at about 900 metres. Into this surface has been cut a number of valleys, over-deepened by glaciers. To the west the landscape is more jagged with ridges and peaks, including Ben Nevis with a height of 1344 metres. This area is dissected by U-shaped valleys, including the valley of the River Nevis, deep lochs and a fjorded coastline.

North-west of the Great Glen the rock structures are varied and the scenery constantly changes. This area, like the rest of the Highland zone, contains much evidence of highland glaciation, including corries, hanging valleys and waterfalls.

FARMING

There are many constraints on agriculture. The land is high, soils are poor, rainfall is heavy, reaching 4000 mm in the west, the winds are strong and temperatures low because of the elevation. Agriculture is confined to hill farming with the lower ground used for shelter and growing feedstuffs. Sheep are more important than cattle with about one third of the Scottish flock in the Highlands, compared with 19 per cent of the beef cattle and 6 per cent of the dairy cattle.

CROFTING

The small, family-run farms, mainly to be found on the islands or along the west coast, are known as crofts. The crofts are smallholdings of 2–4 hectares which may not provide sufficient income for the crofters. Additional income is obtained from fishing, the textile industry – making Harris Tweed or Shetland knitwear, and tourism.

The main crops grown are oats, potatoes and other vegetables. Additional grazing is available in some areas as a result of the grouping of crofts into 'townships' with common grazing land. A Crofters Commission, set up by the Government, has encouraged land improvement and the survival of the crofting communities.

INDUSTRY

With virtually no coal, the main source of power throughout the Highlands is hydroelectricity. The advantages of the area for hydroelectric power development include the heavy precipitation, extensive lochs and deep valleys for water storage, hard bed-rock for building dam facilities and steep gradients which give the stored water the thrust required to turn the turbines.

Some of the HEP is used to smelt aluminium at Kinlochleven.

Hydroelectricity has encouraged the development of other industries in the Highlands and Islands. The Forestry Commission has helped to regenerate many Highland forests.

Light industries have also been developed in Fort William and at many other Highland locations as fig. 2.18A shows, but some modern industries have closed down in recent years — aluminium smelting and paper making at Fort William for example.

The rapid development of oil and natural gas in the North Sea and the large-scale investment in terminals in the Shetlands, Orkneys and north-east Scotland have brought employment to these areas and elsewhere. The oil has also brought with it new problems of pollution, land conservation and long-term planning. The impact of the oil industry is summarized in unit 2.4 (p.26).

TOURISM

The Scottish Tourist Board has encouraged the building of new hotels and facilities in the Highlands to bring tourist money into the area. Aviemore in the Cairngorms has been developed for winter sports with new accommodation and recreational facilities. Fort William is an important tourist centre at the foot of Ben Nevis. New accommodation, including camping and caravan facilities, has been introduced.

Tourism in this region is likely to expand with improvements to roads, ferries, accommodation and recreational facilities.

PROBLEMS

1 Depopulation

The population of the Highlands and Islands, which declined steadily up to 1971, showed a slight rise between 1971 and 1981. However, the total is still only 5.4 per cent of Scotland's population.

The table below shows the percentage changes for the Highlands and Islands administrative districts between 1981 and 1990.

Emigration to the cities of the south, or overseas, accounted for much of the decline. The fall in new developments on the oil fields has resulted in a sharp drop in the population of the Shetlands. Tourism has increased the population in Strathspey but its decline in the remote areas and Western Isles continues.

Region	% change 1981–1990
Badenoch and Strathspey	+ 13.5
Caithness	− 3.1
Inverness	+ 10.5
Lochaber	− 2.4
Nairn	+ 4.7
Ross and Cromarty	+ 4.2
Skye and Lochalsh	+ 11.3
Sutherland	−2.0
Orkney	+ 2.0
Shetland	− 15.5
Western Isles	− 2.8

2 Loss of young people

Not only has the population declined, but also in the more remote areas the proportion of young people is falling. This is particularly so in Orkney and it remains to be seen whether the oil boom will permanently reverse this trend. The cause for the decline is lack of employment and opportunities in the area and the pull of the higher wages and attractions of the cities in the south. The effect on the local communities

The British Isles 55

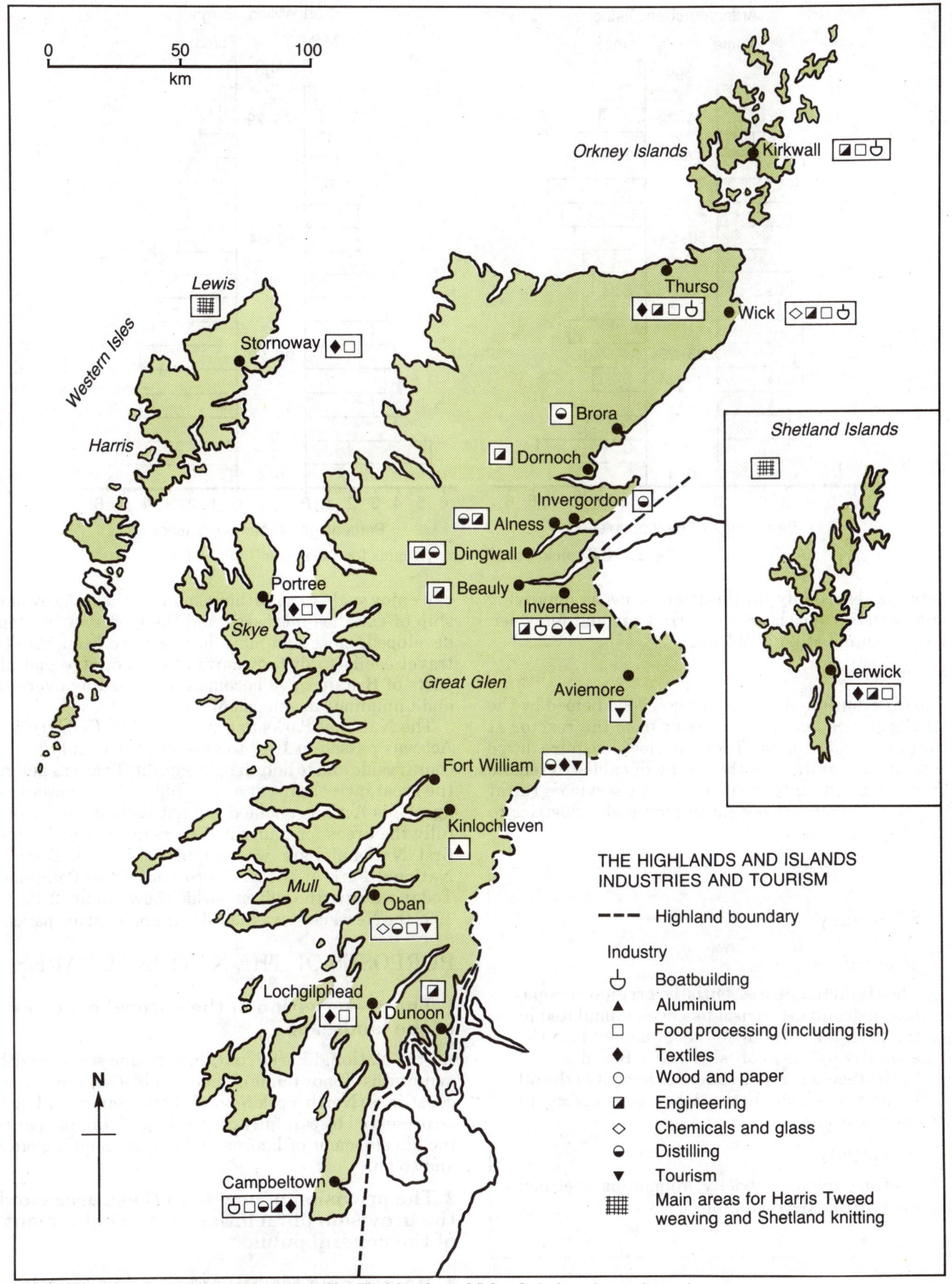

Fig. 2.18A The Highlands and Islands industries and tourism

is that only a small proportion of the people who remain are economically active.

3 Main towns and services

The main towns and services are on the eastern side of the region, with only small settlements like Ullapool on the west. As a result the hinterlands of these towns extend over long distances and include the islands.

4 Transport and communications

Transport costs can be high because of the distances between settlements and to the main towns. The road

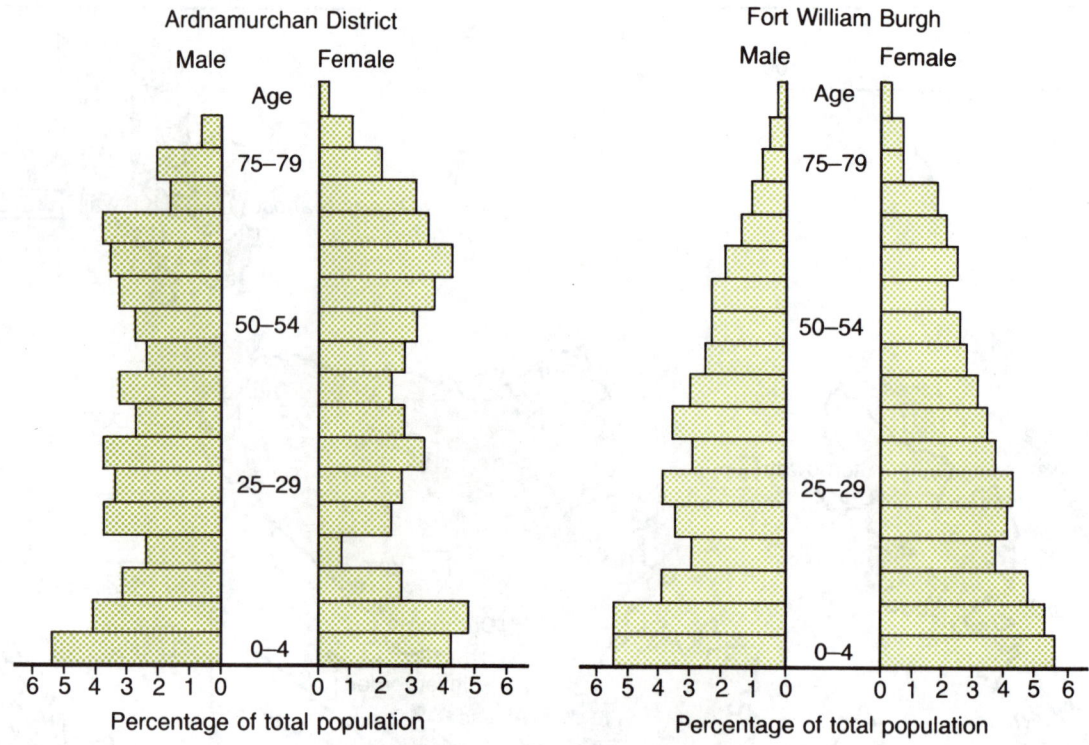

Fig. 2.18B Typical population pyramids for the region

network, especially on the islands, needs improving and economy measures to restrict air and ferry services create further problems.

5 Power

The distribution of electricity has been helped by the HEP schemes and atomic power from the reactor at Dounreay, Caithness. These projects require large amounts of capital and the laying of cables to remote areas adds further to the expense. The service is run at a loss to encourage people to stay and industries to move into the region.

Summary

Basic ideas

The Highlands are essentially a region of population decline. Tourism has been stimulated in the region by the injection of money into the economy by the Scottish Tourist Board.

The recent growth and development of the oil industry has brought new jobs and prosperity to specific areas.

Key terms

Crofting; hydroelectricity; aluminium smelting; oil; tourism; depopulation.

2.19 The National Parks

The enormous growth of towns and cities has led to the belief that we should preserve country areas which are especially attractive. Tourism and leisure activities in such areas need to be planned to ensure that people can enjoy such areas without spoiling them. As ownership of cars has increased and the motorway system developed, more and more people have been able to travel easily to distant parts of the country and all parts of Britain have become threatened by over-use and unplanned development.

The National Parks and Access to the Countryside Act was passed in 1949 to preserve the beauty of the countryside and to help people enjoy it. This was before the great increase in car ownership and the motorway age. This Act has enabled the nation to control carefully the areas for tourism. As a result of the Act the first National Park was set up—the Peak District National Park at the southern end of the Pennines. Today we have the eleven parks, shown in fig. 2.19. In 1992 the New Forest was added to the original ten parks.

PURPOSES OF THE NATIONAL PARKS

1 The preservation of the natural beauties of the landscape

All the National Parks contain very fine scenery with mountains (Snowdonia), moorlands (Dartmoor) or coastlines (North York Moors). This scenery will now be preserved by carefully controlling within the parks the development of houses, industries, camping sites and so on.

2 The provision of access to these areas and the provision of facilities for the enjoyment of the general public

3 Maintaining traditional farming practices in the park areas

When a region was designated a National Park there was no change in ownership of land or property. The residents continued to live and work in it as before. As a National Park, however, the authorities are able to use strict planning controls to preserve the natural beauty. They can do this by:

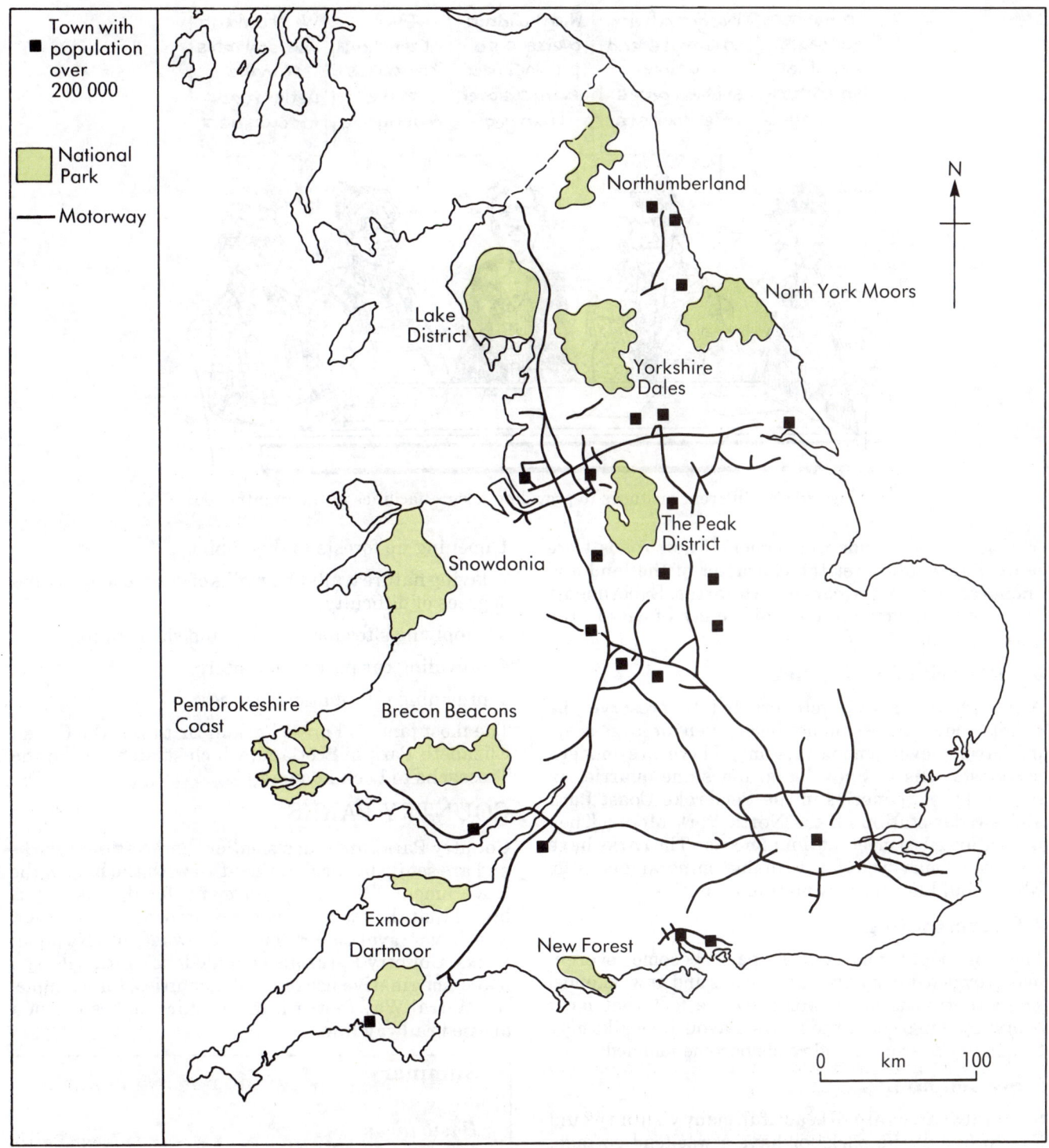

Fig. 2.19A England and Wales: the National Parks

(a) limiting new building in the park;
(b) limiting industrial development in the park;
(c) dictating the building materials to be used for the repair and extension of existing buildings;
(d) setting high standards of design for approved new buildings;
(e) carefully locating and screening car parks for visitors;
(f) employing wardens to supervise the parks.

PROBLEMS OF THE NATIONAL PARKS

The popularity of the parks and the strict maintenance of the quality of the environment have created a number of problems.

1 Depopulation

The restriction of development preserves the scenery for the visitors but limits opportunities for people who live within the parks. Factories cannot be built to provide new work; new electricity pylons cannot be erected across the hills to provide modern facilities; houses and farm buildings have to be constructed using expensive local materials to 'fit into' the landscape. The tourist industry has provided new summer jobs but the lack of work and restriction of development has meant that local people have left the areas.

2 Traffic

Millions of cars visit the most popular parks each year. Traffic jams can be almost as bad as in the centre

Fig. 2.19B Different attitudes to providing leisure facilities in the countryside

Speech bubbles:
- "I came here for peace and quiet. No visitors I say."
- "I've got a living to earn; I spend my time shutting gates after tourists."
- "With holidays overseas so popular, I need every customer I can get."
- "Every citizen should have access to the countryside."
- "We shouldn't use local rates to make better roads for outsiders."

of cities on weekends in summer. If new roads were built they would alter the character of the land and encourage even more cars into the areas. Experiments are now being made to control the use of cars in the parks.

3 Industrial development

Although the parks were created to preserve the countryside, permission has been given for large-scale industrial development in some. There are modern power stations in Snowdonia, limestone quarries in the Peak; oil refineries in the Pembroke Coast Park and a radar station on the North York Moors. They were allowed to meet 'national needs'. The parks have also been surveyed for valuable mineral deposits, which could lead to new mining activities.

4 Overcrowding

The most popular parts of the parks become severely overcrowded during holiday seasons and at weekends. The situation is made worse by the fact that most people stay in or near their cars. Favourite walks may be heavily over-used and roads become jammed.

5 Second homes

Since these areas are so beautiful, many visitors would like to live in the parks or have a weekend cottage. Some city dwellers can pay higher prices for cottages than locals can afford, and gradually artificial villages are being created in which only a few people live permanently and only a tiny minority work locally.

6 Pollution

Overcrowding of the parks can cause pollution—by exhaust fumes from many cars in traffic jams and motor boats on the lakes, and through litter left by careless visitors. The constant use of footpaths can destroy ground vegetation.

FOREST PARKS

Forest parks have been created by the Forestry Commission. There are four parks in Scotland, one in Wales and three in England. The creation of a forest park involves:

1 opening up forests to the public;
2 laying nature trails and walks of graded lengths and degrees of difficulty;
3 supplying sites for camping and caravanning;
4 providing car parks for visitors;
5 providing information services.

The most famous Forest Park in Britain is the Queen Elizabeth Park in Scotland, which stretches from the Trossachs to Loch Lomond.

COUNTRY PARKS

Country Parks are much smaller than National Parks and are set up by local authorities with the help of the Government. By setting up many local parks, it is hoped that they will attract visitors who would otherwise have travelled further and crowded into National Parks. Country Parks also enable local authorities to make imaginative use of local amenities, for example, the Wirral Way footpath in Cheshire makes use of a disused railway line.

Summary

Basic ideas

Increasing demand for use of the countryside for leisure has resulted in the government designating particular areas as National, Forest, and Country Parks.

The popularity of the National Parks has created problems for those who are responsible for maintaining their beauty and character. It is difficult to maintain the right balance between the economic needs of the country or region, the freedom of visitors to enjoy themselves and the rights of those who live in the parks to carry on their normal ways of life.

Key terms

National Park; Forest Park; Country Park; conflicting interests, second homes; pollution; conservation.

2.20 The holiday industry

Until fairly recently, most people had very few holidays in the year. Day trips and one or two weeks' summer holiday was the typical pattern for most working people. From Victorian times onwards, the favourite locations at which to spend this time was at the seaside. As a result, the coastline of Britain became sprinkled with seaside resorts, all of which shared certain common features — a promenade, a pier, entertainment facilities, guest- or boarding-houses in which visitors without much money could stay, and hotels for the better off. Key factors in the development and importance of such resorts were,

1 Proximity to a densely populated urban area,

2 Rapid and cheap mass transport which enabled large numbers of people to visit resorts regularly.

People were less mobile then than they are today, for they did not have cars. Most people had only a limited amount of money to spend and so had little choice of where to go on holiday. As a result, resorts became closely linked with particular industrial regions or individual cities. Skegness became known as 'Nottingham by the sea', while just to the north Cleethorpes was a favourite with the people of Sheffield. For the workers in the Lancashire cotton mills, Blackpool was the chief holiday centre. So after the establishment of the railway network in Britain, there developed a simple relationship between many seaside resorts and the main areas they served.

Since the Second World War this pattern has largely broken down as a result of:

1 The increased mobility of families, which came with car ownership.

2 Higher standards of living, which gave many people a greater freedom of choice.

3 The old-fashioned image of many resorts made them less attractive for holidays, especially to younger people.

4 The motorway network has given easier access to the most attractive holiday areas.

5 New styles of holiday-making have developed (see list below).

6 The establishment of foreign 'package' holidays for millions of people.

CHANGING PATTERNS OF HOLIDAY MAKING

In the last 40 years the major changes in holiday-making which together have almost destroyed the seaside boarding-house tradition include:

1 The development of holiday camps containing all the facilities needed by a family on holiday.

2 The expansion of caravanning holidays as car ownership increased. This led to the building of permanent caravan camps near the sea in areas such as Cornwall and North Wales, as well as the provision of camp sites for touring caravans.

3 The development of different types of self-catering or 'do-it-yourself' holidays, which cut the costs for families and also gave people more freedom to do what they wished. Self-catering facilities now exist in:

  (a) modernized holiday camps;
  (b) seaside flats and apartments, often converted from former boarding-houses and private hotels;
  (c) chalets, log cabins etc. provided by organizations such as the Forestry Commission;
  (d) time-share facilities in converted hotels and large houses;
  (e) rented cottages.

4 'Off-peak' holidays at cheaper rates for special groups such as Old Age Pensioners, and winter-break holidays in hotels and guest-houses throughout the country.

5 The growth of special interest and activity holidays.

6 Increasing competition from the foreign holiday trade.

The effect of these changes is that the holiday industry has spread much more widely through Britain and there is no longer a simple distribution of major holiday centres. Traditional holiday regions such as Scotland, the Lake District and Cornwall are still key areas of the holiday industry, but every region of Britain now tries to attract more income from visitors.

THE TOURIST INDUSTRY

Tourism has now become a major service industry in Britain, and the provision of holidays for foreign visitors has become an important source of foreign currency for the country. The main centre of the overseas tourist trade is London, although efforts are being made to encourage foreign tourists to stay in other parts of the country.

Each year, Britain attracts millions of visitors from all over the world. An important element of this trade is the American tourist trade; over 20 per cent of overseas tourists come from North America.

The total income from overseas tourists in 1988 was £6.2 billion, which was more than half of the income of the entire holiday industry.

The attractions which Britain offers overseas tourists are:

1 Historic sites and buildings. In Europe, two world wars destroyed many ancient buildings but Britain has a wealth of intact historic buildings.

2 British traditions and ceremonies associated with the Royal Family.

3 Since the Commonwealth countries and the USA are English-speaking, there is no language barrier as on the Continent. Most European visitors speak some English.

4 Many visitors come to search for their 'roots' — tracing families to which emigrant ancestors belonged.

5 The excellent air networks provided by Heathrow and Gatwick airports in particular.

6 The modern hotel facilities now available in London and other large cities.

7 Shopping and entertainment facilities.

EFFECTS OF THE CHANGES IN THE HOLIDAY PATTERNS

Increased mobility of the people of Britain, increased leisure time and greater interest in outdoor activities have encouraged the setting up of National, Country and Forest Parks (unit 2.19). The increased use of these amenities, however, has created pressure on the land and caused environmental problems which threaten the quality of the landscape. This is the result of over-use and over-development.

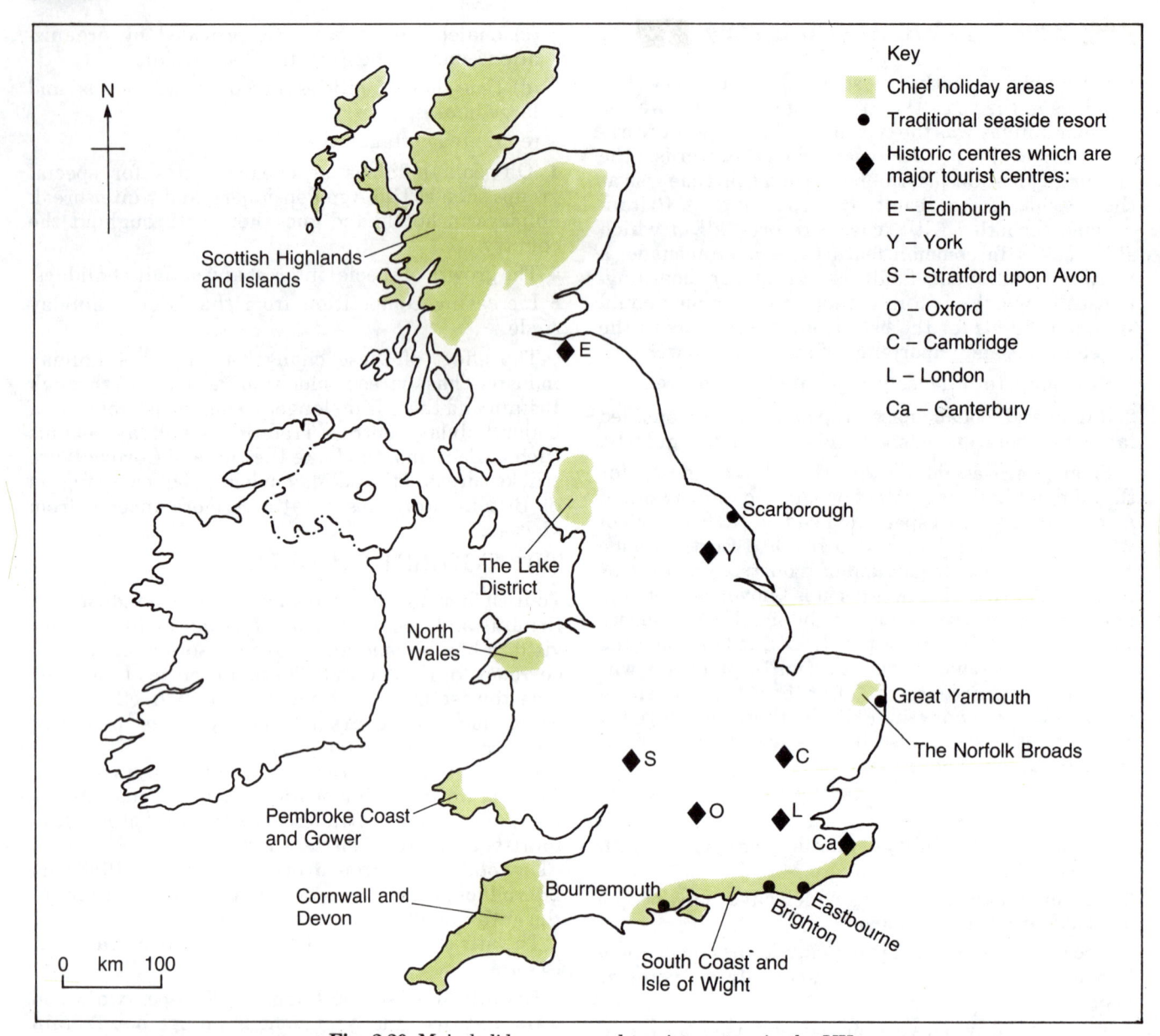

Fig. 2.20 Main holiday areas and tourist centres in the UK

Changing holiday patterns have made it necessary for traditional holiday areas and resorts to adapt to new demands. Some have failed to do this and older seaside resorts such as Hastings have suffered.

The expansion of holiday activities and tourism has become an important source of income and has provided many new jobs. To some extent, this growth has compensated for the national loss of jobs and wealth which has resulted from the decline of manufacturing industry.

EFFECTS OF THE EXPANSION OF TOURISM

1 The development of the foreign tourist trade and the subsequent boom in hotel building have increased competition for attractive sites in our cities, especially in London (Unit 2.8). Some residents complain that hotels have taken up the land needed for more houses.

2 The overconcentration of the foreign tourist trade in London has increased traffic and pedestrian congestion and strained the transport system.

3 The most popular tourist centres outside London have also become congested and overcrowded in the peak tourist season. This destroys the atmosphere and character of ancient cities such as York – the very qualities the tourists want to experience.

4 Tourism has grown rapidly but is a risky business. Tourists are kept away from Britain by publicity on violence, terrorism, etc., and are also put off by changes in the value of the pound which may make holidays more expensive. As a result the hotel industry has to face years of slump or boom in rapid succession.

5 Tourist coaches and cars add to the traffic density and congestion on our busiest motorways such as the M1 and the M25.

Summary

Basic ideas

The holiday industry has become more diversified and widespread. The foreign tourist trade is now a major service industry in Britain. The growth of the holiday industry has created environmental problems.

Key terms

Resorts; mobility; holiday camps; self-catering; foreign tourists; off-peak holidays.

ized.

3 WESTERN EUROPE

3.1 Population distribution in Norway and Sweden

POPULATION DENSITY

The density of the population living in a region is measured by taking the average number of people per unit area. The unit area which is normally used is a square kilometre, so that if, for example, 2 000 people are living in an area of 10 square kilometres the population density is 2 000 ÷ 10 = 200 per sq. km. This

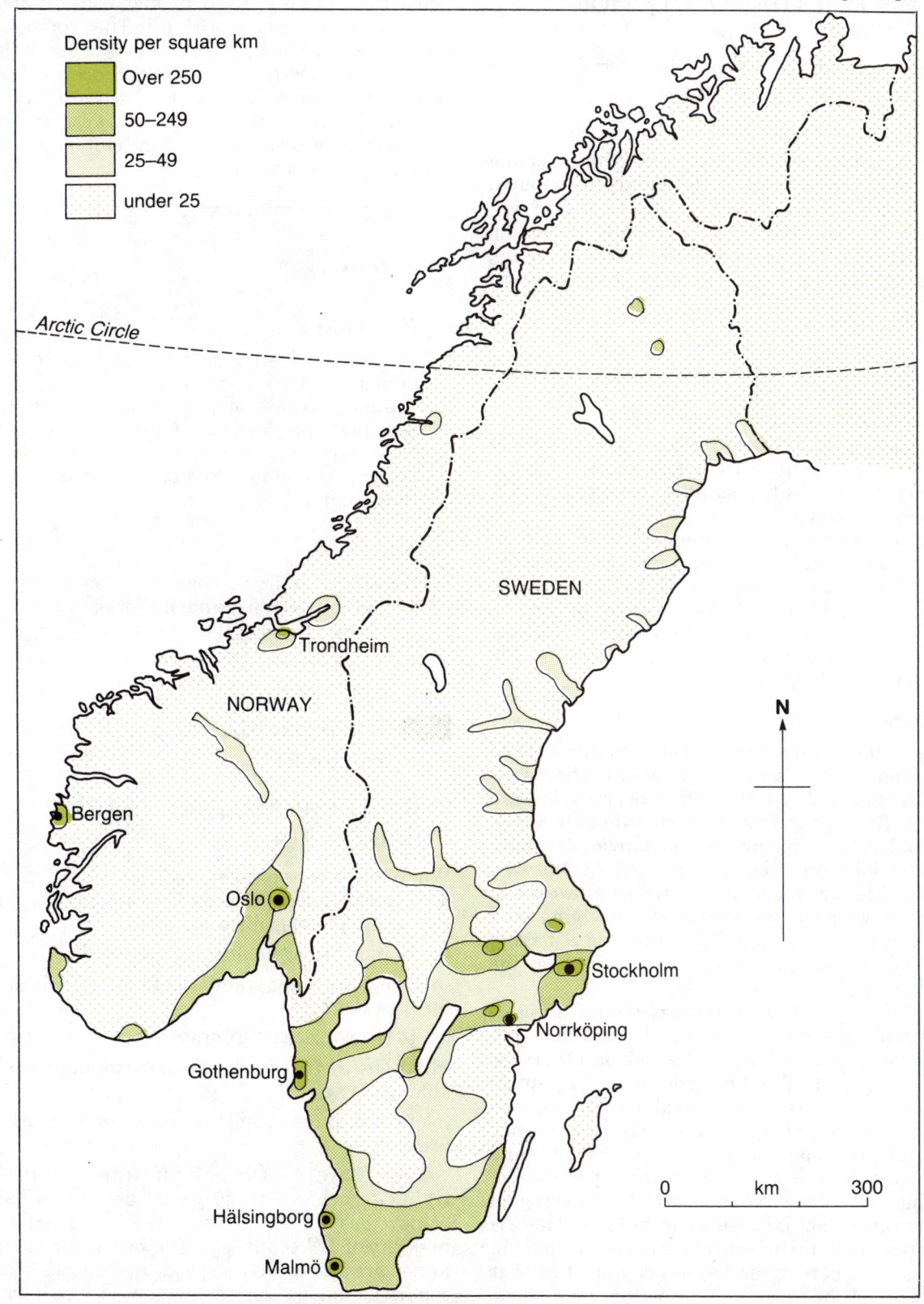

Fig. 3.1 Sweden and Norway: population density

measure is an average and does not indicate the variations in density that may occur within the area being measured. For example, in the UK the density of population is 229 per sq. km, but in some inner city areas it reaches over 5 000 per sq. km, whereas in the Highlands of Scotland it falls as low as 5 per sq. km.

Densities in Norway and Sweden are comparatively low, 13 per sq. km. and 20 per sq. km. respectively, making Norway one of the most thinly-peopled countries in the world.

REASONS FOR THE POPULATION DISTRIBUTION

A number of factors have helped to determine where people live in Norway and Sweden.

Relief

Much of the interior of Norway is mountainous and consequently the population is mainly distributed around the coast or on the only extensive area of lowland, near Oslo (see unit 3.14). Sweden is less mountainous, except in the interior of the northern region, but soils are thin and poor in many of the lowland areas.

Climate

Norway has a maritime climate, while that of Sweden is more continental. The mildness of southern Norway gives it a growing season of eight months, compared with six months in central Sweden. Both countries extend into the Arctic Circle and these northern regions experience low temperatures in winter (−12°C in northern Sweden).

In summer, temperatures throughout both countries reach 16°C or higher. The high latitudes result in many hours of daylight in summer, with 24 hours in the north, contrasting with only five hours of twilight at midwinter. Rainfall is heavy in western Norway, Bergen having 2100 mm, but is much lighter in the east, with 635 mm at Stockholm.

Resources

Farming in both countries is limited by the lack of suitable land, poor soils and a climate which limits the growing season as well as the variety of crops that can be grown. Both countries have considerable forest resources, but farming and forestry provide few jobs, so rural population densities are low. In Norway, higher densities are found around the south-west and south coasts where there is sufficient low-lying land for settlements to develop. Here there is a fishing industry, shipbuilding, and industries based on the Norwegian off-shore oil resources.

In Sweden, population density around the areas of iron-ore extraction in the north at Kiruna and Gällivare is increased, in an area which is otherwise sparsely populated. The lowland region of central Sweden, with its water power, small deposits of iron ore and extensive timber resources, has a wide range of specialized manufacturing industries, and consequently there is a relatively dense population. This is the 'core' area of Sweden, with the Oslo region having an equivalent importance in Norway. There is a concentration of urban centres, and good communications in both core areas have encouraged further development, at the expense of the peripheral regions, particularly the north.

POPULATION TRENDS

In both countries, people are deserting the north and the remote highland regions for the southern lowlands. There is also a move from rural to urban centres. In central and southern Sweden, more than 70 per cent of the population now lives in urban areas, with the bigger centres like Stockholm and Gothenburg attracting people from all over the country.

Both countries have the problem of slow depopulation of their northern regions and the corresponding drift to urban centres in the south. Fewer workers are needed in farming, forestry and fishing, and rural areas have declined as a result. The Norwegian and Swedish governments have schemes to assist the more remote rural areas, particularly those in the north. Development areas, similar to those in Britain, have been designated with investment grants for industry, transport subsidies and other measures to check the decline of population.

Summary

Basic ideas

Physical and economic factors help to determine population density.

Concentration of population in core areas results in the run-down of peripheral regions.

Governments are concerned at the decline of peripheral regions and take measures to assist these regions.

Key terms

Density; resources; core; peripheral; internal migration; urbanization; development area.

3.2 Agricultural problems in the EC

THE COMMON AGRICULTURAL POLICY (CAP)

When the EC was formed, five goals were drawn up for a common agricultural policy among the member countires. These goals were:

(a) to increase agricultural productivity;

(b) to ensure a fair standard of living for farmers and farm workers;

(c) to check price fluctuations;

(d) to ensure that supplies of farm produce were available when needed;

(e) to guarantee supplies to consumers at reasonable prices.

There have been many difficulties for the EC in trying to achieve these goals, and what has been achieved so far has not made the CAP popular in the majority of EC countries. The problems which have arisen are ther esult of the wide differences in farming conditons among the member countires. Farming in the UK for example, is more highly mechanised and efficient than farming in France or Portugal. Some countries, such as Denmark and Ireland are important exporters of agricultural produce, while others like the UK are importers. Farming is more important in the economy of Greece, with 29 per cent of the workers employed on the land, than in Luxemburg, where only one per cent work in agriculture.

Country	% of workforce employed in agriculture	Average farm size (hectares)
Belgium	3	15.4
Denmark	8.2	24.9
Ireland	26	22.5
France	9	25.4
Greece	29	4.3
Italy	15	7.4
Luxemburg	1	14.1
Netherlands	6	15.6
Portugal	27	5.1
Spain	18	14.8
United Kingdom	1.5	68.7
West Germany	6	15.3

Table 3.2 Average farm size and employment in agriculture in the countries of the EC

The main farming problems in the EC are as follows:

1 Small size of farms

Small farms are not capable of producing a reasonable income for a family, unless they are used for intensive cultivation such as market gardening. In the Netherlands, for example, farms of less than 20 ha can be highly efficient because they use large amounts of capital in the form of machinery, fertilizer and irrigation equipment. Larger farms are essential in areas growing cereals and similar field crops.

Table 3.2 shows that average farm sizes vary considerably, from 4.3 ha in Greece to 68.7 in the UK. About two-thirds of farms in the EC are under 10 ha in size, making them less efficient. In France, the government has tried to increase farm sizes. Land for sale is bought to enlarge nearby farms, and farmers have been paid compensation if they retire and allow their land to be used to enlarge other farms in the neighbourhood. The EC has provided money to retrain farm workers no longer needed on the land. In 1992 just over 50 per cent of French farms were over 50 ha in size and only 4 per cent less than 10 ha.

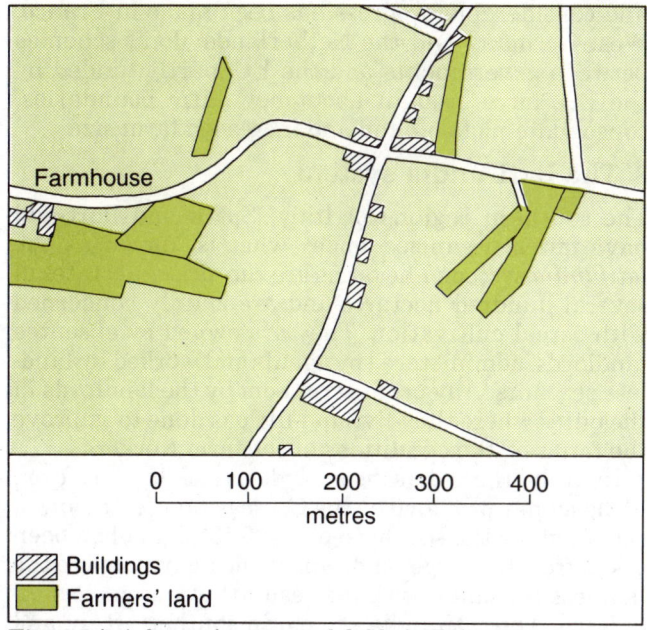

Fig. 3.2A A farmer's scattered fields in Brittany

2 Fragmentation

In many EC countries, farms consist of tiny scattered strips, which makes the use of machinery difficult and wastes the farmer's time. Fragmentation is a particular problem in northern Spain and Portugal, Greece and France, and originated in a number of ways, including:

(a) inheritance laws dividing land equally among heirs;

(b) piecemeal land reclamation;

(c) earlier communal farming systems.

Efforts are being made to consolidate farm holdings

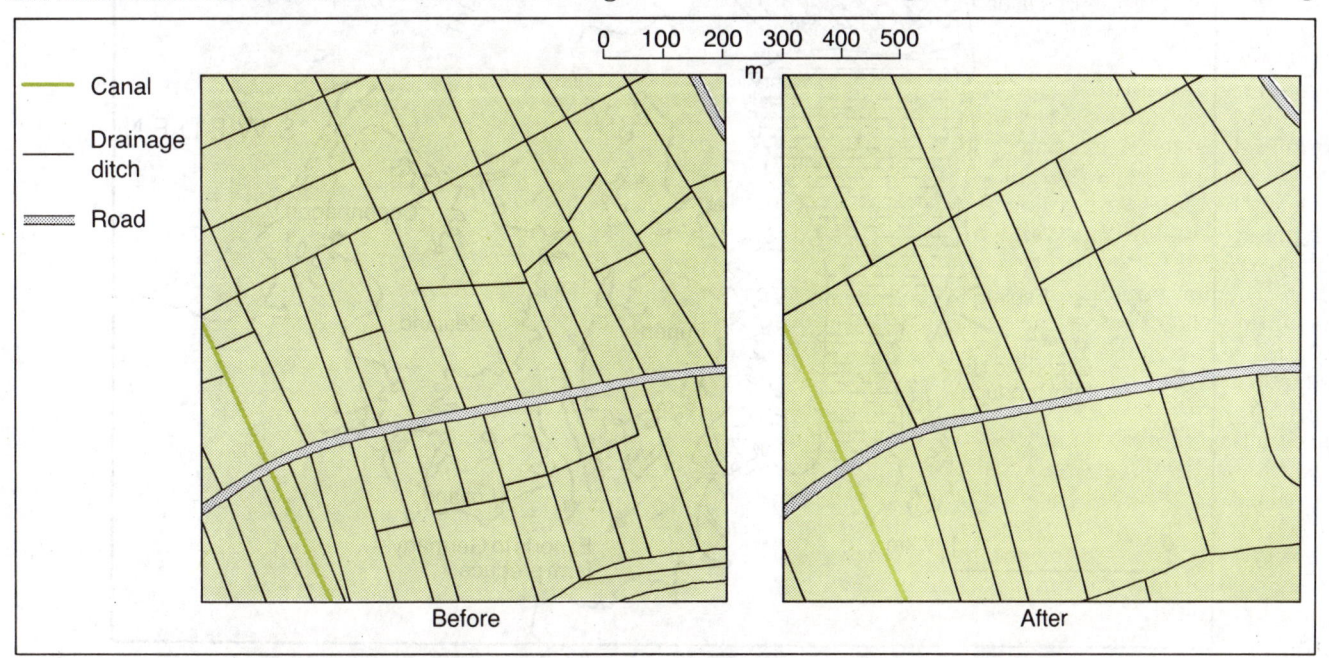

Fig. 3.2B Field boundaries in the Netherlands, before and after consolidation

and considerable progress has been made in France, West Germany and the Netherlands. Joint schemes between governments and the EC, partly funded by the EC, have brought about new farm boundaries, consolidate plots of land and increased farm size.

3 The Latifundia system

The southern regions of Italy, Spain and Portugal have farms organized under what is known as the *latifundia* system. The farms are run as large estates of several hundred hectares and are mainly concerned with cereal cultivation. They are owned by absentee landlords, administered by agents and worked by landless peasants. Any profits are spent by the landlords in the cities where they live and little is done to improve the farms or the conditions of the farm workers.

In Italy there has been widespread land reform, using money provided by the *Cassa per il Mezzogiorno*, the 'fund for the south' (see unit 3.13). Land has been taken from the large landowners and distributed to the landless peasants, with the result that output has increased. The latifundia system in southern Italy and Sicily is so much a part of the way of life that it has not been possible to eliminate it completely, and large estates can still be seen.

In Spain and Portugal the problem has not, as yet, been tackled on the same scale and much of the land, including new irrigation projects carried out with state funds, is in the hands of large landowners.

4 Pricing problems

Most of the CAP funds are spent supporting EC farmers through a complex system of guaranteed prices. The price of farm products is set sufficiently high to encourage farmers to produce a surplus. High prices benefit the large farmer, while allowing the inefficient small producer to stay in operation. Over-production has caused a number of problems. The surplus products such as milk, butter, wine, sugar and beef have to be stored in suitable warehouses, causing the 'wine lakes' and 'butter mountains' we hear about on TV. Storage costs are high and excess amounts are often sold cheaply to other European countries such as the CIS. The prices paid to EC farmers are often higher than world prices, so EC food is comparatively expensive. If prices were cut drastically, many farmers would go out of business, with social and political consequences, especially in countries with large numbers employed in farming.

Summary

Basic ideas

The EC has encountered problems in trying to achieve a Common Agricultural Policy.

Farming systems vary considerably from one EC country to another.

Pricing policies have resulted in surplus production in the EC.

Key terms

Fragmentation; consolidation; latifundia system; guaranteed prices; overproduction.

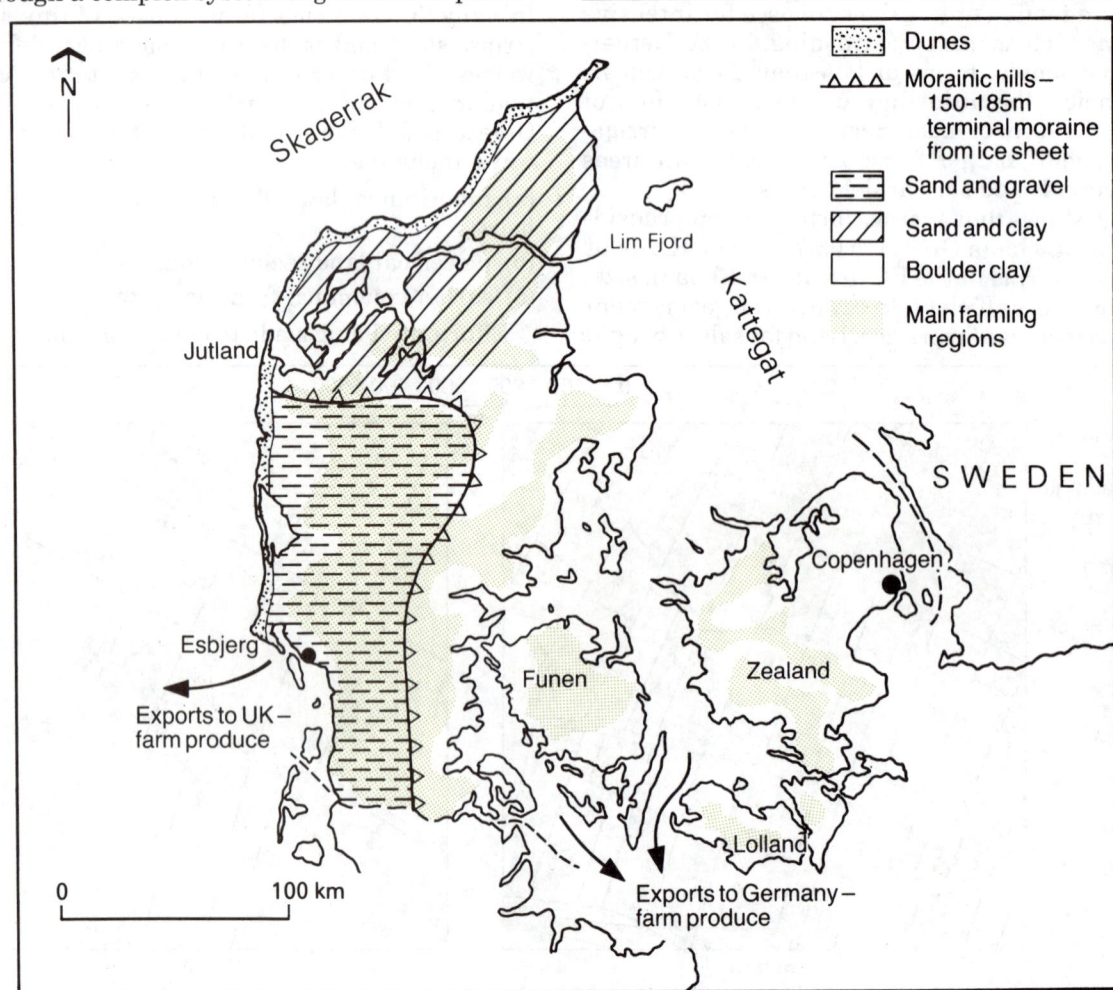

Fig. 3.3A Denmark: agriculture

3.3 Farming in Denmark

THE PHYSICAL INFLUENCE ON FARMING

The natural fertility of Denmark's soil is not high. East Jutland and the islands are the most fertile areas, with a boulder clay cover containing lime from the chalk bedrock. Western Jutland consists of morainic hills and sandy outwash material which forms heathland and marshes. About a quarter of this region is used for grazing or for growing rye and root crops. The climate of Denmark is similar to that of East Anglia, with more severe winters. The January average is 0°C with 18°C in July. Rainfall averages 558 mm.

THE HUMAN INFLUENCE ON FARMING

1 Government policy after 1880 changed farming from wheat growing to a highly organized dairy industry for the British and German markets. Esbjerg was developed as a port for the UK trade.

2 Scientific farming, with the use of fertilizers and a balanced rotation of crops, has made the boulder clay area highly productive.

3 A highly developed cooperative movement has organized small-scale farming and produced standardized products. The cooperatives have large-scale buying and selling powers and undertake mechanized processing of milk, eggs and bacon. Government inspections maintain standards and help to uphold the quality and reputation of the produce overseas.

4 Selective livestock breeding has produced the Danish Red cow and Landrace pig which, like the other farm animals and the poultry, are fed mainly on fodder crops grown in Denmark.

5 Folk high schools provide education for young people and train them in up-to-date farming methods.

6 EC membership has strengthened the traditional markets of the UK and Germany.

7 There are close links between farming and industry, e.g. dairy engineering, milling and brewing.

IMPORTANCE OF LIVESTOCK FARMING

The majority of Danish farms are small, within the size range of 5 to 30 ha. The most important crop is barley, grown mainly for animal feed. Other fodder crops such as beet, hay and clover are also grown. Oil seeds such as rape are of growing importance. Nine-tenths of the total crop yield is used for livestock fodder and 90 per cent of the value of Danish agricultural production comes from livestock. Costs are increased by the need for large quantities of fertilizer as well as fuel for tractors and machinery. These inputs must be imported.

Farming is becoming more specialized as labour and other costs increase. Instead of mixed farming, there is a concentration on such things as barley growing or the production of beef cattle. About two-thirds of agricultural output is exported, mainly to other members of the EC. Danish agriculture is supported by heavy subsidies from the Common Market.

Farm produce is not as important in Denmark's export trade as it once was. About one-third of Denmark's exports by value comes from its farms, whereas manufactured goods account for 60 per cent of exports by value.

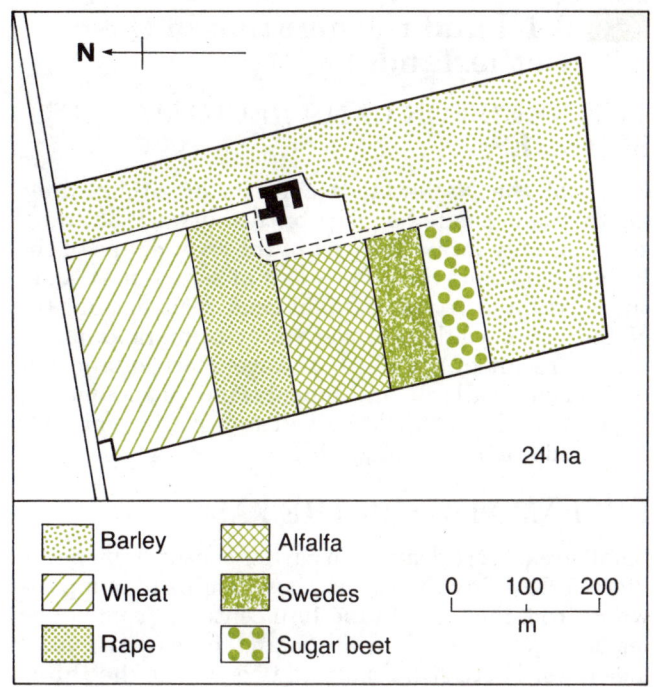

Fig. 3.3B A farm in Zealand

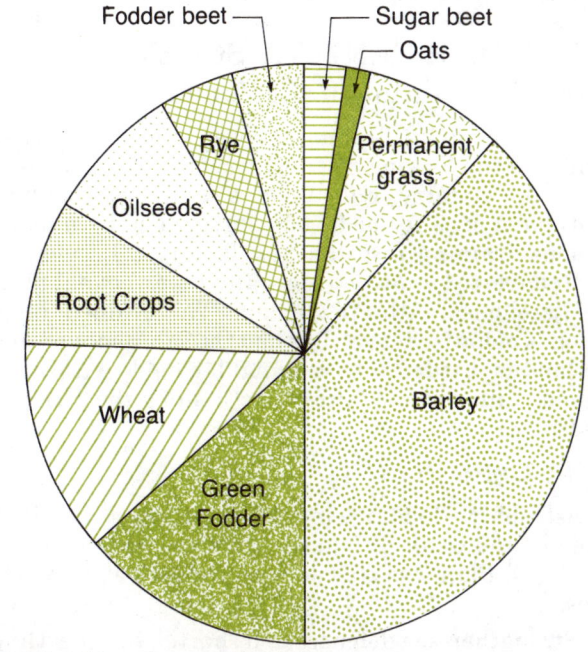

Fig. 3.3C Land use on Danish farms

Summary

Basic ideas

Farming in Denmark has been considerably influenced by government policy.

Cooperative farming has considerably benefited the many small-scale producers.

Farming is becoming more specialized and scientific.

Key terms

Cooperative farming; livestock fodder; specialist farming.

3.4 Land reclamation in the Netherlands

THE NEED FOR LAND RECLAMATION SCHEMES

Much of the Netherlands consists of either sandy heathland deposited as part of the outwash of an ice sheet, or clay formed as part of the river deltas of the Rhine, Maas and Scheldt. A belt of sand dunes edges the North Sea coast. Without land reclamation, the Netherlands would be under water, or marshland.

As a result of drainage, however, fertile land has been made available and supports one of the densest populations in the world, as well as providing valuable farm and horticultural products.

RECLAMATION IN THE PAST

Small areas were drained in earlier centuries by building a series of dykes and using windmills to pump the water from the land. In the 19th century steam power made it possible to drain inland lakes and water meadows. There still remained two gaps in the Dutch coastline, that leading to the Zuider Zee, and the delta area of the south-west.

TWENTIETH CENTURY SCHEMES

1 The reclamation of the Zuider Zee

First a large dyke, 31 km. long was built with a road along the top linking the northern and southern halves of the country. Four polders (units of reclaimed land) have been formed, each surrounded by a dyke; streams draining into the new lake (the Ijsselmeer) have converted it into a fresh-water lake. A canal links the Ijsselmeer with Amsterdam. The drained land, which is below sea level, has had the salt removed and the land is divided into rectangular fields with well-planned villages and farms spaced along the straight roads.

2 The Delta Plan

Catastrophic flooding in the south-west in 1953 revealed the weak link in the country's sea-defences. The Delta Plan was started with the following objectives:

(a) Strengthen sea defences and shorten the coastline by building four main, and several subsidiary, dams.
(b) Provide access to Antwerp and Rotterdam but seal off the other delta inlets to form inland lakes.
(c) Limit salt penetration of the land by converting some of the lakes to fresh-water.
(d) Make this water available for irrigation and town supplies.

Polders
1 Wieringermeer
2 North East
3 East Flevoland
4 South Flevoland
5 Markerwaard

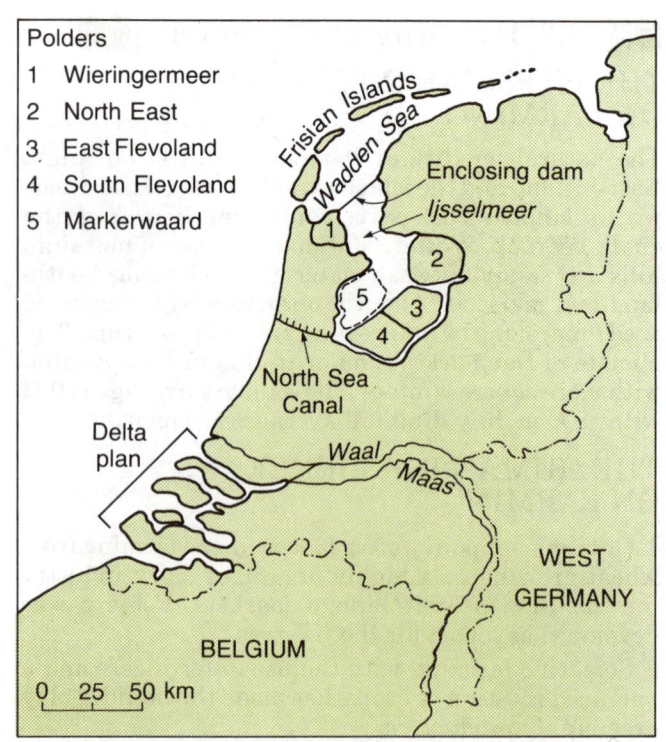

Fig. 3.4B Main reclamation areas

(e) Develop a major recreational area with yachting and bathing facilities.
(f) Reduce the isolation of the south-west by building new roads, settlements and light industries.
(g) Reclaim small amounts of land.

3 River reclamation

The flood plains of the Rhine and Maas are a major problem, with silt raising the level of the river beds and exposing the land to further flooding. A series of winter and summer dykes have been built and need constant control.

4 Heathland reclamation

Stretches of heath with peat bogs known as 'geest' still remain in the east and south. Some areas have been planted with conifers, while the higher peat moors have been reclaimed by improving the drainage of the sandy podsols with deep ploughing and fertilizers.

LAND RECLAMATION AND THE ENVIRONMENT

In the past the Dutch were very proud of their land reclamation programme, draining wetlands and making new farmland from areas that were once part of the sea-bed. In recent years ecologists, fishermen and recreation groups have been speaking out against

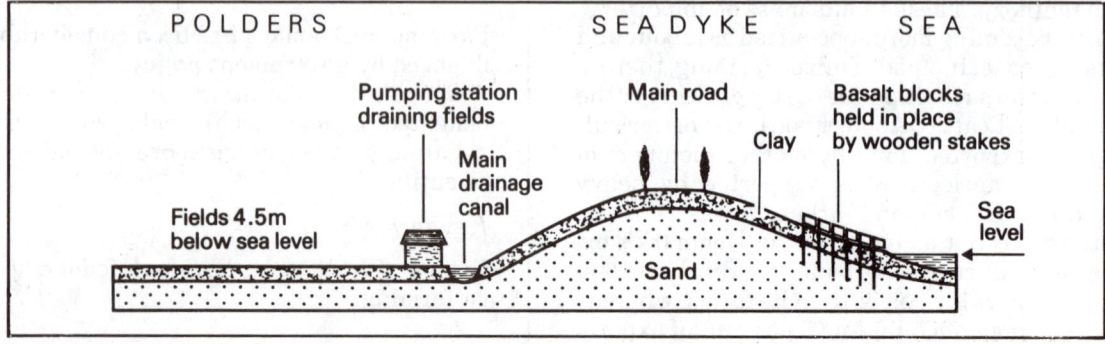

Fig. 3.4A Cross-section of polders and a sea dyke in the Netherlands

Western Europe

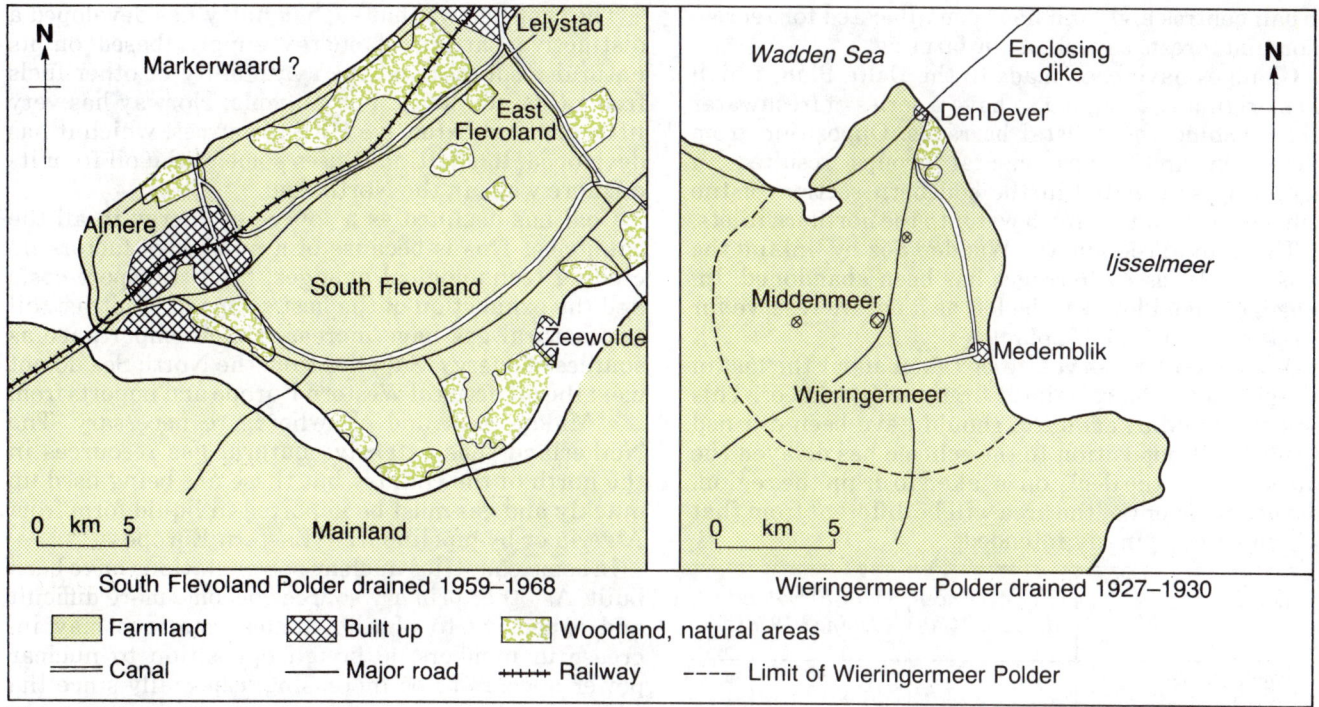

Fig. 3.4C South Flevoland Polder

Fig. 3.4D Wieringermeer Polder, drained 1927-1930

reclamation schemes and as a result some schemes have been changed while others have been abandoned.

The first Ijsselmeer polders to be drained were used almost entirely for farming. Few trees were planted and the landscape still looks uninteresting and windswept. As the Dutch have become more urbanized, there has been a shift away from agriculture with the result that the more recently drained polders contain

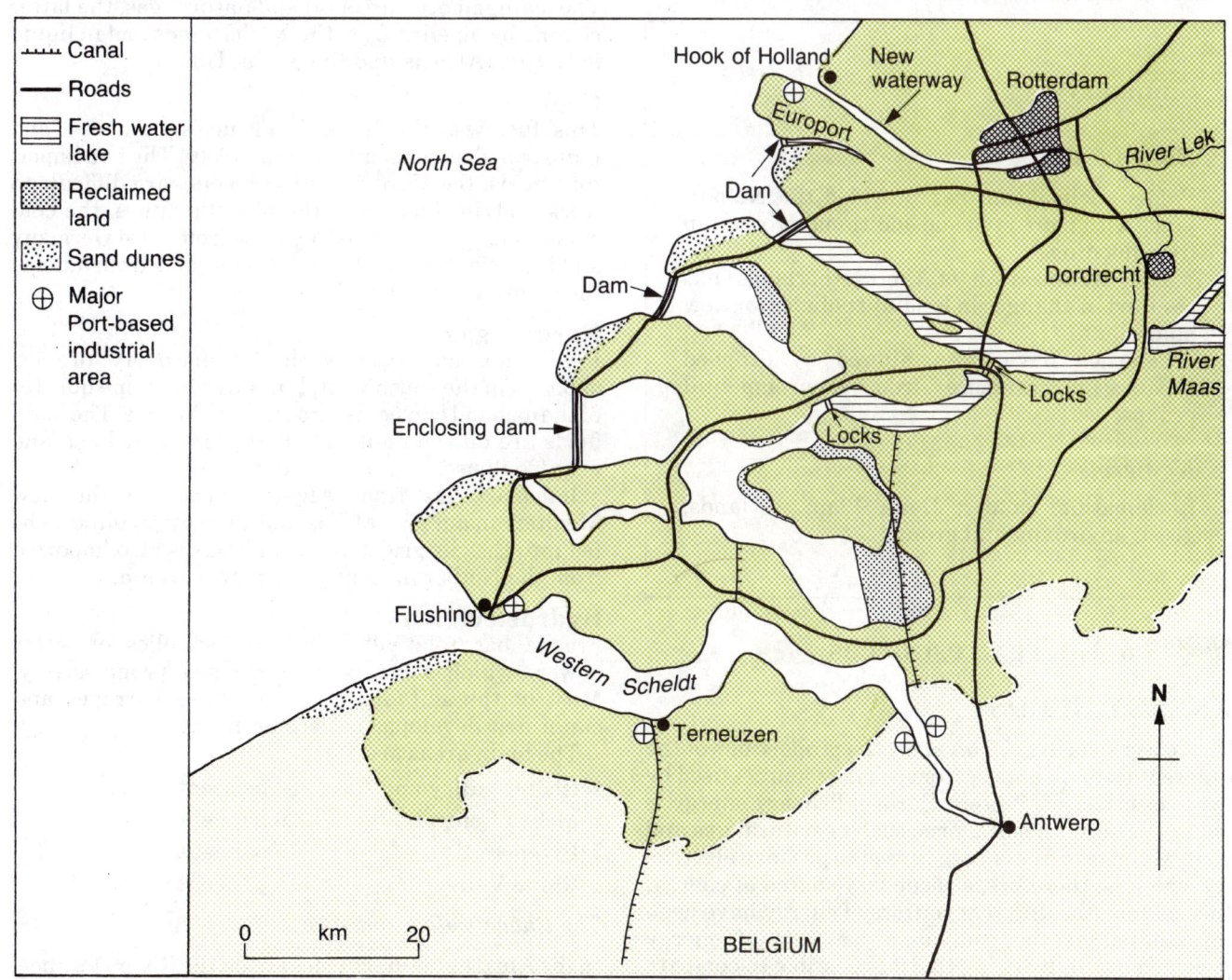

Fig. 3.4E The Delta Plan

urban centres and land has been allocated for recreation and forests as well as for farming.

Changes have been made to the Delta Plan, which was originally designed to have a series of freshwater lakes behind the coastal barrages. Opposition from fishermen and environmental groups resulted in retaining salt water in the southern section of the scheme and limiting fresh water to the northern inlets.

The plan to reclaim the Wadden Sea by linking the Frisian Islands by barrages has been abandoned. Instead, the mudflats will be left as a nature reserve for birds, seals and marsh plants.

A decision has, as yet, to be taken about the last of the polders to be reclaimed from the Ijsselmeer. This polder, the Markerwaard, should have been drained by 1985 but opposition to the scheme has delayed the work. Even if the decision is taken to drain the region, the development of the area will be different from that which was originally intended.

Land use	Wieringermeer (drained 1930)	South Flevoland (drained 1968)
Agriculture	87	50
Woods, natural areas	3	25
Settlement/ Industry	1	18
Dykes, roads, water	9	7

Table 3.4 Different land use patterns on polders (%)

Summary

Basic ideas

Polder reclamation has provided the Netherlands with more land and additional protection from flooding.

The urbanization of the Netherlands has resulted in changes in land-use policies for new polderland.

Schemes have been altered or dropped because of pressure from environmental groups.

Key terms

Reclamation; polder; Delta Plan; wetlands; geest; environmental groups.

3.5 Energy resources

ENERGY NEEDS

The bar graphs in fig. 3.5A show the proportions of the different forms of energy from primary sources used by nine countries of Western Europe. Primary energy is energy used in its basic form, such as natural gas and coal. Much primary energy is used to produce electricity which is, therefore, a secondary source of energy. In the table, the different sources of energy have been represented as the equivalent amounts of energy provided by oil. By doing this it is possible to compare the various primary sources.

The table shows that each country has developed a distinctive pattern of energy supply, based on its natural resources and the availability of other fuels from other countries. For example, Norway has very little coal but extensive HEP resources, which it has developed. In addition it uses some of the oil from its offshore wells in the North Sea.

Coal has declined as a source of energy in all the countries. This is because of a number of factors including technological changes, high transport costs and the exhaustion of the best seams. In contrast, oil and natural gas have increased their importance as sources of energy. Supplies from the North Sea do not meet the oil needs of Western Europe and imports from the Middle East and elsewhere are necessary. The Netherlands has extensive natural gas resources in the north of the country but these are being used up quickly and gas must be imported in liquid form from Algeria or by pipeline from Eastern Europe.

In some countries nuclear power stations have been built. As other primary sources become more difficult and expensive to obtain, nuclear stations may increase in numbers, although opposition to nuclear power appears to be increasing, especially since the Chernobyl disaster.

FRENCH ENERGY RESOURCES

France's domestic energy resources meet only 38 per cent of the country's needs, the rest must be imported. The main imports are of oil and natural gas, the latter coming by pipeline from the Netherlands and in liquid form from Algeria and the Soviet Union.

Coal

This fuel was the basis of France's economic and industrial development until the 1950s. The two important fields, the Nord and the Moselle, are difficult to work and, in the case of the Moselle mines, the coal makes poor coke. Coal is imported from West Germany and just over half the French needs come from outside the country.

Natural gas

Production has risen with the discovery of new deposits in the south-west, but only about one quarter of the demand can be met from inside France. The main fields are on the flanks of the Pyrenees at Lacq and near Toulouse.

Imported gas from Algeria comes to the new Mediterranean port of Fos and then by pipeline to be fed into the gas grid near Lyons. Gas is also imported from the Netherlands and the Soviet Union.

Hydroelectricity

France has relatively abundant supplies of water power, which have been harnessed progressively. Most of the suitable sites now have barrages and major new developments are unlikely.

The main areas are:

1 Rhône Valley and Alps   50 per cent
2 Massif Central   20 per cent
3 Pyrenees   15 per cent
4 Rhine Valley   15 per cent

The Rhône Valley and Alps

In the Alps the main schemes are on the River Durance, north and north-east of Marseilles, and on the River

Western Europe 69

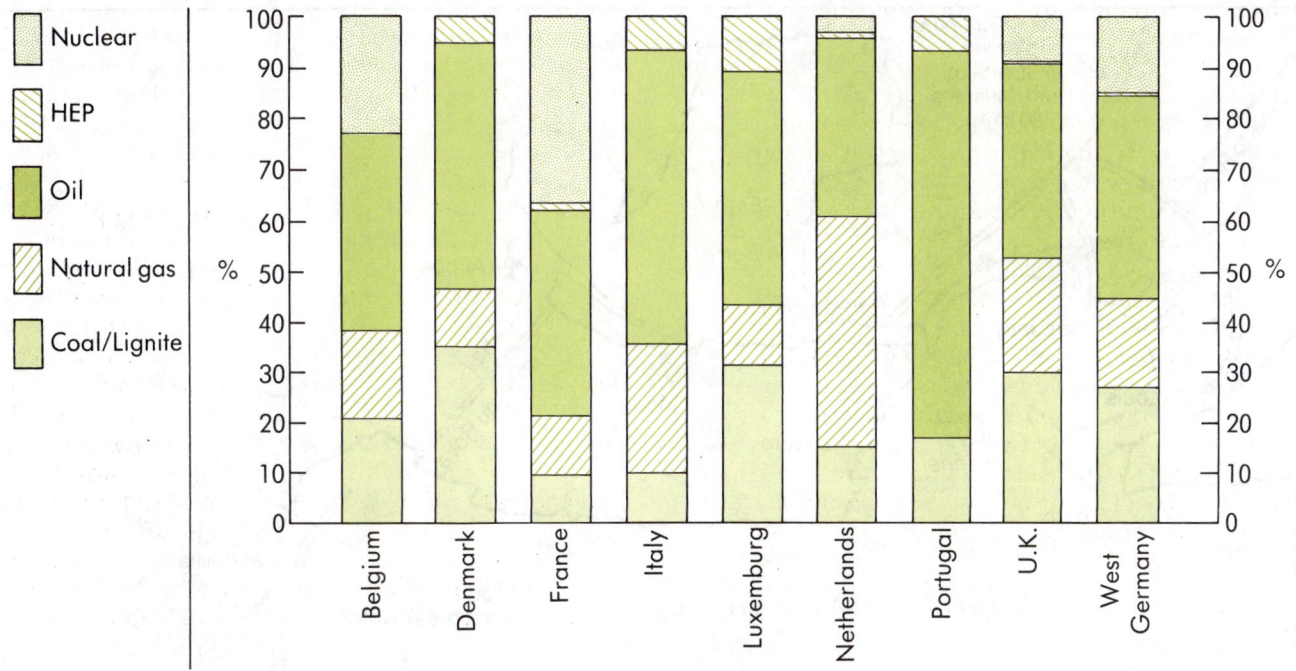

Fig. 3.5A Primary energy consumption 1990

Isère. The Alpine section of the river Rhône, shortly after it leaves Lake Geneva, is harnessed at Génissiat.

The multi-purpose schemes on the lower Rhône rely more on the volume of water in lateral canals than on the river itself. At Donzère, midway between Lyons and the sea, a large power station has been built and the river diverted into an artificial waterway.

Massif Central

The main hydroelectric stations are along the rivers which run down the western side of the Plateau. The largest centre is Marèges in the upper valley of the Dordogne.

Pyrenees

There are many small HEP stations which provide power for the electrochemical and electrometallurgical industries at Pamiers, Tarascon and Toulouse. In this region, as in the Alps, less power is produced in winter when the ground is frozen and run-off is limited.

Rhine Valley

In the rift section of the valley between Basle and Strasburg a few schemes are in operation diverting the waters of the Rhine into canals which are harnessed to generate electricity. Ottmarsheim, Krems and Fessenheim are such centres.

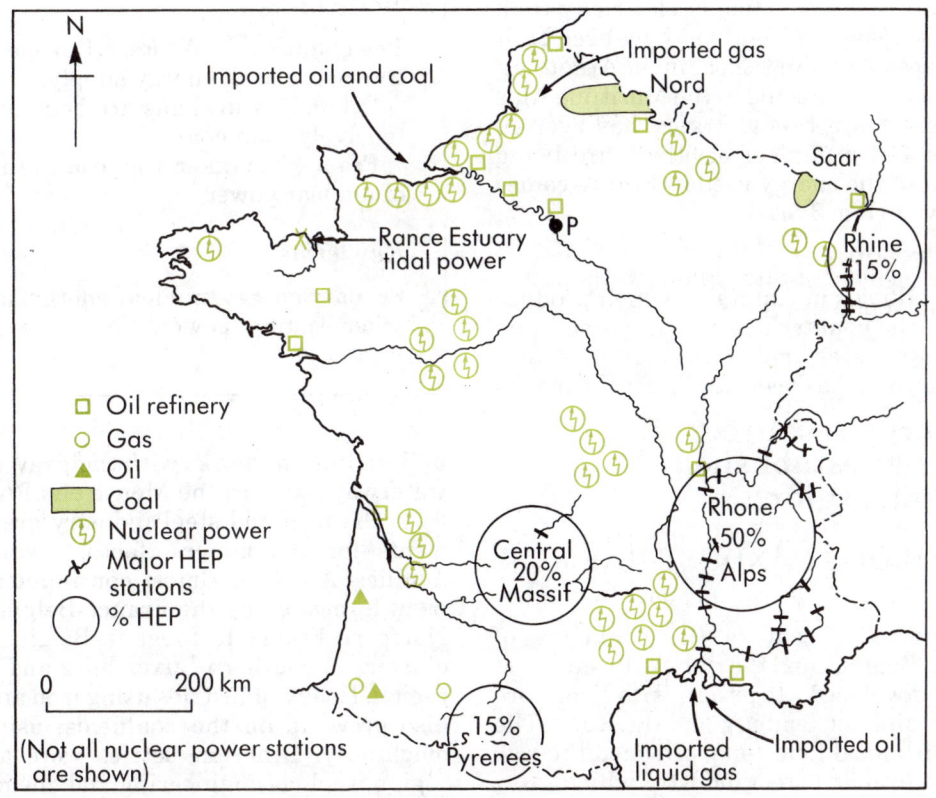

Fig. 3.5B France: energy resources

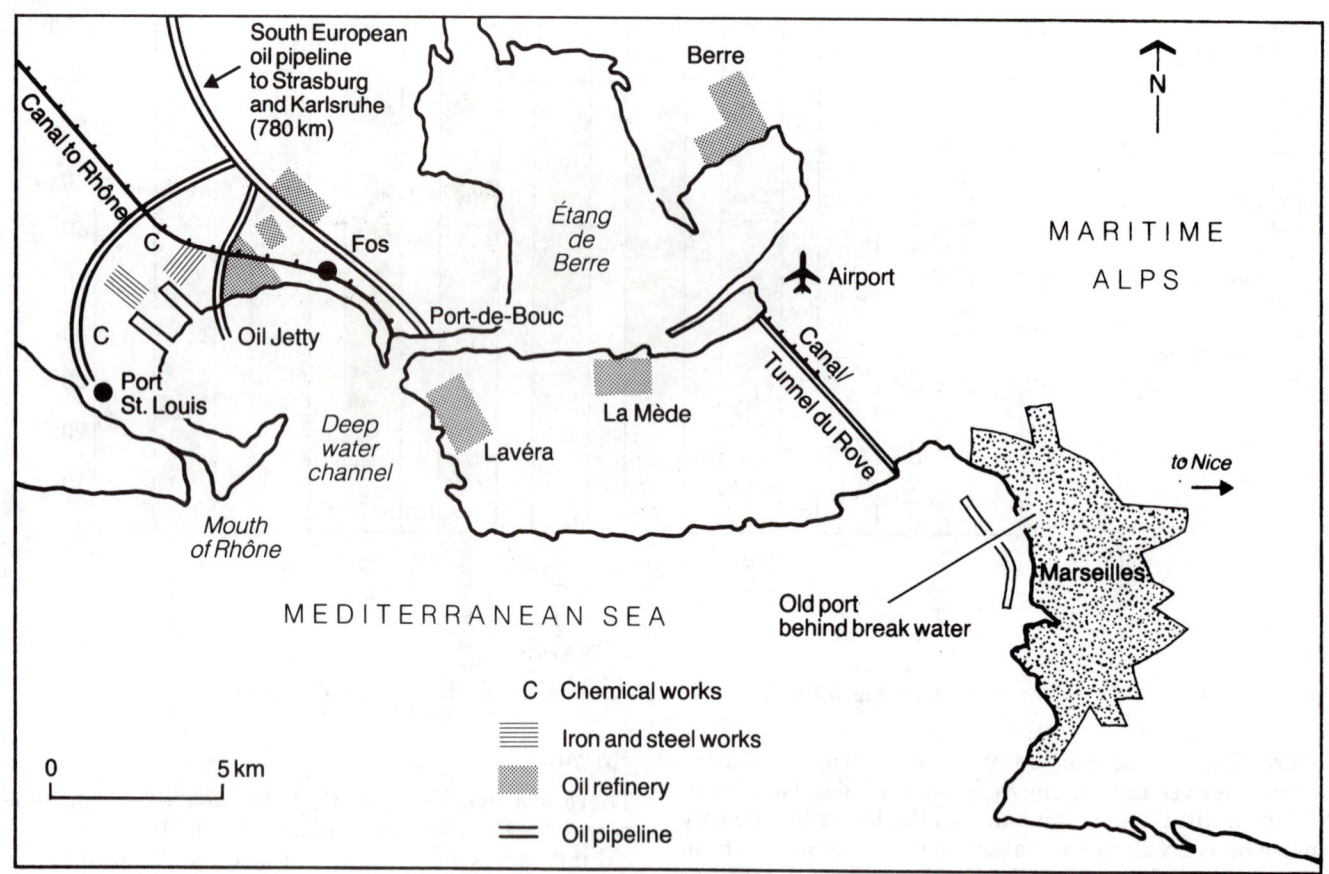

Fig. 3.5C Oil refineries near Marseilles

Nuclear power

The fuel used in nuclear reactors comes from radioactive metals, the most important of which is uranium. Only small amounts of uranium are required and France has considerable reserves in the Massif Central. With very limited energy resources, which are some distance from the areas of highest demand, it is not surprising that France has taken the lead in Western Europe in the production of electricity from nuclear power. Nuclear power-stations have been built in a number of places, including Chooz in the Ardennes, Fessenheim in Alsace, Marcoule in the Maritime Alps and Chinon in the Loire valley. France has over 40 nuclear reactors and a number of others are being built. 37 per cent of the energy used in France comes from nuclear power (Fig. 3.5A).

Other energy resources

There are small oilfields in Aquitaine which produce three per cent of the country's needs. The remaining oil comes from overseas, much through the new Europort du Sud which has been built near the mouth of the River Rhône. Although output is very small, France also has a power station using tidal power on the Rance estuary in northern Brittany.

Summary

Basic ideas

The countries of Western Europe have distinctive patterns of energy supply.
Oil and natural gas are being used more extensively than coal.
France has taken the lead in the production of nuclear power.

Key terms

Primary energy, nuclear energy, multi-purpose schemes, tidal power.

3.6 An old-established industrial region

THE GROWTH OF AN INDUSTRIAL REGION

During the nineteenth century the coalfields of northern France, Belgium and the Ruhr valley in West Germany were developed, together with iron ore resources in Lorraine, Luxemburg and the Ruhr. The coal and iron, with local limestone, provided the raw materials for the iron and steel industry which grew up on each of the coalfields. Canals and railways were built to link the works with their raw materials and to waterways such as the Meuse and Rhine.

As the iron and steel industry grew, so did settlements for the miners, factory workers and their families. A belt of almost continuous urban development formed along the Franco-Belgian coalfield from Northern France to Liège in Belgium, with separate clusters in southern Luxemburg and the Rhine-Ruhr region. Heavy industries using iron and steel products also grew up on the coalfields, using steam-driven machinery. Other industries were attracted to the region, such as engineering and chemicals.

The traditional textile industry of Flanders was

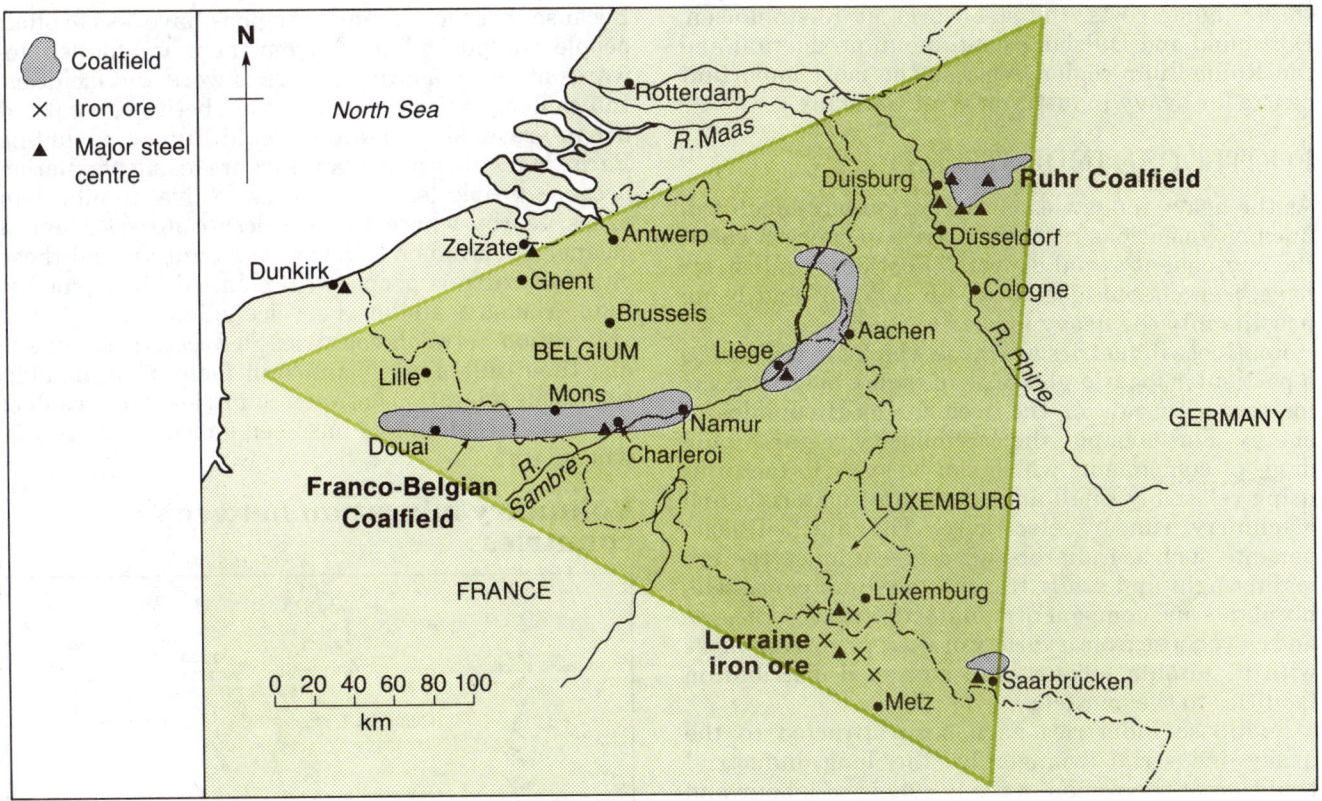

Fig. 3.6 The heavy industrial triangle

mechanized, and moved to the coalfield where power was cheap. Production of cotton cloth took the place of linen and Lille, Douai and Valenciennes became cotton cities. The ports of Antwerp and Rotterdam, linked to the region by canals and rivers, made the import of raw cotton and the export of finished goods relatively cheap and easy.

At the beginning of the twentieth century this was the most important heavy industrial region in Western Europe. It is sometimes described as the heavy industrial triangle (see fig. 3.6), and acted as a magnet to other industries.

INDUSTRIAL CHANGE

The region has lost some, but not all of its industrial importance in the last forty years. There has been a rapid decline in coal production and the steel industry has also reduced its output, as table 3.6 shows.

Country	Coal (m tonnes)		Steel (m tonnes)	
	1974	1990	1974	1990
Belgium	7.5	1.0	16.2	11.4
France	23.6	10.5	27.0	19.0
Luxemburg	—	—	6.4	3.6
W. Germany	92.8	76.6	53.4	38.4

Table 3.6 Declining output of coal and steel

The decline in coal production is partly because new sources of energy, particularly oil and natural gas are being used instead. Cheaper coal can be imported from the USA and Poland. Steel production has declined because of the increase in cheap steel imports from countries like Brazil and North Korea. Table 3.6 shows the coal and steel outputs for the whole of each of the countries which means that the figures for France and West Germany include areas outside the heavy industrial triangle.

New steel plants have been built on the coast at Dunkirk in France and close to the coast at Zelzate in Belgium. This trend to coastal sites is also to be found in other West European countries, including the Netherlands and West Germany. These new sites have facilities for importing overseas ore and coal and exporting finished steel products.

The textile industry has also had to change to meet competition from cheap cloth made in mills in India and other Asian countries. The number of workers has nearly halved since 1954, following the introduction of automatic machinery and more efficient working methods. The engineering, chemical and metal-smelting industries which grew up during the industrial revolution are still an important feature of the heavy industrial triangle. Like the steel industry, they have reduced their labour force and changed their products to meet the needs of modern industry. For example, the metallurgical region of Liège produces castings for machine tools, and special steels required by the electronics industry.

INDUSTRIAL INERTIA

The heavy industries of the triangle have remained, despite the fact that many of the reasons why they grew up there no longer apply. This is an example of industrial inertia (see unit 2.5). They have stayed because it is expensive to move, difficult to find a suitable labour force elsewhere and many of their customers are also in the same region. In the Ruhr, for example, coking coal is still available from the coalfield, but local iron ore was exhausted many years ago and ore must be imported through Rotterdam. This increases costs, even though it can be carried by barge and does not need to be transported by rail. Despite these higher costs, the steelworks at Rheinhausen, Dortmund and Duisburg continue in production and the Rhine-Ruhr region remains the most important centre for heavy industry in West Germany.

FOOTLOOSE INDUSTRIES

As the heavy industries of this region have declined, unemployment has risen giving rise to concern about the consequent social distress. 'Footloose' industries have been encouraged to set up factories and bring new life into the heavy industrial triangle.

Footloose industries are those which are not tied to a particular location because of high transport costs for raw materials or the need for local supplies of energy. For example, the car industry requires hundreds of components which can be made in factories using relatively small amounts of raw materials and machinery run by electricity. The finished components, such as radiators, windscreens and tyres, are mainly light and easily transported. Both car assembly plants and component manufacturers are footloose and can choose from a variety of sites, preferring those with a suitable labour force and good distribution facilities to the markets.

Footloose industries have been attracted to the heavy industrial triangle by the long industrial tradition of the region, a ready supply of labour and good transport facilities. The governments of France, Belgium and West Germany have spent considerable sums of money building new industrial premises, providing grants to attract new industries and cleaning up many of the eyesores such as tip heaps which are a legacy of the industrial revolution. As a result, footloose industries have been established in the triangle. They include car component factories in the Lille-Douai area, pharmaceutical goods at Liège and Opel cars near Bochum in the Ruhr.

Summary

Basic ideas

The growth of heavy industry in NW Europe took place on coalfields using local iron ore deposits. Heavy industries remain in this region, despite the fact that many of the reasons why they grew up have disappeared. Footloose industries have been encouraged to move into the region to check local unemployment.

Key terms

Heavy industry; industrial triangle; industrial inertia; footloose industry.

3.7 Movements of population

TYPES OF MIGRATION

There are two types of population movement, international migration from one country to another and internal migration from one part of a country to another part. Internal migration takes place between one region and another, between towns and rural areas and between towns or conurbations. Poorer regions such as the Central Massif of France or the heathlands of North Germany provide less opportunities for people than the cities and wealthier industrial regions. Because these more remote regions have less to offer, people are 'pushed' away from them and 'pulled' towards other areas where there is work and facilities. Internal migration also takes place between rural and urban areas. Many large cities in Europe, including Paris, Marseilles and Frankfurt are losing population because people leave the cities to live in suburban areas nearby where there is less congestion and a cleaner environment. New towns built around these cities also attract people with planned developments, industrial sites and local service industries.

Migration between countries in Western Europe is also the result of 'push' and 'pull' factors but, in addition, some migration between countries is the result of war or persecution and has been forced on the people who migrate.

Voluntary migration between countries

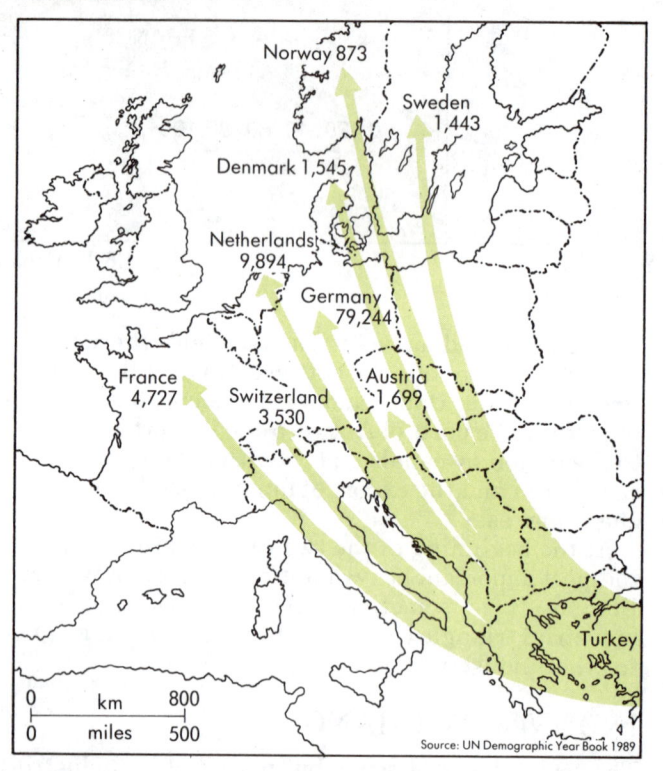

Fig. 3.7A Numbers of long-term immigrants from Turkey in West European countries – 1988

Fig. 3.7A shows the the countries of Western Europe which have 'pulled' people from their homes in Turkey. The economic attractions of regular work with high wages in contrast with lack of employment and lower living standards in Turkey resulted in many young people, mostly men, moving to the industrial centres of Western Europe in the 1970s. In the host countries the immigrants were welcomed at first because they solved a labour shortage and provided cheaper labour for less desirable jobs. For both the country from which the migrants come and the host country there are advantages and disadvantages.

Advantages for country losing migrants

1 As young people of child bearing age leave, the high birth rate may be lowered.

2 There is less pressure on jobs and resources.

3 Migrants send back money to their families and support them with foreign funds.

4 Migrants learn new skills which they may bring back to their own country.

Disadvantages for country losing migrants

1 Families are split up, often with the women and children left behind when male family members migrate.
2 Young, active people, often those with skills and education, form the largest group of migrants.
3 An elderly population is left behind, increasing the death rate.
4 The country may become partly dependent on money sent back by emigrants.

Advantages for host country

1 The labour shortage is solved and both service and manufacturing industries benefit.
2 Unpleasant jobs can be given to immigrants, leaving local people to do the more skilled and highly paid jobs.
3 Migrants are prepared to work long hours and are usually young and fit.
4 The host country discovers a new culture with its foods, music and leisure activities.

Disadvantages for host country

1 When unemployment rises, immigrant workers are resented.
2 Some ethnic groups do not mix with the local population, forming ghettoes in the industrial cities.
3 Migrants use local social services, causing resentment.
4 Migrants are often young men which can create social tension.

Case study – Gastarbeiter in West Germany before unification

As Fig. 3.7A shows, the majority of Turkish migrants chose West Germany where standards of living were high and work was readily available. The Germans call these migrant workers gastarbeiter (guest workers). The gastarbeiter are found mainly in the chief cities such as Frankfurt, Munich and Dusseldorf and work mainly in unskilled jobs in the steel, plastics and car industries. The West German government banned the recruitment of gastarbeiter in 1973 but families continue to join their husbands and fathers. In 1980 grants were offered to Turks wishing to return home but very few took advantage of the offer. The scheme has now been dropped and immigrant workers face an uncertain future as the economic climate becomes more difficult. There has been local resentment at the Turkish migrants. They tend to remain isolated by language culture and religion and have not become fully absorbed into the German population. Furthermore, the unification of Germany has produced a new set of problems, including that of finding work for the people of Eastern Germany where living standards and job opportunities are lower than in the West.

Forced migration

Fig. 3.7B shows where refugees have gone following the breakup of Yugoslavia in 1991–92. The ethnic divisions in Yugoslavia were suppressed under the Communist regime but have boiled over now that communism has been discredited. As a result, Serb, Croat and Muslim groups are in conflict and hundreds of thousands of people have fled the country. These refugees have created problems for their host countries and neither refugees nor their hosts want the migration to become permanent. However, previous refugee migrations indicate that it is inevitable that

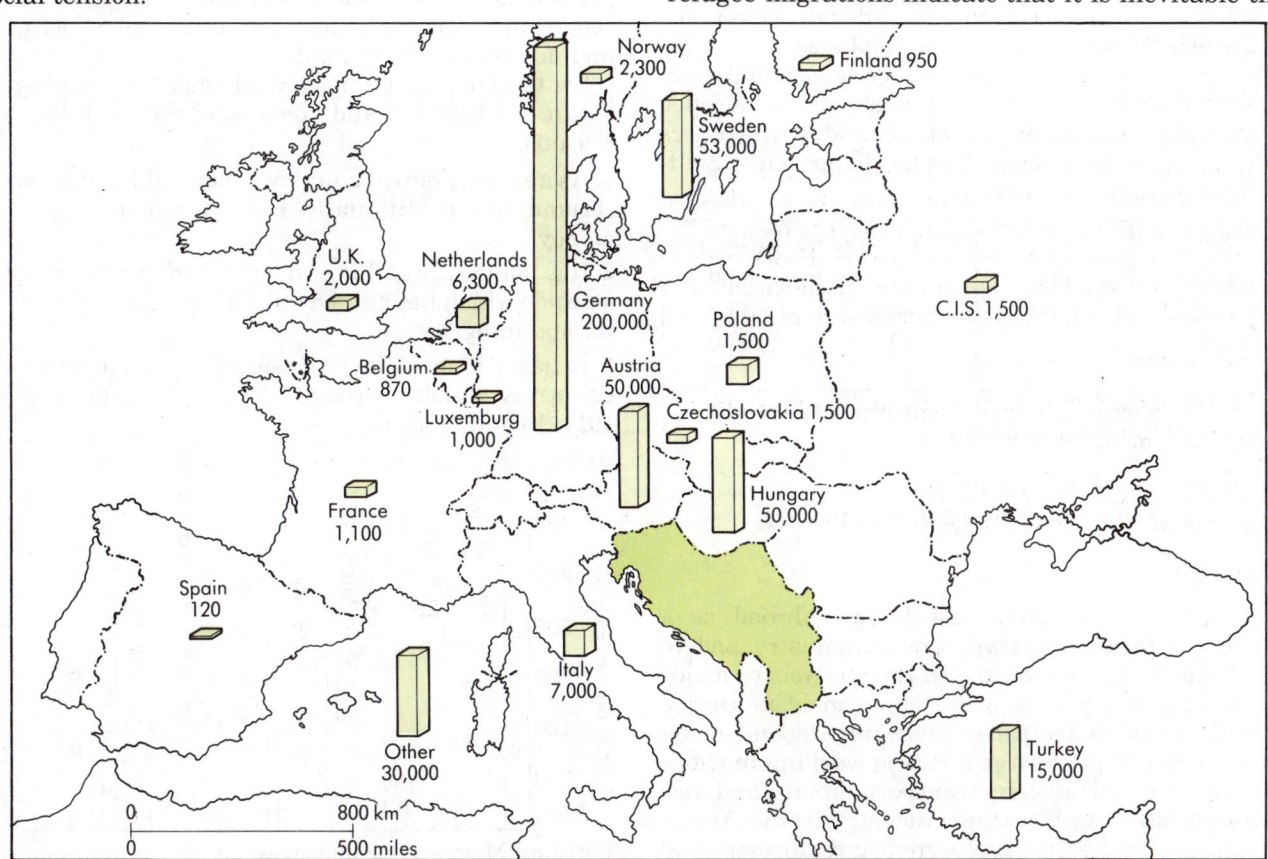

Fig. 3.7B Distribution of refugees from what was Yugoslavia, August 1992

some of these people will not return to their homeland and will settle elsewhere. The refugee problem is not confined to Western Europe. The United Nations estimates that there are over 14 million refugees in the world. In recent years Vietnam, Somalia, Ethiopia, Afghanistan and the Middle East (Palestinian arabs) have been the centre of refugee problems.

There are other examples of forced migration, but these are not to be found in Western Europe. They include moving people after a natural or man-made disaster, e.g. the Chernobyl nuclear disaster or the Philippine earthquake in July 1990. Governments can resettle people for political reasons. For example, in Indonesia large numbers of people have moved to the eastern islands which are relatively underpopulated. It has also happened by expelling groups, such as the Ugandan Asian community in the 1970s, or the acquisition of land by war, e.g. the Arab refugee problem in Israel and neighbouring countries, particularly Jordan.

> **Summary**
>
> *Basic ideas*
>
> Migration can be internal or international. It can also be forced or voluntary. There are advantages and disadvantages for migrants and their hosts, for the migrants' country of origin and the host country.
>
> Migration can be forced by war, disaster or governmental pressures. Refugees have been increasing in numbers as a result of wars in Europe and elsewhere.
>
> *Key terms*
>
> Migration; host country; push and pull effects; gastarbeiter; refugees.

3.8 Service industries in Switzerland

In Western Europe, as in other more developed regions of the world, more people are employed in service industries than in either the primary or secondary sectors. Furthermore, there is a tendency for service industries to increase in importance and for the others to become less significant. This has happened in Switzerland, as table 3.8 shows.

Year	Primary	Secondary	Tertiary
1960	14.6	46.5	38.9
1970	8.6	46.0	45.3
1980	7.2	39.8	53.0
1989	5.5	35.1	57.3

Table 3.8 Percentages employed in primary, secondary and tertiary industries 1960–1989

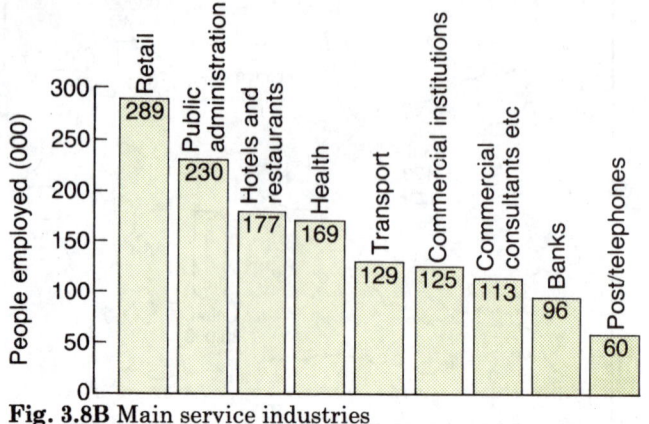

DISTRIBUTION OF THE SERVICE INDUSTRIES

Tourism

Switzerland is probably best known abroad as a country with an important tourist industry and to some extent this is reflected in the analysis of major service industries in fig. 3.8B. Employment in service industries which are partly or mainly dependent on tourists includes the large numbers working in shops and other retail outlets, transport, hotels and restaurants. Tourism is a major industry in the Alpine region (see fig. 3.8C), where agriculture, forestry and manufacturing are limited. In the canton (administrative region) of Graubünden, for example, which includes centres such as St. Moritz, Davos and Klosters, 62 per cent of the working population are employed in tertiary industries. In the Jura canton where tourism is limited and industry more important, only 39 per cent are employed in service industries.

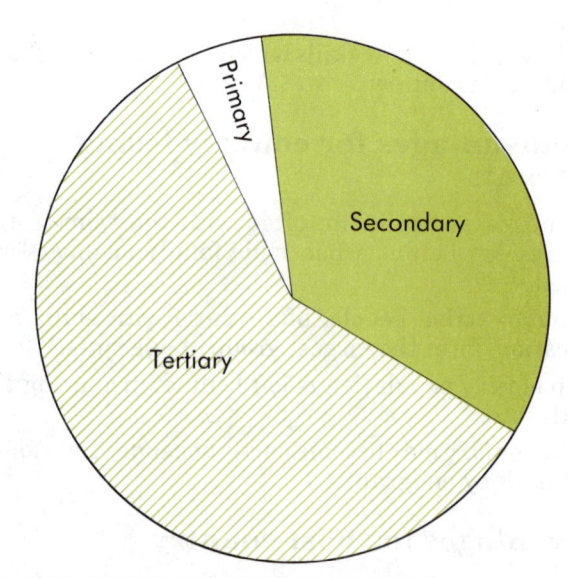

Fig. 3.8A Distribution of the Swiss work-force, 1989

Commerce

The Central Plateau is the region where most people live. Some of its cities such as Geneva, Lucerne and Interlaken are tourist centres, but they are also known for their banks, commercial institutions and international organizations like the Red Cross. As regional shopping centres with national and international commercial interests, they are pre-eminently cities dependent on service industries. In Geneva, for example, 78 per cent of the workforce is employed in the tertiary sector, in Lausanne 75 per cent, in Zurich 73 per cent and in Lucerne 70 per cent.

Switzerland has gained a worldwide reputation as a centre for banking and commerce, for the following reasons:

1 As a small, neutral country in central Europe, Switzerland has traditionally been a safe location for money.

2 It is politically stable and has taken an independent attitude which has gained for it a reputation for security and integrity.

3 It has a long history of neutrality, even when the countries which surround it have been at war, eg 1914–18 and 1939–45.

Fig. 3.8B Main service industries

Western Europe 75

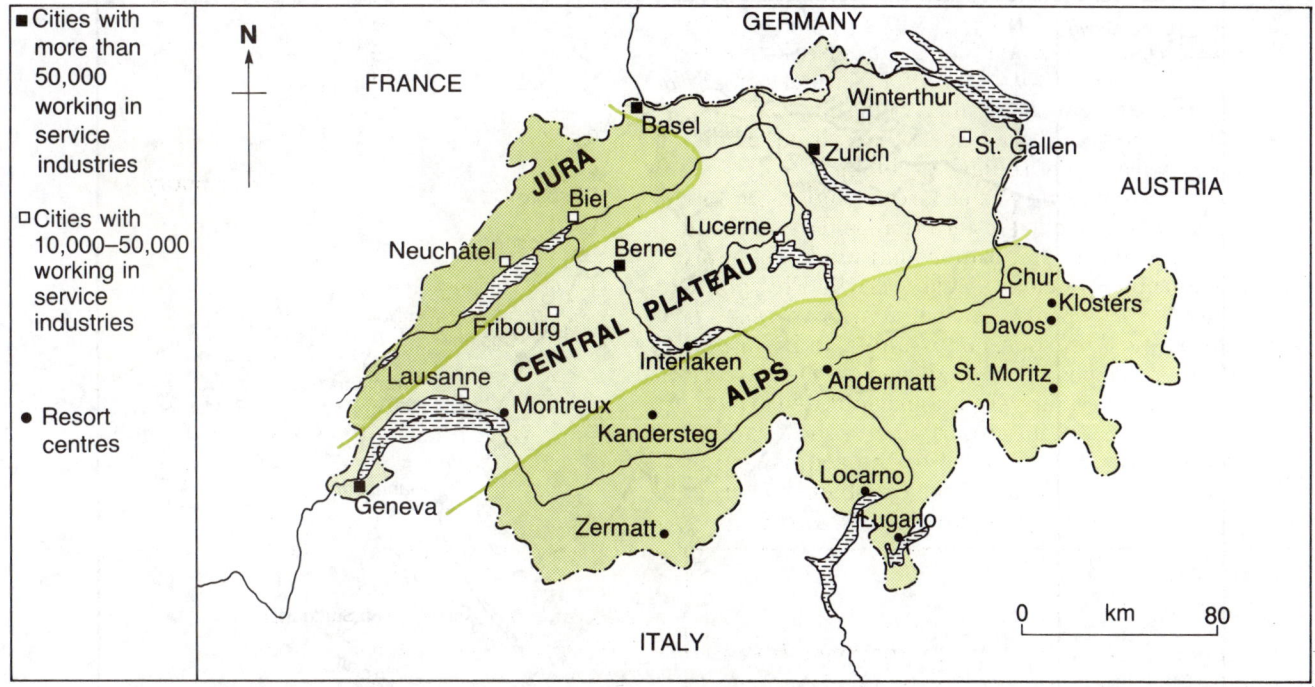

Fig. 3.8C Distribution of main service industry centres

4 Taxation on large incomes and fortunes is low.
5 The banking system is renowned for its secrecy. Customers can have numbered accounts which may not be revealed to taxation authorities in Switzerland or abroad.

Specialist health care

The clear atmosphere and unpolluted mountain air have gained a number of mountain resorts in Switzerland a reputation as health centres. Some of the people working in medicine and nursing, which are included in 'Health' on fig. 3.8B, are employed in these resorts. In Davos, for example, there are 14 clinics and sanatoria, as well as a tuberculosis research centre to which patients are sent from all over the world.

Summary

Basic ideas

Types of employment can be grouped into three categories: primary, secondary and tertiary.
 In Western Europe more people are employed in service industries than in either of the other two sectors.
 Tertiary industries are found mainly in large urban areas.

Key terms

Primary; secondary; tertiary; tourism; commerce; specialist health care.

northern Germany. In these countries they are an important means of carrying heavy and bulky goods. The network is at its densest in the Netherlands, where 34

3.9 Inland waterways

THE WATERWAY NETWORK

The inland waterways of western Europe form an extensive network in Belgium, the Netherlands and

Fig. 3.9A Major waterways of Western Europe

Waterways able to take barges of 1350 tonnes or more

Rivers
1 Seine
2 Rhône
3 Po
4 Rhine
5 Neckar
6 Danube
7 Main
8 Mosel
9 Elbe
10 Weser
11 Meuse

Canals
12 Mittelland
13 Dortmund-Ems
14 North Sea
15 Kiel

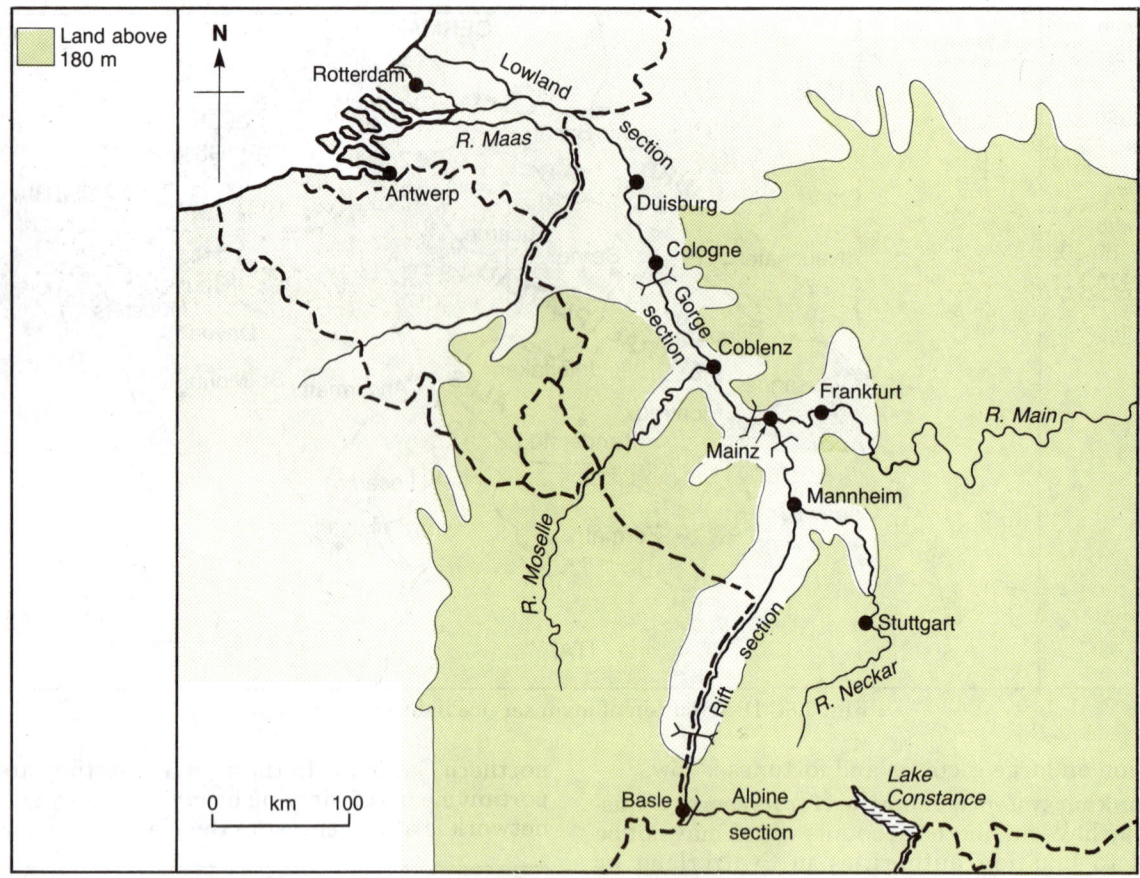

Fig. 3.9B The Rhine Valley

per cent of all goods transported travel by water. Considerable improvements have been made to the waterway network in recent years, particularly in West Germany, to make it competitive with the other forms of transport.

Water transport is slower than rail or road, but the cost per tonne for each kilometre the goods are carried is lower than for other means of transport.

THE RHINE VALLEY

The importance of the Rhine Valley as an international routeway and as a natural frontier is in its unique link as an artery from central Europe through Germany to the Netherlands. The river provides water for drinking, industry and irrigation; it is used as a dumping ground for effluent and sewage; it has been harnessed for HEP and is also a routeway used by pleasure boats as well as commercial traffic. Inevitably, some of the uses made of the river are in conflict with one another and control is made more difficult by the fact that for some of its course it is an international boundary.

The Alpine Section

After leaving Lake Constance, the Rhine is harnessed to provide hydroelectricity at a number of stations, of which Schaffhausen is the best known. Industries such as the production of machinery have developed in this area. This section of the river contains rapids and is not used by river traffic.

The Rift Valley

This section, from Basle to Mainz, is 304 km long and 32–48 km wide.

1350 tonne barges can reach Basle, but ice and low water in winter limit navigation to eight months. Canals have improved the navigation in sections where the river is shallow or meanders. HEP is produced at Ottmarsheim and Kembs.

Strasburg is the main river port in eastern France, being linked by canals to Lorraine and the Rhône. The Neckar is also navigable, and Mannheim with engineering, electrical and food-processing works is an important river port.

The Gorge Section

This section from Bingen to Bonn, is 112 km long.

Despite swift currents, this is a busy routeway. The steep sides are cultivated with vineyards clinging to the hillsides. Road and rail routes also use the narrow valley floor. Castles are a reminder of the earlier control of movement along the valley.

The Lowland or Plain Section

This section is from Bonn to the Delta area, and is dominated by the Ruhr coalfield industrial area and the heavy industrial belt extending into the Netherlands. The valley is also important for fast rail and autobahn routes, which supplement the slower river traffic.

THE RHINE AS A WATERWAY

The River Rhine and its tributaries form the most important inland waterway in Europe. It carries four times as much as all the other waterways combined and is a busy routeway between the North Sea and central Europe. New technology and improvements in engineering are changing the haulage system used on the river. The traditional method of haulage has been to use a powerful tug to pull behind it up to four large steel barges, each carrying 1 500 tonnes of cargo. This system requires 18 men, three on each barge and six on

Fig. 3.9C The Gorge section of the River Rhine

the tug. A more efficient system has been introduced, called a push-train. This consists of a specially-designed push-tug equipped with radar and closed circuit TV which pushes two pairs of barges connected together in front of it. These push-trains can carry between 8 and 11 000 tonnes of cargo and only need a crew of seven on the push-tug. Powerful diesel engines have increased the tonnage and also the speed with which the cargo can be transported.

Journey times for push-trains on the River Rhine (hours)

Journey	Up-stream time	Journey	Down-stream time
Rotterdam–Duisburg	31	Duisburg–Rotterdam	15
Duisburg–Cologne	14	Cologne–Duisburg	6
Cologne–Mannheim	37	Mannheim–Cologne	13
Mannheim–Basle	52	Basle–Mannheim	9

Coal is no longer as important a cargo on the Rhine as it was fifty years ago. The main materials moving upstream from Rotterdam are iron ore and metal scrap, oil and oil products, grain and fodder crops. The ore is destined for the Ruhr industrial region, while the oil and oil products go to refineries and chemical works in the same region. Downstream, the most important cargoes are of building materials (mainly sand and gravel), coal, chemicals and manufactured goods. A number of inland ports have grown up along the Rhine and its tributaries. The largest, Rotterdam, has as its hinterland the whole of the Rhine valley (see unit 3.10), whereas the other ports have more localized hinterlands.

Inland port	Tonnage handled (1983) m tonnes
Rotterdam	233·4
Duisburg-Ruhrort	20·5
Cologne	12·0
Strasburg	11·7
Frankfurt	10·2
Mannheim	8·6
Basle	8·0

Summary

Basic ideas

The Rhine and its tributaries make up the most important waterway network in Europe.

Water transport is slower than other methods, but costs per tonne kilometre are lower.

New haulage systems are making the waterways more efficient and are reducing costs.

Key terms

Waterway network; push-tug; push-train; hinterland.

3.10 Rotterdam

AN ENTREPÔT PORT

Rotterdam is the busiest port in the world and continues to grow as new docks are added and the approach channel is deepened to take larger ships. It owes its importance to its position at the mouth of the River Rhine, as the terminal for the network of inland waterways described in unit 3.9. It is predominantly an entrepôt port, that is, most of the cargoes handled at Rotterdam are in transit, bound for destinations elsewhere. Ocean-going ships arrive to off-load grain, iron ore and other goods into steel barges which carry them to factories in other parts of western and central Europe. Manufactured goods from the industrial regions such as Mannheim, which are destined for overseas markets, move in the opposite direction.

GROWTH OF THE PORT

Rotterdam also owes its predominant position as a port to the availability of suitable land downstream on which to expand. The small medieval harbour was 30 kilometres from the open sea, approached by a winding channel. In 1872 the New Waterway was formed, by dredging and straightening this channel. New docks were built at Botlek and industries grew up downstream from the city centre.

During the 1939–45 war, Rotterdam was badly damaged and the city had to be rebuilt after the war.

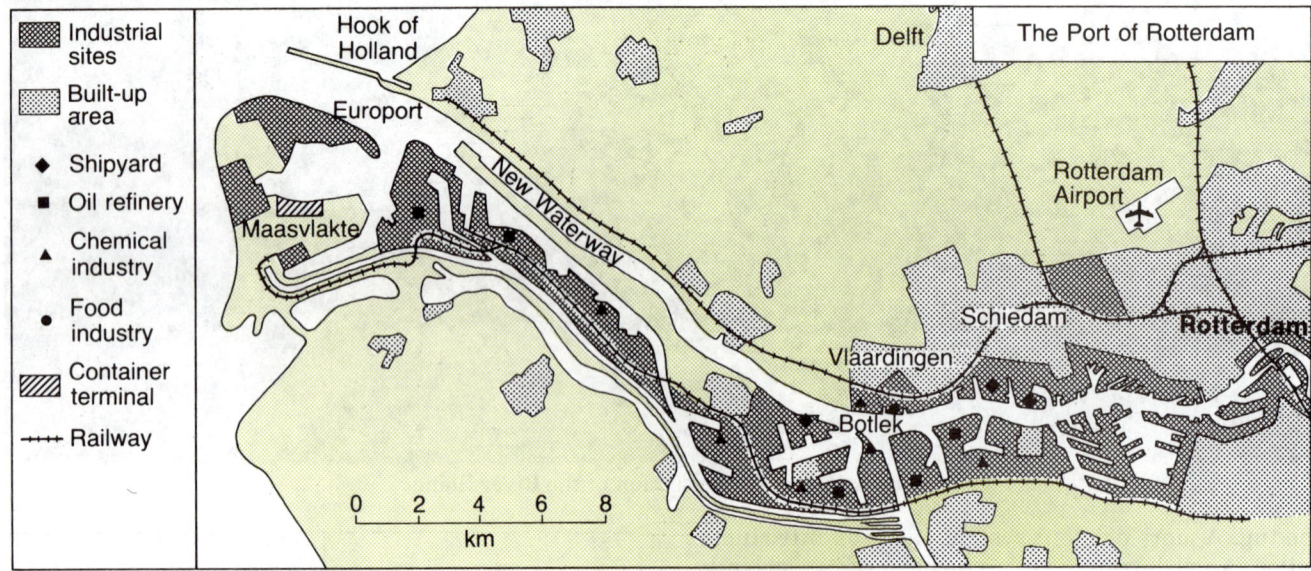

Fig. 3.10 The port of Rotterdam

The old dock areas were congested and could not deal with the increasing size of cargo ships, particularly large bulk carriers used for transporting ores and grain, and supertankers carrying crude oil.

Marshland was drained on the left bank of the New Waterway and factories and oil refineries built. This region, called Europort, was planned as the major port for the EC. In recent years there has been a further extension to the port by reclaiming land from the sea to make the island of Maasvlakte. A large container terminal has been built covering 80 hectares, because there was no room to expand the old terminal close to Rotterdam. A deep-water channel has been dredged to give the approach to the New Waterway a depth of 21 m. As a result, ships of up to 310,000 tonnes can now enter Rotterdam. Less oil is being carried along the waterways, instead it is pumped from the refineries through pipelines to the Ruhr, Cologne and Belgium.

PORT INDUSTRIES

Like many other ports, Rotterdam has developed industries based partly on the needs of shipping using the port, such as shipbuilding and marine engineering, and partly on raw materials which enter the port, such as oil refining, chemicals and flour milling. Oil refineries and petrochemical works line the south side of the New Waterway, causing oil spillage and air pollution problems, which the oil companies are attempting to solve.

REASONS FOR ROTTERDAM'S IMPORTANCE

Here is a summary of the reasons why Rotterdam is such an important port:

1 It is a natural gateway to the Rhine and the connecting waterways of western Europe.

2 There is a large hinterland stretching as far as Switzerland and Austria and including the Ruhr industrial region.

3 It has kept up with port technology. Europort has been built, largely on reclaimed land, and transit facilities have been improved.

4 It has highly developed port-based industries, such as oil refineries, chemical plants and shipbuilding and repair yards.

5 It has been designed as the main port of the Common Market countries and the road, rail and water network provides access the main EC countries.

Summary

Basic ideas

Rotterdam is an entrepôt port and handles more cargo than any other port.

The position of the port and the availability of land for expansion account for its continuing supremacy.

Key terms

Entrepôt; bulk carriers; supertankers; Europort; container terminal.

3.11 Urban development — Paris

Paris grew up at a crossing point on the River Seine at the island of Ile de la Cité, which made a good defensive position. Successive kings and governments of France carried out a policy of centralization, concentrating the wealth, power and culture of France in Paris.

Today Paris is the administrative, commercial and cultural centre of France, as well as the centre of the communication system. The city has a population of 2.1 million, but there are 9.6 million in Greater Paris. In the planning region of which Paris is the centre there was a population increase of over 5 per cent between 1982 and 1990. This region is growing much faster than nearly all the other planning regions, because it attracts people from other parts of France. It is an example of a core region growing at the expense of peripheral regions. There is a number of reasons why Paris and its region are developing so rapidly.

1 Paris is a great industrial centre. Industries are varied, ranging from car manufacture (Renault, Citroën) to clothing and footwear for the fashion trade. Oil is piped from Le Havre to refineries along the Seine and petrochemical industries have developed. Consumer goods such as washing machines and furniture are made and food is processed.

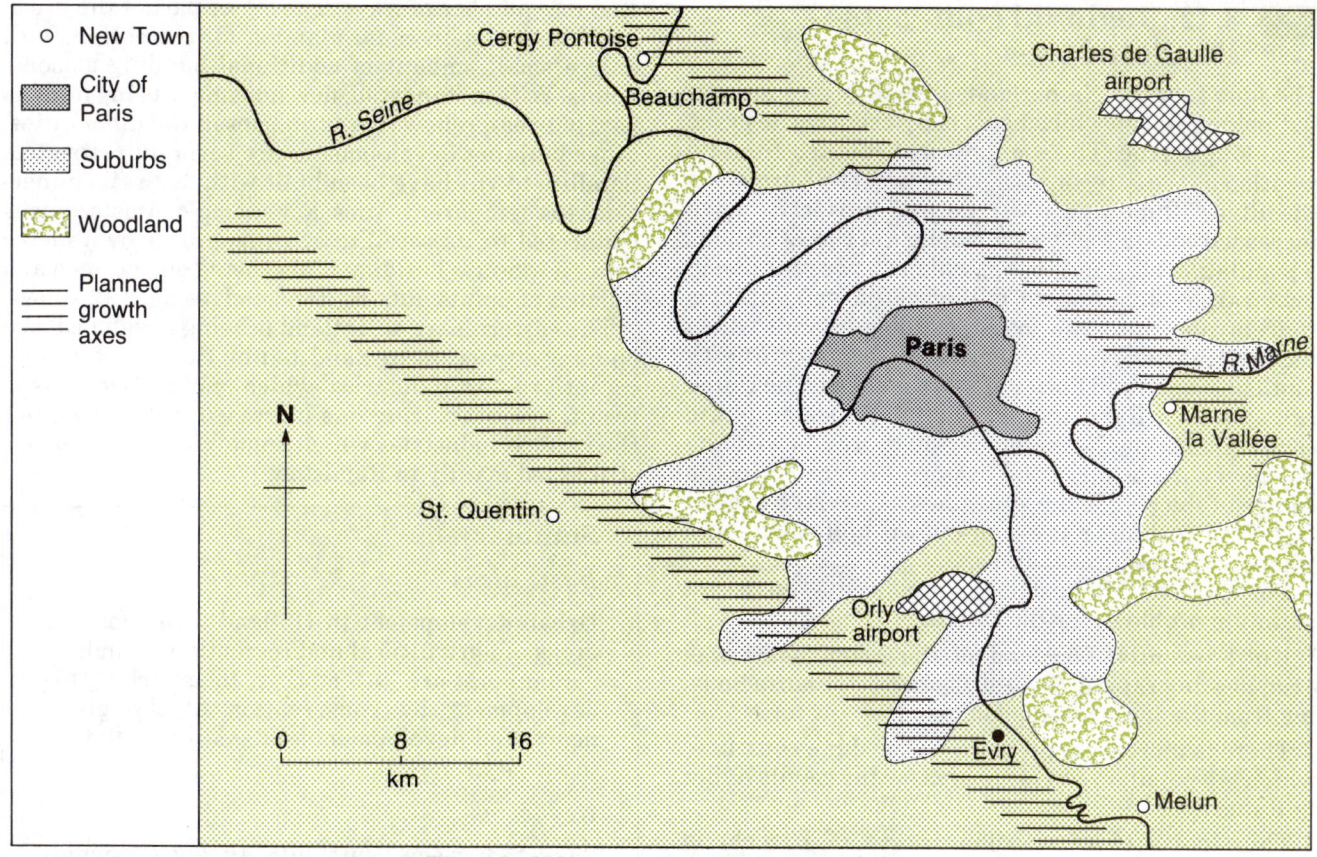

Fig. 3.11 Urban growth in the Paris region

2 The central administration, research departments, banking, insurance and commerce all employ many professional and managerial workers, with nearly two-thirds of the work-force in service industries.

3 Paris is a major cultural centre for France and western Europe. Its universities, art galleries and museums are of international importance.

4 The large fashion houses, shops and markets make Paris a great retail centre. Like other historical cities, Paris has a large tourist industry.

5 Paris is a major inland port dealing with over 19 million tonnes of grain, coal and similar goods each year. Its two major international airports, Charles de Gaulle and Orly, make it the second busiest European city for air passengers, after London.

URBAN PROBLEMS

The rapid growth of Paris and its region has produced a number of problems:

1 Overcrowding in the inner city, with decaying housing and poor facilities.

2 Severe traffic congestion, with commuter flows of over three million people each day.

3 Concentrations of industry, mainly in the northern and western suburbs.

4 Suburban sprawl, with rapid population increases in the outer suburbs.

5 A limited public transport system. The Paris Métro has never been as extensive as London's Underground.

Planners have attempted to solve these problems in the following manner:

1 Older housing areas have been modernized, old factories in the inner city pulled down and new offices and flats built.

2 A new ring road, the Boulevard Périphérique, has been built around the older part of the city. This is linked to the motorway network.

3 Industry has been dispersed to other parts of France, and five new cities, roughly 15 to 35 kilometres from the centre of Paris, have been developed. These cities will have their own industries.

4 By concentrating population growth into these new cities, suburban sprawl can be checked and the countryside around Paris conserved.

5 Extensions to the Métro network and new fast suburban railways, one of which connects Charles de Gaulle airport to Orly, have been built.

In addition, a number of cities in other parts of France have been selected to expand and act as 'metropoles d'équilibre' (counterbalancing cities) to Paris. It is hoped that these cities, and a number of smaller ones, will attract migrants who would otherwise move to the capital.

Summary

Basic ideas

Paris has functions typical of many capital cities.

The rapid growth of the city has created a number of problems,

Planners are attempting to solve these problems by local, regional and national strategies.

Key terms

Core; periphery; inner-city decay; overcrowding; congestion; industrial concentration; suburban sprawl; dispersal of industry; counterbalancing cities.

3.12 Regional contrasts— Randstad

The idea that the Netherlands is mainly a country of flat polderland on which herds of Friesian cattle graze is no longer true. The country has benefited from its position as the gateway to much of western Europe via the River Rhine and its trade and prosperity have increased considerably as a member of the EC. It has a population of 14 millions of which 88 per cent live in urban areas. Just under 6 million of this population is concentrated into two loops of built-up land, which include Haarlem, Amsterdam and Utrecht in the north and The Hague and Rotterdam in the south. The Dutch call this area Randstad, 'Ring city'. Randstad is the core region of the Netherlands and contrasts with the periphery made up of the eastern provinces. In the centre of the ring is the 'green heart', a fertile area of farmland including the well-known bulb fields and intensive horticultural areas.

The growth of Randstad has produced a number of planning problems for the Dutch:

1 Until recently, farmland in the green heart was disappearing rapidly to meet the needs for more housing from the increase in population.

2 There is increasing pressure on the dune coastline, which is a popular recreation area for the people living in Randstad.

3 The Gooi area of woodland north of Utrecht is another attractive environment in danger from urban sprawl.

4 Inner districts of the main Randstad cities have poor housing standards and have become run-down as people have moved out to the wealthier suburbs.

5 Good road and rail networks have encouraged long-distance commuting from low-density suburbs, but these facilities have encouraged the development of yet more low-density suburbs.

The planners are dealing with the problems of Randstad in a number of ways. The major part of the green heart is to remain as farmland or for recreation, with only a small amount of additional building at some points. Within Randstad, new housing is being built as part of urban renewal programmes in the inner cities, other building developments are severely restricted. Satellite towns have been built with fast rail connections to their parent cities. For example, Amsterdam is connected to its satellite at Bijlmermeer by a metro line. New house-building is also being encouraged at a number of points outside Randstad, as fig. 3.12 shows.

The eastern part of Holland is being developed as a counter-attraction to Randstad by the use of special incentives for industries which move there. As a result, manufacturing has increased in the east, but the service industries which employ more people are still based mainly in Randstad.

Summary

Basic ideas

Urban development in Holland threatens key areas of agricultural and recreational land.

Planners are attempting to restrict this development by conservation of the green heart, and developments outside Randstad, or inner-city renewal.

Key terms

Randstad; green heart; long-distance commuting; satellite towns; urban renewal.

3.13 Regional contrasts — Southern Italy

POVERTY AND BACKWARDNESS

The south of Italy, which the Italians call the *Mezzogiorno*, has always been the most backward part of the country. By 1950, when Italy began to reconstruct after the Second World War, the Mezzogiorno was a region of poor housing, poverty, malnutrition and unemployment. Industrial and agricultural production were backward and did not offer the opportunities needed by the rapidly increasing population.

THE *CASSA PER IL MEZZOGIORNO*

Between 1950 and 1984 successive Italian governments, the World Bank and after 1970 the EC, invested large sums of money in the south of Italy to provide work and improve the living standard of the people. In 1950 the Fund for the South (*Cassa per il Mezzogiorno*) was set up. There were three stages in the development of the south, with a different emphasis at each stage.

1950–7 Agriculture

In this stage most of the money was spent on land reform, irrigation and land improvement schemes. Land was compulsorily bought from landowners and given to landless families. Cash-crop farming was encouraged and there was an increase in the output of such crops as table grapes, tomatoes, salad vegetables and tobacco. New farms and roads were built, sewers laid and drinking water provided to villages. These improvements to the infrastructure helped the marketing of crops and raised local living standards.

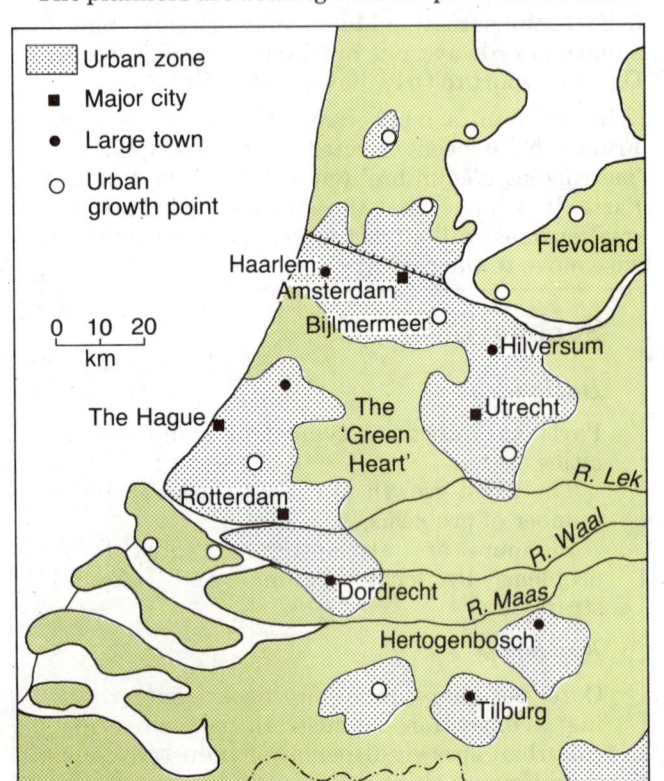

Fig. 3.12 Randstad, Holland

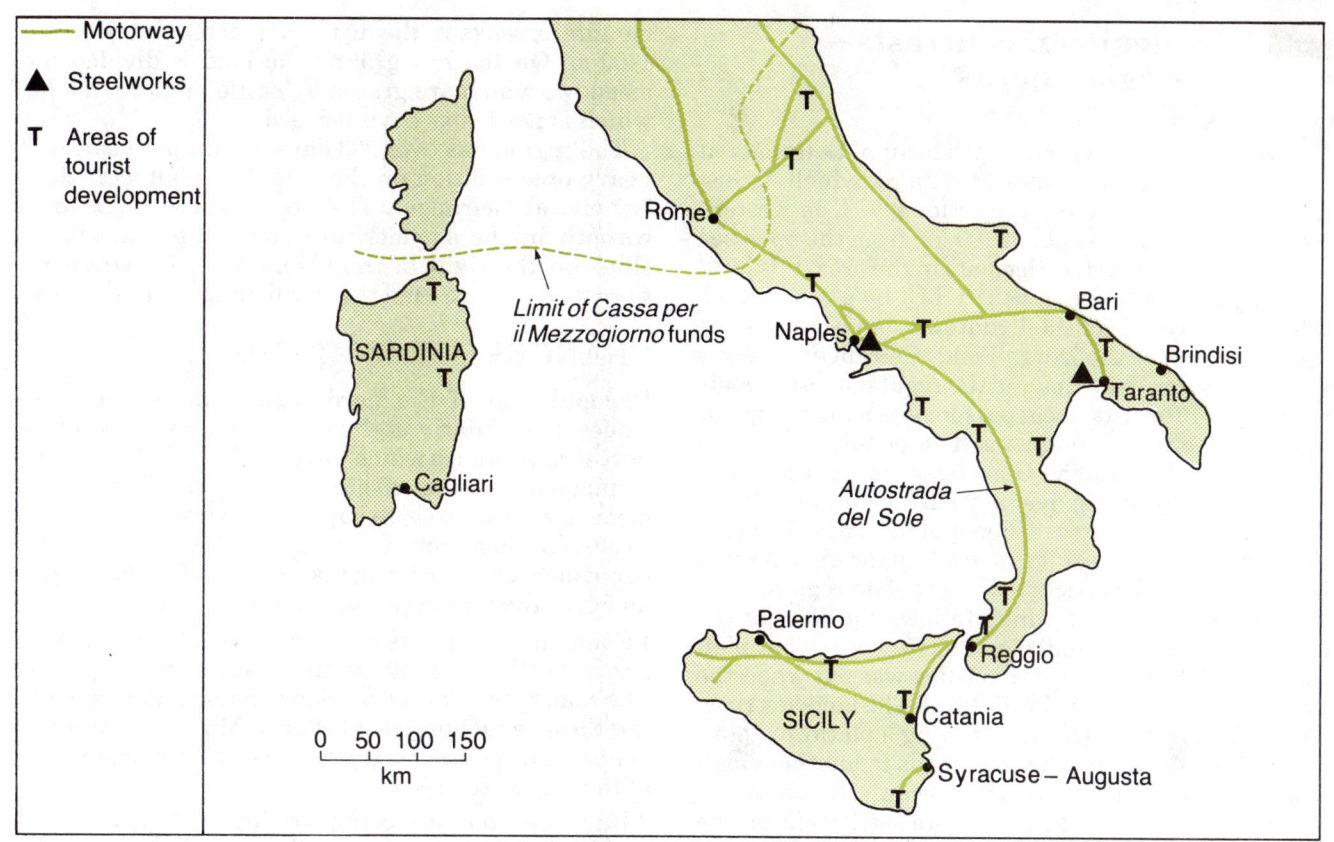

Fig. 3.13 The Mezzogiorno

1957–65 Industry

Improvements to the infrastructure and agriculture continued, but the emphasis was on the development of industry. Firms in other parts of the country were given financial incentives to relocate in the south and a percentage of any industrial development had to be in the south. Centres were earmarked as 'growth poles' and were given aid to encourage them to develop as new areas for industrial development. Bari, Brindisi and Taranto were three such towns. As a result, a large steelworks was built at Taranto, petrochemical plants at Brindisi and engineering works at Bari. Car firms built factories in the region, Alfa-Sud near Naples and Fiat at Cassino. Most of the investment projects, however, were for heavy industries, which have suffered from cut-backs in recent years.

1965–84 Tourism

While agriculture, industry and the infrastructure continued to receive aid, there was a shift in emphasis towards tourism. A major motorway, the *Autostrada del Sole* was built from Milan to Reggio. Extensions of the motorway network to the east coast and Sicily helped to break down the isolation of the south. The region has many historic sites, attractive beaches and a great deal of sunshine to attract tourists. Grants and loans were made available for the restoration of ancient monuments, the building of museums, enlarging and modernizing hotels and the development of tourist villages.

The South today

Up to 1974 people were leaving the south to find work in northern Italy or abroad and between 1950 and 1974 over four million people emigrated from the south. Return migration has not been on a large scale, due to higher rates of employment elsewhere. Many of the large industrial plants built in the 1960s are operating on reduced capacity. Petrochemical works built in Sardinia are either idle or generating on a very limited output, but the discovery of oil off the coast of southern Sicily has resulted in increased activity around Syracuse, where oil platforms are produced.

Agricultural yields have increased, but over-production of tomatoes and wine grapes has added to EC surpluses. Almost the entire production of Italian citrus fruit comes from the south but a proportion of the crop is unusable because of its quality, and other EC countries, Israel and the USA supply the European market. Much of the Italian crop is processed. Corruption and the Mafia are still part of the southern way of life and there are sharp contrasts in the south between the flourishing Adriatic coast and the backwardness of Calabria, Sicily and Sardinia. The major changes have not removed the contrasts between the north and south. Although the Fund for the South has now been stopped, it had a considerable effect on the region and may parts have reached a reasonable level of prosperity.

Summary

Basic ideas

Development of the Italian south has been in three phases, concentrating first on agriculture, then industry and finally tourism.

Emigration from the south has been checked and the standard of living has increased. However, old customs linger on and the north is still a richer region.

Key terms

Infrastructure; poverty; malnutrition; growth pole; isolation.

3.14 Regional contrasts — Norwegian fjords

GEIRANGER

Figure 3.14 shows the small settlement of Geiranger at the upper end of the Geiranger Fjord, which is just north of lat. 62° N and close to long. 7° E in western Norway. Geiranger is about 100 km from the open sea and is typical of fjord settlements in the area. It is built on a deltaic fan and can be reached by a road which follows the Gudbrandsdal routeway and crosses the upland region of the Dovre Fjeld. Geiranger receives visitors from cruise ships and the regular coastal boats which carry tourists, local passengers, mail and goods from Bergen and Trondheim. The population of the community in which Geiranger is located has remained static at just over 2 000 in recent years. It has not suffered from the rural depopulation of some other fjord areas, neither has it experienced the kind of rapid increase which has occurred in the Oslo region.

In fig. 3.14 the road which follows the edge of the fjord on the right is built on a narrow wave-cut platform called a strandflat. This ledge was cut when the land was at a relatively lower level. The land has risen since the end of the Ice Age, leaving a platform above the present sea level. The road leads to another small settlement and then zig-zags upwards to cross the mountains, ending at another fjord settlement on the Norddalsfjord and passing through a region of summer pastures on the mountainside, called the saeter. The mountain peaks in the distance reach heights of over 1400 m. On the low ground the land is divided into meadows which are grazed by cattle and provide hay which is needed as a winter feed.

The region has over 200 days of rain per year, with heavy precipitation on the mountains but as little as 500 mm at Geiranger. The fjord head is a pocket of warmth in the summer, especially the south-facing slope on the right of the photograph. In winter the fjord never freezes and there is little snow at sea-level.

CHANGES IN THE FJORDS

Depopulation of the fjord regions of Norway continues, particularly in the more remote regions of the northern latitudes which have not benefited from jobs connected with the offshore oil industry. The government is anxious to give support to rural communities to prevent them from disappearing completely. A number of measures are being taken to check depopulation and give the regions a less uncertain future:

1 Communications are being improved. Ferries are larger and roll-on/roll-off landing stages are being built. The road network is also being extended. For example, the E6 is being improved between Mo i Rana and Kirkenes, in response, partly, to the strategic importance of the region to NATO.

2 HEP resources are being developed, particularly in connection with electrometallurgy and electrochemical works like those at Høyanger and Årdal. At these

Fig. 3.14 Geiranger at the head of the Geiranger fjord

places, and at Mo i Rana where there is a large iron and steel works, new communities have been created. The employment which has resulted from the North Sea oil developments has been mainly in the southern fjord region.

3 Farms are being consolidated, allowing more machinery to be used, but as a result fewer workers are needed. The demand for fresh fruit and vegetables from towns and tourist hotels has increased and local freezer plants have overcome transport problems. Some farmers are rearing silver fox and mink for their pelts.

4 Guaranteed farm incomes and subsidies have made farming in the fjord regions less risky and now buildings and machinery are appearing.

5 Farming cooperatives are becoming more widespread and marketing is more efficient, resulting in a steady demand for milk, butter and cheese. Forestry management groups are also becoming profitable. They grow trees instead of crops and carefully control the felling rate.

6 Tourism is increasing in importance. Package-deal holidays in chalets and farms are becoming more popular and saeter farmhouses are being repaired and rented out as summer cottages. Cruise companies are being encouraged, as are fishing, climbing and camping holidays in the mountains. The Norwegian fjord country is very appealing to visitors, but is not an easy region in which to live and rural depopulation is likely to continue for some time.

Summary

Basic ideas

Population in many Norwegian fjord regions is either static or falling sharply compared with the Oslo region.
Measures are being taken by the government to check depopulation, but rural numbers continue to decline.

Key terms

Strandflat; saeter; depopulation; communication improvement; HEP development; farm consolidation; subsidies; cooperatives; forestry management; tourism.

3.15 Mediterranean tourism

Over 100 million people take a Mediterranean holiday each year, with the majority of the tourists coming from the cooler and less sunny regions of the UK, Scandinavia, Benelux and Germany. The most popular stretches of Mediterranean coastline are those of Spain, which are visited by over 40 million holidaymakers a year. During the main holiday season, from April to October, the resident coastal population of many resorts is doubled. This inevitably puts pressure on the resources, while boosting employment in the hotel trade and other service industries concerned with tourism. The Spanish resorts, like those elsewhere, have grown at a very rapid rate since large-scale package tours became more popular in the early 1970s. Benidorm, with a population of over 40 000 and hotels which can sleep 60 000, was a remote fishing village only 25 years ago.

The Mediterranean tourist regions are some distance from the core industrial areas of western Europe. They form the periphery and are often regions with lower living standards where, in the past, farming and fishing were the main occupations. For the EC countries of Greece, Italy, Spain and Portugal, tourism is an essential part of the economy, providing much-needed foreign currency. There are disadvantages and advantages in tourism for the people who live near the coast, as well as for the local environment. These can be listed as costs and benefits.

COSTS
1 Pollution

About 85 per cent of the sewage from 120 coastal sites around the Mediterranean is discharged into the sea, with inadequate or no treatment at all. Industrial waste also enters the Mediterranean from oil refineries, chemical plants and other factories. Because the Mediterranean is almost land-locked and tideless, the pollution tends to accumulate, making bathing in some areas unhealthy. Beaches are polluted with tar and litter and pollution has also affected marine life, particularly shellfish, which should not be eaten raw.

2 Haphazard building

Hotels, shops and apartments have been built in large numbers, often with little thought for planning. As a result, scenery has been spoiled by tall hotel blocks and traditional building styles have been ignored.

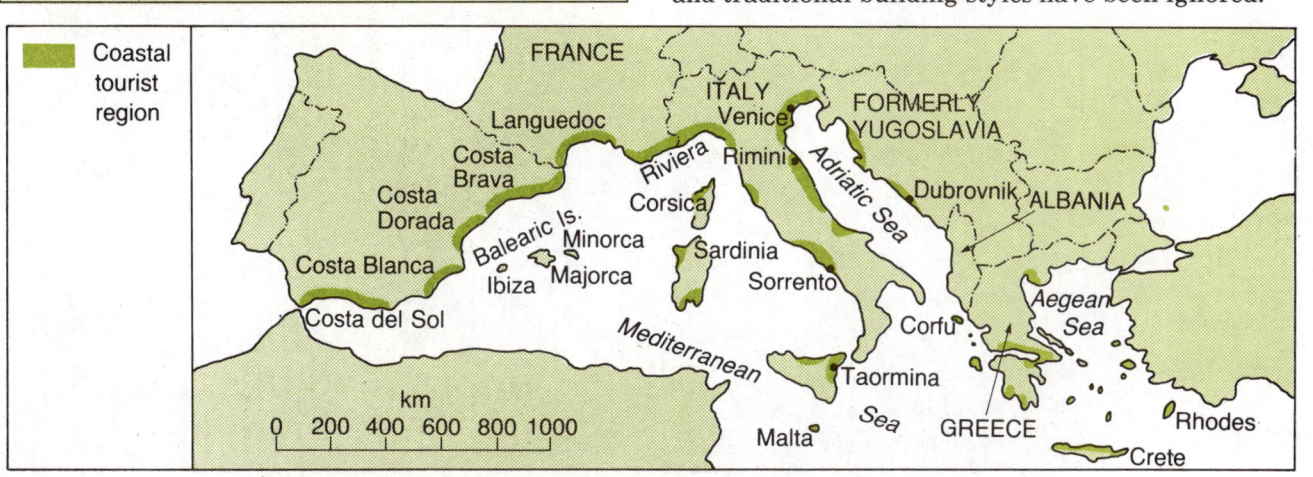

Fig. 3.15 Main resort regions around the Mediterranean coast of Europe

3 Changes in land use

Because land prices have soared, good farmland has been built-over and countryside with scenic beauty has disappeared. Some habitats are threatened, for example the beaches on Greek islands used for egg-laying by sea turtles.

4 Congestion

The increase in the number of vehicles has resulted in some new roads, but many streets are congested and rural roads damaged by heavy traffic. Some tourist sites such as the Acropolis in Athens and St. Mark's Square in Venice have become overcrowded and made less attractive by the number of visitors.

5 Noise

There is an increase in noise, with clubs and discotheques operating late at night and charter flights arriving and taking-off from local airports.

6 Souvenir shops

There is a spread of souvenir shops, take-away restaurants and similar facilities needed by visitors but of less interest to local people.

7 Breakdown of traditions

Local customs and traditions may disappear or be altered to meet the needs of the tourists: for example, the so-called 'flamenco' dancing put on in some tourist hotels in Spain.

BENEFITS

1 Employment

There is much more employment in regions where previously there were few opportunities for work other than farming or fishing.

2 Standard of living

Local people are likely to experience a higher standard of living as tourist money flows into the coastal regions. Farmers benefit by growing crops such as vegetables and fruit needed by the hotels.

3 Infrastructure

The infrastructure is improved to provide roads, promenades, hospitals and other facilities needed by the visitors.

4 Entertainment

Theatres, night clubs, casinos, cinemas and many other forms of entertainment are developed and are of benefit to local people as well as visitors.

5 New interests

New ideas and interests are introduced such as local radio, clubs and amateur dramatic groups.

6 Conservation

Funds are found to restore old buildings, local craft workers find new markets for their products and traditional customs may be revived to interest the tourists.

Tourism is a growth industry in countries bordering the Mediterranean, but it has been received with mixed feelings by many of the people whose homes are on its shores.

Summary

Basic ideas

The shores of the Mediterranean are the most popular recreation areas in Europe.
There are costs and benefits from the development of coastal towns as tourist centres.

Key terms

Pollution; haphazard building; congestion; noise; breakdown of traditions; employment; conservation.

4 THE DEVELOPING WORLD

4.1 The development gap

DEFINITIONS
The advanced industrial nations of the world such as Germany and the USA are said to belong to the *developed world*. In contrast, most of the countries which make up Africa, Asia and Central and South America are said to be members of the developing world.

The *development gap* is the difference in economic activity and wealth which exists between the developed world and the developing countries. The gap is largely due to the fact that developing countries have not undergone modern industrialization. Some developing countries have poor resources but in many, the resources are not fully made use of because inefficient methods of production are still used. The development gap shows up most clearly in the mass poverty which characterizes so many less developed countries.

CHARACTERISTICS OF LESS DEVELOPED COUNTRIES

The degree of development of a country is difficult to define and measure. The developing countries are advancing, but each country is doing so at a different rate. In most, there has been some industrial growth in recent times, national wealth and food production have increased as new techniques have been adopted. Nevertheless, the following characteristics still typify most of the less-developed lands:

1 little modern industry;
2 high birth rate and rapidly increasing populations;
3 farming is the chief economic activity;
4 much poverty;
5 low educational and technological levels;
6 poor diets causing malnutrition;
7 poor transport facilities;
8 lack of services and modern amenities such as good quality housing and pure piped water.

MEASURES OF DEVELOPMENT
Gross National Product (GNP)
We often talk about the standard of living of people we know, but this is very difficult to measure. One measure of how wealthy a country is is its GNP, which is the net value of all goods and services produced by the country in one year. It is important to know how many people have to share the national income, so the GNP is divided by the number of inhabitants to give a measure called the *per capita income* (PCI).

Development indicators
There are various statistics which are used to compare the level of development of one country with another. These include:

— The amount of energy used by industry
— The percentage of people who go to college or university
— The percentage of people working in farming
— Number of people to each doctor
— Number of newspapers sold per 1000 population (this gives an idea of the literacy rate)
— Average amount of food available per head of population.

A model of underdevelopment
The model in fig. 4.1B was designed to describe and explain the process of development. It simplifies the situation to help us understand why some countries remain poor and why the developing countries do

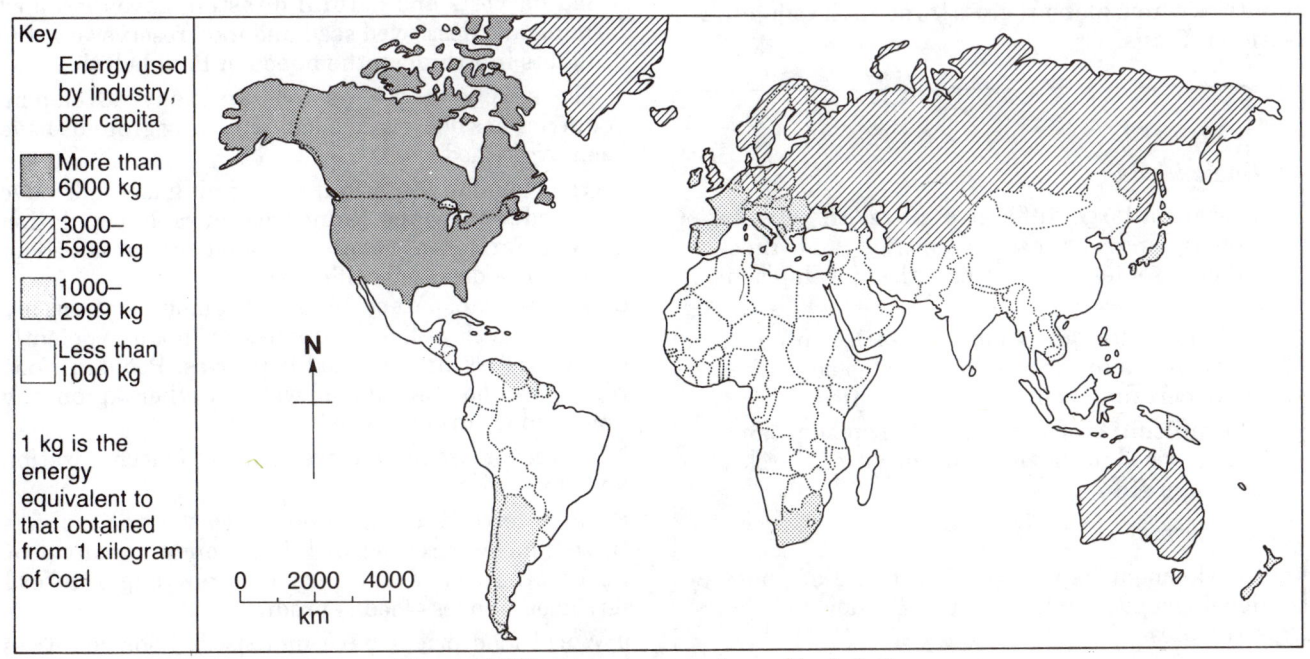

Fig. 4.1A Where most energy is used by industry

The developing world

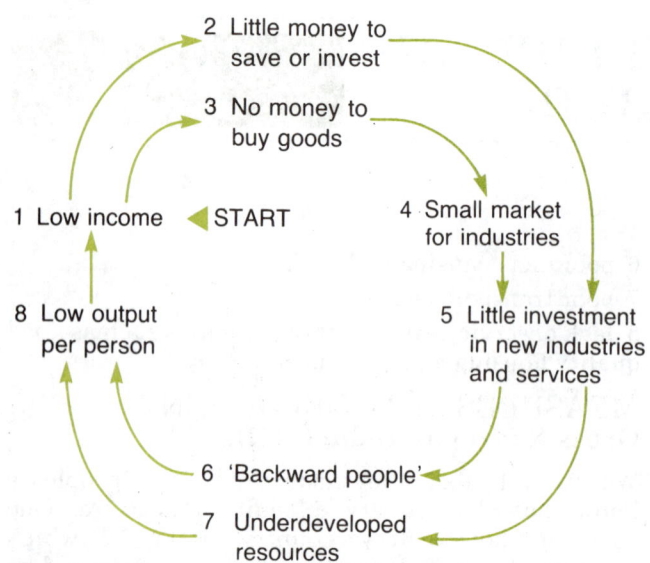

Fig. 4.1B The vicious circle of development

not have enough capital to invest and bring about development quicker. It is called the 'vicious circle' because it is so difficult for a developing country to break out of the cycle.

HOW DEVELOPMENT MAY BE ACHIEVED

Three main needs have been identified as a basis for development:

1 Industrialization: this is seen as the chief agent of change.

2 Capital: vast amounts of money are needed to help less-developed countries progress. This may come from international aid or from investment by large international companies (multinationals). See unit 4.15.

3 Trade agreements: the agreements guarantee markets and fair prices for goods from the developing countries.

Four main approaches have been used to achieve more rapid development:

1 The creation of **National Plans** to give a country clear goals and purpose. India and Tanzania are countries which plan progress through the adoption of National Plans.

2 Export stimulation or import substitution: countries can decide whether to export raw materials to earn money to buy goods they need, or to spend less on imports by making things themselves for the home market. See unit 4.10.

3 Low technology: traditional crafts and industries may be expanded and modernized to avoid importing expensive goods e.g. the textile industries of India.

4 Revolution: some countries have turned their backs on the western economic system and have tried to change their countries' futures through revolution e.g. Ethiopia and Cuba.

4.2 Hunger and poverty

Two-thirds of the people of the world live in the developing countries. It has been estimated that in these countries 400 million people live on the brink of starvation. Many are undernourished, that is, they do not receive sufficient calories a day to maintain good health. Sixty-three per cent of the people in the developing world are also said to be malnourished, that is, they are seriously lacking in essential nutrients, usually protein, which people in rich countries get from eating foods such as meat, cheese and milk.

Hunger can kill. When a person loses 30 per cent of his or her body weight, starvation begins. If the intake of calories drops below the daily expenditure of energy, hungry people burn up their own body fats, muscles and tissues as fuel. Shortage of carbohydrates affects the mind. Hungry people become confused and less energetic and may not realize how ill they are. Their kidneys and livers do not function properly and they are susceptible to diseases. Babies also suffer. A pregnant mother who is malnourished may produce a weak baby which has not developed properly.

REASONS FOR WORLD HUNGER

1 The rapid growth of population has outstripped the increases in food production.

2 The availability of new land for agricultural development and water resources for farming is limited.

3 Bad harvests and natural disasters have disrupted farming and destroyed seed and food reserves e.g. the droughts in Ethiopia, the floods in Bangladesh.

4 The supply of fish as food in many developing countries has decreased because fishing grounds have been overfished.

5 Traditional (often primitive) farming methods have low productivity and cannot match rapid population growth. Farmers are badly educated and cannot adapt easily to modern scientific ideas.

6 Because transport systems and communications are not well developed, food supplies are not as efficiently distributed as in advanced countries. People in one region may be short of food while another region may have a food surplus stored.

7 The recent rise in oil prices hindered mechanization and modernization.

8 Many fertilizers are oil-based, so the prices of fertilizers have increased with inflation and many poor developing world farmers can no longer afford fertilizers. So less food is produced.

9 World food prices have increased. Poor countries cannot afford to buy extra food on the world markets.

Summary

Basic ideas

There is a large difference in wealth between modern industrialized countries and those which are less developed—the development gap.

Although the developing countries differ in character and degree of development they share certain common characteristics.

The difficulties of achieving development can be summarized in the model of the vicious circle of development.

Key terms

Development gap; GNP; PCI; circle of underdevelopment; national plans; development strategies.

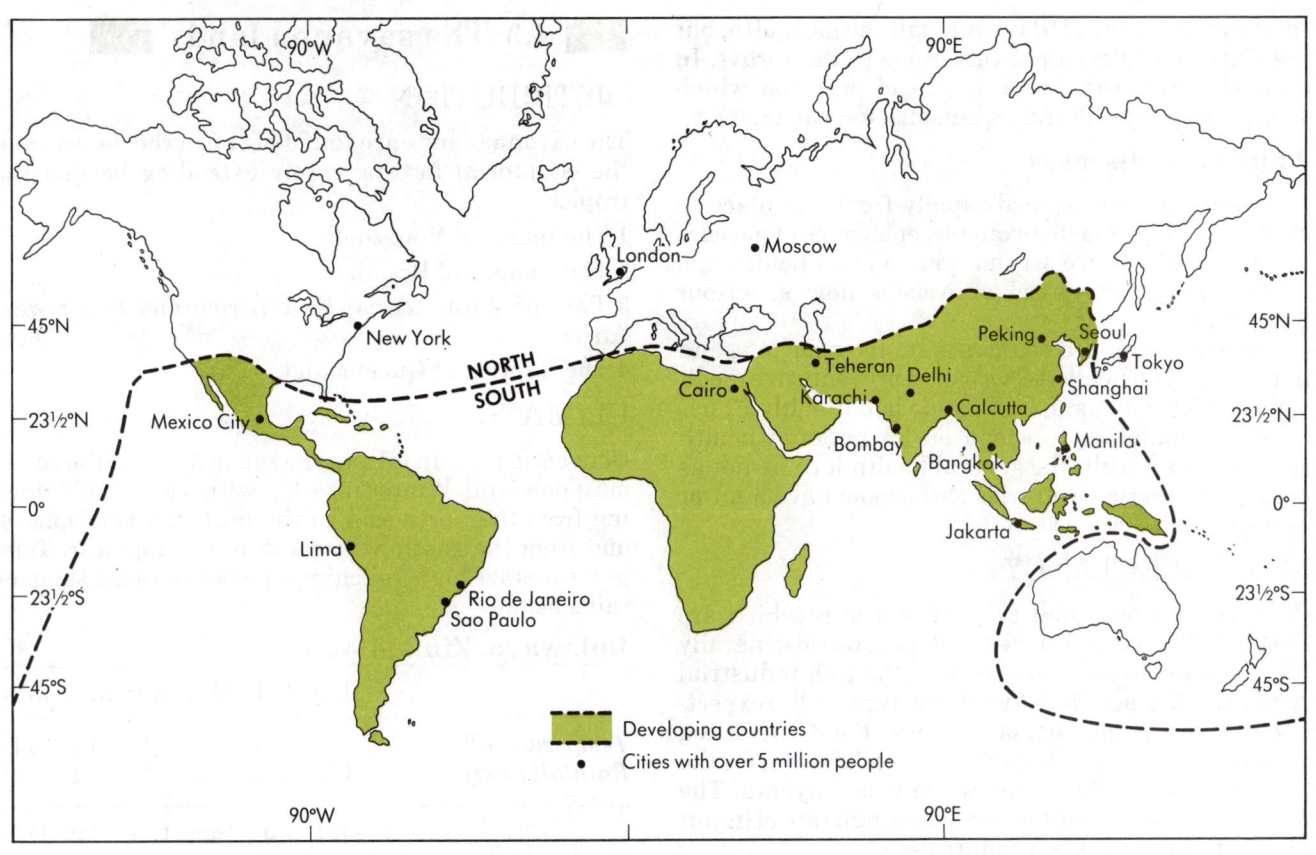

Fig. 4.2A Developing countries—the north–south divide

10 Many developing countries are heavily in debt. They find it hard to get the new loans they need from rich nations to pay for development projects such as irrigation and flood control schemes.

11 Best land is often taken for cash crops: hungry people grow tea for export to earn foreign currency to pay foreign debts.

12 The cash from cash crops goes to the men who spend it away from the farm. Most farming is done by women who do not receive the money.

13 Since many farmers do not own their land they cannot get loans to improve productivity.

THE CIRCLE OF POVERTY

Many farmers in developing countries find themselves in a circle or cycle of poverty (See fig. 4.2B).

Fig. 4.2B The vicious circle of poverty for farmers in the developing world

Because they have poor food supplies they suffer from malnutrition. This means they are not fit enough to work very hard, so the farmwork is not done properly and the crops give poor yields. Consequently the family has poor food supplies.

The cycle can also be shown in terms of farming techniques. Since the farmer is poor he cannot buy modern tools or improved seeds. He depends on poor equipment, poor quality draught animals and cannot afford fertilizers. As a result yields are low and he has little for sale. This means he gets very little cash and has no chance of saving. Without savings he is too poor to buy modern tools and seed.

In many developing countries it is therefore very difficult to improve food supplies.

EFFECTS OF INADEQUATE FOOD SUPPLIES

People are healthy when they have a balanced diet of nutrients — carbohydrates, proteins, fats, minerals and salts. In the developing world, some foods are very expensive or scarce, especially foods which are high in protein, such as meat and fish. Even where people have a sufficient quantity of food to eat, they may not be healthy, because their diet is not balanced. A shortage of proteins or vitamins will cause deficiency diseases such as kwashiorkor (protein deficiency), beriberi (vitamin B deficiency) or even night-blindness due to a lack of vitamin A. Other diseases widely experienced in the developing world include:

1 Diseases caused by insects

In the developing world in general and in Africa in particular, many serious diseases are caused by insects. A very common one is malaria, which is spread by the *Anopheles* mosquito, which breeds in marshes, stagnant pools and puddles. At one time, it seemed that

The developing world

spraying areas with DDT would kill the mosquito, but they have now developed resistance to the sprays. In Central Africa the tsetse fly spread protozoa which causes sleeping sickness in humans and cattle.

2 Epidemic diseases

Infectious diseases spread rapidly from one place to another. In Uganda, for example, epidemics of measles and tuberculosis are serious causes of ill health and death. The rapid spread of Aids is now a serious problem, too.

The less-developed countries are too poor to spend much money on health services and preventative medicine. In 1990 for example, Uganda had roughly £1 per head of population to spend on its national health service. As a result, the general health level is not as high as in the rich countries and people have a lower capacity for work.

LIFE EXPECTANCY

Because of a poor diet and the illnesses which are linked with it, people in the developing world generally have shorter lives than people in the rich industrial countries. It is possible to work out average life expectancies for different parts of the world. For 37 advanced nations the average life expectancy is 72 years, for the 31 poorest countries of the world it is 45 years. The main reason for this difference is the high rate of infant mortality in the poorest countries.

Summary

Basic ideas

Millions of people in the developing world live on the brink of starvation.
Rapid increase in population has exceeded increase in food production.
Many food producers find themselves in a cycle of poverty.

Key terms
Undernourished; malnourished; hunger; epidemics; deficiency diseases; life expectancy.

4.3 The savanna lands

DISTRIBUTION

The savanna lands are found between the deserts and the equatorial forests, rarely extending beyond the tropics.

1 The llanos of Venezuela.
2 The campos of Brazil.
3 Part of West Africa, East Africa and South-west Africa.
4 The interior of Queensland.

CLIMATE

Convectional rain falls in the summer, when the sun is most powerful. Winters are dry, with trade winds blowing from the north-east in the northern hemisphere, and from the south-west south of the Equator. Temperatures are high, reaching a peak before the summer rains begin.

Bulawayo, Zimbabwe

	Jan	Feb	Mar	Apr	May	Jun
Temperature °C	22	23	22	19	16	14
Rainfall (mm)	140	110	82	18	9	2

	Jul	Aug	Sep	Oct	Nov	Dec
Temperature °C	14	15	19	22	23	22
Rainfall (mm)	0	0	4	22	80	122

Latitude of Bulawayo: 20° 10'S. Total rainfall: 589mm

VEGETATION

The true savanna is a parkland with scattered trees and grass. With high temperatures all the year round and a dry season, the trees are adapted to retain moisture. Many, like the acacia, have elongated branches which shade the roots. The baobab, sometimes called the 'upside down' tree because it looks as though its roots are sticking in the air, has a thick bark and holds moisture in its trunk. The bushes are often thorny and have small narrow leaves.

Elephant grass grows to a height of five metres but most of the grasses are shorter and coarse. The grass

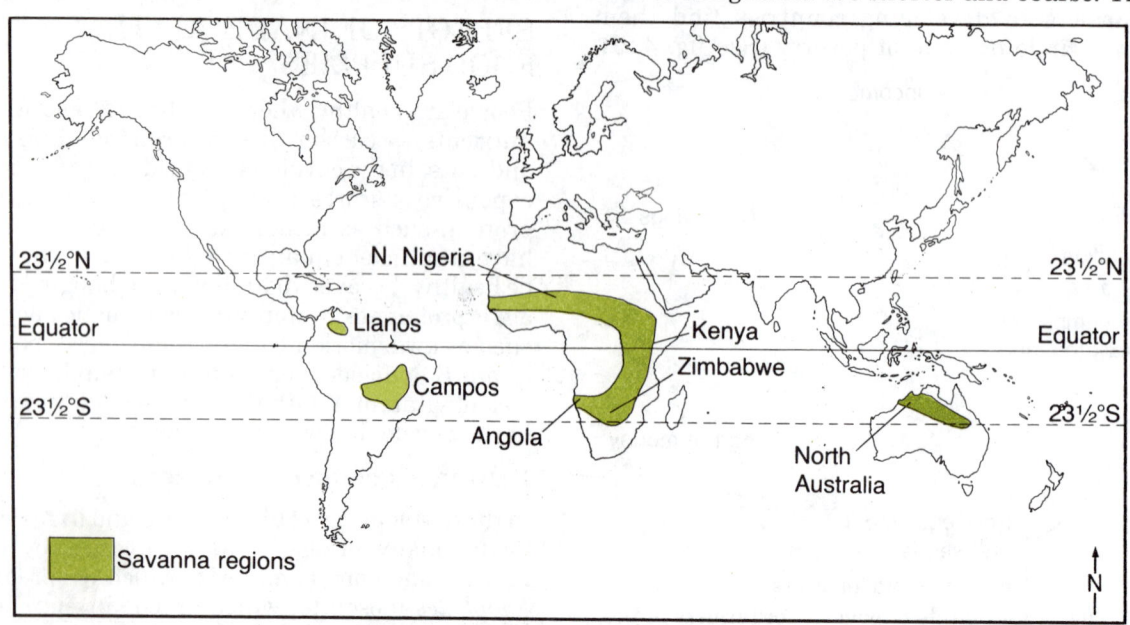

Fig. 4.3A Savanna grassland regions

dies down in the dry season and grows rapidly when the rains come.

Near the equatorial rain forests there are extensive patches of woodland, whereas on the desert fringe there are only a few, stunted trees.

SOILS

The soils are mainly red laterites with the nutrients leached out, leaving hydroxides of aluminium and iron. The soils are porous so irrigation is difficult; they are not very fertile.

DEVELOPMENT

The tropical grasslands, especially in Africa, are the home of herds of animals such as the zebra, giraffe, elephant, gazelle and wildebeest. Tourists are eager to see and photograph these animals and countries like Kenya and Tanzania have developed tourist industries.

Tourism may be a mixed benefit, however. Developing countries may become over-dependent upon the income earned from rich western tourists and neglect traditional ways of life. Increased numbers of visitors may also alter the character of the unspoiled lands which have been designated game parks.

Cattle rearing is the traditional way of life of many tribes in the savanna lands, but growing crops such as corn, cotton, groundnuts and tobacco is becoming more important, together with stock rearing on a large scale in South America and Queensland, Australia.

THE SAHEL (Read unit 5.5 as well)

Figure 4.3B shows the Sahel region of Africa, stretching across the continent on the southern edge of the Sahara desert. The rainfall varies on average from 100 mm per annum on the desert edges to 500 mm on the southern side of the region. These low rainfall totals hide the large variations which may occur from year to year. Since 1968 the actual rainfall has been well below average and the result has been a prolonged and severe drought, causing famine, disease and death.

The drought has meant that the peoples of the region have not been able to grow their staple (basic) foods — millet and sorghum. The cattle pastures were over-grazed and the bare patches of land encouraged soil erosion, so the pastures were destroyed. Trees were cut down for fuel and this also led to soil erosion. The result has been *desertification* of the region. Traditional ways of life have been destroyed. For example, the nomadic Tuaregs have had to leave their grazing lands and move to the towns. Many of those who have left the land now live in shanty towns. Forms of aid available to these regions are listed in unit 4.15.

Summary

Basic ideas

The savanna lands are natural parklands to which the rains come with the overhead sun.
The tropical grasslands have become extensive cattle rearing areas.
Tourism has become an important source of income, based on the new game parks and national parks.

Key terms

Convectional rain; parkland; laterites; cattle rearing; game parks; drought; desertification

4.4 Farming in the monsoon lands

The monsoon climate which is experienced in South-East Asia and northern Australia is caused by the seasonal reversal of winds. In winter, most monsoon regions experience dry conditions as the winds blow from the land to the sea. Heavy rainfall occurs in summer as a result of moisture-laden onshore winds blowing into the land mass.

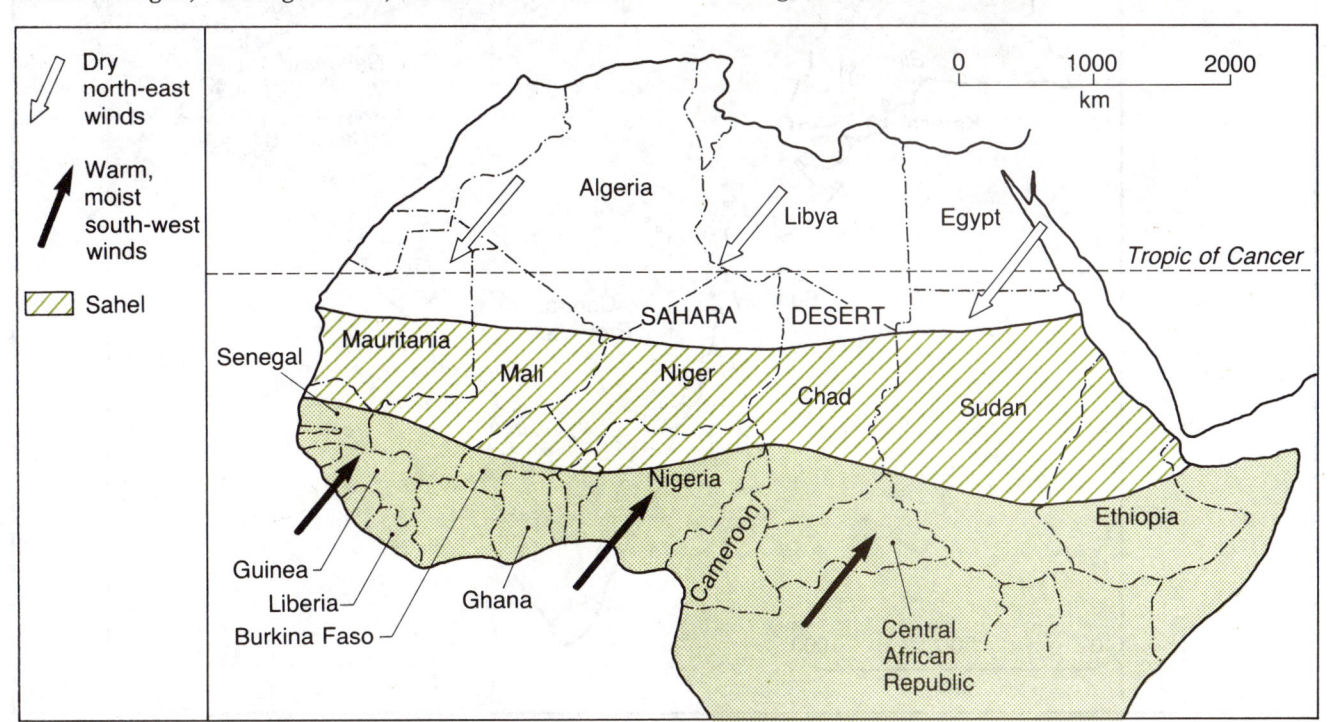

Fig. 4.3B The Sahel region of Africa

90 The developing world

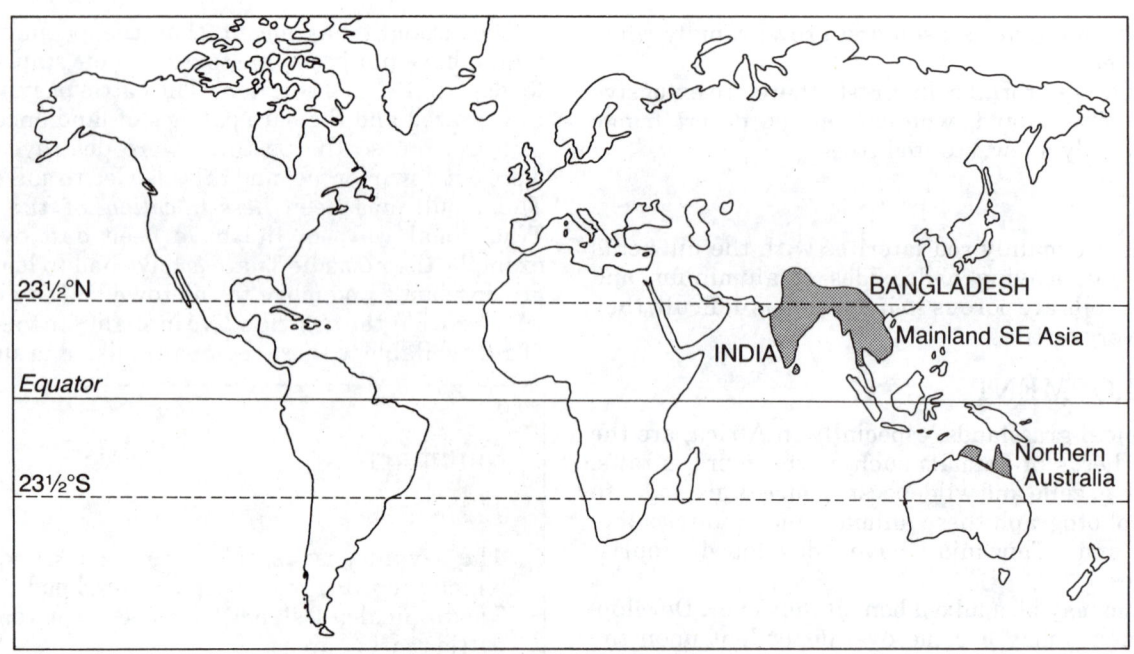

Fig. 4.4A Monsoon regions

THE CLIMATIC PATTERN
The dry north-east monsoon provides
1 a 'cool' season in January and February and
2 a 'hot' season from March to June.
The wet south-west monsoon provides
3 a 'hot-wet' season from June to September and
4 cold, showery weather from October to December as the monsoon retreats.

Because of the climate, two crops a year can generally be grown, for the winter temperatures are high enough for temperate crops to be grown.

The 'hot' season without rain makes irrigation necessary. The 'hot-wet' season provides a surplus of

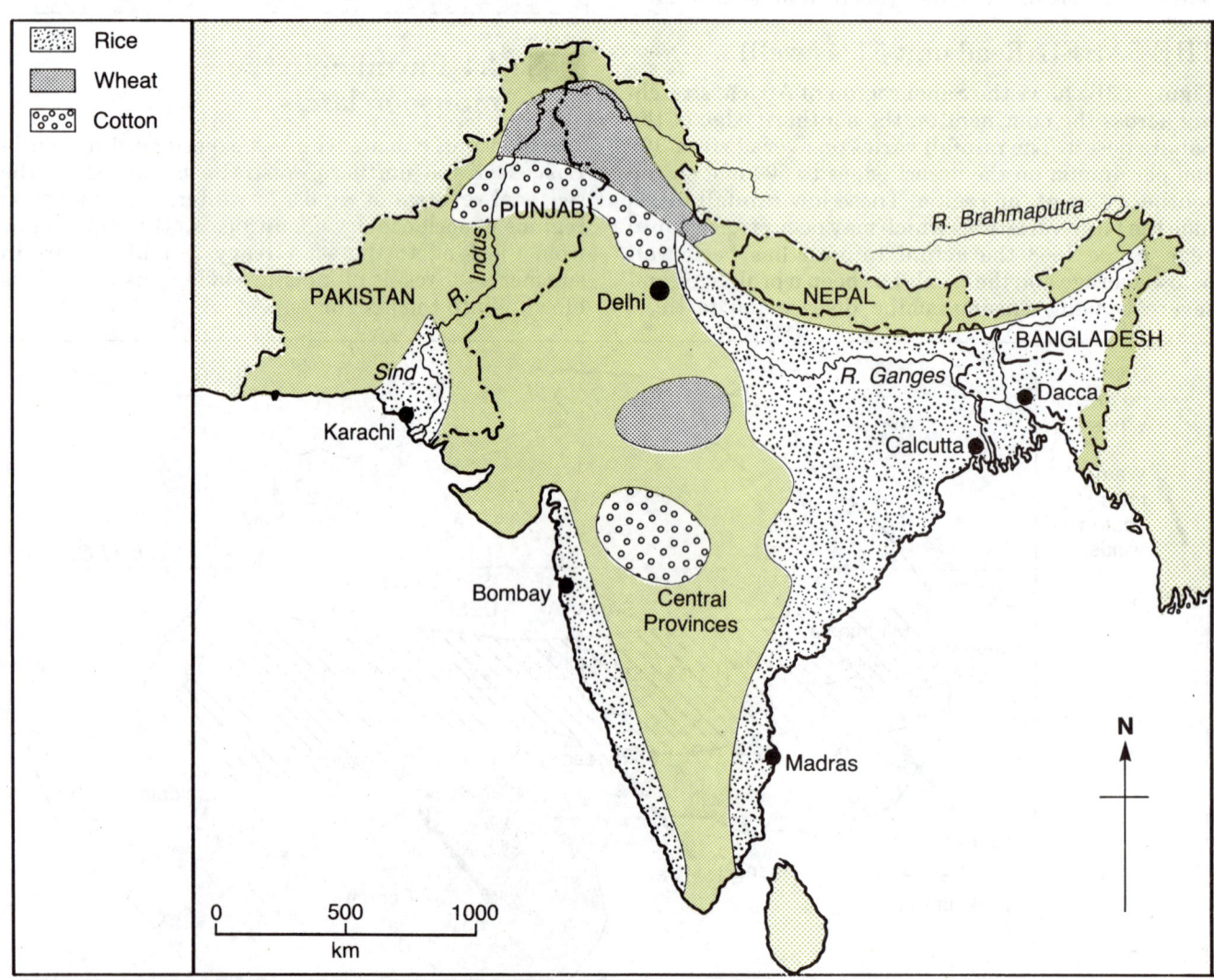

Fig. 4.4B India, Pakistan and Bangladesh: distribution of important crops

water which can be stored and used to irrigate the land.

Farming in many areas is based on three types of irrigation:

Tank irrigation, in which water is stored in small reservoirs and ponds. This is very common on the Deccan Plateau.

Wells: one quarter of all the irrigated land is watered from wells. The water is often raised by the use of oxen, although modern 'tube' wells are now sunk. Wells are very important sources of water in parts of the plains of the Indus and Ganges.

Canals provide water for half of the irrigated areas. New development projects have greatly increased the provision of canals.

EXAMPLE — FARMING IN INDIA

Farming on the Indian sub-continent is based on the rhythm of climate created by monsoons. The two periods of monsoon each year give the region four seasons.

Farming is less productive in India than in developed countries such as England. One farmer in India produces on average little more than enough food for one family. In England one farmer produces enough food for ten families.

Reasons for the low output include:

1 The poor quality of the soil. It contains little humus and the monsoon rains wash the minerals out of the soil.

2 Farms are very small, perhaps 0.25 hectares and divided into scattered strips. This leads to inefficient working and makes it difficult to introduce mechanization and modern techniques.

3 Because of the lack of timber and since farmers are too poor to buy fuel, animal dung is burned as a fuel and not used as manure.

4 The cow is sacred to the Hindus, so there are too many cows, which eat scarce food resources.

5 Poverty. Farmers cannot afford better seed, better tools or fertilizers, nor can they risk using new methods which may fail.

Crops

1 Rice is the chief crop and the basic item of diet for many. Most rice is grown on the coastal plains and in the Ganges valley.

2 Wheat is the chief food crop of the dry areas and of the dry season. It is a winter crop which is sown in October and harvested in March.

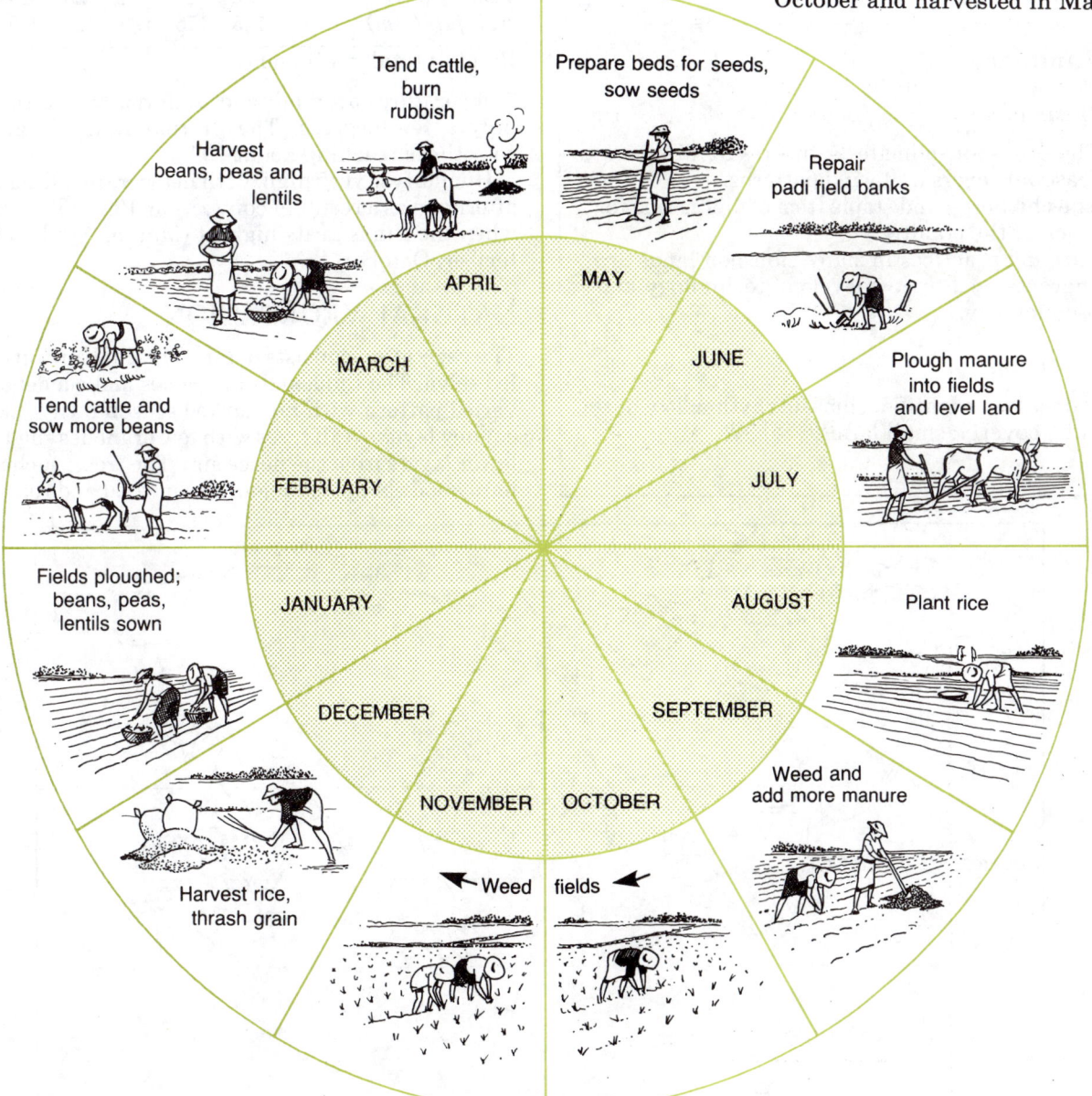

Fig. 4.4C The rice farmer's year

Where it is too dry for rice and the soils are too poor for wheat, millet is grown.

3 Indian farmers grow linseed, groundnuts and sesame because their diet does not contain much fat.

4 Sugar cane is widely grown but yields are very poor and sugar refining methods so crude that it is only produced for local consumption, except where modern developments have formed part of a multi-purpose project.

5 India is the second greatest cotton producer in the world after the USA. The chief growing areas are in Uttar Pradesh, the Central Provinces and the Bombay region.

6 Nearly all the jute grown in the world is produced in the Brahmaputra-Ganges delta region.

7 Tea is India's most valuable cash crop. The chief producing areas are Assam and Darjeeling in the Himalayan foothills.

The Farming Year

The annual cycle of farming of a rice farmer is shown in fig. 4.4C. The quiet period on the farms lasts from March to May. If possible, many of the men look for work in the large cities for that period, to increase the family income.

Summary

Basic ideas

The monsoon climate is the result of strong seasonal reversal of wind patterns.
The chief crop and staple item of diet is rice for much of the country.
Farming practices in many monsoon lands are characterized by low levels of technology and productivity.

Key terms

Monsoon; irrigation; climatic rhythm; low outputs; poverty; small farms.

4.5 The tropical rain forest ecosystem

DISTRIBUTION

The regions of tropical rain forest lie within approximately 5° north and south of the Equator:

1 coastal region of Colombia;
2 lowlands of the River Amazon;
3 West Africa and Zaïre (Congo) basin;
4 Malaysia, Indonesia and New Guinea.

AREAS

Amazon Valley, Indonesia, central and west Africa, Sri Lanka, Philippines are the principal rain forest areas.

CLIMATE

Kisangani (Zaïre)

	Jan	Feb	Mar	Apr	May	Jun
Temperature °C	25	25	26	27	26	25
Rainfall (mm)	55	80	180	155	130	120

	Jul	Aug	Sep	Oct	Nov	Dec
Temperature °C	23	23	24	25	25	25
Rainfall (mm)	125	175	190	220	200	85

Rainfall total = 1715 mm

Temperatures are high and uniform, with a range of only a few degrees. The diurnal range is greater, sometimes reaching about 7°C.

Humidity is very high, with heavy rain falling in the afternoon as a result of convection. Rainfall is highest when the sun is at its highest (March, April and September, October).

NATURAL VEGETATION

The vegetation consists of forests, which are often called selva. The thousands of species make a dense and varied pattern with no marked seasonal rhythm. The canopy layer of tall trees with few branches shades the lower layers from the fierce sun. The trees, such as the hardwood ebony, mahogany, ironwood and rosewood,

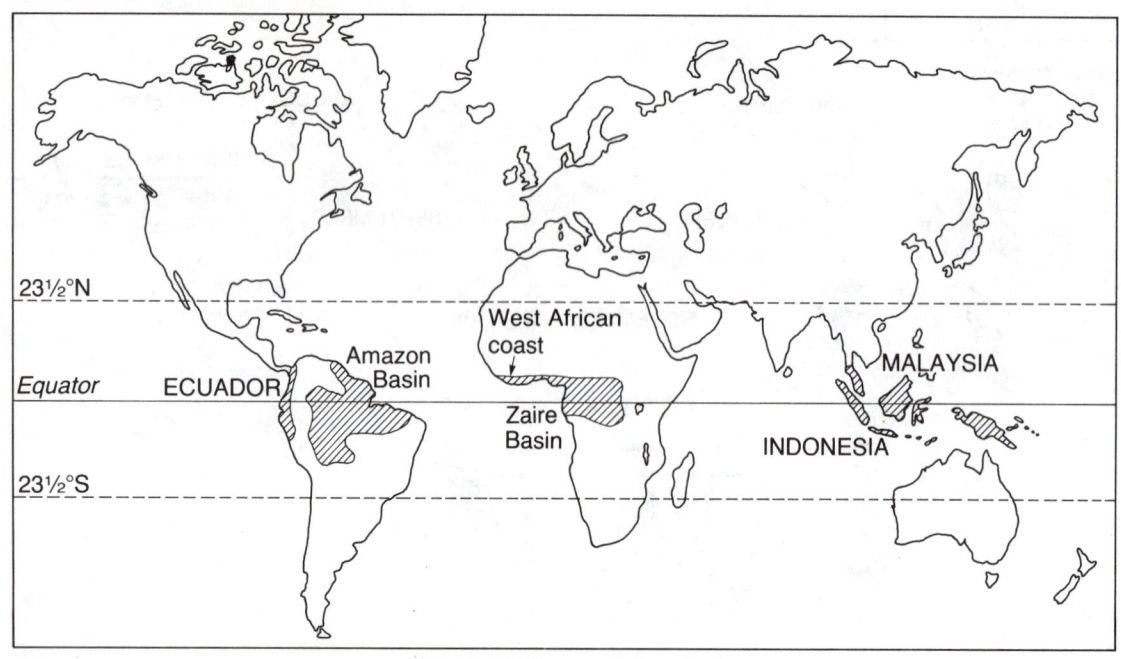

Fig. 4.5A Equatorial regions

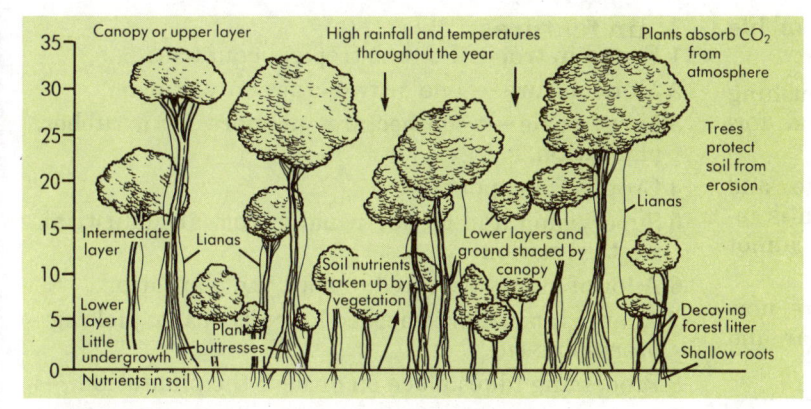

Fig. 4.5B The equatorial rain forest ecosystem

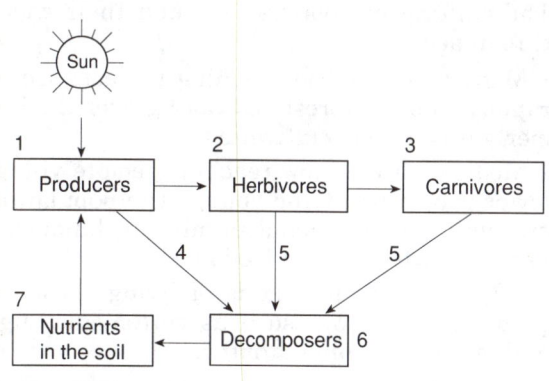

Fig. 4.5C

are important for such things as furniture and panelling. The roots form thick plank-buttresses at ground level.

Shorter trees form an intermediate layer below the canopy. Lianas, rope-like climbers, hang from the tress, while orchids grow out of crevices in the tree trunks. At ground level there are ferns and other plants, but the undergrowth is not thick. Everything is damp and green with some trees in flower, others in fruit, while yet other may be shedding their leaves.

Along low-lying muddy coasts, where the tide rises and falls, grow mangrove forests. The trees are short with a tangle of roots showing at low tide. The roots trap the mud and the swamp gradually extends seawards.

SOILS
High temperatures and humid conditions result in chemical weathering and leaching, the water draining away most of the valuable nutrients. The result is a red-coloured soil containing iron, which is fertile when first planted but which rapidly loses its fertility.

THE RAINFOREST ECOSYSTEM
An ecosystem is a community of plants and animals which share the same environment. The plants and other living organisms in the lands which have an equatorial type climate are part of the equatorial forest ecosystem. Fig. 4.5C shows a model of the ecosystem. Sunlight provides energy for the system. Plant foods called nutrients in the soil, together with water, help the producers to grow. The producers are plants such as trees on which herbivores feed. In the rainforest the herbivores include an enormous variety of insects, in addition to animals such as monkeys. Carnivores eat the herbivores and each other. Carnivores of the rainforest include the jaguar and the puma. The decomposers such as fungi and bacteria quickly break down the dead materials in the high temperatures and rainfall of the region to make more nutrients. So the cycle begins again.
1 The sun's energy is converted into food by the process of photosynthesis by the vegetation.
2 Fruit, leaves and other vegetation are eaten by monkeys, caterpillars and a vast range of insects.
3 The herbivores are eaten by meat eaters, e.g. the ocelot.
4 Leaves fall and dead vegetation accumulates on the forest floor.
5 Other living organisms die and add to the litter layer on the forest floor.
6 Decomposers such as bacteria break down the litter.
7 The result is the formation of nutrients which dissolve in water to provide plant food for the vegetation.

FOREST RESOURCES
Lumbering for hardwood such as mahogany and rosewood is important but difficult because the trees are scattered, the soil soft and damp and the forest dense. Some of the trees are heavier than water and do not float. Some plantations have been developed fro the growth of the palm oil tree, from the fruit and kernel of which a valuable vegetable oil is extracted.

Native people clear patches of forest by cutting and burning to grow yams, bananas and cassava.

TRADITIONAL WAYS OF LIFE
In the past, people lived in the equatorial forests either by collecting food such as fruit and berries and hunting fish, birds and animals or by growing food as *shifting cultivators*.

Shifting cultivation: definition
This is a method of subsistence farming practised in the humid tropics. It involves clearing and cultivating small plots of land for two or three harvests and then abandoning the site to allow the soil to refertilize itself. It is sometimes called 'bush-fallowing' or 'slash and burn'.

Method
1 Clearing made by cutting down small trees and bushes.
2 Burning undergrowth leaving tree stumps in ground.
3 Crops such as yams, manioc, beans, maize, planted in ashes.
4 When ground is exhausted the cultivators repeat the operation in other part of the forest.

Advantages
1 Allows people to survive in a hostile environment.
2 Uses soil fertility.
3 Avoids erosion.
4 Does not require expensive or elaborate tools.

Disadvantages
1 Few people per hectare. A family of five may need 20 hectares to survive.
2 Diet is a poor and no animals can be kept.
3 Seasonal shortages of food.
4 Original vegetation is eventually replaced with poorer secondary plants.
5 No conservation; the land is being exploited

RECENT CHANGES
Better communications have opened up some of the forest areas, such as the Amazon lowlands, and people have become sedentary, growing subsistence crops and cattle ranching.

The hunters and gatherers face the end of their traditional way of life because:
1 Less land is available for hunting and fishing as areas are opened up by modern developers.
2 They catch diseases from the new settlers, from which the forest dwellers are not immune.
3 It is planned that some of the forest dwellers will be concentrated in forest reservations so that the rest of the land can be developed.

The shifting cultivators also find their way of life threatened:

1 Modern timber and ranching projects are pushing rapidly into the forest and taking over the land formerly used by the cultivators.
2 Medical care is now reaching remote villages and fewer people are dying young. The population is increasing but traditional farming techniques cannot keep up with the extra food needs.
3 To raise their standards of living, some are now growing cash crops such as cotton and sugar and giving up traditional farming.

Summary

Basic ideas

Equatorial lands are characterized by a constantly hot, wet and humid climate which results in a natural vegetation cover of thick forests.
The difficulties caused by the physical environment have until recently inhibited the economic development of these regions, especially the Amazon basin.
New economic developments are destroying traditional ways of life.

Key terms

Convection rain; selva; lumber; hunting and gathering; shifting cultivation; development.

4.6 Exporting food crops and forest products

INTRODUCTION

After the Industrial Revolution, the newly industrialized countries needed industrial raw materials and food for their growing urban populations. Tropical colonies were established to meet some of these needs. By importing cotton, rubber, timber, and minerals from their colonies, the industrial nations were able to provide their industries with cheap raw materials. At the same time, tropical and sub-tropical foods such as sugar, cocoa, tea and fruit provided food for the cities.

Today much of the trade in these commodities is still controlled by multinational companies of the developed countries, such as Brooke Bond and Lonrho. The former colonies have become independent countries, but their economies still reflect the purposes for which they were once developed as colonies.

PLANTATION AGRICULTURE

Definition

This is a highly organized form of agriculture involving the growing of one crop in tropical or sub-tropical regions. The crop grown is often processed on or near the plantation and then shipped to Europe, North America or one of the other industrialized parts of the world. This system was developed in colonial times.

Main features
1 Found in tropical or sub-tropical countries.
2 Monoculture — one or two crops only grown.
3 Large scale — 400 hectares or more for a rubber plantation.
4 Crop is for export.
5 Supervision and money usually from an industrial western nation.
6 A lot of money required to start the plantation.
7 A large labour force needed for cultivating, picking, processing *etc.*
8 Processing takes place on or near the plantation.

Advantages
1 Quality of crop and product is high.
2 Care taken with crop to improve output and keep down diseases.
3 Much more efficient because capital provides the expert knowledge and methods.
4 Steady supply of crop to market by staggering planting.
5 Provides employment for large numbers of people who are not skilled.

Disadvantages
1 The crop can be attacked by disease, pests or storms and all profits are lost.
2 Soil can become poor and erosion occur.
3 'White' supervision brings political tension.
4 Local people are often exploited.
5 Need for more labour has resulted in immigration, causing social problems, *e.g.* Indians working on sugar plantations in South Africa.
6 Fluctuations in world prices often cause problems.

Main crops grown
Tea, coffee, cocoa, bananas, rubber, palm oil, sugar cane.

Recent changes
1 Change of ownership — sometimes taken over by governments of independent nations.
2 Growth of smallholdings for such crops as cocoa.
3 Government-sponsored plantations using money borrowed from overseas.

A FOOD-EXPORTING TROPICAL COUNTRY — SRI LANKA

Sri Lanka is an island about half the size of England. It has a population of more than fifteen million people and is an overcrowded island, for many of its people depend for a living upon what they themselves grow. Sri Lanka's chief imports are machinery, petrol and transport equipment.

The country's main exports are food crops. It is the second largest exporter of tea in the world — 70 per cent of Sri Lanka's export earnings come from tea. Coconut products (copra, desiccated coconut, coconut oil) are also important exports, together with spices (cinnamon and cloves).

Reasons why Sri Lanka is a food exporter
1 The colonial past

Sri Lanka was a British colony (Ceylon) and the tea industry is still mainly British owned.

2 Latitude

Sri Lanka lies between 5° 55' and 9° 55' North, that is, just to the north of the Equator. It is well located to grow 'equatorial' crops that are needed by Britain.

Fig. 4.6A Sri Lanka: exports

3 Relief

Sri Lanka consists of a mountain core rising to over 2400 metres in places, surrounded by coastal lowlands. Different types of crop can be grown at different altitudes: coconuts on the coastal plain, rice on the lowlands, rubber in the foothills, tea in the hills.

4 Climate

Temperatures are high throughout the year, because of latitude. Rainfall varies from more than 5180 mm in exposed areas to less than 1000 mm in parts of the dry zone. The dry zone covers 75 per cent of the country and is characterized by summer drought and unreliable rainfall, so commercial farming is found only in the wet zone. Since so much of the country is unproductive, Sri Lanka has to export cash crops to buy the food it requires but cannot grow.

5 Position

Sri Lanka is a crossroads for world shipping so it is easy to export agricultural produce all over the world, *e.g.* tea to the USA, UK and Australia.

6 Demand

Although technology has produced substitutes for products such as rubber, tropical foodstuffs are still needed by the developed world.

FOREST PRODUCTS IN A TROPICAL COUNTRY – MALAYSIA

Malaysia is a federation of 13 states which became a new nation in 1963. The states were formerly British colonies. Two of the states, Sabah and Sarawak, are in northern Borneo.

Physical background

The Malay Peninsula is a corrugated highland area with very little flat land, though there are areas of undulating lowland. The mountains rise to over 2100 m.

The island of Borneo has coastal lowlands and a highland core rising to 4090 m.

The climate is equatorial although the east coast is also influenced by the north-east monsoon (November-March). Temperatures are high, averaging about 32°C all year. Rain falls throughout the year; the annual average is more than 2540 mm, and the wettest areas get as much as 6580 mm a year. The climate is monotonous; never cold, never excessively hot, with constant high humidity.

Natural vegetation is high evergreen forest and there are mangrove swamps in coastal areas. Up to 600 m, the evergreen forests are composed of dipterocarp trees (trees with winged seeds). This forest is a 'triple canopy' forest. Trees rise to 50-60 m in height, with their lowest branches as much as 30 m above the ground. Beneath them lies the second canopy of shade-loving trees of 6-15 m in height. The ground canopy is made up of bamboo, mosses, ferns and other large-leaved plants.

Over 600 metres above sea level, chestnut and oak trees become common. These forests extend up to 1250 m above sea level, where they give way to forests of small gnarled trees which are only 5 m high and are covered with mosses and lichens.

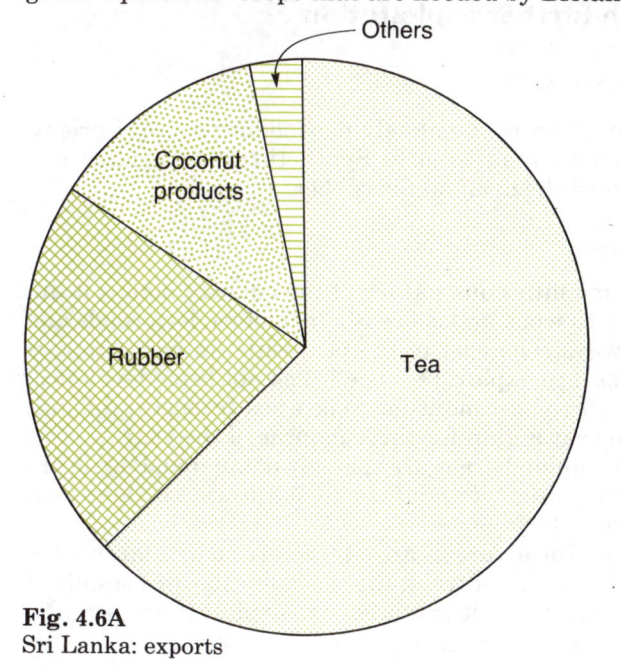

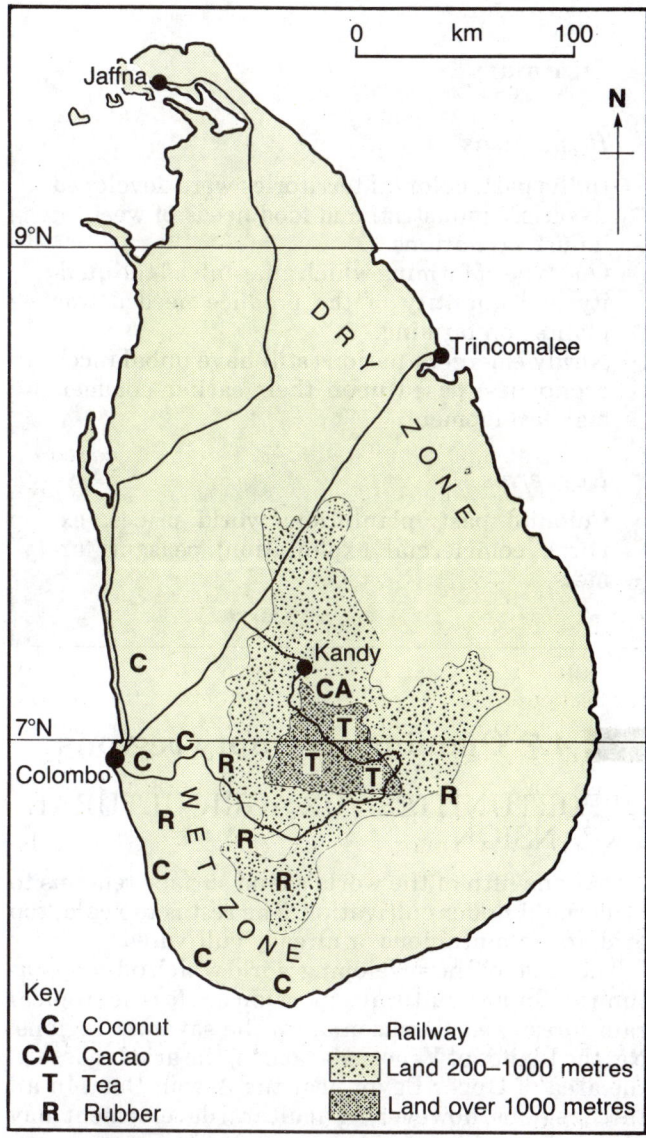

Fig. 4.6B Sri Lanka: export crops

Key
C Coconut
CA Cacao
T Tea
R Rubber
— Railway
Land 200–1000 metres
Land over 1000 metres

The developing world

Fig. 4.6C Tapping a rubber tree

Economic exploitation of the forest

The forests or 'jungle' were first seen as a barrier to economic development by the British, who wished to exploit the vast tin resources of Malaysia. Roads and railways had to be cut through dense forests to link mining centres with the ports from which the tin was exported. The tin deposits lay on the western side of the Malay Peninsula, so the eastern side remained undeveloped.

In 1878 the British introduced rubber to Malaysia. This industry also was concentrated on the western side of the peninsula, where roads, railways and ports existed. To make room for the plantations, the existing forests were cut and burned, for at that time the Malay hardwoods were of no commercial importance.

The chief forest products today are rubber, palm oil (plantation), timber and copra.

Malaysia produces 40 per cent of the world's rubber. Half of this amount is not produced on plantations, but by peasant farmers who live on the eastern side of the peninsula and grow a few rubber trees as a 'cash crop'. Coconut palms are grown on sandy soils near the sea and the chief product is vegetable oil.

Timber is cut around the edges of the equatorial forest up to a height of 600 m in all parts of Malaysia. The forests yield a variety of high-quality hardwoods. On the peninsula, the timber is moved by road; in Sabah and Sarawak the logs are floated down rivers. Most of the towns have sawmills and timber yards. Next to tin and rubber, timber is now the chief export of Malaysia.

Two-thirds of the forests of Malaysia remain completely untouched, but cutting is carefully controlled because the tree cover controls the flow of ground water and protects the soil from erosion. The forests therefore have to be conserved carefully.

Problems connected with further exploitation

Rubber

Production is completely dependent on world prices, which fluctuate greatly. Synthetic products have also reduced the demand for rubber.

Timber

The mountainous nature of the country makes it difficult to work and there is a lack of modern roads and railways. The east of the peninsula, in particular, is difficult to exploit because it has not been developed. The north-east monsoon makes sea transport difficult from that region for three months of the year.

The upland areas are sparsely populated. People are moving from the country to the town, so there is a labour shortage.

Equatorial forests are characterized by a large number of species of trees; there are few natural stands of one variety, so it is not easy to exploit the most valuable commercial species.

Summary

Basic ideas

In the past, colonial territories were developed to satisfy industrial and food needs of western industrial nations.
One type of farming which guaranteed the quality and quantity of the produce needed was plantation farming.
Newly emergent nations still have unbalanced economies, based upon their earlier commercial development.

Key terms

Colonial past; plantation; world prices; exports; commercial exploitation; peasant farmers.

4.7 Opening up empty regions

OPPORTUNITIES FOR AGRICULTURAL EXPANSION

About one-fifth of the world's land surface remains to be brought under cultivation. The rest is too cold, too arid, too mountainous or already cultivated.

The areas of the developing world which offer opportunities for agricultural expansion are (a) the tropical rain forests, e.g. Amazonia, (b) the savanna regions, e.g. the Llanos of Venezuela, and (c) the arid lands, e.g. the area of Upper Egypt near the Aswan Dam. In all these regions, however, agricultural development may also cause serious problems.

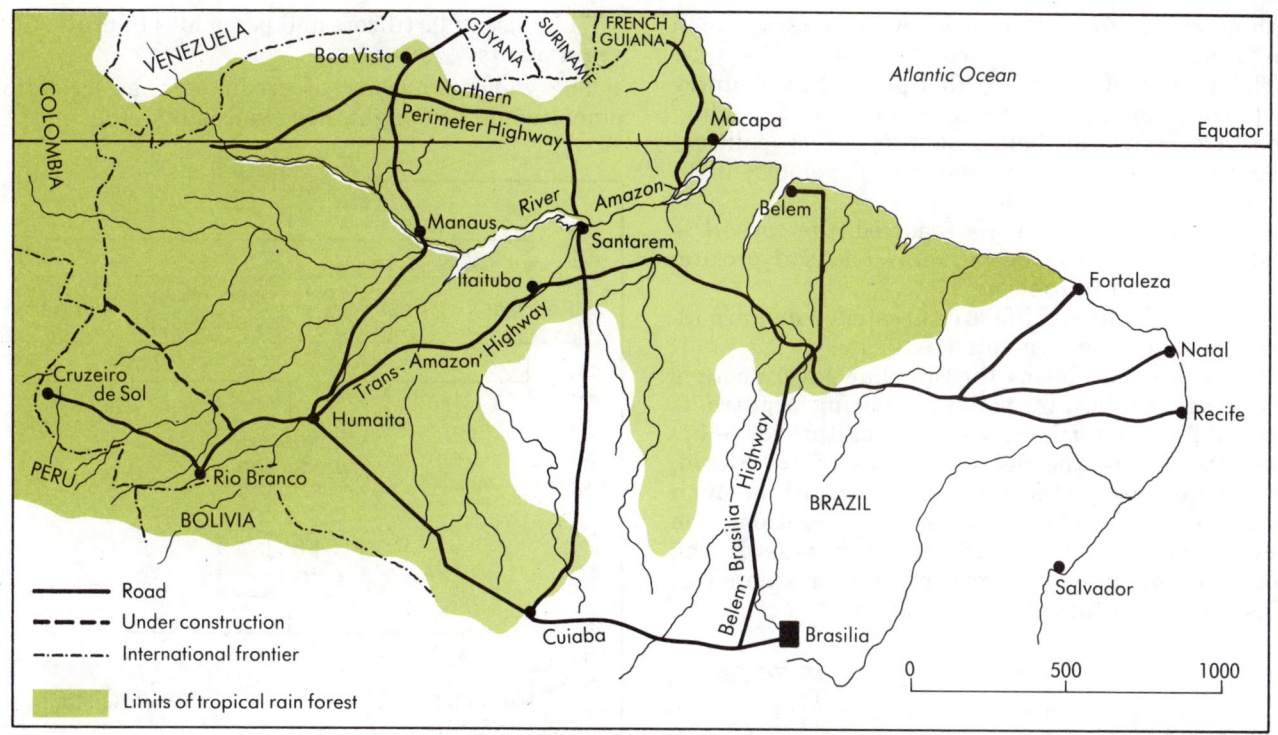

Fig. 4.7 Road network in Amazonia

Amazonia

The rain forest of Amazonia is much less densely populated than the rain forest of the Congo basin. The low density of population has been caused by (a) the 'robber economy' of the early European settlers and (b) the decline in the number of indigenous Indians because of European brutality and diseases.

Efforts to encourage settlement and cultivation in the past were unsuccessful, mainly because of the system of land ownership. European landowners own the river banks and inland areas, leaving the peasants with no land and no access to the rivers, which have been the only means of transport.

Small-scale experiments have shown that food and tree crops can be grown in this region. Away from the alluvial flood plain, cocoa, coffee and rubber grow well, while closer to the rivers rice, maize and beans can be grown.

Developments by Brazil

With a population of 124 millions, Brazil is the fifth largest country in the world. The very high population densities in cities like São Paulo and Rio de Janeiro contrast with the emptiness of the interior, particularly the Amazon basin. The overall density of population is only 14.6 per sq km; compared with 229 in the UK.

To utilize the resources of its share of Amazonia, Brazil has embarked on the building of a major road network. The main highway, the Trans-Amazon, is over 5500 kilometres long and runs from Recife to the border with Peru. It was finished in 1975. Other roads are being developed; some, like the Trans-Amazon with two lanes are seven metres wide and have a gravel surface. Land on each side of the Trans-Amazon has been reserved for government-organized settlements. A commercial centre is being established at approximately every 100 kilometres.

Landless families, mainly farm labourers from north-east Brazil, are given 100 hectares, of which two hectares are cleared. The government helps the pioneers to build their houses and to obtain credit for the purchase of food, seeds and equipment. The majority of settlers are not, however, supported by the government. They have been attracted to the new roads by the prospect of free land. Conditions for the new settlers are harsh. Despite the lush appearance of the forests, the nutrients in the soil are rapidly leached out by the heavy rainfall and soil erosion is an ever-present danger.

Large clearings for pasture have also been supported by government funds. The government hopes that cattle rearing will produce meat that can be sold overseas as well as in Brazil. Brahman cattle which can withstand the high temperatures have been introduced. In many areas, however, pastures have deteriorated and the government programme has been abandoned.

The opening up of the forest lands of Amazonia has not, as yet, resulted in the large-scale immigration for which the region was planned. Some of the largest settlements are the mining towns where iron ore, bauxite, manganese, tin and gold are extracted.

All the new developments seem designed to take what is valuable from the region as quickly as possible. This is a typical 'robber economy'.

Problems associated with the development

Ecologists are concerned at the widespread destruction of the tropical rain forest ecosystem, and the possible disappearance of the Amazonian forests because it could cause climatic changes and seriously affect the world's atmosphere balance. So far, deforestation has been most extensive in the eastern and southern fringes of the region, leaving the west relatively untouched.

The land-hungry poor of Brazil are unlikely to support any moves to conserve the rain forest. They need to use the land to produce food and earn money. They will therefore exploit the initial fertility of the soil, with no regard for the problems which may occur in the future.

The large landowners in other parts of the country see the opening up of Amazonia as a means of avoiding land reform nearer home, so they exert political pressure on the government for development to proceed as fast as possible.

When the forest cover is removed, the topsoil is washed away by the heavy rains and soil erosion becomes a serious problem.

Traditional ways of life are threatened and are already disappearing (see unit 4.5).

Despite these problems, the Brazilian government is determined to follow the policy of clearing large tracts of forest for new settlement and agricultural development. As one of the debtor nations of the world, Brazil's need to increase its natural wealth is much more important than any other consideration. The 'New Republic' government, however, regards the settling of 'social debt' — poverty, homelessness etc. — as more important than settling foreign debt.

Summary

Basic ideas

The Amazon Basin is seen by Brazil as an area of great potential wealth.
Its development could cause serious environmental and human problems.
Because of the need to develop resources swiftly in Brazil, economic exploitation of Amazonia is given greater priority than factors such as conservation.

Key terms

Robber economy; development; transport network; immigration; deforestation; environmental problems.

4.8 The Green Revolution

The Green Revolution was the term given to the programme of modernization of farming in the developing world. The revolution began in the 1960s. The aim was to increase food production at a faster rate than the rate at which the population grew in developing lands.

FEATURES OF THE GREEN REVOLUTION

1 Agricultural scientists produced new strains of grain which gave much heavier yields at harvest time. The first wheat strain, Mexipak, was developed in Mexico. It trebled the yield of wheat. The first new rice strain was grown in the Philippines (IR8) and more than trebled rice yields. The new seeds are now used in many developing countries. They are called HYVs (heavy-yield varieties).

2 Extension of irrigation so that water would be available at the place and time needed for the crops.

3 Wider use of fertilizers and pesticides to protect the grain plants.

4 The wider provision of credit so that irrigation pumps could be bought, new wells sunk etc.

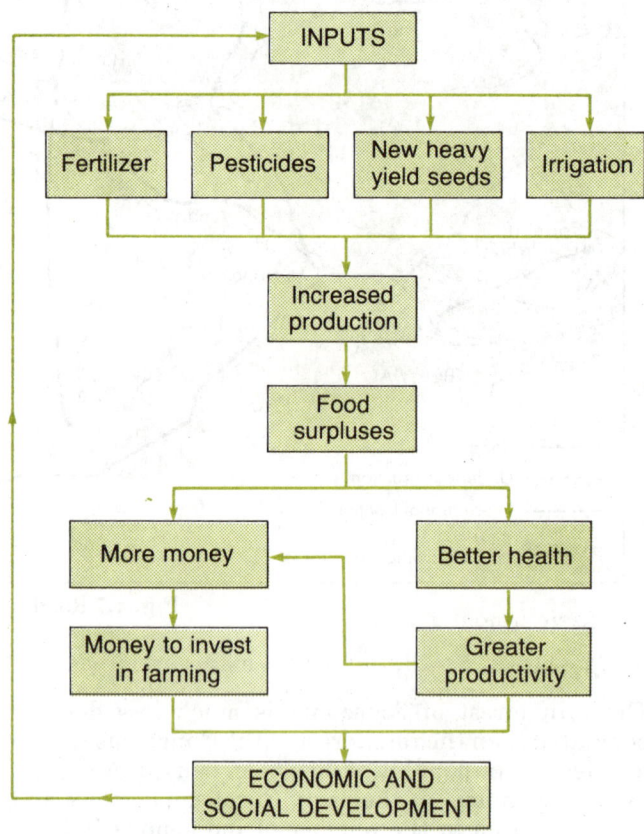

Fig. 4.8 A model of agricultural development

THE EFFECTS OF THE GREEN REVOLUTION

1 In India the introduction of HYV wheat resulted in an increase of 200 per cent in the production of wheat within a few years. This added substantially to the food supply of the country. The rice HYV strains have not been as successful as wheat because they are short-stemmed and easily damaged by the floods which are common in the main rice growing areas. Even so, in some areas such as the Punjab, the rice yield has increased greatly.

2 The wider use of fertilizers created a huge market for a new fertilizer industry. Fertilizer factories have sprung up all over India and have provided new jobs.

3 The extension of irrigation has increased the demand for electricity in the country areas to work pumps. Rural electrification has therefore proceeded rapidly and improved the standard of living a little.

PROBLEMS ASSOCIATED WITH THE GREEN REVOLUTION

1 HYV crops need heavy fertilization. Poor farmers cannot afford chemical fertilizers. Without the proper application of expensive fertilizers, yields drop by 30 per cent.

2 Yields are also affected by the fact that low standards of education result in some farmers being careless in operating irrigation techniques.

3 When yields are high in a particular district, the price for grain falls. The farmer has to sell his surplus

straight away because he needs money, so he gets the poorest prices and is not much better off than in the past.

4 If the harvest is poor, the farmer has to borrow from the village moneylenders to buy seeds and fertilizers. He finds it difficult to pay off the debt and has to work to pay the interest.

5 The concentration of HYV grains means that the supply of foods rich in carbohydrates has been increased. From a nutritional point of view the greater need is for protein-rich foods, such as lentils and peas.

6 The farmers who have benefited least from the Green Revolution are those who needed it most — the poorest farmers. The rich farmers have become wealthier so in some country areas the gap between rich and poor has increased.

7 Fertilizers have had to be imported in many underdeveloped countries. This has added to the problem of finding a way to pay for what is needed.

Summary

Basic ideas

The Green Revolution was a major attempt to improve farming techniques and productivity in the developing world.
The Green Revolution was based upon the scientific development of new heavy-yield strains of food crops such as rice, wheat and maize.
The effects of the 'revolution' are being limited by the inability of very poor farmers to cultivate the new crops as they should.

Key terms

Modernization; revolution; heavy-yield varieties; mexipak; fertilizers; fertilizer industry.

4.9 Developing transport networks

INTRODUCTION

In modern industrial countries, transport networks are highly developed, for the networks have been developed over a long period of time. Establishing transport networks is very expensive and in the developing world it is impossible for countries to build railways, roads and establish airline systems which compare with those found in the richer countries.

THE IMPORTANCE OF A WELL DEVELOPED NETWORK

1 It reduces the isolation of remote areas and helps bind the territory of newly-independent countries together.

2 Many developing countries get much of their income from exporting primary products such as minerals and food products, and they need to import fuel oil and fertilizers. A poorly-developed network makes the operation of this trade more difficult.

3 Efficient systems of distribution within a country can offset the worst effects of disasters and natural hazards, because help can be got to the problem areas quickly.

4 The supply and distribution of goods by a well-developed network can raise the standard of living throughout the country.

FACTORS WHICH HAVE DETERMINED THE DEVELOPMENT OF TRANSPORT NETWORKS IN THE DEVELOPING LANDS

1 The transport systems are a product of the colonial period and were designed to:
(a) establish political administration by the colonial power;
(b) provide a means for getting export crops and minerals to the coast, to be shipped to the colonial power which, in return, provide the colony with manufactured goods;

2 The basic pattern, therefore, was a spinal transport system which linked interior areas with ports, for example, north-south routes in the eastern half of West Africa and east-west routes to the Atlantic ports in the western half of West Africa.

3 Most colonial powers wanted to control roads and railways completely and did not always use the shortest or most economical route. In Guinea, Senegal and Burkina Faso, for example, the French would not build routes to the nearest ports, which were in British colonies, and instead built roundabout routes to French ports such as Abidjan and Cotonou.

4 Transport systems were confined to the territories of single colonial powers, so there were no efficient international transport links in many areas.

5 Since independence, these patterns have been maintained because:
(a) the economies of the new countries may still be dominated by the old colonial powers;
(b) the new developing countries are not wealthy enough to change the basic transport pattern;
(c) in many areas there has not yet been sufficient economic expansion or change in the pattern of production to make big changes necessary. One exception is Nigeria, which has been able to use its oil wealth to build new networks.

A MODEL OF THE DEVELOPMENT OF A TRANSPORT NETWORK

Although every country is different, it is possible to identify a general pattern of network development in the developing world. This model is called the Taaffe model and it was worked out from studies of Brazil, East Africa, Ghana, Nigeria and Malaysia. This model identifies four main stages of development:

Stage 1 — Small ports and trading stations

In many countries at this stage, rivers and waterways were the main forms of transport with small coastal settlements handling the colonial trade. These ports had small hinterlands and had no connection with each other.

The developing world

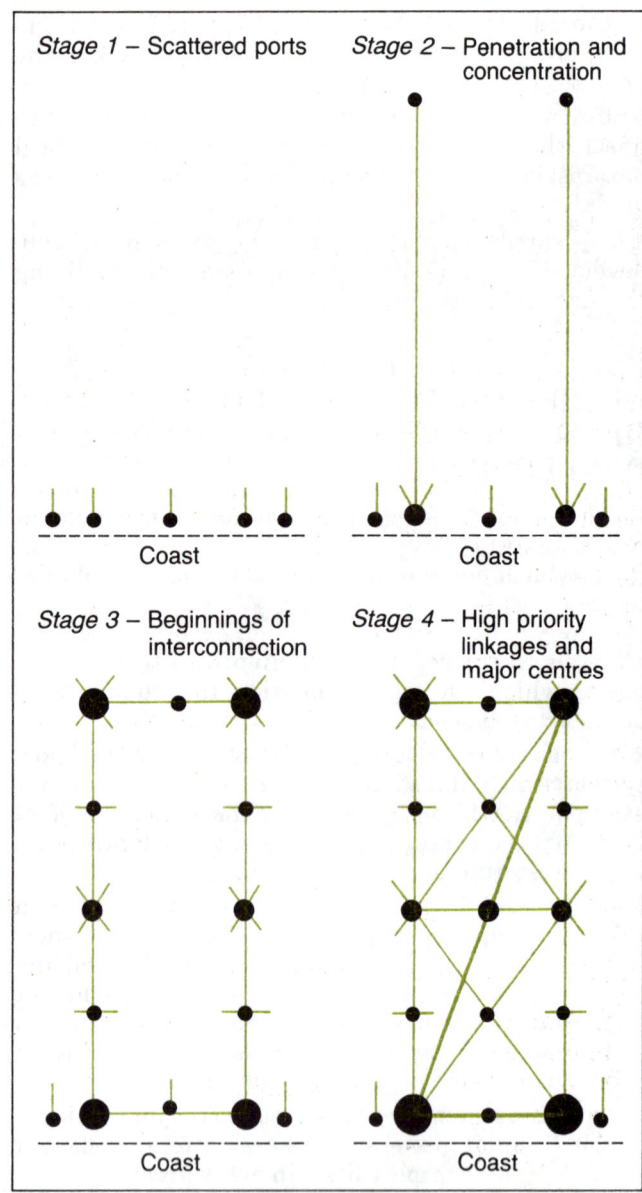

Fig. 4.9A Taaffe's model of the development of a transport network

- Stage 1 – Scattered ports
- Stage 2 – Penetration and concentration
- Stage 3 – Beginnings of interconnection
- Stage 4 – High priority linkages and major centres

Stage 2 — Penetration and port concentration

A few ports are selected, from which new lines of communication are built inland to link the ports with the areas which produce the chief exports. At the same time, the colonial power could establish its power over inland areas away from the coast. Because of the concentration on a few ports, better port facilities could be built and trade improved. The ports which were not chosen died.

Stage 3 — Beginning of interconnection

In this phase, feeder routes develop which lead direct to the chief ports and the chief inland centres which have developed along the routeways. Similar commercial centres grow along the routeways between the main towns. Some of the inland centres also begin to link up.

Stage 4 — Accessible centres grow rapidly, high-priority linkages emerge

The linkages between centres continue to grow and the most accessible centres become the main points of economic growth. Ports grow as trade increases. All the chief inland towns are linked, but some routes become especially important — the high-priority linkages e.g. the Lagos-Ibadan expressway in Nigeria.

THE VALUE OF THE MODEL

1 It emphasizes the principles which have been at work in many developing countries;

2 It takes into account the colonial factors, which were so important in the early days;

3 It applies to more than one form of transport;

4 It gives us a general pattern which makes it easier to identify unique features which may only apply to a single country.

WEAKNESSES OF THE MODEL

1 It cannot be used to understand the pattern of transport development in an inland country such as Zambia.

2 In some countries, such as Kenya, a series of ports did not develop and trade was concentrated at the one port of Mombasa; the model does not work for such countries.

3 Within the same developing country one part of the network may be at a different stage to another. Figure 4.9B shows that the railways in north-east Brazil are at a different stage from those in the south-east around Rio de Janeiro and Santos.

Fig. 4.9B Railways in Eastern Brazil, showing different stages in network development

The developing world 101

Summary

Basic ideas
Present economic development may be hampered by historic networks.
The continued economic dominance of the advanced nations has resulted largely in the maintenance of colonial networks.
The Taaffe model may be applied to a number of different countries and to different forms of transport.

Key terms
Network; colonial period; Taaffe model; port concentration; interconnection; high-priority linkages.

4.10 Establishing New Industries

THE IMPORTANCE OF INDUSTRIALIZATION

Many governments of developing countries see industrialization as the key to economic growth. Industrialization is the increase of that proportion of total GNP created by the manufacture of goods. The governments of developing countries argue that, as was the case in western Europe, USA, Japan and the USSR, the income and job opportunities will grow when their countries have become industrialized.

OBSTACLES TO INDUSTRIALIZATION IN THE DEVELOPING WORLD

1 Developing countries lie on the edge or periphery of the world economy, which is concentrated in the core regions of Europe, North America, Japan and neighbouring countries. The core areas are so powerful that they may stifle opportunities for industrialization in periphery areas, which they use as their markets;

2 Poor infrastructures on which to build modern industries — road and railway networks are not well developed; electrical power and basic services needed by factories are not readily available; they do not have information technology networks to compare with those of the developed nations;

3 Shortage of skilled labour, with lower educational standards;

4 Limited capital and managerial expertise to get industries going;

5 Limited local markets for new industries, because many people have low purchasing power and transport networks do not make exporting easy;

6 Capital, technology, and skilled people may have to be imported in the form of aid and this may increase dependence on developed nations (see unit 4.15);

7 Trade barriers: rich countries often impose *import duties* which restrict imports, e.g. Ghana cannot afford to export manufactured chocolate to the UK and Germany.

A MODEL OF INDUSTRIALIZATION

In South America it is possible to recognize three stages in the industrialization of developing countries. All the countries in South America have experienced stage 1 and moved on to stage 2. Brazil and Argentina have entered the third stage.

Stage 1 — The start of industrialization

This is the phase in which industries developed to process exports and to make basic goods for the local market. These industries are low-technology industries. The manufacture of corned beef in Argentina and Uruguay, and the concentration of copper ore for export from Chile are examples of this phase. Bottled drinks, cigarettes and cheap clothes which are sold in local areas are also typical products of this stage. Because the new factories are sited in towns, people move from the countryside to urban areas. Many of the factory owners are immigrants from developed countries, who also import machinery and skilled workers to run the factories.

Stage 2 — Import substitution

In this phase new factories are built to make things which are needed in the country and which had previously been imported. The advantages of this development are:

(a) it provides factory work for local people;

(b) it can make goods cheaper because local workers are not paid as much as the workers in factories in the industrial countries;

(c) it cuts the import bill and makes the developing country economically stronger.

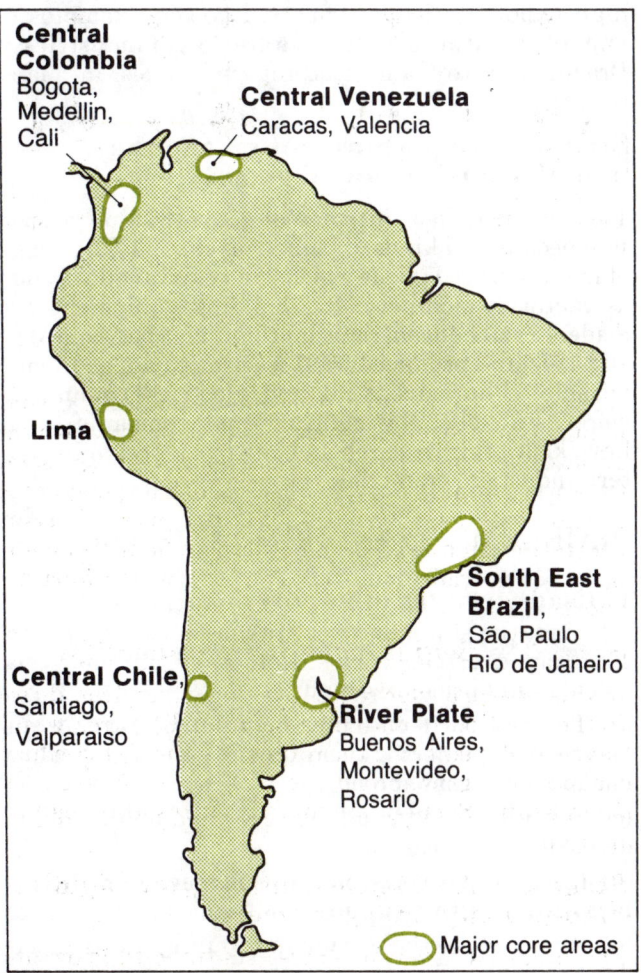

Fig. 4.10A Chief industrial core areas of South America

Fig. 4.10B Rio de Janeiro showing part of the Ipanema Beach with hotels and shops behind

South American countries entered this stage when they were cut off from their suppliers by two world wars. Since 1950, new industries have been encouraged by grants, tax allowances, subsidies and high import duties on imported goods. Examples of import substitution industries are the car industries of Brazil, and toy and clothing industries in many countries.

Stage 3 — Export promotion and the manufacture of capital goods

This is also called the stage of general industrialization because all kinds of industries expand. The range of manufactured goods widens and capital goods such as factory machinery and building equipment are made. Brazil concentrated on this phase between 1968 and 1973 and produced what was called an 'economic miracle'. Pharmaceutical and electrical industries were established by multinational companies that have kept their research and chief production in western industrial countries.

PROBLEMS OF INDUSTRIALIZATION

1 Disadvantages of import substitution

(a) Since the new industries are subsidized and protected from overseas competition, they are not very efficient and prices are high;
(b) The standard of living may actually go down, because consumers can no longer get good quality, cheap goods from abroad;
(c) Subsidies and tax allowances are a financial burden for the government;
(d) It sometimes costs more to buy machinery for the factories than to continue to buy goods from abroad;
(e) It may make the developing country more dependent upon the advanced industrial countries, because money has to be borrowed:

(i) to build the new factories;
(ii) to attract skilled foreign workers;
(iii) concessions to foreign companies may have to be paid for by obtaining foreign loans.

2 Disadvantages of a policy of general industrialization

(a) It may create heavy foreign debts;
(b) The country may become too dependent upon foreign multinational companies;
(c) Multinational companies take their profits out of the country, so there is little local benefit.

3 Problems of industrial concentration in major cities

(a) Mass migration into the cities, and the creation of shanty towns and other social problems;
(b) The contrast between the rich and poor regions is highlighted, which may result in political divisions;
(c) Traffic congestion and pollution in the chief cities — see unit 4.13.

As a result of these problems, some governments are now subsidizing firms to move from core to peripheral parts of the country; and are building new towns as industrial growth centres e.g. Ciudad Guayana in Venezuela.

THE EFFECTS OF INDUSTRIALIZATION

In South America, the increase in industrialization has not achieved the hoped-for results because:

1 So many concessions have been made to industry, that taxes are not adding to the wealth of the nation.
2 New jobs have not been created in large numbers, because new technology is automated.
3 Factory products have killed off old handicrafts such as shoemaking.

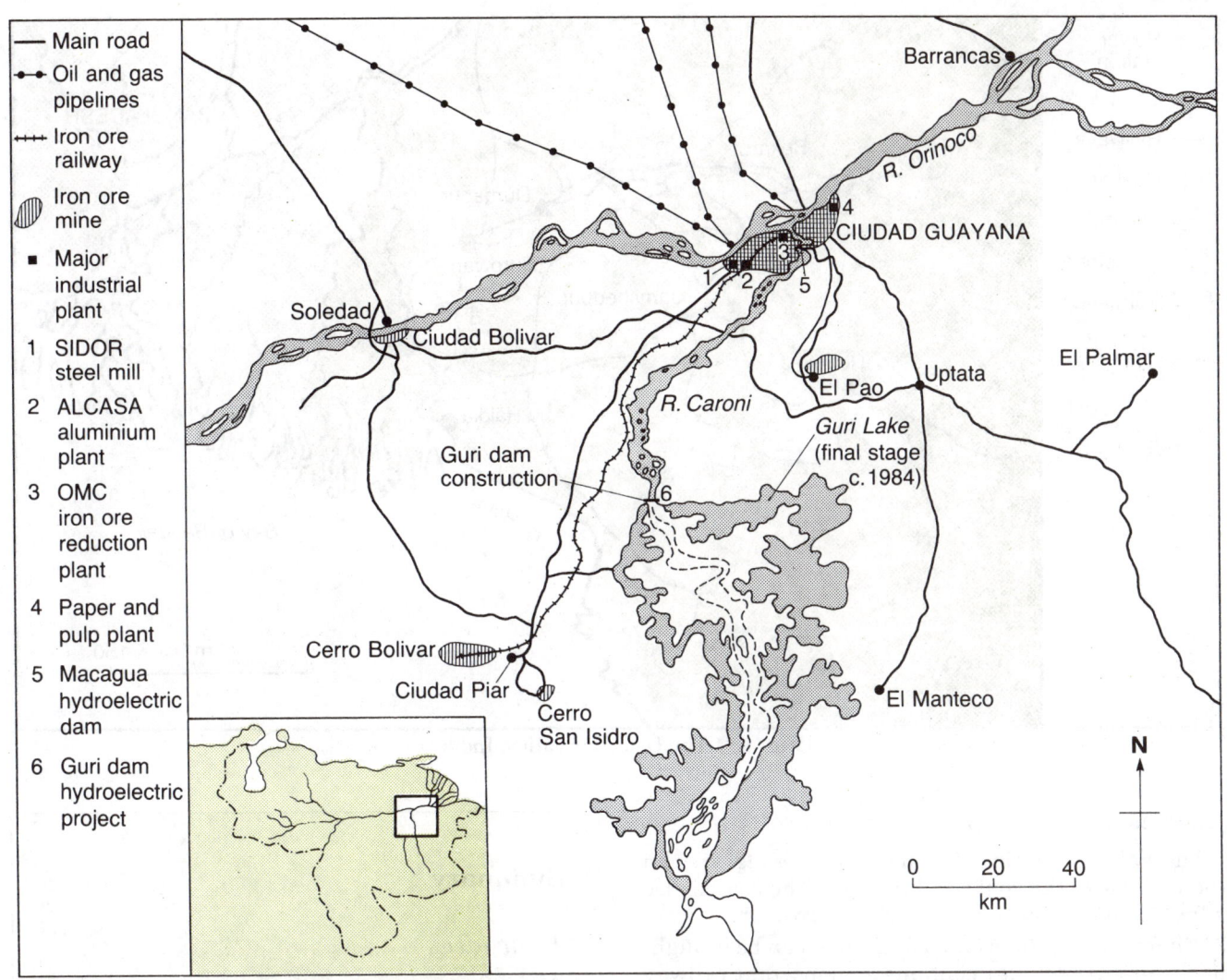

Fig. 4.10C Industrial activities in Ciudad Guayana and vicinity in Venezuela

Key to map:
- Main road
- Oil and gas pipelines
- Iron ore railway
- Iron ore mine
- Major industrial plant
1. SIDOR steel mill
2. ALCASA aluminium plant
3. OMC iron ore reduction plant
4. Paper and pulp plant
5. Macagua hydroelectric dam
6. Guri dam hydroelectric project

4 New consumer industries have added to health problems by increasing smoking and alcoholism.

5 Economic inequalities have not been reduced. the gap between rich and poor has been emphasized.

6 Most of the benefits of industrialization have been exported to their home countries by the multinational companies.

Summary

Basic ideas

Many governments of developing countries see industrialization as the key to economic growth.
It is possible to identify three stages in the industrialization of many developing countries. In some countries, the increased industrialization has not produced the hoped-for economic and social results.

Key terms

GNP; core and periphery; infrastructure; import substitution; export promotion; foreign debt; economic miracle.

4.11 Multi-purpose development schemes

DEFINITION

A multi-purpose development scheme is a modern project undertaken by a developing country with the financial and technical assistance of advanced industrial nations. Such projects are intended to increase the wealth of the country and the standard of living of its inhabitants. It is termed 'multi-purpose' because the project is designed to produce more than one result. For example, a large dam may be built to control flooding, to store water for irrigation and to provide a source for hydroelectricity with which to power new industries.

The Damodar valley, India

The Damodar River is a tributary of the River Hooghly, by which the city of Calcutta stands. India is still a land of villages, with only 20 per cent of its people living in towns and cities. The country has to face the massive problem of raising the standard of living of its 700 million people. In common with other developing countries, India is anxious to develop major industries as a means of increasing the wealth of the nation. One of the most important projects has been developed in the Damodar valley.

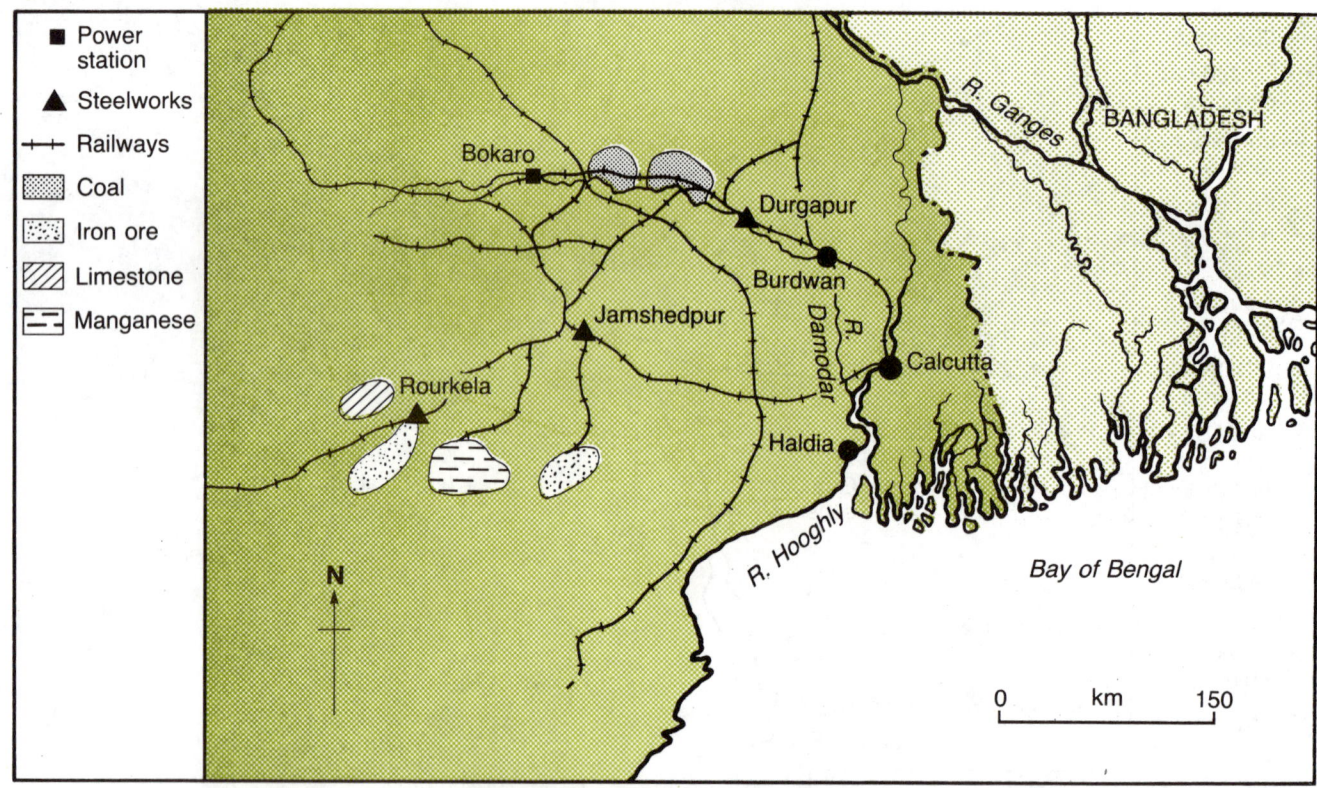

Fig. 4.11 The Damodar valley, India

Reasons for the Damodar valley project

1 The valley contains the chief coal-mining area in India. Some of the coal is coking coal. The coal is also a fuel for power stations such as Bokaro.

2 Other raw materials for making steel can be brought in cheaply. The valley contains an important railway line from Calcutta to the north. The railway is used to bring together iron ore, limestone and manganese. A steelworks already existed at Jamshedpur and other works have now been built at Rourkela and Durgapur and another is planned for Bokaro.

3 Since India is not a rich country and has little experience of developing major industrial complexes, assistance has been given by the UK, USSR and the German Federal Republic.

4 There is a convenient market for the steel which is produced. It is taken by road and rail to steel-using factories in Calcutta. It can also be exported from Calcutta.

5 The establishment of the steelworks is only part of the development. A number of dams have been built on the Damodar river in the Bokaro-Durgapur areas. At some of these dams there are hydroelectric power stations, which also serve the industrial complex.

6 The dams control the flow of the river. In the monsoon season, water is held back in the reservoirs to stop the river flooding its lower valley. In the dry season the water is released to irrigate the farmland. Before the dams were built, monsoon floods killed thousands and caused disease and famine.

7 Because there is now a regular and guaranteed supply of water, canals have been cut to develop a large area of farmland around Burdwan. This has increased the supply of food in the region and made the farmers more prosperous.

The Damodar valley project is therefore a 'multipurpose' scheme.

Summary

Basic ideas

A multi-purpose scheme is designed to provide a number of uses for a project.
Multi-purpose projects are intended to increase substantially the economic prosperity of a developing country.

Key terms

Development; multi-purpose; increasing national wealth; international aid; flood control; hydroelectricity.

4.12 Urbanization and the growth of shanty towns

At present, the developing countries are not as urbanized as the developed countries of the world. Despite its huge cities, for example, 80 per cent of the people of India still live in villages, while 80 per cent of the people of Britain live in towns. In the developing world, however, people are now moving to the cities, which are growing at a faster rate than the cities of the industrial countries.

REASONS FOR URBANIZATION IN DEVELOPING COUNTRIES

1 The chief reason is the decline of the death rate. Improvements in diet, health, sanitation and so on mean that fewer infants die soon after birth. Better

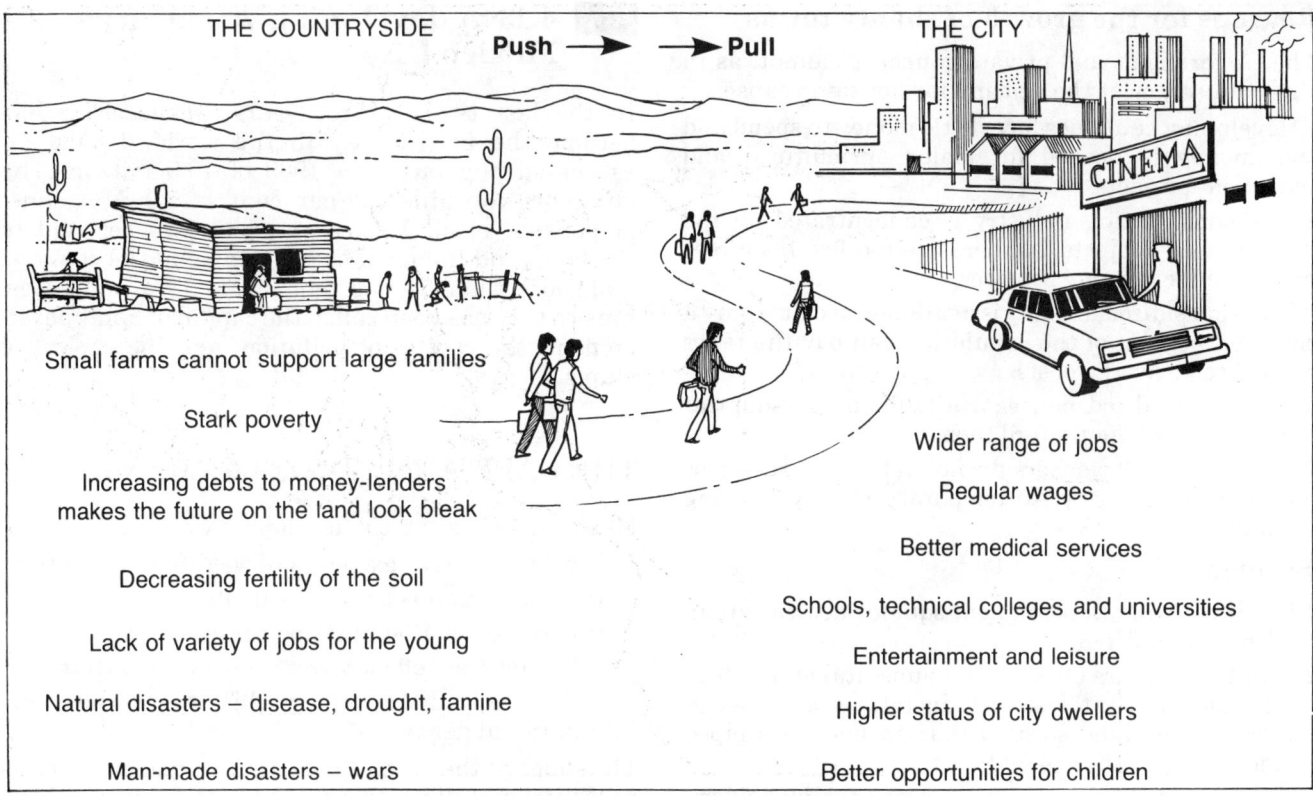

Fig. 4.12A The push-pull model of migration

THE COUNTRYSIDE — Push → Pull — **THE CITY**

- Small farms cannot support large families
- Stark poverty
- Increasing debts to money-lenders makes the future on the land look bleak
- Decreasing fertility of the soil
- Lack of variety of jobs for the young
- Natural disasters – disease, drought, famine
- Man-made disasters – wars

- Wider range of jobs
- Regular wages
- Better medical services
- Schools, technical colleges and universities
- Entertainment and leisure
- Higher status of city dwellers
- Better opportunities for children

medical services also mean that people live longer. Throughout the developing world, births now greatly exceed deaths, so there is a rapid population increase. This increase is greater in the cities than in the countryside, because medical and health services are better in the cities, so the cities are growing faster than the rural settlements.

2 People move from the country to the towns because the towns offer higher standards of living, higher wages and more varied job opportunities. This is not always so, but is a view firmly held by rural emigrants.

3 Others leave the country because of natural disasters such as drought, flood, earthquakes and famine and make for the cities to start a new life.

EFFECTS OF URBANIZATION

1 Overcrowding in the poorer areas of the cities. A survey in India showed, for example, that over half the families lived in single rooms. Migrants making for the cities stay with relatives or people from the same village and this adds to the overcrowding.

2 City authorities are faced with tremendous housing and welfare problems.

3 Unplanned 'squatter' settlements develop within the cities where there is space (*e.g.* the bustees of Calcutta), or, more usually, on the edges of cities (*e.g.* the barriadas of Peru). These settlements are called shanty towns.

Fig. 4.12B A shanty town in Bangladesh

Reasons for the growth of shanty towns

The Government and private concerns cannot, as in this country, meet the demand for houses because:

1 Developing countries have little money to spend and this money is needed for major agricultural and industrial projects.

2 The construction industry is concentrated on the development projects, so there are too few resources available for housing schemes.

3 Little subsidized housing is available, because only a small proportion of the population can pay the taxes needed to cover the costs.

4 When subsidized houses are built, many squatter families still cannot afford them.

5 Some migrant workers do not intend to stay permanently in the city, so temporary shanty housing suits them.

Problems

1 Families living in permanent squalor deteriorate in health and vitality.

2 Shanty towns are often built on unsuitable sites, e.g. the ground may be too steep to install a gravity sewer system, or the land so high that an adequate piped water supply cannot be laid on.

3 The danger of contaminated water causing epidemics.

4 Because the shanty towns are on the edges of large cities, people have to travel long distances to work and so use their wages on travel instead of improving their living conditions.

5 Shanty town dwellers do not pay rates or taxes so the city has less money for improvement projects.

6 Overcrowding in squalid conditions on the edges of cities can lead to political and social unrest.

Ways of improving the situation

1 Encouraging birth control to reduce the rapid population growth.

2 Developing rural areas, so that fewer migrants are attracted to the cities.

3 Spending more of the national resources on housing and social welfare.

4 In view of the poverty of the state and of those living in the shanty towns, providing sites with concrete roads, piped water and sewerage so that shanty towns can develop in an orderly way and to a healthier standard.

Summary

Basic ideas

Urbanization is the chief common feature of developing countries;

Urbanization has led to overcrowding and the establishment of unplanned squatter settlements, called shanty towns;

The contrasts between rich and poor in the cities can lead to social and political unrest.

Key terms

Urbanization; death rate; overcrowding; shanty towns; health problems; birth control.

4.13 A developing world city — Mexico City

In the last two or three years, Mexico City has become the largest city in the world. It had an estimated population in 1989 of 19.5 million. The city now contains 22 per cent of all Mexicans; 66 per cent of all Mexican students, 70 per cent of the bank and financial organizations in the country, and more than 50 per cent of Mexico's industries. Mexico City has been called the capital of underdevelopment, the capital of pollution, and the capital of slums.

THE CAPITAL OF DEVELOPMENT

Mexico City is a typical developing world city:
— it contains great extremes of wealth and poverty;
— the population is growing rapidly;
— it is ringed by illegal slum cities;
— it cannot cope efficiently with major disasters;
— it is the capital of a country which has considerable international debts.

The shops of the 'Zona Rosa' in the city centre are as exclusive and expensive as those of Paris and New York. There are also expensive restaurants, magnificent churches and modern office blocks. Yet two million people in the city have no running water, three million have homes with no sewage system and 40 per cent of the population are unemployed or only have occasional work. The *pepenadores* live by picking over rubbish dumps and selling the reusable bits of metal and plastic they find. Many beggars live and die on the city streets.

The city does not have a well-developed infrastructure and when crises or disasters happen they cannot be handled as well as in a city in a rich, developed country. The recent earthquake disaster highlighted problems of corrupt building companies, poor planning decisions and delays in mounting large-scale rescue operations.

Like many other developing countries, Mexico is now deeply in debt. Mexico owes $US 1200 per head of population. The peso has been greatly devalued and the country cannot afford to undertake projects which would help improve its social and economic problems.

THE CAPITAL OF POLLUTION

At the end of the Second World War, the Mexicans decided on a policy of industrialization, which was concentrated in the cities and in Mexico City in particular. Poor peasants were attracted to the cities and populations increased rapidly. Improved medical care cut the death rate and kept more babies alive. As a result, Mexico City has become a huge industrial centre. There is a permanent cloud of greyish-brown fog over the city. Just breathing in Mexico City is said to be the equivalent of smoking two packets of cigarettes a day. Roughly 30 000 children and 70 000 adults in the city die each year from diseases caused by pollution.

Causes of pollution

1 130 000 factories exist in the city area.

2 Pollution laws are not strictly enforced.

Fig. 4.13A
Mexico City

3 Neither the factory owners nor the government can afford expensive anti-pollution equipment.
4 Most of the three million cars and 7 000 diesel buses in the city are old and have inefficient engines.
5 The city is 2500 metres above sea level, so the air is thin. As a result, the engines produce extra amounts of carbon monoxide and hydrocarbon pollution.
6 The city is surrounded by mountains, which hold the blanket of fog over the city.

Efforts to reduce pollution

1 New laws in 1983 to limit factory pollution and to fine factory owners heavily if they break the laws.
2 'Plan Texcoco', designed to stop the dust storms during which dust and burning pollutants are blown into people's eyes.
3 Pemex, the national petroleum company, has reduced the amount of sulphur in diesel fuel.

CAPITAL OF SLUMS

Mexico City has a massive housing problem. The average family size is 5.5 persons and 26 per cent of all families live in single rooms. Even professional people find it difficult to get reasonable accommodation. As a result the city is now ringed with illegal slum cities. These are founded by the *paracaidistas* — the 'parachutists', who invade private land suddenly and build huts and shacks as quickly as possible. The slums have no services and there are health and political problems for the government.

REASONS FOR THE GROWTH OF THE POPULATION OF MEXICO CITY

1 Rapid immigration into the city as a result of industrialization.
2 'Push' from the country areas, where there is extreme poverty.
3 A high birth rate.
4 Ineffective population control — 90 per cent of the people are Roman Catholic.
5 Decline in the death rate from 9.6 to 6.7 per 1000 during the 1970s.

EFFECTS OF THE GROWTH OF THE CITY

1 Mexico City has lost 75 per cent of the woodland in its region since 1945, and this has reduced the amount of water available.
2 More water has to be pumped from the sub-soil, and parts of the city have now sunk 30 feet.
3 Traffic congestion — a six-lane orbital motorway, called the *Periferico* has been built, on which there are massive traffic jams.
4 Public services, especially sewerage, are inadequate.
5 Fifty per cent of the people have no medical services.
6 Government departments are bureaucratic and slow, some are corrupt. As a result the problems grow faster than solutions can be found for them.

Summary

Basic ideas

Mexico city is now the largest city in the world, and typifies the problems facing the developing world.
Attempts to achieve development through industrialization have created further problems.
The growth in population has led to the creation of many shanty towns.

Key terms

Infrastructure; pollution; slum cities; industrialization; international debts; corruption.

4.14 Tourism in the developing world — Tanzania

Many developing countries now see tourism as a means of earning money from wealthier nations. This currency is needed to buy manufactured goods and industrial machinery. Citizens of countries such as the USA, Japan, Germany, the UK and Australia travel throughout the world on holidays, for cheap air fares have made it worth travelling long distances for short stays of two to three weeks.

Tanzania is one of the countries in which the tourist industry is being developed. Its attractions include:

1 Landscape. It contains the highest mountain in Africa (Mount Kilimanjaro) and borders the three largest lakes in the continent (Lake Victoria, Lake Malawi and Lake Tanganyika).
2 It contains two of the world's largest game sanctuaries (Serengeti and Ngorongoro) and one of the world's most important prehistoric sites (Olduvai Gorge). There are eight game reserves in all in the country.
3 Tanzania borders the Indian Ocean, and north of Dar es Salaam there are vast unspoiled sandy beaches.
4 The climate is not inhospitable for white people. There are two dry seasons a year — the cool season from June to September and the hot, dry season from mid-December to February. Although the climate at the coast is otherwise hot and humid, the highlands provide much cooler conditions.
5 Dar es Salaam and Zanzibar provide links with the Arab world, so visitors can have both an 'African' and 'Arab' holiday.
6 For many visitors there is no serious language barrier. Tanganyika (now Tanzania) and Zanzibar were former British colonies. English is widely spoken in cities and tourist areas, while German is spoken in the chief hotels on the coast.
7 Tanzania has its own brand of socialism. Some visitors are very interested in seeing *ujamaa* villages which are a sort of African kibbutz.
8 The Tanzanian Tourist Corporation has built modern, western-style hotels in the most attractive tourist centres.

The developing world 109

perienced an increase in its national debt and finds it increasingly difficult to maintain the infrastructure of tourism — the luxury hotels, travel arrangements, expensive food and drink expected by wealthy western tourists on holiday.

> **Summary**
>
> *Basic ideas*
>
> Developing countries have established tourist industries as a major source of income.
> There are serious problems assoaciated with the successful establishment of the industry.
> Western holidaymakers often expect standards of comfort and luxury which are difficult to supply in the developing world.
>
> *Key terms*
>
> Foreign currency; game sanctuaries; terrorism; political instability; international debt; infrastructure.

Fig. 4.14 Tanzania: tourism

PROBLEMS AFFECTING THE DEVELOPMENT OF TOURISM

The development of tourist attractions affects and even destroys traditional ways of life, *e.g.* if the animals are strictly protected in the game preserves, tribes that have lived as hunters are unable to follow the old way of life. Tourists are attracted by traditional crafts — Makonda wood carvings, Masai beadwork and fabric weaving. To cater for western tastes and to meet new demand the old crafts become artificial.

Tourism in Tanzania is affected by the political instability of East Africa. It is not on friendly terms with Uganda so East African package tours have had to be altered.

It is not easy to develop tourism on a capitalist basis for western visitors in a socialist country.

Tanzania is not yet able to offer the quality or range of holiday accommodation available in neighbouring Kenya, so most western visitors are attracted to Kenya.

The growth of terrorism throughout the world has made western travellers, particularly Americans, more cautious about travelling in the developing countries.

Like many developing countries, Tanzania has ex-

4.15 Aid from the Developed World

DEFINITION

International aid is the provision of expertise, manufactured goods, food and sums of money by richer developed nations to the developing world, to help the poorer countries achieve economic and social progress.

REASONS WHY RICH COUNTRIES GIVE AID

1 Many people in Western Europe believe that countries like France, Britain, Holland and Belgium, which were formerly colonial powers, now have a duty to help the colonies they once exploited.

2 Non-colonial powers, such as the Scandinavian countries, believe that helping the poorer countries is a moral duty.

3 The aid helps developing countries establish sound governments and stronger economies, which favour a good climate for world trade and world peace.

4 If living standards are raised in developing countries, they will buy more goods from the industrialized nations and so the developed world will benefit itself by giving aid.

5 If a developing country becomes dependent upon a western or communist country for long-term help, the influence of the donor (giver) nation will be increased in that country. So it is a way of extending political influence.

6 Technical experts from the developed country are able to obtain interesting and well-paid jobs running the development projects paid for by the international aid.

SOURCES OF AID

There are four main sources:

1 Aid from one country to another
The aid money is usually spent in the country which gives it, to buy machinery, industrial raw materials etc.

Fig. 4.15A
Bob Geldof and his Band Aid activities

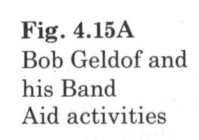

2 Technical assistance

Sending skilled teachers, nurses, scientists, engineers and other skilled experts who are in short supply in the developing country. Some of the experts work to train local people in their skills, but others manage and direct the aid programmes operating in the country.

3 Voluntary organizations

Most of these collect money in the richer countries to buy food and equipment and to pay experts to help developing countries. In Britain, organizations such as Oxfam and Christian Aid work in this way. Band Aid was an example of how millions of pounds of voluntary aid for the developing world can be organized.

4 International organizations

Organizations such as the International Bank of Reconstruction, and the International Development Association, arrange to provide loans for the developing countries. Interest has to be paid on the loans, and since the prices the developing countries get for their commodities have fallen, some developing countries now find that the interest they owe is almost impossible to pay.

TYPES OF AID

International aid falls into two main categories (see fig. 4.15B) — private aid and official aid.

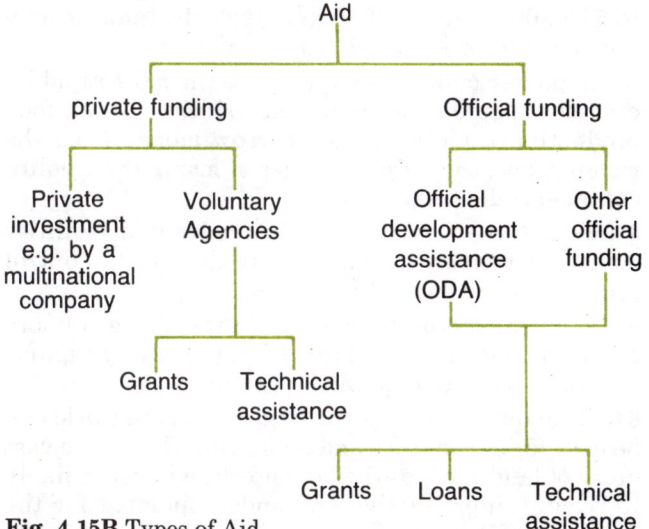

Fig. 4.15B Types of Aid

Official aid is either given as bilateral aid (one country to another) or as multinational (multilateral) aid, in which the funds are contributed by a number of countries and coordinated by an international organization such as the United Nations. The most important part of the aid programme of national governments is the Official Development Assistance (ODA), which is given as grants or loans on generous conditions. It has been suggested that western countries should give 0.7 per cent of their GNP as ODA, but this has never been agreed. The percentage given by different countries varies considerably.

Private aid may come from a number of sources. Powerful multinational companies and banks may provide the capital needed for a development project in a country in which they are especially interested. Voluntary organizations also give private aid.

PATTERNS OF AID

1 Until the late 1960s, most aid was tied to particular projects, especially large prestigious projects such as the Aswan High Dam and the Volta River project. The rich countries liked this type of aid, because they could sell their technology to the projects and control how the money was spent.

2 Since the 1970s, the emphasis has been upon aid for rural areas and is called 'non-project' aid, because it goes to an overall development programme and not to a single project.

3 Aid is not given by western countries only. The oil-producing countries of OPEC, the CIS and China are also involved in giving aid.

4 Since 1970 there has been a growing rift between the rich and poor countries of the world — the 'North' and 'South'. The developing countries of the 'South' argue that aid should be increased and that they should be given better trading agreements with the 'North' so that the wealth of the world can be shared more fairly.

Summary

Basic ideas

Aid from the developed countries takes a variety of forms.
Aid programmes also benefit the economies of the donor nations.
Aid is seen by the developing countries as one means of providing them with a fairer share of the world's wealth.

Key terms

International aid; technical assistance; official aid; private aid; non-project aid; 'north' and 'south'.

5 SOCIAL AND ENVIRONMENTAL ISSUES

5.1 The growth of world population

Figure 5.1 shows how rapidly the population of the world has grown since 1750. Before that time, the total population was more or less stable. Over the last 200 years, however, the rate of growth has become increasingly rapid. Estimates suggest that the rate will continue to increase until the end of the century.

REASONS FOR THE RAPID INCREASE IN POPULATION IN MODERN TIMES

1 The middle of the 18th century saw the start of the agricultural and industrial 'revolutions' in Western Europe, which affected the rest of the world. Scientific developments in farming enabled the production of food crops and meat to be increased tremendously, so the land could support far more people.

2 The new industries required many more workers and raw materials. New forms of transport made it possible to collect food supplies and raw materials from any part of the world. Migrants from the industrial countries took the new technology and knowledge to 'empty' lands such as the Pampas and Prairies and established new nations in North America, South America and Australasia. The new countries themselves began to grow rapidly.

3 Modern developments in science included a vast increase in medical knowledge. Fewer infants now die at birth and elderly people live longer. There has, therefore, been a tremendous 'natural increase' of population.

4 Modern technology and communications also enable us to offset the worst effects of famine, flood and pestilence, so that fewer people now die from natural hazards.

5 Many societies do not believe in birth control, so the population grows rapidly.

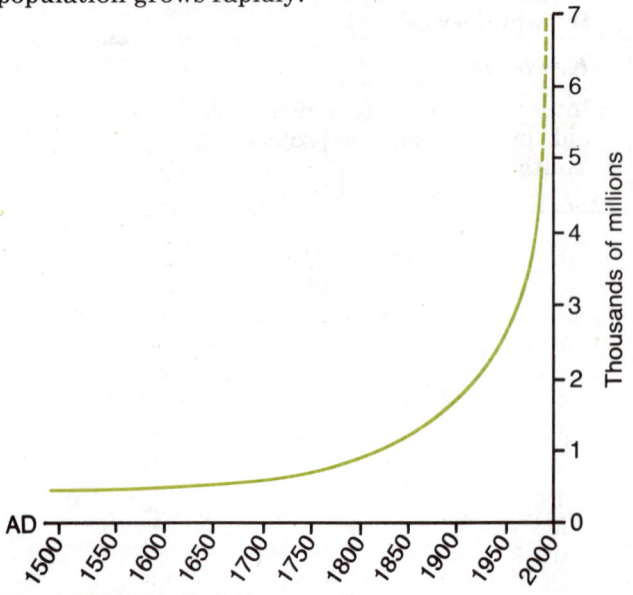

Fig. 5.1 World population growth

PROBLEMS OF POPULATION GROWTH

There are approximately 5 321 million people in the world today. The problem is not so much the size of the population, but its rate of growth. There has been a population explosion in this century and it is estimated that by the year 2025 the world will have a population of approximately 8 300 million people. At present there are over 12 000 additional mouths to feed every hour and the majority of these are in less-developed countries which have little food to spare and cannot afford to buy extra food and resources on world markets.

The main problems are as follows:

1 The world does not have unlimited resources. As the earth becomes the home of more and more people, sources of raw materials will decline and shortages will occur. Eventually some resources, such as oil, may be used up altogether.

2 The developed countries use up more of the world's resources than the poorer countries, even though their populations are smaller and are increasing more slowly. Per capita income in the United States rose from $7000 to $19 800 between 1955 and 1988. In India it only increased from $170 to $290.

3 The poorer countries which have the most rapid increases in population are unable to increase their food production rapidly. If they borrow money from the rich nations, they are in danger of losing their political independence.

4 Low levels of education and inadequate facilities make it extremely difficult to introduce birth control programmes to some less-developed countries.

5 Tradition, the pattern of life in the villages (more children means more breadwinners) and religious beliefs also discourage birth control.

6 Only about one-fifth of the land area of the world can be used for agriculture and habitation. There are vast areas of land, such as the hot deserts, which are likely to remain unproductive and underpopulated for the forseeable future.

7 The difficulty of adequately housing and providing food for the increasing population can lead to unrest, high crime rates and the breakdown of law and order. To some extent this has already happened in parts of South America and Africa.

8 Rapid population growth leads to increasing urbanization. This reduces the amount of farmland and puts pressure on such facilities as recreational areas. It also increases the likelihood of social problems and the deterioration of facilities such as health care.

DEALING WITH THE PROBLEMS OF POPULATION GROWTH
1 Increasing agricultural output

This can be done in two ways, opening up new areas for farming, such as the desert margins and forested areas, and secondly by increasing yields from land already farmed. The Green Revolution (see unit 4.8) is an example of increasing yields by scientific methods.

2 Migration

In some countries, less-developed regions can be more fully utilized, for example the interior of Brazil. Migration on a massive scale is unlikely to solve the problem.

3 Limiting population growth

The Roman Catholic, Hindu and Muslim religions are all opposed to family planning. Some countries, such as India, Thailand and Indonesia have introduced widespread family planning campaigns. China has been even more drastic by encouraging families to have only one child. Eighty-five countries of the developing world now provide some form of public support for family planning programmes.

Country	1960	1990	2010 (projected)
Brazil	73	150	293
China	688	1,119	1,571
Egypt	26	54	110
Nigeria	52	118	508
U.S.A.	181	251	308
C.I.S.	214	291	375
World	3,037	5,321	9,312

Table 5.1 World population (millions)

Summary

Basic ideas

World population is growing rapidly and creating a number of problems as a result.
If the population continues to increase at the present rate, standards of living will decline.
Population growth is particularly rapid in many developing countries, and customs and beliefs may inhibit birth control techniques.

Key terms

Birth control; Green Revolution; migration; urbanization.

5.2 Exhaustion of natural resources

RENEWABLE AND NON-RENEWABLE RESOURCES

Natural resources are the materials that nature provides under, on or above the earth's surface, and which humans use in order to live and to create wealth. They are the minerals, rocks, soil, water, vegetation, living creatures and air which constitute our planet. These resources are not limitless and as the earth's population increases, some resources are becoming more scarce. Some resources, such as trees and living creatures, are renewable, while others, such as minerals and fossil fuels (oil, natural gas, coal), are limited in their supply and are non-renewable resources.

DIMINISHING RESOURCES — TREES

Figure 5.2 shows the variety of resources which are available from the tropical rain forests (see unit 4.5). As these forests are destroyed, some of these resources will become in short supply and may disappear altogether. Some resources, such as medicines, which still await discovery in the rain forests may never be discovered if these forests disappear.

Timber is the greatest resource of the rain forests. There is an increasing demand for hardwoods such as mahogany, teak, iroko and sapele, and costs are rising. Hardwood trees need over 100 years to reach maturity and are a diminishing resource, because they are being felled faster than they can be replaced.

Softwood supply about 70 per cent of the world's timber needs. They come from the coniferous and mixed forest regions of the northern hemisphere. Some conifers mature in 30 to 50 years and there is extensive replanting in Scandinavia, Canada and the CIS. In Britain the Forestry Commission owns about 1 million hectares of woodland, some of which has been planted in areas which are not previously forested. Provided softwood forests are replanted and waste paper is recycled, this renewable source of timber can continue to be used indefinitely.

ENERGY

In 1984 the world used about twice as much energy as it did in 1965.

Primary energy sources 1984 (as percentages of the total)				
Oil	*Natural gas*	*Coal*	*HEP*	*Nuclear*
39	20	30	7	4

There is worldwide recognition that fossil fuels must be conserved, although opinions vary as to how long existing resources will last. If the demand for energy continues to double every 20 years, it is essential to develop new sources of energy. Many countries have regarded nuclear power as the energy source of the future, but the disaster at the Chernobyl nuclear power station in the CIS in 1986 is likely to make many people opposed to the further development of nuclear power stations.

Alternative sources of energy which are being developed in relatively small-scale projects include:

1 Solar radiation — Negev desert, Israel
2 The wind — Burnley, Lancs.
3 Tidal power — Rance estuary, Brittany
4 Geothermal energy — North Island, New Zealand
5 Wave energy — experimental stage only

RESOURCE CONSERVATION

As the world's population increases and standards of living rise, increasing demands are made on the world's natural resources. Both renewable and non-renewable resources are being depleted and conservation – the careful use and protection of resources — is

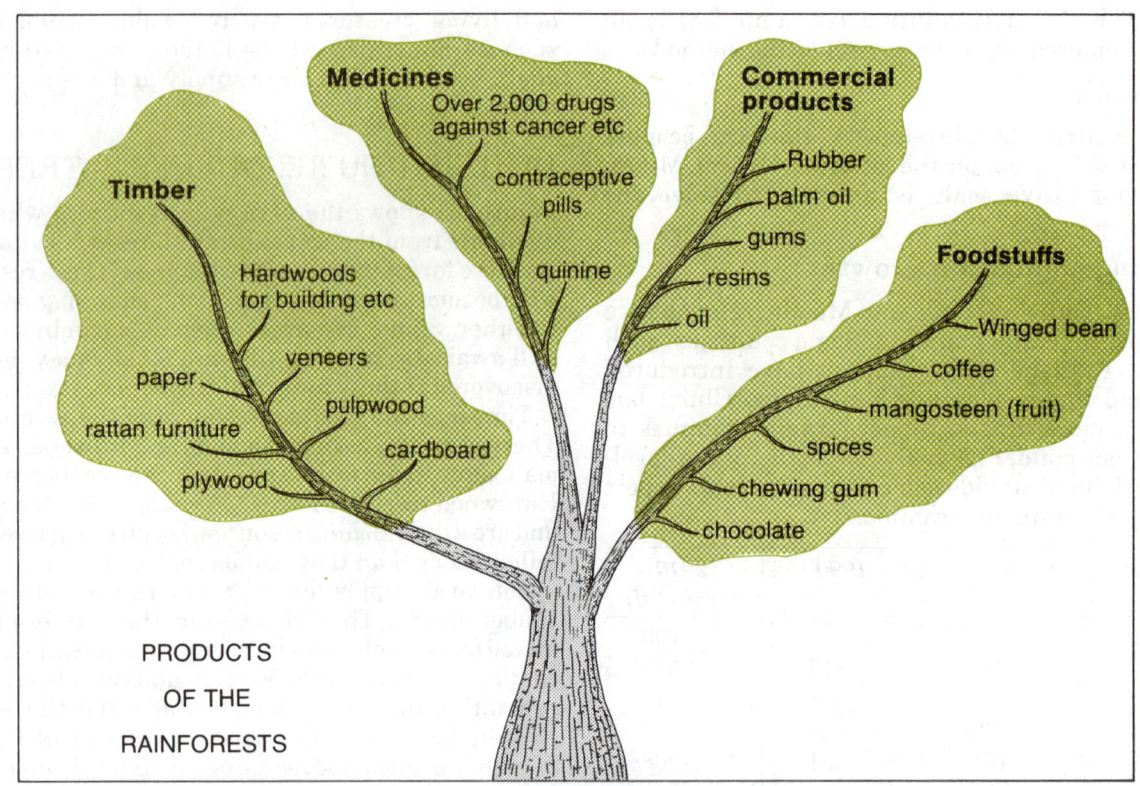

Fig. 5.2 Products of the rainforests

more widespread, especially in the developed world. Efforts are being made to conserve the rain forests, but there is limited enthusiasm from developing countries, which can benefit in the short term from the wealth of these forests. The recycling of metal containers, car tyres, and bottles are practical attempts at conservation.

Conservation not only protects existing resources from extravagant exploitation, waste and destruction, it also makes these resources last longer so that they will be of benefit to future generations.

Summary

Basic ideas

Resources are either renewable or non-renewable.
Some renewable resources are being used up faster than they can be replaced.
Fossil fuels are a non-renewable resource and alternative sources of energy are being developed.
Conservation is one way of safeguarding resources for the future.

Key terms

Renewable; non-renewable; fossil fuels; recycling; alternative energy; resource conservation.

5.3 Hostile environments

Many areas of the developing world consist of environments in which it is difficult to maintain life or to improve living standards, because of lack of resources, unreliable rainfall regimes, lack of cultivable land, or the presence of pests and disease.

Recently, a great deal of attention has been focused on the problems of Africa, where the tragedy of the people who live in the Sahel has led to massive public fund-raising activities (see unit 4.3).

HUNGER IN AFRICA

Rainfall well below average affects many parts of Africa, as fig. 5.3A shows. The Food and Agricultural Organization of the United Nations lists 20 African countries which, in 1985, were affected, with 30 million

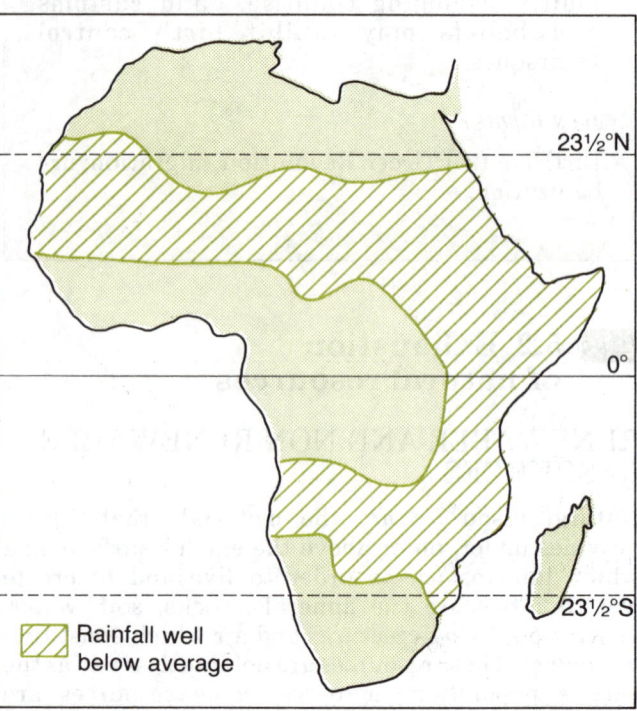

Fig. 5.3A Africa — rainfall

people in those countries at risk of starvation by drought. The savanna lands are particularly prone to unreliable rainfall from year to year. Over 100 million Africans have an inadequate diet and the production of food has declined rapidly in the last 25 years. Although drought is the immediate cause of the present distress, there are several underlying causes which are not related to the hostile environment. These include:

1 Use of the most fertile land for cash crops such as cotton and peanuts instead of food crops. This is a legacy of the colonial system, which is perpetuated by the ownership of land by multinational companies. Only 54 per cent of Africa's land grows food crops.

2 Poverty, which prevents the purchase of fertilizers, high-yielding varieties of seeds and irrigation equipment.

3 Excessive dependence on women for food production. Growing food is the traditional task of women in many African societies, with only limited contributions by the men. Many men have had to find work in the towns or on plantations, leaving four out of ten households without an adult male.

4 Environmental damage has reduced food production, by over-grazing, cutting down trees for fuel and burning cattle dung instead of returning it to the soil. Soil erosion increases after the trees and other vegetation are removed.

PESTS AND DISEASE

Tsetse fly

Pests and disease which kill or debilitate animals and humans are prevalent in many parts of Africa. The tsetse fly has limited cattle rearing in areas such as the Sahel, where arable farming is difficult. The tsetse fly breeds in lakes and marshes and produces a disease in cattle and wild animals called *nagana*. Parasites are also transmitted to humans, causing sleeping sickness and other diseases. Widespread use of pesticides could reduce the threat from the tsetse fly.

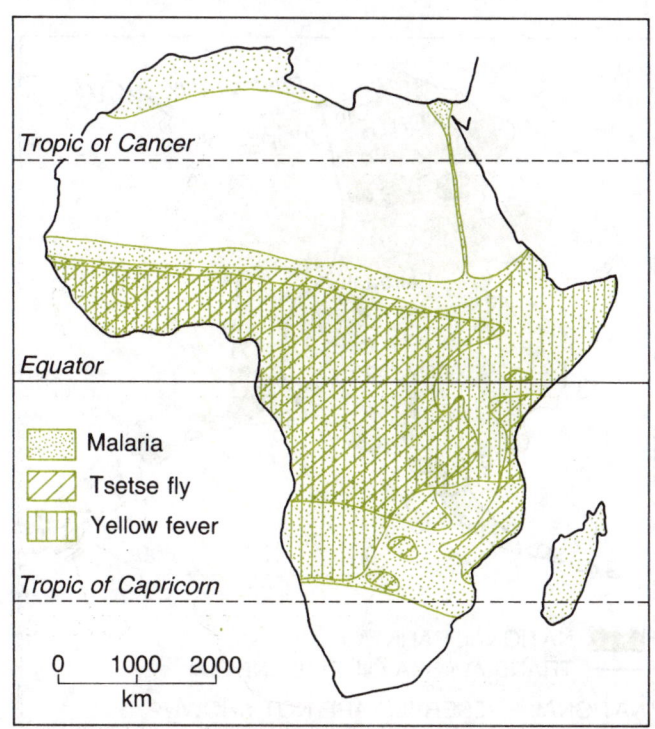

Fig. 5.3B Africa — major diseases and pests

Mosquito

Millions of Africans are infected with the malarial parasite injected into the blood by the female mosquito. The mosquito also carries other diseases, including yellow fever, which is endemic in parts of Africa (fig. 5.3B). Campaigns to eliminate malaria were successful in the 1950s and 1960s, when DDT was sprayed on the walls of houses. However, mosquitoes have adapted to these pesticides and are resistant to them. It may not be possible to wipe out malaria completely, but it can be controlled by using new pesticides and anti-malarial drugs. Yellow fever, another mosquito-borne disease, has been practically eradicated from urban areas, but it is still a major threat in Africa.

Locust

Locusts are large grasshoppers which breed in parts of North Africa and the Middle East. A swarm of locusts can eat over 200 tonnes of vegetation every day and can devastate a large area in a very short time. Desert locusts invade parts of the Sahara desert and the savanna lands in Africa north of the equator. Locust-control teams use satellite photographs to pin-point swarms, and aircraft to spray large areas quickly. Like the other environmental hazards of Africa, more could be done to eliminate the locust if additional money to buy equipment and insecticides was available.

Summary

Basic ideas

Some environments are difficult for human survival.
Modern scientific methods can reduce environmental hazards.

Key terms

Rainfall regimes; cash crops; over-grazing; soil erosion; tsetse fly; malaria; locust control.

5.4 Land use and ownership conflicts

Figure 5.4A shows the different pressures on land, which result in conflicts of interest. Land is a scarce resource, particularly in the urbanized regions of the developed world where there is sufficient wealth to exploit its potential in a variety of ways. People who have an interest in one particular form of development, or in preserving the existing land use, form pressure groups which attempt to influence the final decision on how the land is used. For example, oil exploration companies with permission to set up drilling rigs in parts of southern England are meeting opposition from conservation groups, farmers and local councils, who fear the region may be turned into a miniature Texas with 'nodding donkeys' (oil pumps) and storage tanks creating eyesores. On a larger scale, conflicting demands for land can become national or

Social and environmental issues

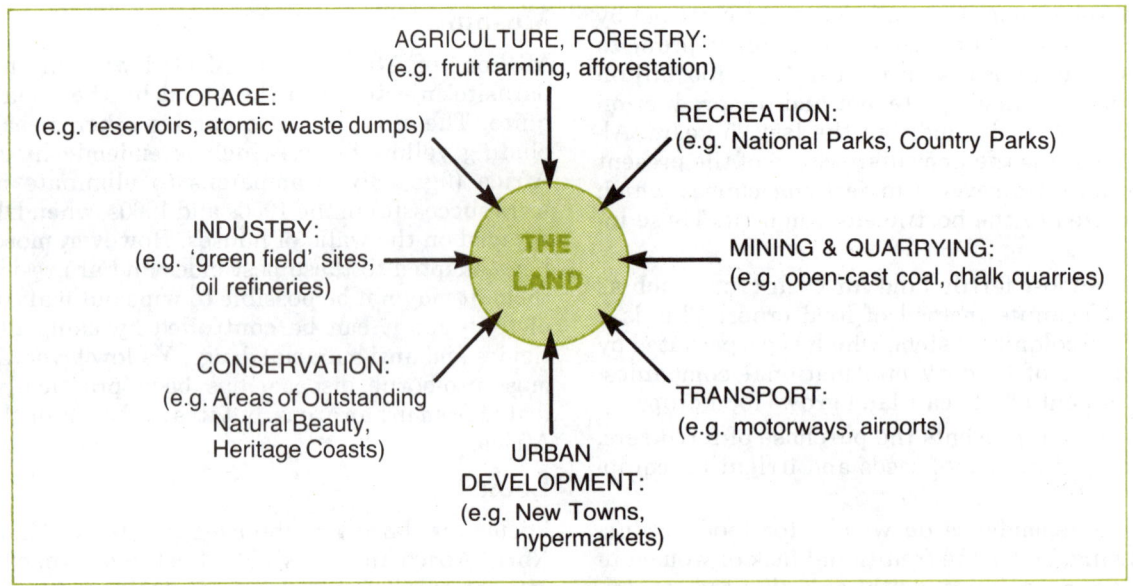

Fig. 5.4A Conflicting demands for land

Diagram showing arrows pointing to THE LAND from:
- AGRICULTURE, FORESTRY: (e.g. fruit farming, afforestation)
- STORAGE: (e.g. reservoirs, atomic waste dumps)
- RECREATION: (e.g. National Parks, Country Parks)
- INDUSTRY: (e.g. 'green field' sites, oil refineries)
- MINING & QUARRYING: (e.g. open-cast coal, chalk quarries)
- CONSERVATION: (e.g. Areas of Outstanding Natural Beauty, Heritage Coasts)
- TRANSPORT: (e.g. motorways, airports)
- URBAN DEVELOPMENT: (e.g. New Towns, hypermarkets)

international issues. One example is the problem of nomadic people in regions as varied as the Arctic wastes of North America and Europe, the rain forests and the hot deserts.

LAND USE IN ALASKA

Land ownership

For many years, the native people of Alaska, consisting mainly of nomadic groups such as the Inupiat and Kutchin, regarded themselves as second-class citizens of the USA with no legal rights to the land, which technically belonged to the Federal Government. They became poorer as their territory was exploited by US companies anxious to profit from the minerals, timber and fish of this under-developed American state. The discovery of vast quantities of oil in the 1960s on the North Slope, near Prudhoe Bay, brought further protests, because land was needed for a pipeline right across Alaska to the ice-free port of Valdez on the south coast.

In 1971 the US government passed the Alaska Native Claims Settlement Act. This gave the 85 000 native people of Alaska nearly 18 million hectares of land and a thousand million dollars compensation. The people became shareholders in 13 regional and some 200 village profit-making corporations which were set up to administer the land and money. In return for this land and money, the other native claims were dropped and the land needed for the pipeline was granted.

The Settlement Act stated that individuals (the shareholders) could not sell their stock for 20 years — that is until 1991. The profit-making corporations which were set up invested money in timber, fisheries, reindeer herds, mining, hotels and other ventures, many of which have prospered and paid dividends to their shareholders. Millions of dollars have also been used to provide electricity, schools, water, satellite telephones and other amenities to remote settlements. This increase in material comforts has also brought with it boredom, alcoholism and the breakdown of some families as people have abandoned their traditional customs and way of life. For those who still hunt whales, a quota system has been introduced; conservation groups protest at the continuation of this aspect of the traditional nomadic way of life.

The cost of living and unemployment are higher in Alaska than anywhere else in the United States, and although schools teach the traditional customs, many children finish their education in colleges in other American states and do not want to return to Alaska. Many people complain that they once collectively owned the whole of the state, whereas now they only own small pieces of it.

Recreation areas

A further complication relating to land use in Alaska has been the decision by the Federal Government in Washington, DC to designate 41 million hectares (an area larger than California) as ten national preserves and eight national parks (fig. 5.4B). The government believes that conservation of these areas now will check exploitation and will give the state valuable recreation potential. It should also prevent having to buy land in the future, when prices are higher, to

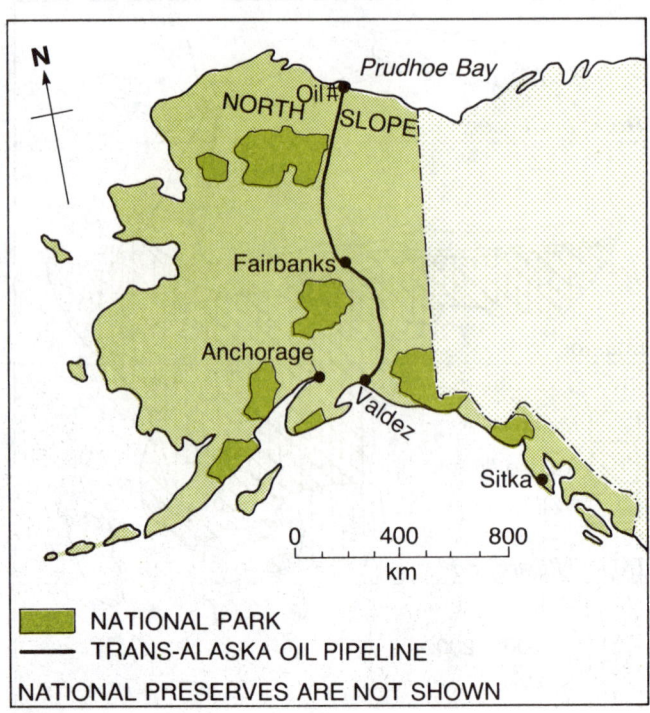

Fig. 5.4B National Parks in Alaska

(Map of Alaska showing NATIONAL PARK areas, TRANS-ALASKA OIL PIPELINE from Prudhoe Bay via North Slope, Fairbanks, Anchorage to Valdez; also showing Sitka. NATIONAL PRESERVES ARE NOT SHOWN. Scale 0–400–800 km.)

protect it for conservation; this has happened in other American states. Alaskans who live off the land will be able to continue hunting, fishing and gathering. The Alaskans are unhappy at these developments, because they believe that important exploitable natural resources in the national preserves and parks will be locked away for good. They also consider that they have not been given enough say as to how the land should be used. They say that they are also concerned about the environment and want to see their land wisely managed. They distrust the Federal Government, which has not had a good record in the past for looking after their rights.

Summary

Basic ideas

There are many pressures on the use of land and these pressures are often in conflict.
Land-ownership disputes in Alaska have brought about changes, not always to the benefit of the nomadic inhabitants.
Conservation for recreation purposes is a further area of dispute.

Key terms

Pressure group; native rights; breakdown of traditions; conservation.

5.5 Soil erosion and conservation

Much soil erosion is the result of bad farming methods, due to ignorance, neglect or greed. Mistakes were made in the past by European settlers who tried to use similar methods to those they used at home in new lands. Immigrants to such regions as the United States, tropical Africa, Australia and New Zealand found that the farming methods they were used to could lead to soil erosion in regions with different climatic conditions. In recent years, speculators have bought land in the High Plains ranges of the US, planted crops such as soy beans when prices were high, and then left the land fallow. Erosion can quickly occur in these circumstances once the soil is left exposed.

WATER EROSION

Erosion by rainwater occurs when soil is bare and has no vegetation or other form of cover to protect it. It is most common in the following conditions:

1 Where rain falls as large droplets which have enough power to blast soil particles apart.

2 Where the rainfall comes in very heavy storms and falls more quickly than it can be absorbed by the soil. This happens in hot countries, where much rain falls during heavy convectional thunderstorms.

3 Where slopes are sufficiently steep for the water to collect in small streamlets and run downhill.

Water erosion has become an increasing problem in the Sahel, where surface vegetation has died during the droughts, been removed as firewood or eaten by

Fig. 5.5 Contour strip-cropping in America

hungry herds of cattle. Large gullies have formed, making arable farming difficult in some areas.

Soil conservation measures to prevent water erosion include:

1 Leaving corn stalks and stubble on the fields after harvesting, and planting crops between the rows.

2 Contour ploughing — ploughing round slopes instead of up and down.

3 Alternating crops in strips, with a cover crop such as clover next to a crop growing in bare soil, such as corn. This is called strip-cropping. Fallow land is often left with a cover crop.

4 Building terraces, so that the fields are nearly flat and water sinks into the soil instead of running off.

WIND EROSION

Like water erosion, this occurs when soil is left bare. It is most common in the following conditions:

1 Areas of low rainfall, or long periods of drought which allow the soil to become very dusty.

2 Where there are strong winds over large stretches of open countryside such as plains.

3 Where soils are loose and not bound together with organic material such as manure.

In the 1930s, the mid-west of the United States suffered severely from wind erosion. Top soil was blown as far as Boston, over 2000 kilometres away on the Atlantic coast. The area of erosion is still known as the 'Dust Bowl'. Soil conservation methods to prevent wind erosion include:

1 Growing lines of tress, called shelterbelts, across the path of the wind. This is a useful methods close to crops but loses its effect at a distance.

2 Leaving straw and other dead vegetation on the soil

3 Leaving stubble and plant stumps in the ground and planting crops between the rows (as for water erosion).

4 Alternating fields of grain with fallow fields, at right angles to prevailing winds.

GOVERNMENT AID

In the United States, the Soil Conservation Service carries out research on soil and soil erosion, and advises farmers on conservation techniques. As a result of their efforts, roughly one-third of American cropland uses conservation methods. The Federal Government provides subsidies for farmers who practise erosion control, but soil erosion remains a problem in many areas.

Summary

Basic ideas

Much soil erosion is the result of bad farming techniques. Soil erosion can be checked in a variety of ways.

Key terms

Gullies; conservation; contour ploughing; strip-cropping; terraces; Dust Bowl; shelterbelts

5.6 Irrigation

Some of the world's irrigation schemes are on a very large scale and are evidence of human interference in the water cycle. The largest schemes involve ponding back water behind a dam and the control of its flow downstream from that point. Many schemes are multi-purpose, involving the generation of energy and sometimes recreational facilities.

Irrigation can also produce problems, and large-scale development like the construction of the High Dam at Aswan in Upper Egypt have far-reaching effects.

THE ASWAN HIGH DAM

The Aswan High Dam, which was completed in 1971, was built to:

1 prevent flooding of the Nile in August and September;

2 provide a regular flow of water for irrigation, eliminating drought which used to occur when the Nile did not flood;

3 Enable crops to be grown throughout the year, instead of during the six months following the summer floods;

4 Increase the amount of irrigated land;

5 provide large amounts of electricity for both Upper and Lower Egypt.

All these objectives have been achieved.

Lake Nasser was formed behind the High Dam, with 80 per cent of its water going to Egypt and the other 20 per cent to the Sudan. The irrigated area of Egypt has been increased by one-fifth, to over 30 million hectares and farmers can now grow three crops in a year. Nevertheless, control of the River Nile has also brought its problems.

1 Fertile silt, which used to cover the ground when the river flooded, is now held back in Lake Nasser. As a result, the lake is slowly silting up.

2 Because there is no more silt to cover the fields, Egyptian farmers must buy expensive fertilizers for their crops.

3 In the past, salt in the soil was leached out by the floods. Today it rises to the surface, where if forms a crust making the fields less fertile (fig. 5.6).

4 The modern irrigation channels are breeding grounds for mosquitoes and parasites which transmit diseases and can cause death.

5 Some 60 000 Nubians were displaced when Lake Nasser was formed. Housing and new land has had to be provided, and it has not always been suitable.

6 Fishermen in the Nile delta region have had reduced catches, partly because the Nile silt which used to provide food for the fish is no longer present, and partly because the increased use of fertilizers, herbicides and pesticides pollutes the water.

7 Annual deposits of silt along the shoreline used to build up the Nile delta, extending it slowly outwards. This no longer occurs and for the first time erosion has become a problem. Summer resort villages built on the coast have begun to disappear.

The High Dam has been a significant factor in social changes which are taking place in Egypt. These include:

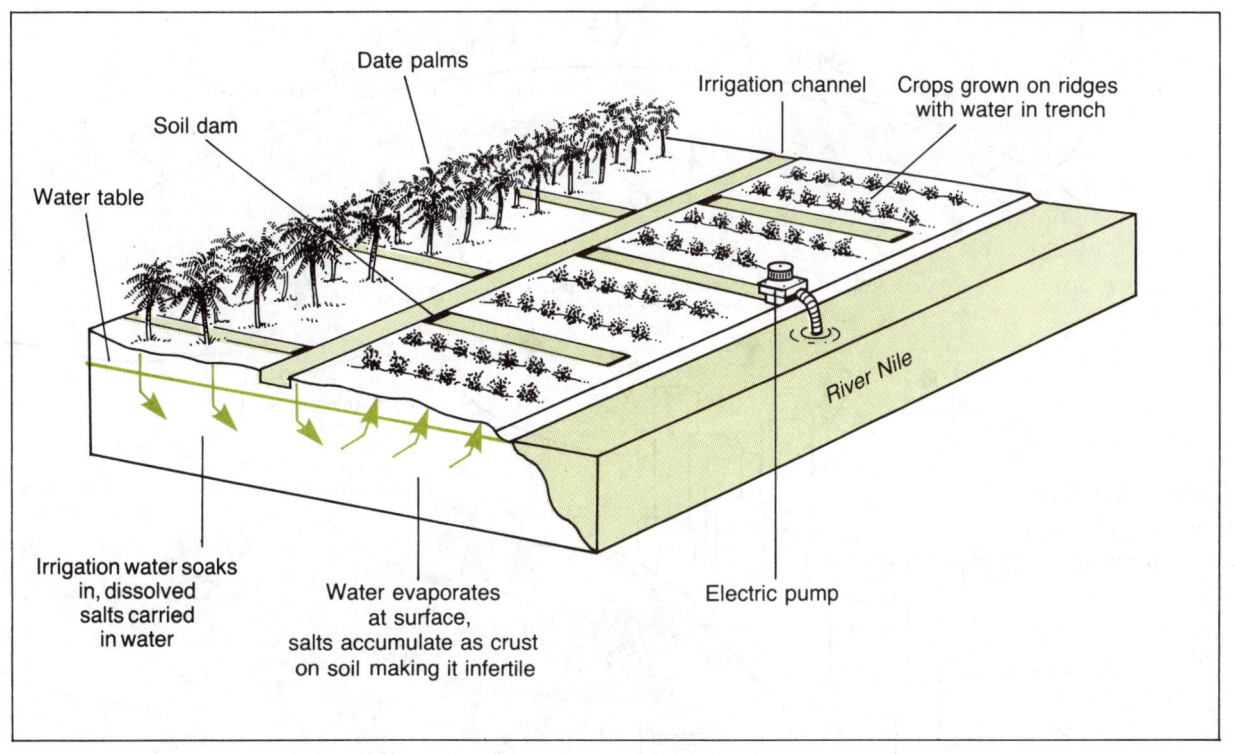

Fig. 5.6 How salts accumulate on irrigated land

1 A rapid increase in the population, which has risen from 19 million in 1950 to 54 million in 1990. The rate of population increase is 2.9 per cent per year (100 000 each month), which is very high (the UK is 0.2 per cent).

2 Farm machinery and irrigation pumps driven by electricity or diesel oil have reduced the need for farm workers. Industries have flourished using cheap electricity, but there is unemployment, especially in rural areas, and many men seek work overseas, particularly in the oil states of the Arabian Gulf.

3 Although electricity and higher crop yields have brought prosperity to the villages, people are moving to the town, especially Cairo. This has resulted in congestion, overcrowding and inadequate facilities. With a population of 10 million, planners calculate that Cairo may reach 20 million in the early years of the next century.

Summary

Basic ideas

The Aswan High Dam has brought problems to Egypt, as well as benefits. The High Dam has also been a significant factor in the social changes which are taking place in Egypt.

Key terms

Multi-purpose; salinity; fertilizers; coastal erosion; population increase; urbanization.

5.7 The Greenhouse effect

THE EARTH'S HEAT BALANCE

The earth receives its heat from the sun in the form of incoming radiation (short-wave radiation) and outgoing re-radiation and reflection from the earth's surface (long-wave or infra-red radiation). There is normally a state of equilibrium between the incoming and outgoing radiation. Some parts of the earth's surface receive more heat than others. For example, the northern hemisphere with large land areas has a positive heat balance whereas the polar regions have a negative heat balance. The heat is transferred away from the tropics by winds and ocean currents to provide an overall balance. Heat is also transferred upwards from the earth's surface into the atmosphere by radiation, conduction and convection.

THE GREENHOUSE EFFECT

The temperature balance on the Earth is partly controlled by much of the out-going reradiation being absorbed by the water vapour and carbon dioxide in the atmosphere. Therefore the effect is very much like the glass in a greenhouse, holding in heat which would otherwise be lost in the atmosphere. This greenhouse effect helps to explain why clear nights are much cooler than cloudy ones.

As long ago as 1896 a Swedish Nobel prize-winner, Svante Arrhenius suggested that more heat energy would be absorbed by the gases given off by the increased burning of coal and this might increase the temperature of the atmosphere. No one took any notice of his ideas until recently when careful measurements of the gases in the atmosphere have shown that there is a build-up, especially of carbon dioxide. It was calculated in 1990 that the rate of *global warming* is about 0.3 °C each decade and this warming has been going on since the Industrial Revolution over 100 years ago. Fig. 5.7A shows the gases which are responsible

120 Social and environmental issues

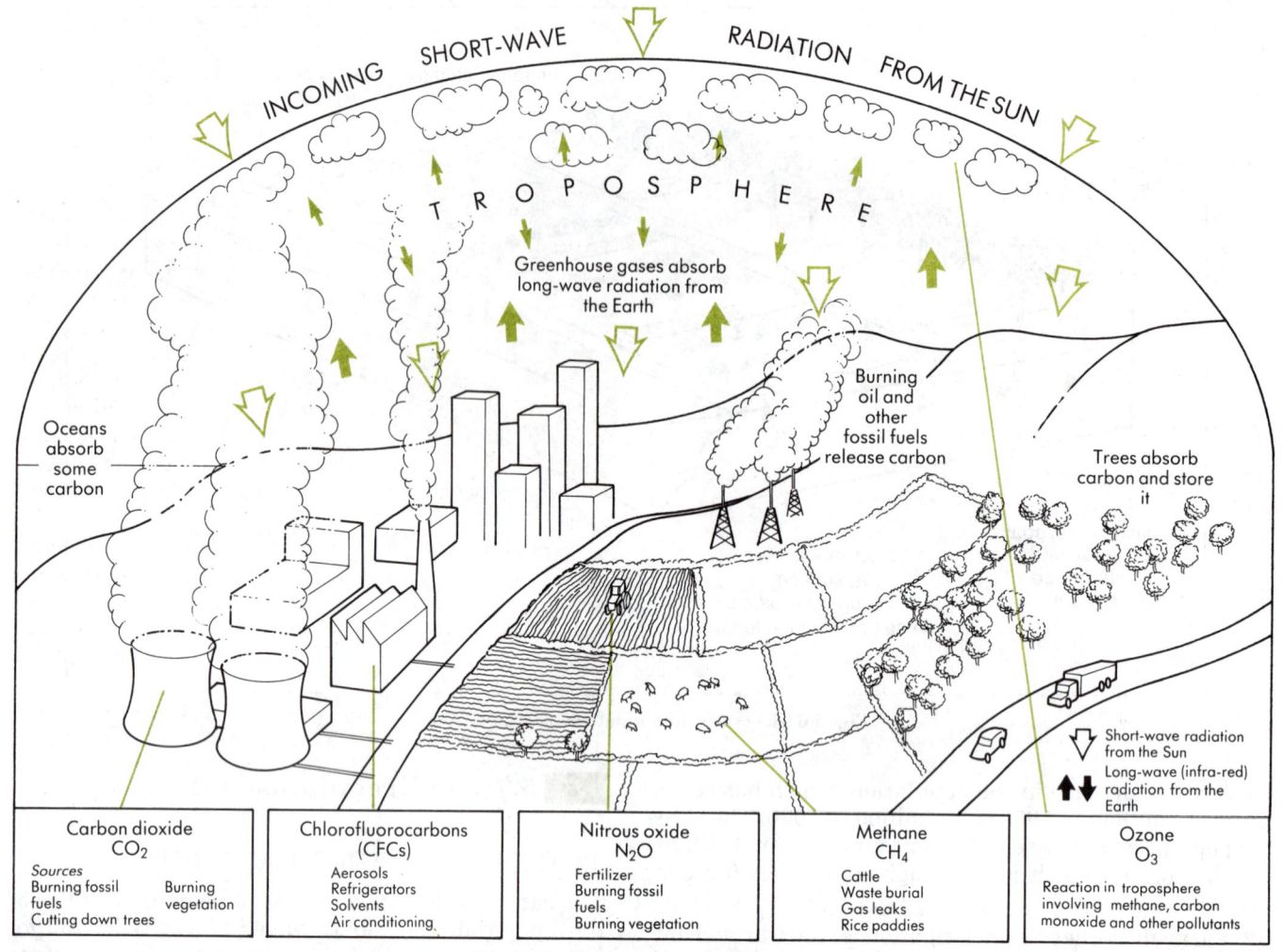

Fig. 5.7A The greenhouse effect

for global warming and how the greenhouse effect is trapping them in the lower atmosphere (troposphere).

As more and more fossil fuels, (coal, oil and gas) are burned in power stations, factories, and internal combustion engines, the amount of carbon dioxide and nitrous oxide in the atmosphere continues to increase. Other gases come from aerosols, waste heaps and the use of fertilizers. As a result, the troposphere between 6 and 18 kilometres above the earth is being polluted by increasing amounts of greenhouse gases.

The oceans absorb carbon dioxide as do plants. Humans and animals breathe out carbon dioxide and produce methane, another greenhouse gas. One reason for concern at the large-scale destruction of the rainforest is because fewer trees means that less carbon dioxide is being absorbed and burning the vegetation adds more pollution to the atmosphere.

POSSIBLE LONG-TERM EFFECTS OF GLOBAL WARMING

As the earth's temperature increases, climates will change and the polar ice caps will melt. This would result in an increase in the sea level, flooding low-lying areas in Britain and other parts of the world. Climatic changes could result in the extension of the northern hemisphere's deserts southwards and mid-latitude countries such as Britain having a warmer climate. One of the problems is that we do not know enough about weather patterns and climates to be able to predict precisely what will happen.

UNCERTAINTY ABOUT THE FUTURE

Some scientists believe the threat from the greenhouse effect is not as serious as articles in newspapers and journals have suggested. They point to the possibility of counter-balancing effects. For example when fossil fuels are burned, sulphur dioxide is one of the gases given off. This gas links up with moisture and specks of dust in the atmosphere to form a haze which reflects some sunlight back into space. A second counter-balancing effect is that ozone, one of the greenhouse gases, is being destroyed by CFCs (chlorofluorocarbons) and that

Summary

Basic ideas

The earth's heat comes from short-wave and long-wave radiation.

Heat is held in the atmosphere by water vapour and gases, mainly carbon dioxide.

The heat balance is being altered by the increase of gases in the atmosphere as the result of human activities.

Global warming can have serious long-term effects and it is very important drastically to reduce emissions of greenhouse gases.

Key terms

Radiation; re-radiation; heat balance; global warming; troposphere; CFCs; fossil fuels; greenhouse gases.

Social and environmental issues

the cooling due to the loss of ozone approximately balances the warming due to the increase in CFCs.

The alarming factor is that, even if the output of greenhouse gases was not allowed to increase and stayed at present emission levels, the concentrations of these gases would carry on rising throughout the 21st century. So would temperatures and the sea level as the warming oceans expand with more meltwater from the polar ice caps. It is exceedingly important, therefore, drastically to reduce emissions of greenhouse gases as soon as possible.

5.8 Air pollution

ACID RAIN

In recent years, there has been growing concern at the damage to plants and fish caused by rainfall which can

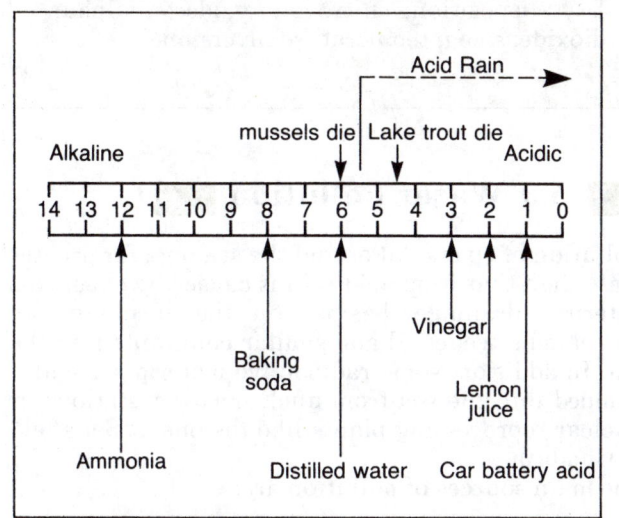

Fig. 5.8A pH Values

be as acidic as weak vinegar. Acidity is measured on the pH scale. This scale ranges from 0 for solids and liquids that are completely acid, to 14 for high alkalinity. A pH of 7 is neutral and is the value of distilled water. Normal rainfall is slightly acidic, with a pH value of 5.6, because it contains carbonic acid formed by the reaction of rain water with carbon dioxide in the atmosphere.

Acid rain has pH values less than 5.6 and the acidity is caused by sulphur and nitrogen gases in the atmosphere. These gases are emitted from the chimney stacks of power stations, smelters and factories. Nitrogen oxides also come from car exhausts. Some of these gases form as a fine dust in the air and collect on buildings or fall on the soil not far from where they were formed. This type of pollution is called 'dry deposition'. It eats away at stonework and shortens the life of metals and paints. Many buildings, including the Statue of Liberty, the Canadian Parliament building in Ottawa, the Houses of Parliament in London and Salisbury Cathedral have had to have extensive repairs to stone and metal which has become corroded.

Gases from furnaces which reach the upper air can be carried by the prevailing winds for long distances. During the journey they combine with water vapour in clouds to form weak sulphuric and nitric acids. These fall to the ground as 'acid rain', or as hail, snow or sleet with an acid content.

This wet deposition can occur up to 2000 kilometres from its source and may not, therefore, originate in the same country as it pollutes. The effects of acid rain are:

1 Coniferous trees turn yellow, the needles fall and the trees die. In West Germany about 80 per cent of the fir trees are estimated to be affected in this way.

2 Polluted water accumulates in lakes, killing fish. In Sweden 9000 lakes are 'dead' and in Norway fish have disappeared from 7000 lakes.

3 Most plant life in the lakes also dies; without green plankton the lakes look abnormally clear.

4 Some mosses and algae grow more vigorously and the food chain in acid lakes is radically changed.

5 Acid rain is harmful to amphibians such as frogs.

6 Plumbing systems can be corroded, with acid dissolving copper into the water.

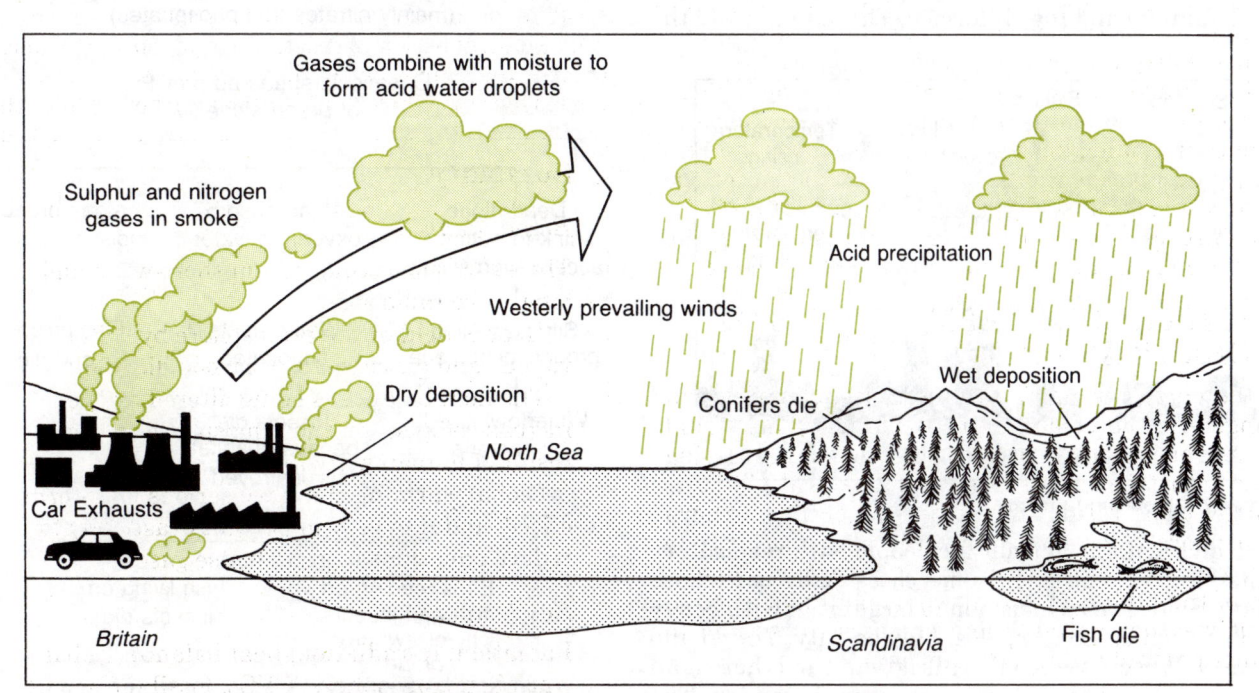

Fig. 5.8B How Britain exports acid rain to Scandinavia

COUNTRIES AFFECTED

The main areas affected are the industrial zones of the northern hemisphere, particularly the north-eastern states of the USA and Eastern Canada, while in Europe acid rain is most severe in Scandinavia, Germany and parts of Central and Eastern Europe. The Scandinavians accuse Britain of causing much of their acid rain. The Generating Boards and the government have accepted responsibility and three power stations will have filters installed as a first measure. EC measurements show that Britain is responsible for about one-tenth of the sulphur dioxide pollution of the air, more than any other European country.

Acid rain is the cause of a dispute between Canada and the United States. Measuring instruments show that half of all chemical depositions in Canada come from the US, mainly blown north-east from coal-fired power stations in the mid-western states. In the USA there are complaints about smelters in Mexico, but smelters on both sides of the border generate 1100 tonnes of pollutants each day. The case against acid rain is not completely proven. The acidification of the environment by coniferous trees themselves is important, especially on some rock types. Many experiments are being carried out to identify the ecological disaster which is taking place.

REMEDIES

In Sweden, one thousand severely affected lakes have been limed to reduce acidity temporarily. Liming is expensive, and only a short-term remedy. It is possible to remove most of the sulphur and nitrogen gases before they reach the atmosphere by putting filters in chimneys. It is calculated that this would increase electricity prices by up to 10 per cent. Environmental groups claim that the cost of acid rain is far greater.

SMOG

When polluted dust from car exhausts and chimneys accumulates near the ground, a form of fog called smog (**sm**oke and **fog**) is formed. This can irritate the eyes and make it difficult for people with respiratory illnesses to breathe. In some cases smog can cause death. Smog is most common in large cities with heavy traffic, such as Los Angeles, Mexico City, Tokyo and Sydney. It occurs when there is no wind and there is an inversion layer caused by temperature inversion. The introduction of smokeless fuels and cleaner car exhaust emissions can help to reduce the risk of smog.

> **Summary**
>
> *Basic ideas*
>
> There are two forms of acidic pollution, dry and wet pollution.
> Acid rain often affects countries which have not been responsible for its formation.
> Smog is a form of air pollution associated with large cities and certain atmospheric conditions.
>
> *Key terms*
>
> Dry deposition; nitrogen oxides; sulphur dioxide; smog; temperature inversion.

5.9 Water Pollution

Pollution of rivers, lakes and the sea on a far greater scale than that from acid rain is caused by chemicals entering drainage basins, or the discharge of untreated sewage, oil and similar pollutants into the sea. In addition, some radioactive materials are also pumped into the sea from nuclear power stations or nuclear reprocessing plants like the one at Sellafield in Cumbria.

The main sources of pollution are:

1 Farm chemicals

Run-off from fertilized fields pollutes waterways and lakes. The main chemicals are nitrates and phosphates, used as fertilizers, and smaller quantities of chemicals used in herbicides and pesticides. Since

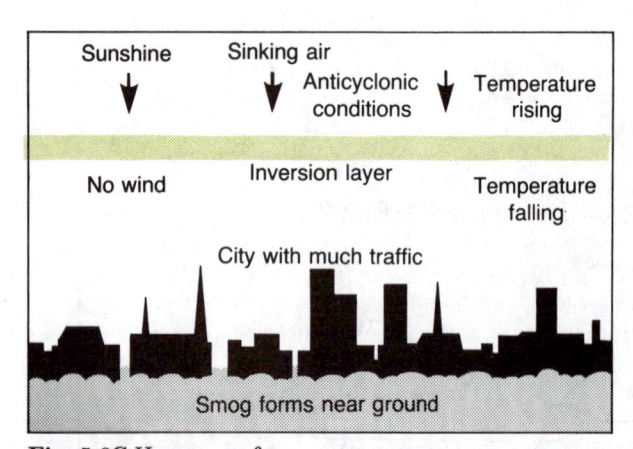

Fig. 5.8C How smog forms

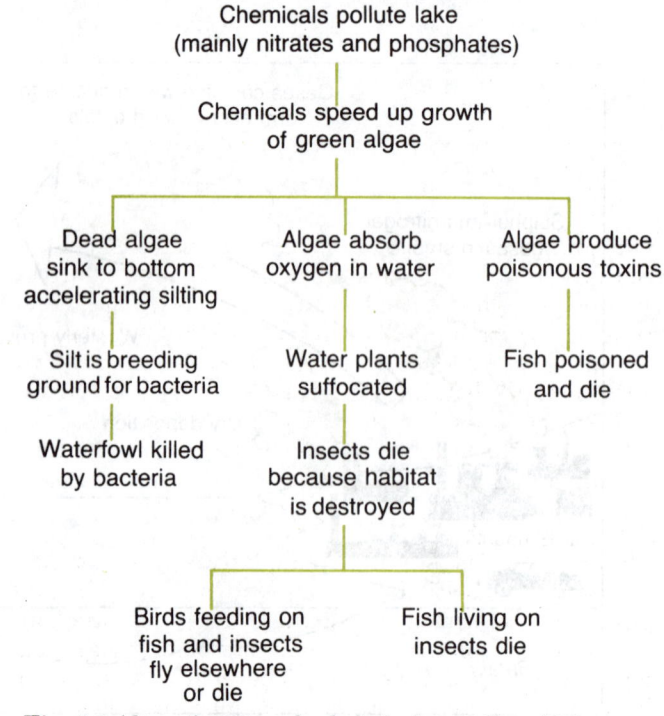

Fig. 5.9 Alterations to a food chain in a polluted lake

1945 the Norfolk Broads have become increasingly polluted, mainly by run-off from the surrounding fields. High nitrate levels cause changes in food chains (see fig. 5.9), destroying wildlife and affecting all but four of the fifty-two Broads.

2 Factory effluents

These consist of chemicals and other industrial waste from factories and mine workings. The River Trent is polluted from a number of sources. It collects a great deal of chemical waste from dyeing and bleaching works in Nottingham and Leicester. Near Scunthorpe, the steelworks discharge ammonia, cyanides and other chemicals into the drainage basin. Power stations in the Trent Valley pour hot water into the river, raising the temperature and driving out oxygen.

3 Toxic chemicals

Dangerous chemical refuse is usually buried in dumps, but in recent years attention has been drawn to leakage from these dumps. Scientists have identified 1000 man-made chemicals in the Great Lakes of North America, most of which came from dumps in the USA. Like acid rain, this form of pollution does not help US-Canadian relations.

4 Domestic sewage

Sewage from urban areas pollutes both drainage basins and the sea. The cheapest way of disposing of sewage is to pipe it, untreated, to the nearest river, or in the case of coastal towns, to pump it a short distance out to sea. Inland towns normally treat raw sewage, so that effluent leaving the works is relatively harmless. Many sewage works are not able to deal with high concentrations of detergents, however. Detergents are rich in phosphates and these fertilize vegetation in rivers and lakes. This vegetation absorbs oxygen, until only a green algae remains. Lake Erie and Lake Ontario have large quantities of algae and are, to some extent, 'dead' lakes.

The EC requires sewage outfall pipes from coastal works to extend for at least 500 metres beyond the low water mark. Most outfall pipes in Britain extend only 100 metres, and raw sewage can easily be washed back on to the beaches. Almost half the beaches in England and Wales fail to reach the standard of cleanliness set by the EC. These beaches include those of such well-known resorts as Blackpool, Rhyl, Brighton, Eastbourne and Clacton-on-Sea.

5 Oil and tar

Oil contamination comes mainly from oil tankers. Spillage as the result of shipwreck, although relatively rare, can be quite disastrous. For example, the beaches of northern Brittany were badly polluted by the oil slick produced when the *Amoco Cadiz* sank in 1978. Illegal cleaning of ships' tanks with seawater close to land is often the cause of the patches of tar which pollute beaches around Britain, the Mediterranean and other parts of the world.

6 Radioactive waste

Water which is slightly radioactive is sometimes discharged from atomic power stations. These discharges are sometimes accidental, but the nuclear reprocessing plant at Sellafield has discharged polluted water deliberately. There have also been leaks which have contaminated local beaches and raised the radioactive level of the Irish Sea.

> **Summary**
>
> *Basic ideas*
>
> Pollution of water is caused mainly by chemicals from farms and factories, or domestic sewage.
> Pollution is also caused by oil contamination and radioactive waste.
>
> *Key terms*
>
> Nitrate; phosphate; factory effluents; toxic waste; green algae; oil slick; radioactive waste; food chain.

5.10 Traffic in cities

Cities throughout the world have the problem of coping with increasing numbers of vehicles on the road and the congestion which results. There are several reasons why these problems occur.

1 As standards of living increase and cars become relatively less expensive because of mass-production methods, the number of vehicles on the roads increases. This is particularly the case in cities, where most people live.

2 The importance of the CBD for shops, offices and other service industries has created additional transport problems because of the large numbers of people who must travel to and from the CBD each working day.

3 The centres of many cities developed before the petrol engine was invented, Streets are narrow and quite unsuitable for large numbers of vehicles.

4 Cities are centres of communication networks where important routes meet. Unless new roads are built round cities, through-traffic can seriously add to the congestion.

SINGAPORE

Many cities have adopted similar strategies to solve the problem of traffic. One example is Singapore. Singapore was founded by Sir Stamford Raffles in 1819. The road pattern developed in a relatively haphazard manner around the port area, but later some planning resulted in new areas with a grid-iron road pattern. Singapore has been an independent country since 1965 and has a population of 2.7 million. There are very high housing densities, averaging 4600 people per sq km (UK: 229 per sq. km) and 50 per cent of the island is built over. The standard of living has risen rapidly and one person in five now owns a car. Large satellite towns have been built on the island by the government to provide housing and services for the population. Industry, commerce and the tourist trade have made the CBD a region of large hotels, shopping malls and office blocks, and the highest congestion is in this region (see fig. 5.10).

The government has dealt with the traffic problem in a number of ways:

1 By building an express highway along the south coast called the East Coast Parkway. It links the

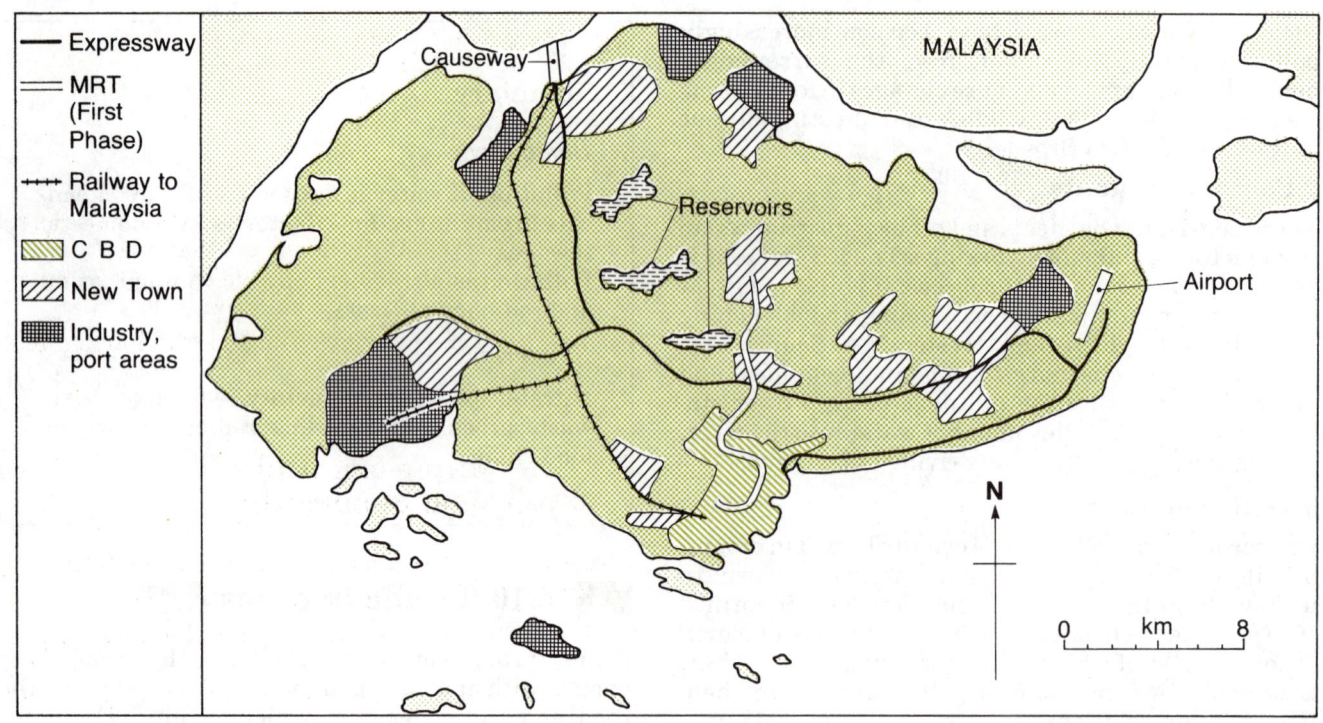

Fig. 5.10 Singapore

international airport with the CBD. Another expressway has been built north of the CBD, with an extension planned to the causeway to Malaysia.

2 By developing a Mass Rapid Transit system (MRT). This is an 'underground' railway which runs partly above ground, and will connect the largest satellite towns to the CBD using a fast train service. It is hoped that by the end of the century, the MRT will be carrying one million passengers per day.

3 By making most of the CBD into a restricted zone, to reduce peak-hour traffic on every day except Sunday. Cars entering this zone have to pay a license fee. Taxi fares are also increased in the zone during the morning peak hours (7.30 to 10.15 a.m.) and between 4 and 7 p.m.

4 By providing multi-storey car parks

The position of the CBD on the south coast of Singapore island restricts the communication network. Consequently Singapore has not had to build an orbital motorway around the city, as has been the case in London, Brussels, Washington and many other major cities.

Summary

Basic ideas

Traffic in cities creates increasingly complex problems.
Measures have been taken to discourage traffic in the CBD and provide alternative means of transport.

Key terms

Communication network; congestion; satellite town; Mass Rapid Transit; restricted zone; multi-storey car park.

6 SELF-TEST UNIT

Introduction

On the pages which follow, a number of questions have been set to help you check how far you have understood the information in the core material contained in units 1 to 5. Questions have been selected covering each of the five themes, and you will find that two types of question are used. There are those which test your understanding and ability to apply information, and there are others which test your ability to remember basic principles and key factors.

Each of the five sets of questions has been given a total mark, which is made up of the individual scores for each question. Answers are provided at the end of the test or can be found by reference to specific units which are indicated at the end of the question. Remember that questions have been chosen at random and do not, therefore, cover all the material in each theme. Nevertheless, tests of this kind are particularly useful, not so much because they tell you how much you understand, but because they help you to find out what you do not know very well, and what needs further revision.

To use this self-test section most effectively, you should plan your work in the following sequence:

1 Revise part of the core material, for example the British Isles, by reading through the text, studying the maps and checking that you understand the ideas and skills involved.

2 When you consider that you fully understand the core material, turn to the self-test questions on the British Isles and write down your answers. It is important that you do not look at the questions before you have revised the core material and, of course, it is equally important that you do not read the answers or look back at the core material until you have completed all the questions.

3 Either mark your answers yourself, or get a friend to mark them for you. If you have less than two-thirds of the total mark for each set, you need to spend much more time revising the core material.

4 If you have a low mark, repeat the revision and test yourself again.

6.1 Map work and physical geography

1 Answer the following questions about fig. 6.1A:

(a) What process occurs at A? (2)
(b) What is the process transferring the water at B? (2)
(c) What process occurs at C? (2)
(d) What is the process at D? (2)
(e) What process occurs underground at E? (2)
(f) What process occurs on the surface at F? (2)
(g) What does the line at G mark the upper limit of? (2)
(h) Name three places on the diagram where water is being stored. (6)

Total score 20

2 Look at fig. 6.1B overleaf, which shows landforms which are the result of erosion.

(a) For each of the diagrams A,B,C, and D, name the landform shown. (4)
(b) Name the major agents of erosion responsible for each landform. (4)
(c) State the direction taken by the agents of erosion in A,B, and D. (3)
(d) Describe how B may have been formed. (3)

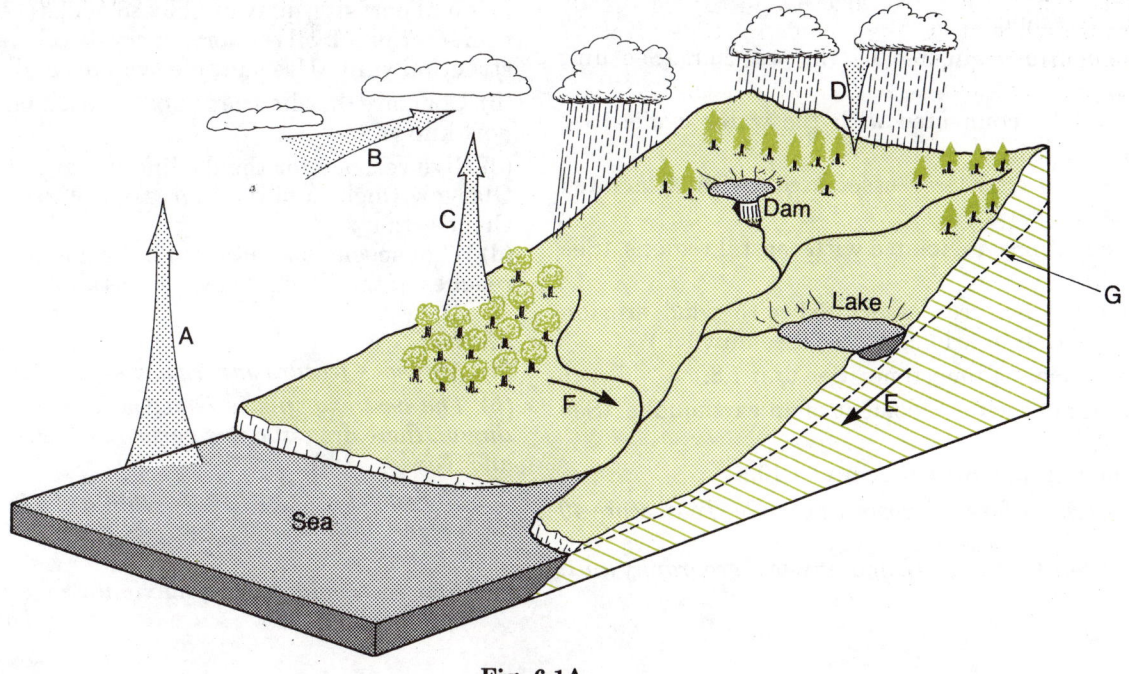

Fig. 6.1A

126 Self-test unit

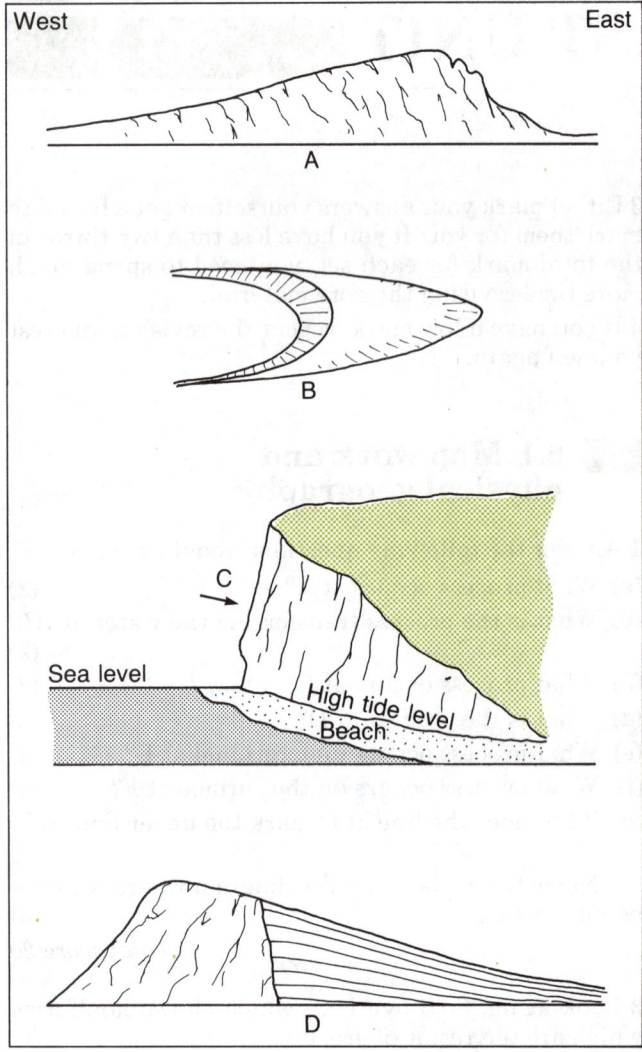

West   East

Fig. 6.1B

(e) Describe three ways in which areas of highland glaciation have been developed by man. (3)

(f) Name one example of each type of development you listed in (e). (3)

Total score 20

3 List five examples of:

(a) Occupations affected by the weather. (See unit 1.3.)

(b) Processes connected with the water cycle. (See unit 1.4.)

(c) Human activities associated with glaciated regions. (See unit 1.5.)

(d) Occupations associated with coastal regions. (See unit 1.6.)

(e) Physical features associated with wind erosion and deposition in arid climates. (See unit 1.7.)

(f) Uses made of limestone. (See unit 1.8.)

(g) Stages in the development of an earthquake. (See unit 1.10.)

(h) Converging plates. (See unit 1.10.)

One mark for each correct example. Total score 40

Total 80 for the map work and physical geography unit.

6.2 The British Isles

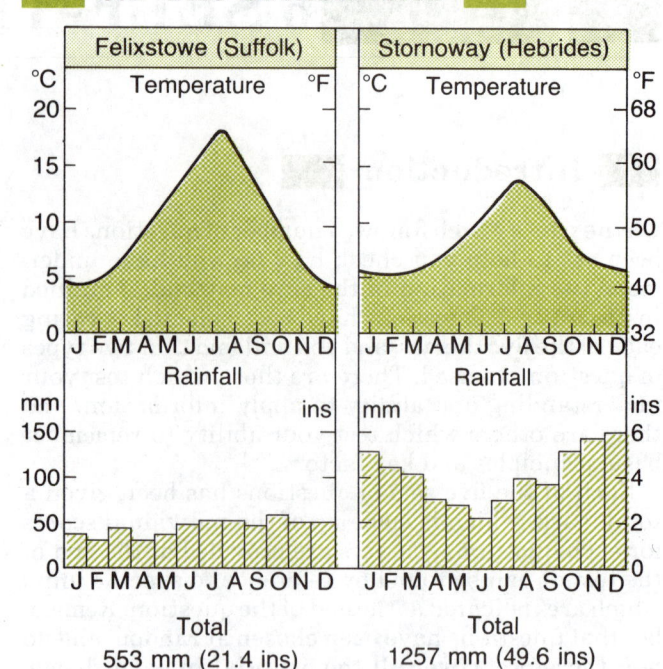

Fig. 6.2A Climate graphs for Felixstowe and Stornoway

1 Study fig. 6.2.A

(a) What is the range of temperature at Felixstowe? (2)

(b) Explain why the summer temperatures at Felixstowe are higher than those at Stornoway. (2)

(c) Explain why winter temperatures at Stornoway are higher than those at Felixstowe (4)

(d) Explain why there is twice as much rainfall at Stornoway as at Felixstowe. (4)

(e) Explain briefly why there are over 30 days with gale-force winds at Stornoway, compared with fewer than 5 at Felixstowe. (5)

Total score 20

2 (a) Study fig. 6.2B showing the framework of an estuarine port model. Complete this model by indicating the most likely location for the following features: original port site; quays; enclosed docks (19th C.); container terminal; oil refinery; concrete oil platform construction yard. (Use suitable symbols and a key.)

(b) Compare this diagram (model) to a named Scottish port known to you.

(c) Give reasons for the decline in cargo handling at Glasgow Docks and the increase at Greenock on the Clyde estuary.

(d) What special advantages do the docks in the upper reaches of the Clyde (Glasgow) retain?

Marks:

(a) 1 for each feature and 2 marks for a correct key (8)

(b) The best example is Glasgow and the Clydeport, though there are estuarine ports on the Firths of Forth and Tay (2)

(c) 1 for each factor up to a maximum of 3 marks for the decline of Glasgow and 3 for the increase at Greenock (6)

(d) 1 for each point up to a maximum of 4 (4)

Total score 20

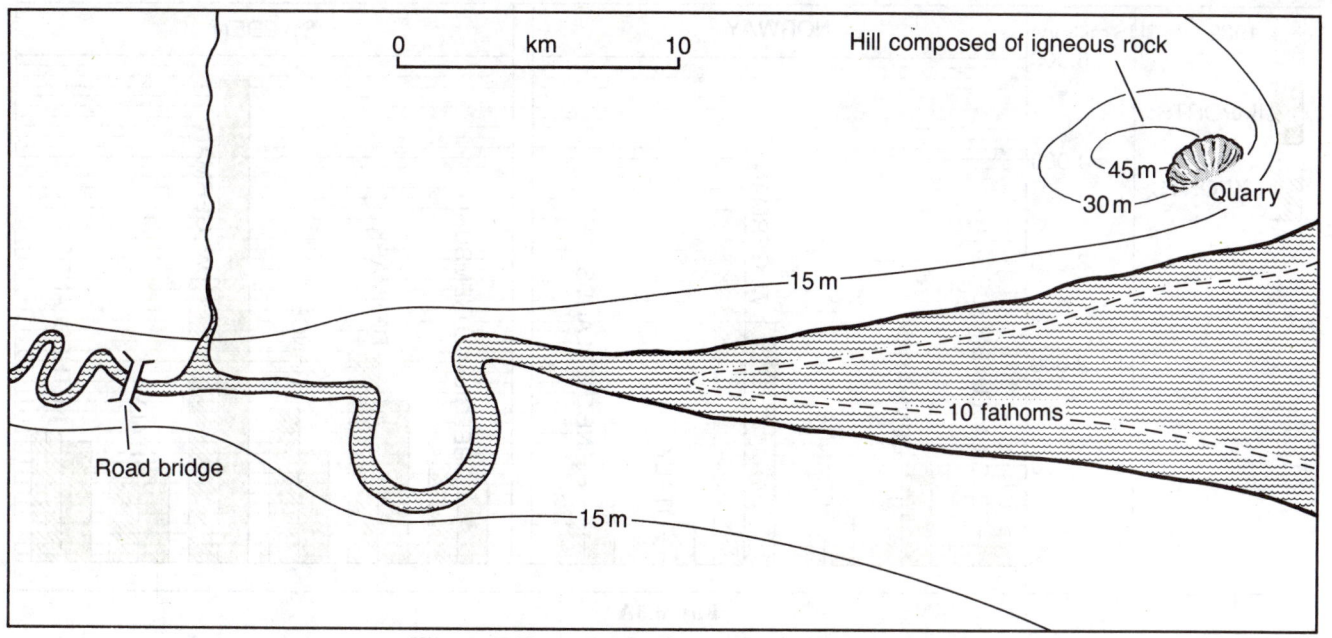

Fig. 6.2B Framework of an estuarine port model

3 Basic Factors

Give five distinctive factors which explain:

(a) What causes the chief climatic features of Britain. (See unit 2.1.)

(b) The conditions which make the western half of Britain important for dairying. (See unit 2.3.)

(c) Why we have become less dependent upon coal as a source of energy. (See unit 2.4.)

(d) Why many of our main industries are no longer located on coalfields. (See unit 2.5.)

(e) Why heavy industrial regions have declined. (See unit 2.7.)

(f) Why the London area has become the chief manufacturing region of England. (See units 2.7 and 2.8.)

(g) Factors which influence the patterns formed by different transport networks. (See unit 2.9.)

(h) The present distribution of population in Britain. (See unit 2.11.)

(i) Why some city centres have been redeveloped. (See unit 2.15.)

(j) Why patterns of holiday-making have changed. (See unit 2.20.)

Score 1 for each correct answer. Total Score 50
Total 90 for the British Isles unit

6.3 Western Europe

1 Study the figures below which show primary energy consumption for the countries listed in 1974 and 1984.

(a) What is meant by primary energy? (1)

(b) Name two other energy sources not listed above that are important for the production of electricity in countries of Western Europe. (2)

(c) Describe the trend in coal consumption in the countries listed between 1974 and 1984. (2)

(d) Describe the changes that have taken place in the consumption of natural gas between 1974 and 1984. (3)

Consumption of Primary Energy
(millions of tonnes of oil equivalent)

Country	Coal 1974	Coal 1984	Oil 1974	Oil 1984	Natural Gas 1974	Natural Gas 1984
West Germany	256.0	83.3	134.3	110.9	32.5	41.1
France	184.1	25.2	121.0	86.2	17.2	23.5
Italy	136.9	15.3	100.8	84.7	15.8	26.5
Netherlands	71.2	5.7	35.4	28.9	32.1	31.2
Norway	28.3	0.5	7.7	8.3	0	0
Switzerland	22.5	0.5	13.0	11.8	0.3	1.0
Denmark	18.1	6.3	16.0	10.4	0	0.2
Totals	647.1	136.8	428.2	341.2	97.9	123.5

(e) Suggest reasons why oil consumption was lower in 1984 than it was in 1974. (4)

(f) Describe the methods of transport used in one of the countries listed for each of these energy sources. (5)

(g) Name three other sources of energy that have not yet been developed on a large scale but which may provide energy in the future. (3)

Total score 20

2 Figure 6.3A shows the value of trade between Norway and Sweden and the countries of Western Europe. Figure 6.3B shows the proposed extension to the road and rail network of Western Europe, known as Scanlink. It involves linking the Danish islands by bridges and building a tunnel between Denmark and Sweden to carry a motorway and high speed trains from Oslo to Lübeck. At Lübeck it would link with the existing network of Western Europe. Travel time between Oslo and Lübeck would be halved.

(a) Which country has the greater amount of trade, Sweden or Norway? (1)

(b) From which country does Sweden import most? (1)

(c) Which country exports most to Germany, Norway or Sweden? (1)

(d) Which countries receive more in value from Sweden than they send as exports to Sweden? (2)

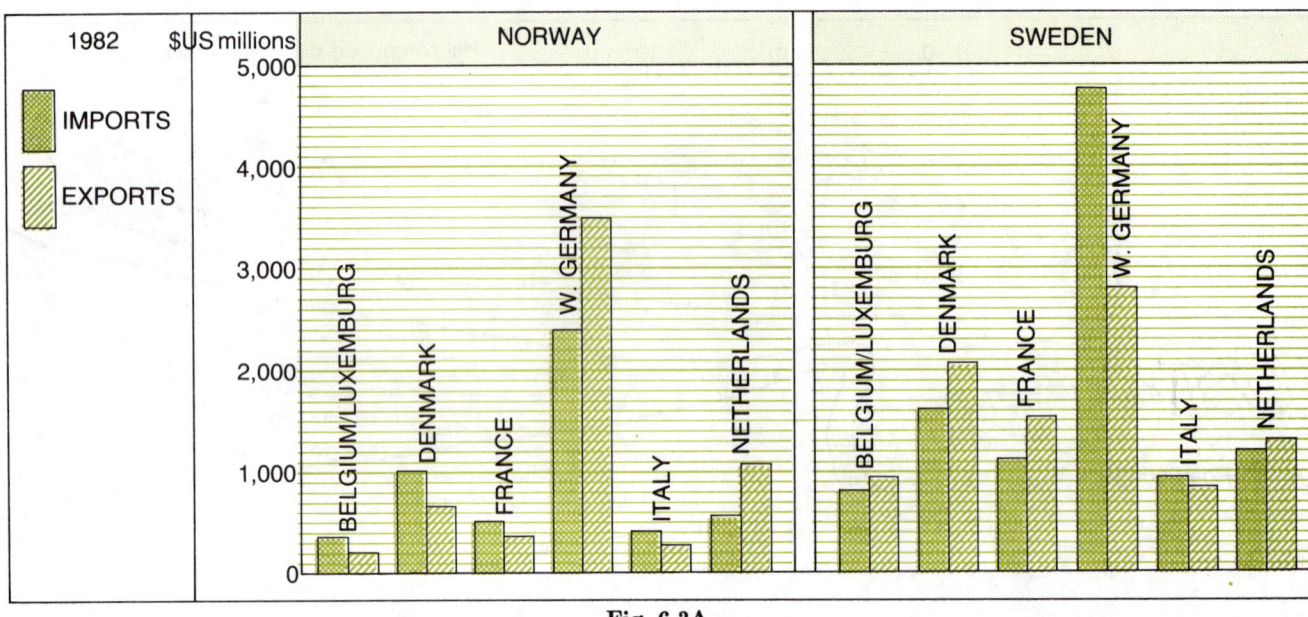

Fig. 6.3A

(e) Which country is likely to benefit most from Scanlink, Norway or Sweden? (1)
(f) Which other neighbouring country not listed on fig. 6.3A could also benefit from Scanlink? (2)
(g) List the advantages of Scanlink to Norway and Sweden. (6)
(h) Explain why conservationists in Scandinavia are alarmed at the effects Scanlink may have on the environment. (6)

Total score 20

3 For each of the following questions list five examples of:
(a) Changed attitudes to land use on polders. (See unit 3.4)

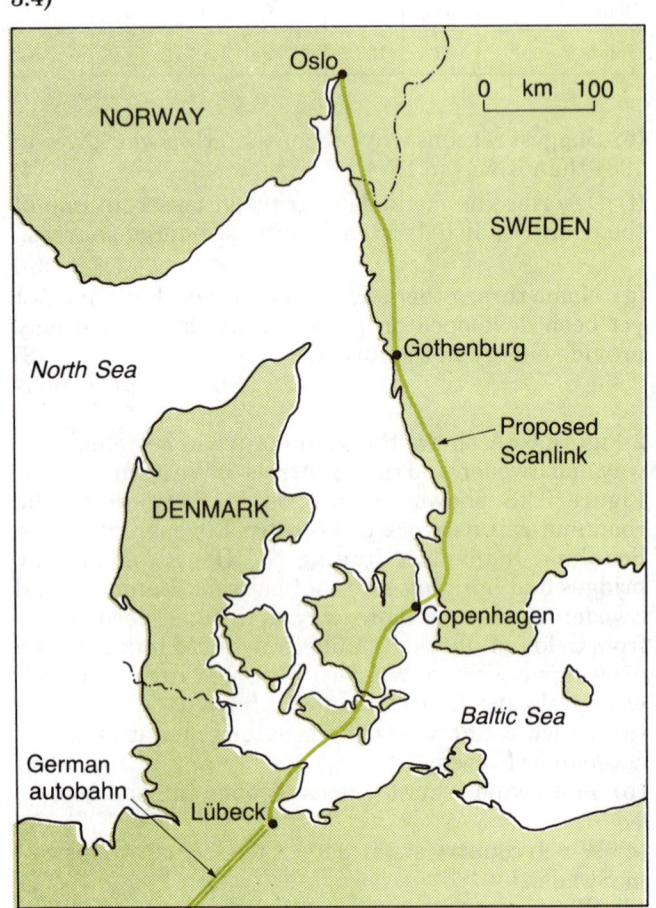

Fig. 6.3B

(b) Reasons why France has increased nuclear energy production. (See unit 3.5)
(c) Why heavy industries have remained in the industrial triangle. (See unit 3.6)
(d) Disadvantages for the country receiving immigrants. (See unit 5.7)
(e) Reasons why Switzerland has developed a range of service industries. (See unit 3.8)
(f) The types of industry developed at major ports. (See unit 3.10)
(g) Action taken to check the growth of Paris. (See unit 3.13)
(h) Planning problems which have resulted from the growth of Randstad. (See unit 3.12)
(i) Problems of the Mezzogiorno. (See unit 3.13)
(j) Attitudes opposing tourist development. (See unit 3.15)

Total 90 for the Western Europe unit   Total score 50

6.4 The developing world

1 Study fig. 6.4A.
(a) Describe the main features of the population-graph (2)
(b) How long did the world's population take to double from
   (i) AD 1500?
   (ii) AD 1800? (2)
(c) How long will the world's population take to double from 1970? (1)
(d) Give **two** reasons to explain why the population of the world is growing so quickly during this century. (2)
(e) What does this table tell you about future trends in population growth?

Area	Western Europe	India	Africa	Brazil
Percentage population under 16 years	25	37	41	42

(4)

(f) World population places great and increasing presure on world food resources. Name the United Nations Agency which seeks to improve agricultural production. (1½)

Self-test unit **129**

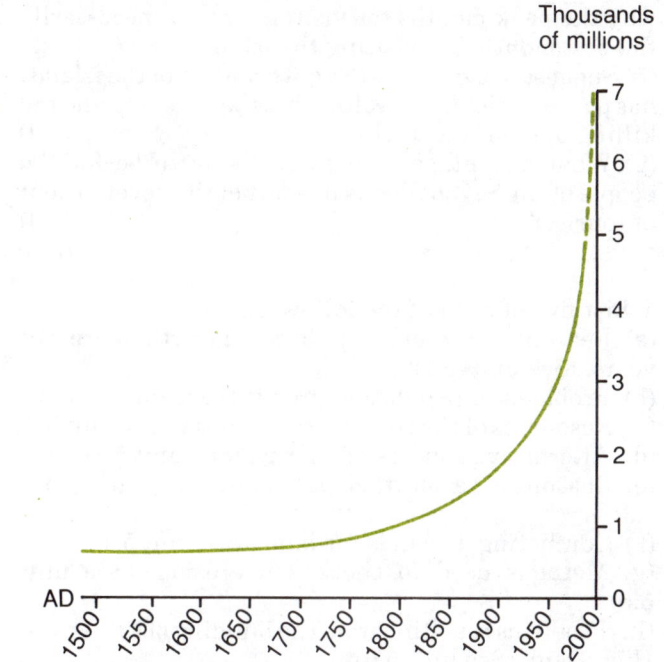

Fig. 6.4A World population growth

(g) In many parts of the world, especially in the developing countries, food production is decreasing rather than increasing. Give **five** possible reasons to account for this. (7½)
Total score 20

2 Study fig. 6.4B
(a) Name one capital city with over 80 per cent of its population in slum and squatter settlements. (2)
(b) What is another name for a squatter settlement? (2)
(c) Which city has the largest population? (2)
(d) Which of the cities marked is a planned new capital city? (2)
(e) Are all the problem cities within the Tropics? (2)
(f) Name the continent(s) with no developing world cities. (2)
(g) Give two reasons why Calcutta is a major problem city in India (4)
(h) Give four characteristics of developing world squatter settlements found on the edges of large cities (4)
Total score 20

3 BASIC FACTORS
Give five distinctive factors which explain:
(a) Why some countries are said to be less developed than others. (See unit 4.1)
(b) Why many people in the developing world live on the brink of starvation. (See unit 4.2)
(c) Why farms in India have lower productivity than farms in England. (See unit 4.4)
(d) Why the traditional ways of life of hunters and gatherers are rapidly disappearing from the equatorial rain forests. (See unit 4.5)
(e) Why developed countries in the past established tropical plantation farming in their colonies. (See unit 4.6)
(f) Why the opening up of empty lands is seen by some as a 'mixed blessing'. (See unit 4.7)
(g) Why the Green Revolution has not been entirely successful. (See unit 4.8)
(h) Why developing countries do not have well-developed transport networks. (See unit 4.9)
(i) Why developing countries see industrialization as the key step to prosperity. (See unit 4.10)
(j) Why shanty towns have grown in countries of the developing world. (See unit 4.12)
Score 1 for each answer
Total score 50
Total 90 for the less developed world unit

6.5 Social and environmental issues

1
(a) Complete fig. 6.5A (p. 130) by filling in the empty rectangles. (*10 marks — 2 for each rectangle*)
(b) Explain what is meant by factory effluents. (2)
(c) Give two reasons why many beaches in Britain fail to reach EC standards of cleanliness. (2)
(d) Describe the ways by which a river can become polluted when flowing through an industrial city. (6)
Total score 20

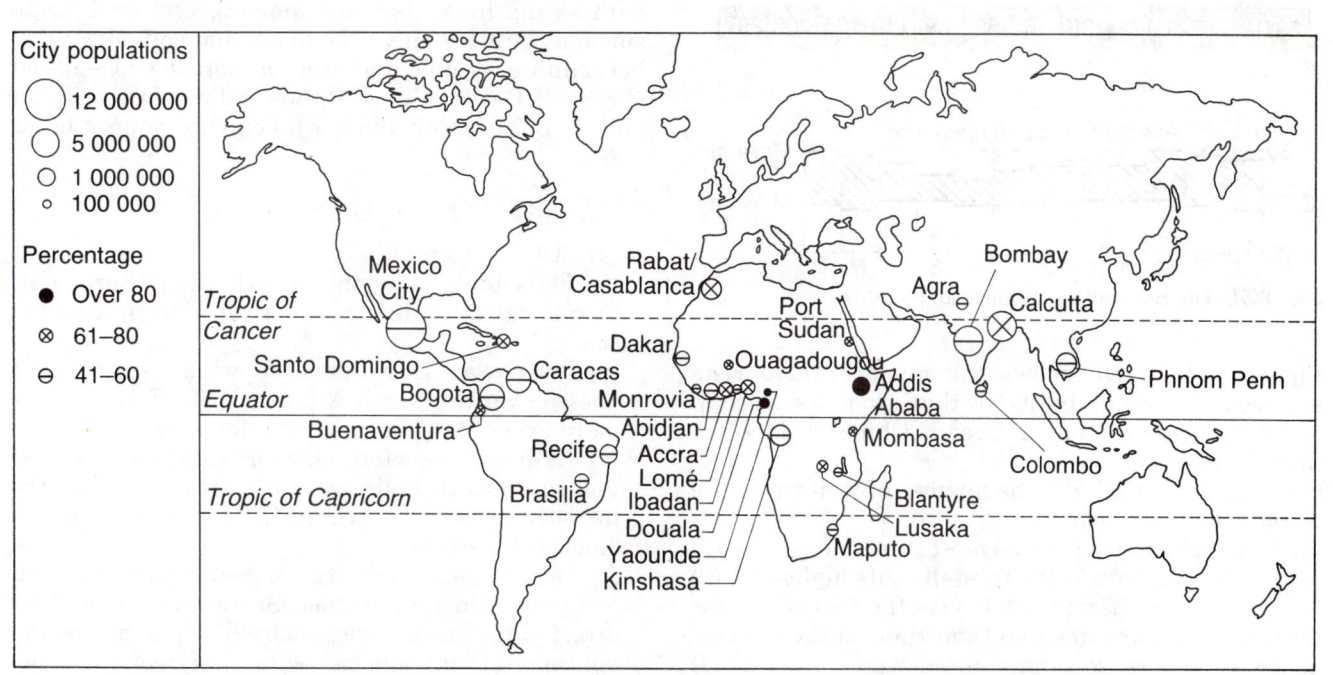

Fig. 6.4b The proportions of slum and squatter populations in some developing world cities, 1981

Fig. 6.5A

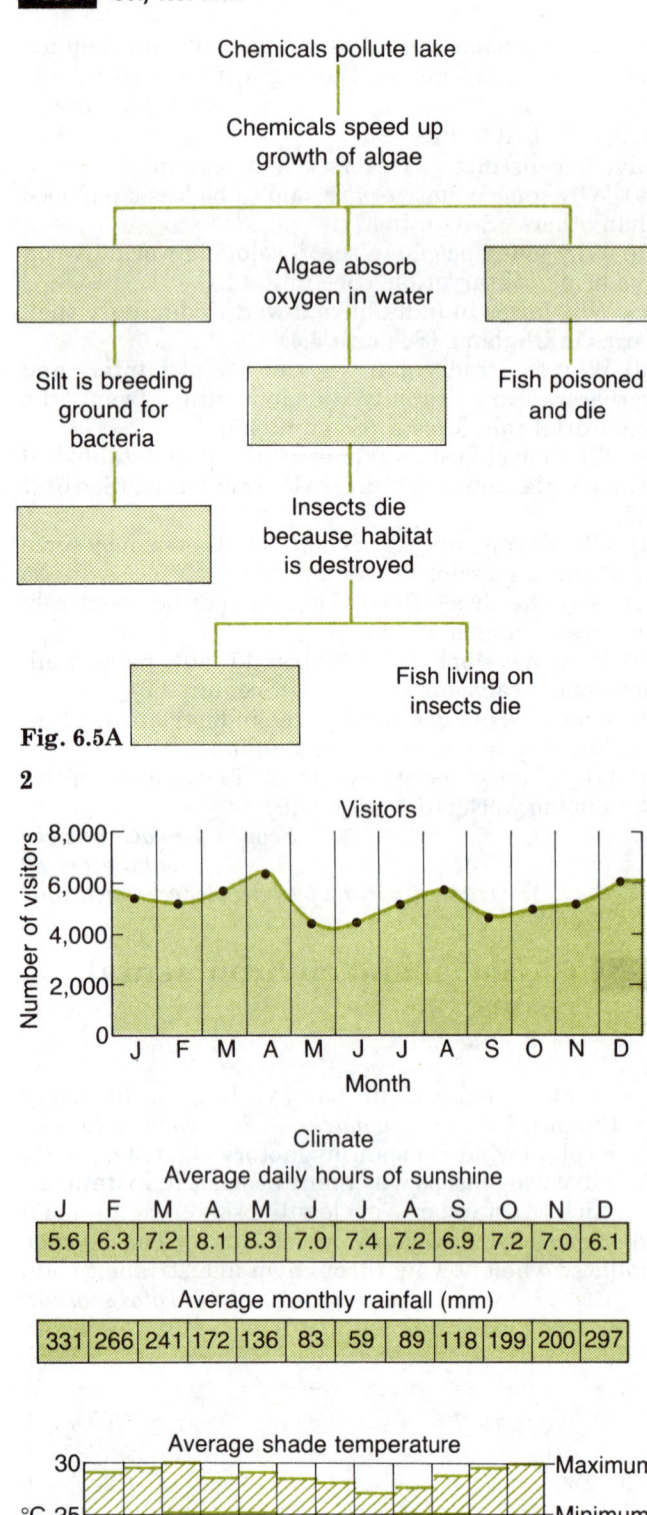

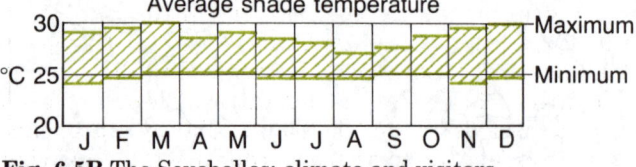

Fig. 6.5B The Seychelles: climate and visitors

Figure 6.5B above shows the number of tourists received each month in 1984 by the Seychelles, a group of islands in the Indian Ocean. Climatic data for the islands is also given.
(a) In which month did the number of visitors to the islands reach its peak? (2)
(b) In which month is there most sunshine? (2)
(c) In which month is the rainfall at its highest? (2)
(d) Which is the best month to visit the Seychelles, for tourists who want to spend their time on the islands' beaches? Give reasons for your answer. (4)
(e) Most visitors are from Europe. Suggest reasons why the peak months for visitors are not necessarily the best months for visiting the islands. (2)
(f) Suggest reasons why the government of the islands has passed strict laws prohibiting spear fishing and the killing of the green turtle. (4)
(g) What advantages are there likely to be for the people of the Seychelles as a result of the development of tourism? (4)

Total score 20

3 List five of each of the following:
(a) Reasons for rapid population growth in recent years. (See unit 5.1)
(b) Problems of population growth. (See unit 5.1)
(c) Resources of the tropical rain forests. (See unit 5.2)
(d) Alternative sources of energy. (See unit 5.2)
(e) Reasons for a shortage of food in Africa. (See unit 5.3)
(f) Conflicting demands for land. (See unit 5.4)
(g) Methods used to check soil erosion. (See unit 5.5)
(h) Problems resulting from the building of the Aswan High Dam. (See unit 5.6)
(i) The greenhouse gases. (See unit 5.7)
(j) Sources of water pollution. (See unit 5.9)

1 mark for each correct factor   Total score 50
Total 90 for the social and environmental issues unit.

Answers

MAP WORK AND PHYSICAL GEOGRAPHY

1 (a) evaporation; (b) condensation; (c) evapotranspiration; (d) precipitation; (e) underground flow (groundwater flow); (f) run-off; (g) water table; (h) lake, dam, sea, water table.
2 (a) A—roche moutonnée, B—barchan, C—sea-cliff, D—crag and tail; (b) A—ice, B—wind, C—water, (the sea), D—ice; (c) A—west-east, B—east-west, D—west-east; (d) Fine particles of sand blown by the wind, checked by a stone or other object and then building up into a barchan; (e) The U-shaped valleys are dammed for HEP; some areas are tourist attractions, with skiing in winter and camping and walking in summer; farming on valley floors and shoulders; timber; mining for gold and other minerals; (f) Génissiat (France); Davos; Upper Rhône valley; Frazer River valley, British Columbia; El Teniente copper mine, Chile.

THE BRITISH ISLES

1 (a) 13.3° Centigrade
(b) Felixstowe is further south than Stornoway. Stornoway is cooled by winds blowing in from the sea.
(c) Stornoway is warmed by winds which have passed over the North Atlantic Drift. Felixstowe is more exposed to continental influences.
(d) Rain-bearing winds come mainly from the west and south-west. Felixstowe is in the drier, eastern half of the country, where the low land does not cause relief rainfall.
(e) Depressions reach Britain mainly from the west, bringing rain and storms; Stornoway is in their direct path. Felixstowe is more likely to be open to continental influences, with anticyclonic conditions dominant more often during the year.

2 (a) The original port side was likely to have been near the bridge over the river. Goods could then be collected and distributed easily.

The quays where the ships berthed developed along the river banks in the old port.

When enclosed docks were needed in the 19th century they would have been built lower down the river on vacant land which could be reached more easily by the new, larger ships.

The container terminal is a modern development. It would be located near the mouth of the estuary on low-lying land. It needs a large site, so the lower shore of the estuary would be best. This is also a good location for an oil refinery since a jetty could be built out into the deep water.

The construction yard would need a supply of stone. On the opposite shore near the river mouth it would be near a quarry. The platforms could be launched into deep water.

(c) Since Glasgow docks are up-river, they can no longer handle the larger ships. As the proportion of cargo carried in modern container vessels increases, so the amount of cargo handled by the old upstream docks declines.

The increase at Greenock is due to the following factors:
1 The estuary is wide and deep (nearly 11 metres) at Greenock. The approach is easy and there is a sheltered anchorage off-shore.
2 There is no need for ships to wait for the tide.
3 The infilling of old dockland has provided room for expansion.
4 It has a modern container terminal.
5 There are sugar and oil-seed refineries near the docks.
6 It has a large modern ship repair dock (graving dock).
7 It has a direct freightliner link with Glasgow.
8 The M8 links it with Glasgow and the Central Lowlands.
9 It is able to export the machinery, metal goods, whisky and other products of its hinterland.

(d) Goods are loaded and unloaded nearer the points where they are produced and sold.

Glasgow is a centre of communication. This makes the collection and distribution of cargo easier. The banks and merchants' offices on which trade depends are in Glasgow.

WESTERN EUROPE

1 (a) Energy obtained directly from a fuel source such as coal, unlike electricity, which is a secondary source of energy; (b) HEP, nuclear power; (c) Trend in all countries is a sharp fall in coal consumption. (d) Those countries using natural gas have increased their consumption, with the exception of the Netherlands. (e) Increase in price; use of other sources of energy (nuclear); more efficient use of oil; slowing of production and therefore reduction in demand for energy. (f) Coal— train or river barge; oil— pipeline or river tanker; natural gas— pipeline. (g) Solar; thermal; tidal; wind.

2 (a) Sweden (b) Germany (c) Norway (d) Belgium/Lux; Denmark; France; Netherlands (e) Sweden (f) Poland (g) Increase in trade; improved communications; faster train and road services with rest of Western Europe. (h) Possible pollution from vehicle exhausts; increased noise; increased forest loss from acid rain; spoiling countryside; visual eyesores.

THE DEVELOPING WORLD

1 (a) The graph shows a reasonably stable situation until about 1750. Since that date there has been tremendous growth at an increasingly rapid rate; (b) (i) 300 years; (ii) Just over 100 years; (c) About 30 years; (d) (i) Better health care which reduces infant mortality and enables people to live longer; (ii) International aid offsets the worst effects of natural disasters; (e) Europe is likely to have the slowest-growing population. Population growth will be fastest in the developing world; (f) F. A. O. (g) (i) Decreasing fertility of soil; (ii) production is interrupted by flood, earthquakes, etc. (iii) production is interrupted by wars; (iv) farmers are turning to cash crops; (v) land is abandoned by peasants moving to the cities.

2 (a) Addis Ababa; (b) Shanty town; (c) Mexico City; (d) Brasilia; (e) No—Agra and Rabat/Casablanca (N.Hemisphere) and Maputo (S.Hemisphere) are not; (f) N.America, Europe, Australasia; (g) (i) Its size; (ii) the high proportion of slum and squatter settlers in its population; (h) (i) Illegally settled; (ii) temporary housing made of waste material; (iii) overcrowded; (iv) insanitary.

SOCIAL AND ENVIRONMENTAL ISSUES

1 (a) Check with fig. 5.9; (b) effluents are the liquid wastes from factories. They may consist of toxic chemicals and also include sewage; (c) sewage not treated before being discharged; outfall pipes do not carry effluent far enough out to sea; (d) factory effluents; water draining from rubbish tips and toxic waste dumps, sewage; hot water from factories.

2 (a) April; (b) May; (c) February; (d) May; there is a good deal of sunshine and very little rain, temperatures are between 24°C and 29°C; (e) European holidays are at Christmas, Easter and in the summer when the schools are not operating. These are peak tourist periods in the Seychelles. Many Europeans want to escape the northern European winter and visit the islands in December and January; (f) to conserve fish and turtle stocks, otherwise they could become endangered species; (g) higher incomes; more employment; greater range of jobs; improved infrastructure (roads etc); more contacts with outside world.

7 AN ANALYSIS OF EXAMINATION QUESTIONS

Positive Achievement

The GCSE examination is designed so that you will be rewarded for your positive achievements, for showing what you know, understand and can do. This poses a problem for the examiners, because not all candidates have the same level of ability and the examination must be designed in a way which gives *all* candidates across the ability range the opportunity to demonstrate their knowledge, abilities and achievements. The GCSE Examining Groups have used three different methods, in the design of their question papers, to differentiate between candidates and give grades which are appropriate to candidates' performance.

1 Different question papers

Some Examining Groups, such as the Scottish Examining Board, the Northern Ireland Schools Examinations and Assessment Council and the Midland Examining Group have designed separate papers for specific grades. For example, the Midland Examining Group's Syllabus A offers a choice of three papers, each targeted at a different range of ability. Paper 1 will normally provide for the range of grades between G and D, Paper 2 for grades E to C and paper 3 for grades D to A. This range can be extended in exceptional circumstances. Candidates will be advised by their teachers as to which of these three papers they should take. In Scotland, Foundation Levels papers will assess grades 6 and 5, Foundation and General Levels papers, grades 6, 5, 4 and 3 and General and Credit Levels papers will assess grades 3, 2 and 1.

2 Differentiation by candidate's response

The Southern Examining Group (Syllabus B) and the London East Anglian Group (Syllabuses A and B), have chosen to give all candidates the same questions, which are not graded in any way. The questions are designed to give all candidates the opportunity of answering them, that is they test the positive achievements of the candidates. However, some candidates will be able to give more detailed descriptions and explanations, as well as providing a deeper insight by being able to analyse, identify problems and make generalizations. Examiners are provided with details of the kinds of answer that are required to obtain particular grades. These details enable them to give credit for different levels of answer. It is extremely important for you to answer the questions as fully as possible and to provide as much detail and explanation as you possibly can.

3 Stepped questions and papers

When stepped questions are used, the early parts of the questions are the easiest, and less able candidates will succeed in answering these parts. More able candidates will also be able to answer the later parts, which are more difficult. The examination paper itself may also be stepped with the questions becoming more difficult towards the end. This form of differentiation is used by some examining groups, including the Northern and Southern (Syllabus A in each case).

Syllabus 0118, offered by the Welsh Joint Education Committee, provides a combination of methods 1 and 3, with stepped questions on separate papers, one of which is for grades C to G, while the other is for grades A to D. In the analysis table of syllabuses on pages x–xi, details are given of the various ways in which the question papers of each examining group are differentiated.

Question Types

STRUCTURED QUESTIONS

Depending on the examination syllabus you are using, all or nearly all of the questions will be *structured*. This means that they examine a topic by means of a series of sub-questions or instructions, and not by selecting an answer from a range of possibilities (i.e. objective tests). Structured questions test not only your knowledge, but also your ability to understand and interpret geographical information, to form conclusions and to organize your ideas and statements in sentences. A considerable number of the structured questions on the examination paper will be concerned with key ideas and issues.

1 Key ideas

The emphasis in the GCSE on understanding underlying ideas or concepts, rather than being able to memorize information by heart, has resulted in a significant change in the design of many of the questions. Key ideas or general principles relate to certain basic situations which recur whether the country under consideration is Sri Lanka or Ireland. Consequently it is not unusual to find that imaginary, rather than real situations are used as examples, with the question either asking for an interpretation of the situation or

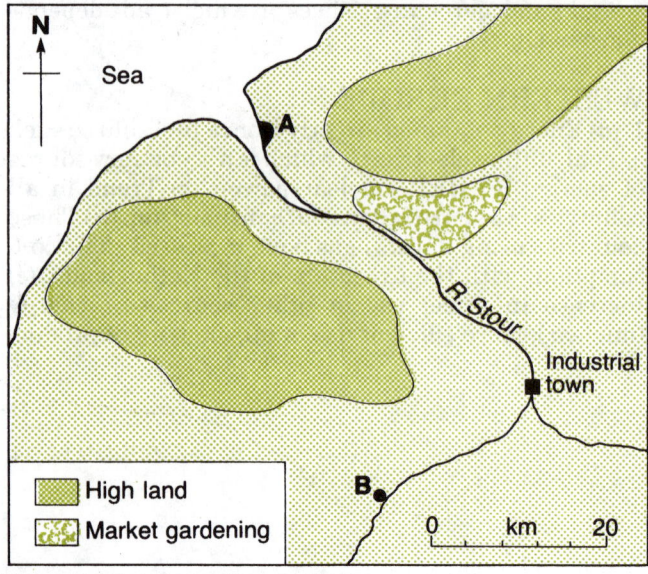

Fig. 7.1 Motorway planning map

posing a problem in connection with it. Here are two examples:
Using fig. 7.1 plan a motorway to join the two towns marked A and B.
(a) Draw the motorway on the map.
(b) Name four factors shown on the map which influenced the route you have chosen.
(c) Explain how the factors you have named in (b) influenced your choice of route.
In this question, the general principles which are being tested are those concerned with the requirements for a routeway — the need for level land, a firm foundation, proximity to settlements and so on.

If you have studied routeways using Ordnance Survey maps, you will have noted how the routes chosen have some features in common and that the ideas involved are basically the same however many maps you study. The question does not, therefore, test factual information, but your ability to understand underlying ideas and to apply them to particular situations.

The second diagram, fig. 7.2, shows a simplified map of the urban zones of a seaside resort which has developed in the last 150 years.
(a) What kinds of buildings would you expect to find in zone A?
(b) Which zone would contain the central business district?
(c) 'An area of old picturesque houses and sailors' taverns, with some small businesses such as boat repairers and ships' chandlers'. Which zone fits this description?
(d) Where would you expect to find some of the most expensive private houses with good sea views? Give reasons for your answer.
(e) Where should any further building be prohibited and an Area of Outstanding Natural Beauty designated? Give reasons for your answer.

Many seaside resorts have features similar to those shown in the diagram, and a study of the growth of settlements would provide the kind of background which is necessary to answer the five parts of the question satisfactorily.

Sometimes a question uses a model to illustrate a general principle. For example, cities have a number of common features, which include a central business district, areas of inner city decay, industrial zones and recent suburban developments. All these can be shown on a diagram which is a generalized model of what most cities are like. The important point about a model is that it is not based on a single example, but on many examples which have been analysed to identify their general characteristics.

When answering a question about a model it is important to relate the model to all the knowledge you have about similar areas or activities. The question may ask for examples of what the model illustrates; if there is an opportunity to show the examiners that you have this knowledge, then make sure you use it.

There are many forms in which general principles can be tested and there is obviously no material which can be learned by heart and used in the examination room. There is, however, a great deal to be said for trying out beforehand as many questions of this type as you can obtain from books or past examination papers. The same question is unlikely to be asked twice but the 'feel' of the question and the problems posed are worth experiencing and investigating, so that the form of the questions is familiar. Examples of questions based on ideas can be found in Section 9 on pages 157–161.

Questions which test your understanding of key ideas usually require written answers and this gives you the opportunity to show how much you know and understand about the subject in the sentences which you write. It is therefore important to include in your answer all the relevant information that is required.

2 Issues

Some structured questions will be concerned with issues, that is with such problems as conservation,

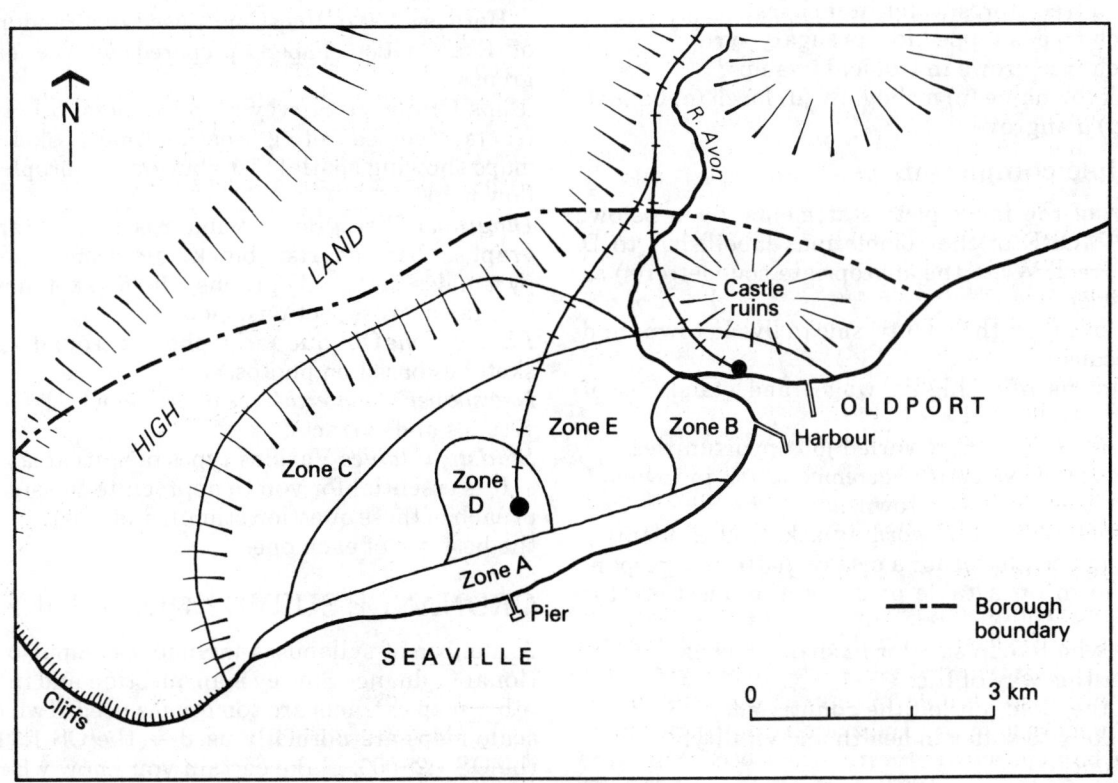

Fig. 7.2 Seaville

population control, natural hazards, pressures on land use and non-renewable resources. A typical question on the important issue of migrant workers might start with a map using flow lines to show the origins of migrant workers in West Germany. Questions would follow on the map and then other sections might include questions on why migrant workers leave their own country, what problems they may find in the host country and the problems they may face when they are no longer required by the host country.

OBJECTIVE TESTS

Two of the examining groups (London East Anglian Group, Syllabus A and the Northern Examining Association, Syllabus A) have included an objective test as part of the examination. Objective tests are made up of questions for which there are precise answers and for which the marking can therefore be objective, that is, not influenced in any way by the personal opinions of the examiner. In many objective test items, you are asked to select one or more answers from a number of possible alternatives. These are called multiple-choice questions and there are three main types:

1 Simple completion

Which one of the following activities is an example of a tertiary industry?
A fishing
B dentistry
C forestry
D building
E tin mining

2 Matching pairs

For each question, choose the letter representing the feature which most appropriately answers it. Each heading may only be used once.
(i) Which tree is coniferous?
(ii) Which tree stores water in its bark?
(iii) Which tree is tapped for its sugary syrup?
(iv) Which tree grows in tropical swamps?
(a) kapok (b) maple (c) mahogany (d) larch (e) baobab (f) oak (g) mangrove

3 Multiple completion

For each of the incomplete statements given below, ONE or MORE of the completions labelled A to D is/are correct. Write the appropriate code letter(s) as your answer.
People move from the countryside to live in towns and cities because:
(A) the towns offer higher wages and standards of living.
(B) the towns offer more varied job opportunities.
(C) there is always better accommodation in towns.
(D) there is less crime in towns.
An alternative form of wording asks you to identify the correct code letter for a certain pattern of responses as shown on a table or below the question, for example:
Families who live in squalor in shanty towns:
(1) prefer this way of life.
(2) wish they had not left the countryside.
(3) are likely to suffer in health and vitality.
A   (1) alone
B   (3) alone
C   (1) and (2) only
D   (2) and (3) only
E   (1), (2) and (3)

Unlike many other question types, multiple choice questions give you the opportunity to identify what you *think* may be the right answer, even if you are not quite sure. It may well be that careful thought about the alternative answers which you are given will enable you to eliminate the unlikely statements and leave only the correct answer.

Be quite certain that you obey the rubric and that, for example, when you are asked to select one answer out of a group, you do not select more than one. The examiner will award you no marks for your answer, even if one of the answers you have given is correct, unless you have followed the instructions given.

Question Stimuli

Nearly all GCSE examination questions in geography which are structured are multi-part. This means that each question is broken up into a number of sections and sub-sections, each of which normally requires only a few lines of writing as an answer. For example, a photograph of an archimedes screw used for irrigation might be followed by the question,

'Explain how the archimedes screw is used to irrigate farm land.'

Subsequent sections of the same question might be based on other forms of irrigation, the difficulties caused by unreliable rainfall regimes and problems of providing aid to disaster areas such as the Sahel.

Multi-part questions often use a large number of question stimuli such as maps, photographs, diagrams and statistical data. A question may start off with a sketch map with questions, followed by questions on a statistical table, further questions on a newspaper cutting and a final section based on the interpretation of a photograph.

Here is a list of the stimuli used in a random sample of Examination Papers prepared by the examining groups:
Maps Ordnance Survey map extracts; other map extracts (overseas etc.); weather maps; sketch maps; maps showing spatial distributions; choropleth maps; flow maps.
Diagrams Pictograms; wind rose; pie graphs; line graphs; bar charts; block diagrams; population pyramids; pyramid graphs; field sketches; block diagrams; cross-sections; models.
Photographs Oblique aerial photos; ground photos and sketches based on photos.
Newspaper material Advertisements; cartoons; articles and extracts.
Statistical tables Various types of statistical data.

It is essential for you to appreciate the significance of each of these question stimuli and to be able to make the best use of each one.

ORDNANCE SURVEY QUESTIONS

A number of syllabuses include a compulsory or optional Ordnance Survey map question and in addition other map extracts are sometimes used. Two different scale maps are normally used — the OS 1:50 000 and the OS 1:25 000. Make certain you know whether one or both of these map types is likely to be used in your examination; the analysis table has details.

Here are some guidelines to follow when answering Ordnance Survey or similar map questions.

1 Spend several minutes looking at the map extract as though it were a picture. What kind of landscape is it a picture of? Does it show high land; coastline; many towns or villages; a region with few or numerous lines of communication? If you know which area of Britain the extract is taken from, try to remember what you know about that part of the country, as this may help you to understand the map. A map extract of part of Devon and Cornwall, for example, may include a section of moorland which may be one of the granite outcrops such as Dartmoor or Bodmin Moor.

2 Keep a check on the time. It is very easy to spend too long looking at the map and working out such things as cross-sections or physical divisions. More than the appropriate amount of time spent on the map question will leave less than a fair share for answers to the other questions on the paper.

3 Know the Ordnance Survey symbols. Although some examining groups provide a key, valuable time can be wasted checking a symbol against the key.

4 Be very accurate when measuring distances. (A length of cotton or the straight edge of a piece of paper are useful measuring aids.) Accuracy is also important when giving grid references, drawing cross-sections, and so on.

5 Do not worry unduly if you cannot answer all the detailed points about the map. Very often answers on such things as the meaning of OS symbols are worth only a small proportion of the total mark for the question.

WEATHER MAPS

Much of what has been said about Ordnance Survey map extracts applies to weather maps, although these are usually less complicated and do not require a long period of careful study before attempting to answer the question. One important point about a weather map is that it shows the weather at a particular time on one day of the year. Your answer is likely to be very different if, say, the weather map shows an anticyclone in January instead of July.

SKETCH-MAPS AND DIAGRAMS

Apart from being asked to interpret sketch-maps and diagrams, you may also need to draw or complete them as part of your answer. They are best drawn with an HB pencil and not with a biro, so that mistakes can be quickly rubbed out. The addition of some colouring may help to make the sketch more easily understood, *e.g.* dark green for a forest, blue for a lake and brown for high land. Only the basic colours of blue, red, green and brown need to be used, and then for shading only. Never use coloured pencils to draw outlines or to write annotations. Figure 7.3 is an example of a quickly drawn, but very effective sketch-map, where colours were not necessary.

Remember that drawing sketch-maps and diagrams takes time, and in an examination it is very important to ration out your time carefully. Drawing good

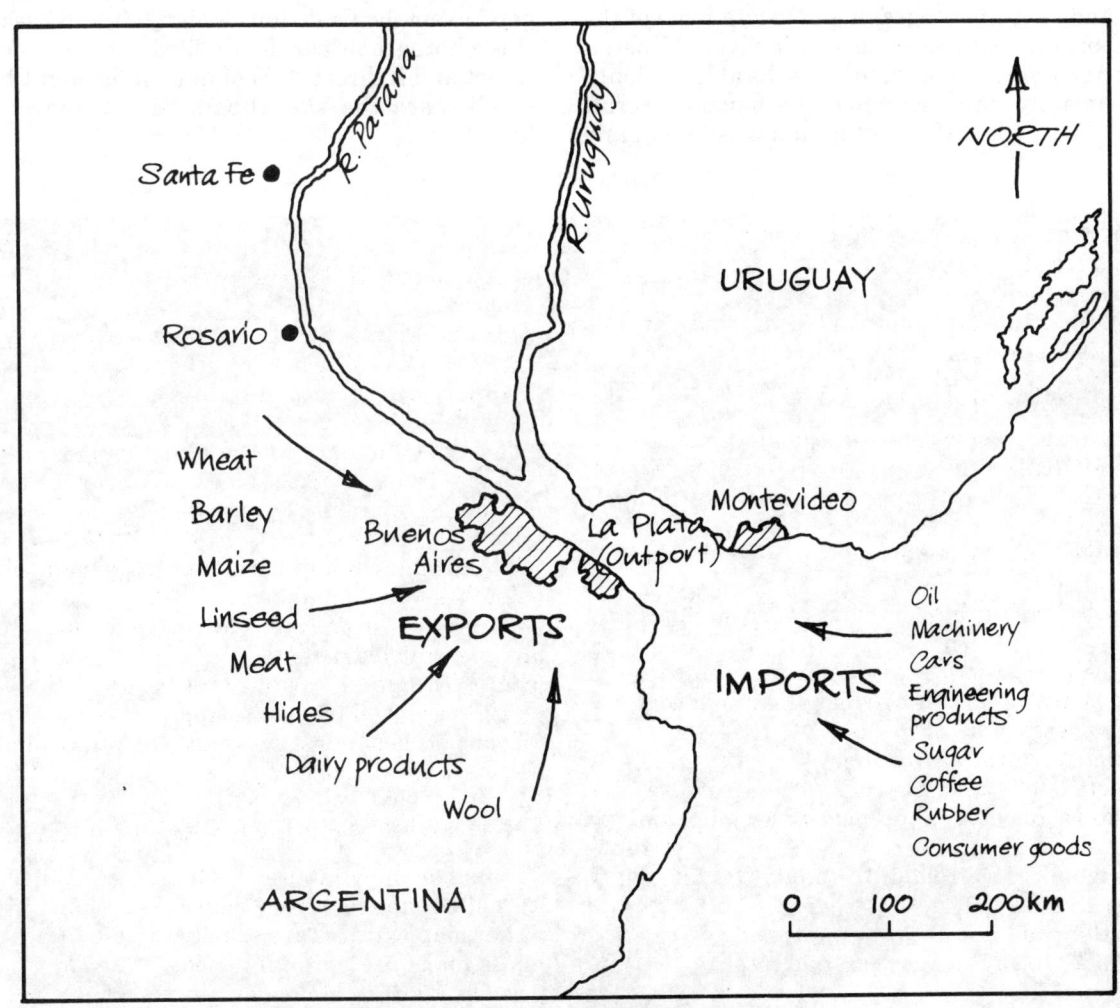

Fig. 7.3 The Pampas: imports and exports

diagrams accurately and quickly is a skill which you should practise whenever there is an opportunity. You may have spent hours drawing careful maps and diagrams for homework. In the examination room you can probably allow yourself only a few minutes, depending on what proportion of the answer must be given to the diagram.

Practise drawing diagrams and sketch-maps by first drawing one neatly and slowly. Then put it on one side, out of sight and try to reproduce it as quickly as you can. Check your first attempt against the original, remembering how long it took you to draw it. During the next day or so time yourself drawing the diagram from memory. After two or three attempts you will be surprised to see how rapidly you can reproduce the original drawing. Do not fall into the trap of repeating information in your written answer which has already been shown on an annotated sketch map or diagram. Examiners do not double mark and the mark is therefore only given once.

INTERPRETATION OF PHOTOGRAPHS

Two kinds of photograph are used in Geography examination papers. The first kind is known as an oblique aerial photo, because it has been taken from an aircraft with the camera pointing at an angle, rather than directly at the ground underneath the aircraft.

This type of photograph is sometimes linked to the Ordnance Survey map question. Part of the city of York, shown in fig. 7.4 can be identified on the 1:25 000 map extract which is at the back of this book. Look at the map and at the photograph and locate some of the more important features such as the river, Minster, castle and gas works. You should also be able to identify approximately which section of the map the aircraft was flying over when the photograph was taken, and the direction in which the camera was pointing.

One way of relating the photograph to part of a map is to concentrate first on something which is easily identifiable on the photograph because it is very large or because it extends for some distance across the landscape. In the photograph of York the Minster is very large, in other areas a hill, clump of trees or a lake might be the first clue to follow in attempting to match the photograph to part of a map of the same area. When the photograph shows an extensive feature like a river valley or a routeway, then make this the first landmark to look for on the map. In the photo of York the river is clearly visible. Once this has been located on the map you can find out which bridge on the map is the one in the foreground of the picture.

To find out which direction the camera was pointing it is best to keep the map on your desk with North pointing away from you and to turn the photograph round beside the map until the rivers, roads and other features are in the same directions as they are on the map. You will find that the photograph of York must be tilted to the right to match it with the North–South axis of the map. What does that suggest about the direction in which the camera was pointing?

The second type of photograph which appears on examination papers is the photo taken on the ground. Unless it is taken from a hillside, this kind of photograph usually shows little of the landscape. It may, however, provide a picture of such things as farming methods, industrial processes, transport systems or living conditions.

The photograph of flooding in Calcutta (fig. 7.5) is a good example. Questions which might be asked about this photograph can be divided into two categories: direct and indirect. Direct questions might be:

'Why are the shop floors raised above the road level?',

Fig. 7.4 Aerial view of York

Fig. 7.5 Flooding in Calcutta

'How do people normally obtain water in this street?',

'What do people use to carry the water back to their homes?'

Indirect questions could be concerned with the monsoon rains, why they are so important and what types of crop are grown in monsoon lands.

Research has shown that most people look at only a part of any photograph. Usually it is the part which they recognize easily and can therefore identify with most readily. If there is a golden rule about answering questions based on a photograph, it is that you should first look carefully at all that the photograph shows and not just at some object or figure which catches your eye.

NEWSPAPER MATERIAL

Figure 7.6 shows one type of question stimulus which uses part of a newspaper article and the accompanying sketch map. As with photographs, the questions on this article can be both direct and indirect. Typical questions on this newspaper extract in a stepped question might include:

Direct questions
1 (a) What source of power would the barrage harness?
(b) What percentage of the electricity demand for England and Wales could be provided by this barrage?
(c) What is one problem in providing electricity from this form of barrage?
(d) Why could this be called a multi-purpose scheme?

Indirect questions
2 (a) List the different ways electricity is generated in Britain at the present time.
(b) Why is it important for alternative forms of energy to be developed?
(c) List three other forms of alternative energy that may be used to generate electricity in the future.

Mersey barrage

Tidal power switch-on plan in 1996

By Peter Davenport and Derek Harris

Plans to build a £450 million barrage across the river Mersey were unveiled yesterday along with the prospect of tidal-powered electricity by 1996.

The Mersey Barrage Company, a consortium of 17 companies and financial institutions, has begun a two-year feasibility study into the project.

The study, which will cost £800,000, will examine two suggested sites for the barrage, one across the mouth of the river from New Brighton to Liverpool and the second, further upstream, from Rock Ferry to Liverpool.

The barrage would take 10 years to complete, provide 5,000 jobs in an area of high unemployment and benefit the tourist industry by creating a huge water lake to be used for water sports.

The barrage, which will be the first in this country, would harness the tidal power of the Mersey to generate 0.05 per cent of the electricity demand of England and Wales, worth £1 million a week.

The Mersey's tidal movements of 30 to 36 ft are among the greatest in the world.

Mr Peter Walker, Secretary of State for Energy, said that tidal power had its problems because its variable nature meant it would not necessarily coincide with peak electricity demands.

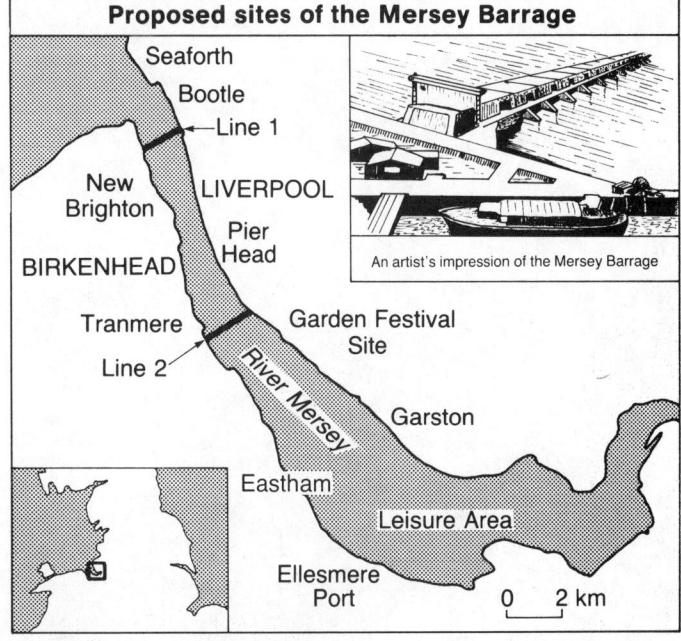

Fig. 7.6 *The Times*, 27 June 1986

STATISTICAL TABLES

The appearance in a geography examination paper of columns of figures seems to frighten a number of candidates, who avoid any such questions even though they may be very straightforward. Statistical questions should not cause any more anxiety than other questions on the paper. They may even cause less. Here is a typical example, with some of the direct and indirect questions which may be set.

Cargo and mail carried 1985/86 (tonnes)
Percentage change over previous year in brackets

Airport	Scheduled services	Cargo Non-scheduled services	Total	Mail
Heathrow	527,448	1,377	528,775 (−2·8)	73,861 (−2·1)
Gatwick	130,743	27,543	158,286 (8·2)	12,642 (2·3)
Stansted	2,984	7,711	10,695 (−26·7)	1,737 (2·8)
Glasgow	7,134	2,550	9,684 (−37·8)	5,011 (−6·1)
Edinburgh	849	1,691	2,540 (210·9)	10,031 (18·7)
Prestwick	11,338	751	12,089 (21·3)	235 (1,136·9)
Aberdeen	3,127	4,588	7,715 (−7·7)	1,445 (1·9)
BAA Airports	683,623	46,161	729,784 (−1·3)	104,962 (6·4)

Source: British Airports Authority

1 (a) What is meant by a scheduled service?
(b) Which airport increased the amount of cargo carried during the period 1984/85 to 1985/86 by the greatest amount?
(c) Which airport saw the greatest decrease in mail carried during the same period?
(d) Which airports showed a greater percentage decrease in the amount of cargo carried in this period than the percentage decrease for all the airports listed?

2 (a) Which of the following goods would you send by air from London to Oslo, rather than by other transport means?
fresh strawberries; furniture; diamonds; motor cars; carpets.
(b) Give reasons for using air transport for the goods you have selected for your answer to (a).

Here are the answers to the questions. How easy did you find this exercise?

1 (a) A scheduled service is one which appears in the timetable and occurs regularly. (b) Edinburgh (c) Glasgow (d) Heathrow, Stansted, Glasgow, Aberdeen.

2 (a) Fresh strawberries and diamonds (b) Strawberries deteriorate quickly and need to reach the market while they are still fresh, other forms of transport (rail and sea) would take at least 36 hours. Diamonds are lightweight and extremely valuable. The shorter the journey time the better, to keep insurance rates down and reduce the risk of the stones being stolen.

8 PRACTICE IN ANSWERING QUESTIONS

The twelve questions that follow have been reproduced from the 1990 and 1991 examination papers. At the examination you will find that the question papers are in the form of books, either with spaces under each section of the question for the answer, or with separate answer booklets for you to use. Space could not be provided in this book for you to write out the answers in full. We suggest that you tackle two questions at a time having done the necessary revision. Time yourself using the time allocation at the beginning of the question and try to write in examination conditions – without background music etc. Detailed answers can be found on pages 154–159, but remember that they are not necessarily the only possible answers. They are our answers to the questions and were not provided by the Examination Boards.

When you check your answers follow the marking scheme closely and work out what percentage of the total marks you achieve. If you have less than 50 per cent you will need to go back and revise the relevant units thoroughly and then try the test again. A total mark between 50% and 80% means that you are making good progress but need to do some further revision before attempting the questions again. Only if you have at least 80 per cent of the marks can you afford to go on to revise other parts of the syllabus.

Question 1
(Time allowed: 33 minutes)

1 (a) (i) What is the name of the weather instrument used to measure temperature? *(1 mark)*

(ii) Where in a weather station would you normally expect to find this instrument? *(1 mark)*

(iii) Use the following figures to calculate the mean temperatures for Tuesday 7 August, 1990. *(1 mark)*

    Maximum temperature   19 °C
    Minimum temperature   8 °C

(b) Look at Fig. 1 below.

Mean monthly temperature – °C

J	F	M	A	M	J	J	A	S	O	N	D
3.7	3.9	6.0	8.7	11.4	14.7	16.0	15.6	13.5	–	–	4.7

Fig. 1

(i) Use this information to complete the graph in Fig. 2. *(3 marks)*

(ii) Use the graph, Fig. 2 to find out the mean monthly temperatures for October and November. *(2 marks)*

(c) Look at Fig. 3.

(i) Explain why the mean annual temperatures of A is higher than B. *(4 marks)*

(ii) Explain why the mean monthly temperatures are higher for A in winter than for C. *(4 marks)*

(iii) Which place, A, B or C is likely to have the highest temperatures in summer? *(2 marks)*

(d) (i) Using Fig. 4, complete the following paragraph using some of the words below. *(3 marks)*

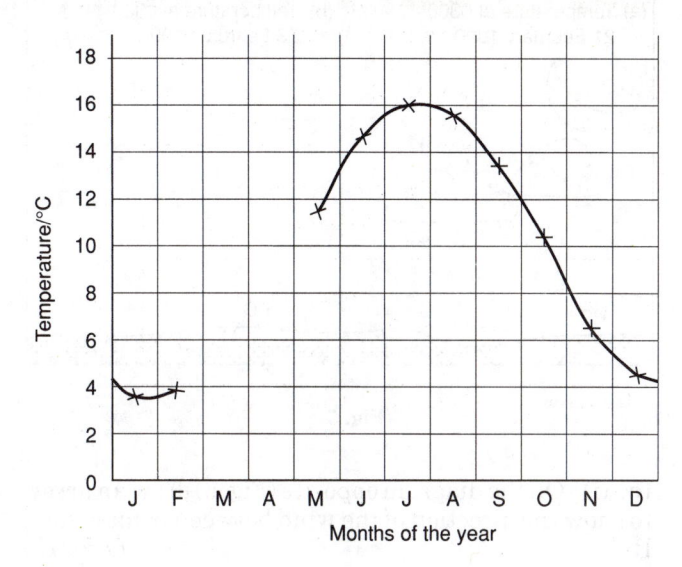

Fig. 2

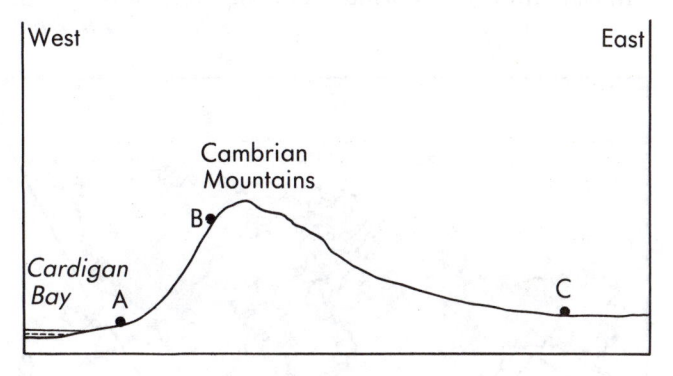

Fig. 3 A sketch cross-section through Wales

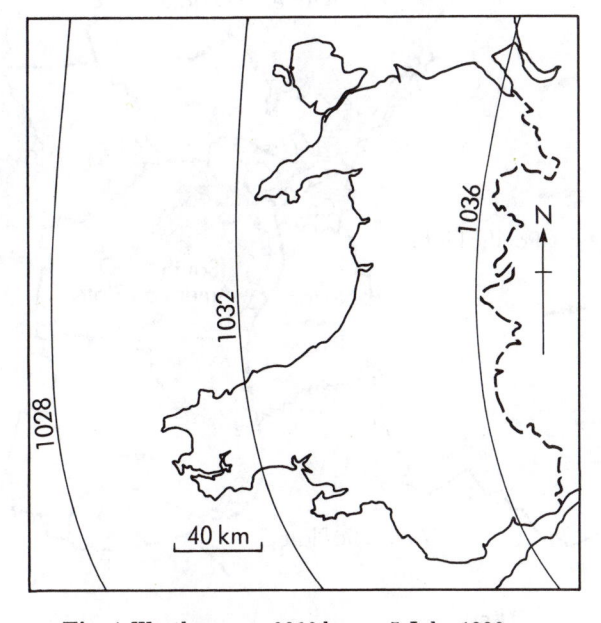

Fig. 4 Weather map, 0900 hours, 5 July, 1990

few; many; high; low; very warm; very cool

The map shows an area of _____ pressure over Wales. There are _____ clouds in the sky and the temperature during the day will be ____.

Practice in answering questions

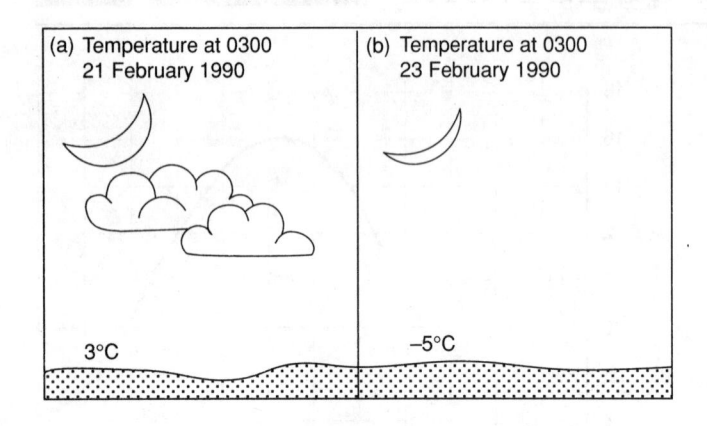

(ii) Using the diagrams below (Fig. 5), explain the differences between the night time temperatures. *(4 marks)*

(a) Temperature at 0300 21 February 1990 — 3°C

(b) Temperature at 0300 23 February 1990 — −5°C

Fig. 5

(e) (i) On the diagram opposite (Fig. 6) draw an arrow to show the direction of the wind between points A and B. *(1 mark)*

(ii) Explain why the wind is blowing in that direction. *(4 marks)*

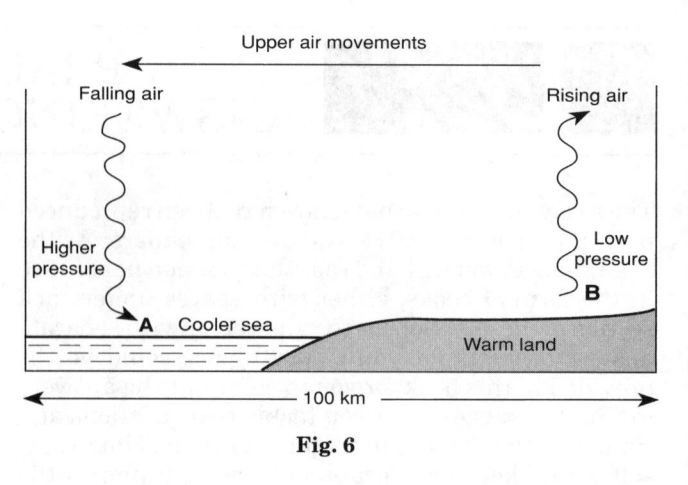

Upper air movements

Falling air — Higher pressure — A — Cooler sea

Rising air — Low pressure — B — Warm land

100 km

Fig. 6

(Total 30 marks)
(Welsh Joint Education Committee, Paper 1, June, 1991, Grades C–G)

Question 2
(Time allowed: 16 minutes)

2 (a) Study Fig. 7 which shows the main plates of the earth's crust and the location of some recent major earthquakes.

Key

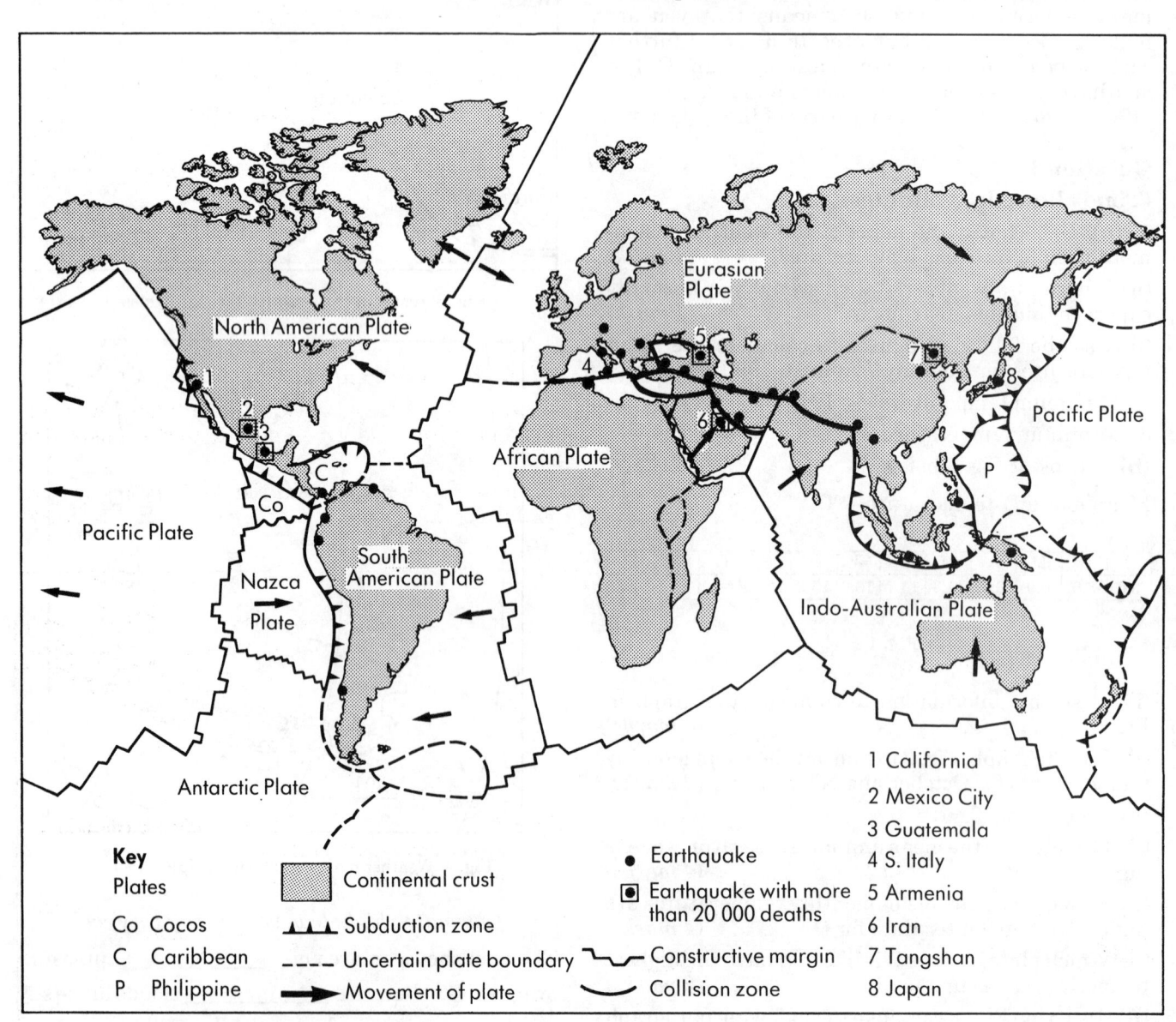

Plates:
- Co Cocos
- C Caribbean
- P Philippine

- Continental crust
- ▲▲▲ Subduction zone
- ---- Uncertain plate boundary
- ➔ Movement of plate
- • Earthquake
- ▣ Earthquake with more than 20 000 deaths
- ⌒⌒ Constructive margin
- ⌒ Collision zone

1 California
2 Mexico City
3 Guatemala
4 S. Italy
5 Armenia
6 Iran
7 Tangshan
8 Japan

Fig. 7

Practice in answering questions 141

Deaths	Richter	Location	Year
50 000		Armenia	1988
30 000		Mexico City	1985
450 000		Tangshan (China)	1976
25 000		Iran	1978
20		Japan	1983
23 000		Guatemala	1976
64		California	1989
3000		S. Italy	1980

Richter scale: 6, 6.5, 7, 7.5, 8, 8.5

Figures refer to number of deaths caused by earthquakes.
Power of earthquake measured on Richter scale.

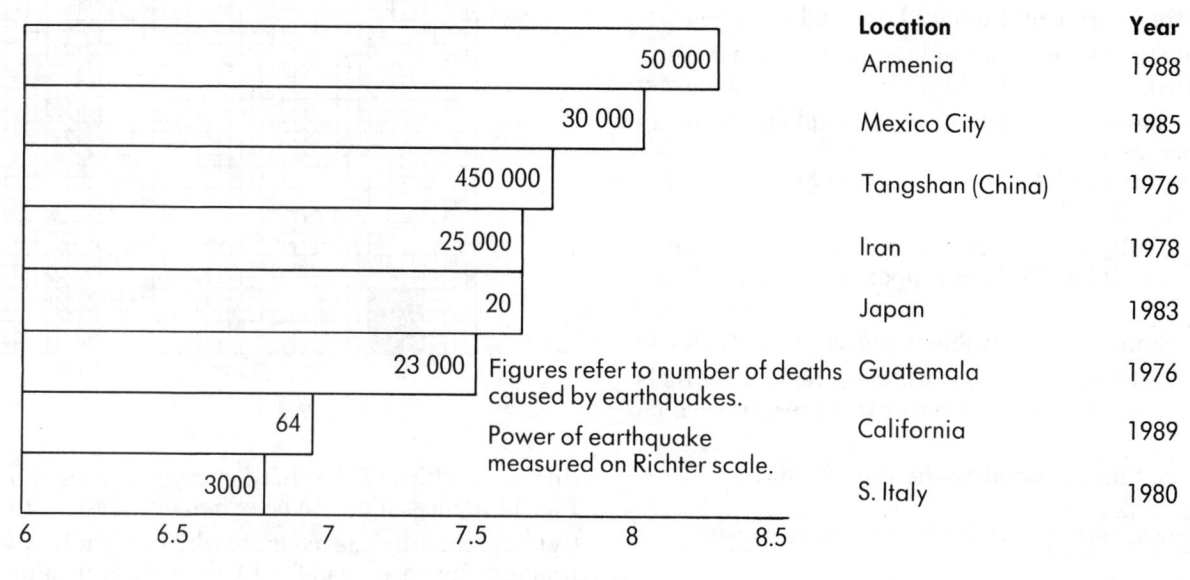

Fig. 8

(i) Define
A 'plate'
B 'subduction zone' *(3 marks)*

(ii) The earthquake in Japan occurred along the subduction zone between TWO major plates. Name the two plates. *(1 mark)*

(b) Fig. 8 gives some information about eight earthquake areas located in Fig. 7.

(i) Why is it difficult to decide from Fig. 8 which was the most serious earthquake? *(1 mark)*

(ii) Name TWO factors, other than the power of the earthquake, which might affect the number of deaths caused by the earthquake. *(2 marks)*

(c) Fig. 9 refers to an earthquake in Mexico City (located on Fig. 7).
With the help of Fig. 9, explain in detail what could cause such an earthquake. *(3 marks)*

(d) Describe some ways to reduce the dangers from earthquakes. *(3 marks)*

(Total 13 marks)
(Midland Examining Group, Syllabus A, Paper 2, June 1990, Grades A–D)

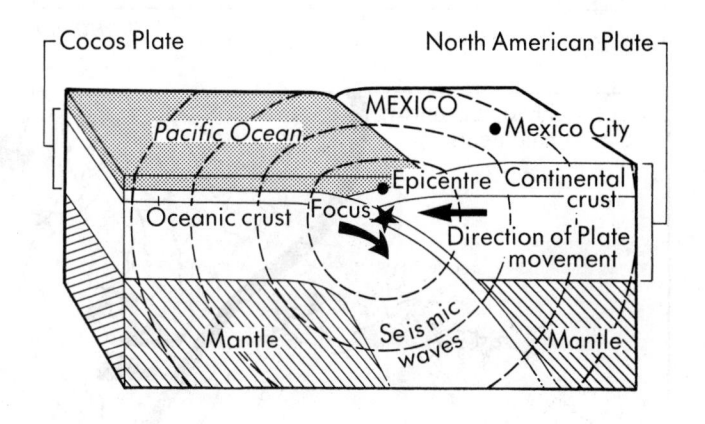

Fig. 9

Question 3
(Time allowed: 20 minutes)

3 (a) Study Fig. 10 which shows a tidal power station on the River Rance. Answer the questions which follow.

(i) State which resource in Fig. 10 is being used to produce power. *(1 mark)*

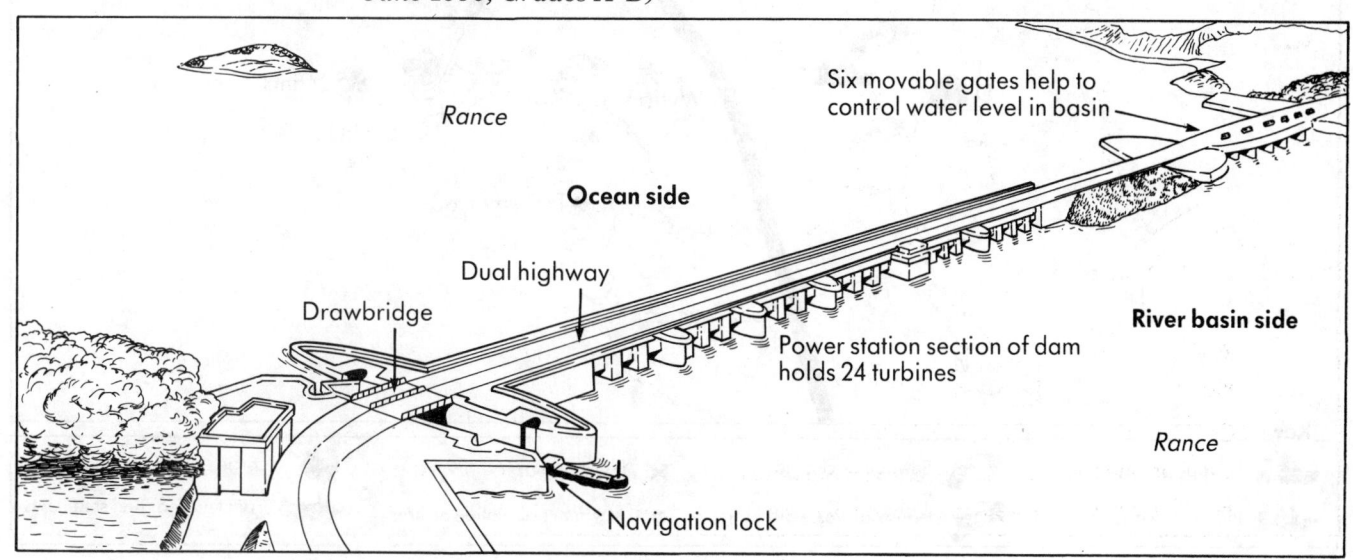

Fig. 10

(ii) State fully how river traffic moves from the ocean side of the barrier to the river basin side. *(2 marks)*

(iii) State fully how the water level in the basin is being controlled. *(2 marks)*

(iv) Developments in technology can exploit previously untapped resources.
State fully why the power station in Fig. 10 is a good example of this. *(3 marks)*

(v) State fully why a person concerned with the environment would be likely to support the scheme shown in Fig. 10. *(3 marks)*

(b) (i) Name one renewable resource. *(1 mark)*

Study Fig. 11 which shows world reserves of three fuels used to produce energy. Answer the questions which follow.

(ii) Using Fig. 11 complete the table below.

Energy Source	World Reserves (in years left)
Oil	
Gas	
Coal	

(3 marks)

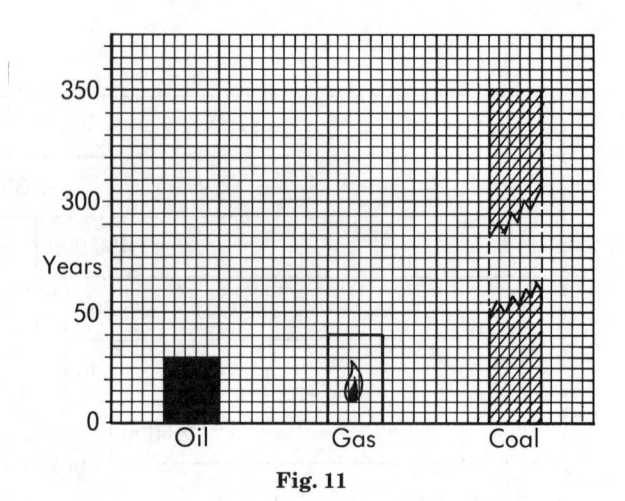

Fig. 11

(iii) State which of the three energy sources shown in Fig. 11 is most likely to be exhausted first. *(1 mark)*

(iv) Explain fully one measure which might be taken to prolong the reserves of a fuel which is in danger of being exhausted. *(3 marks)*

(c)

Study Fig. 12 which shows pollution in the Irish Sea. Answer the questions which follow.

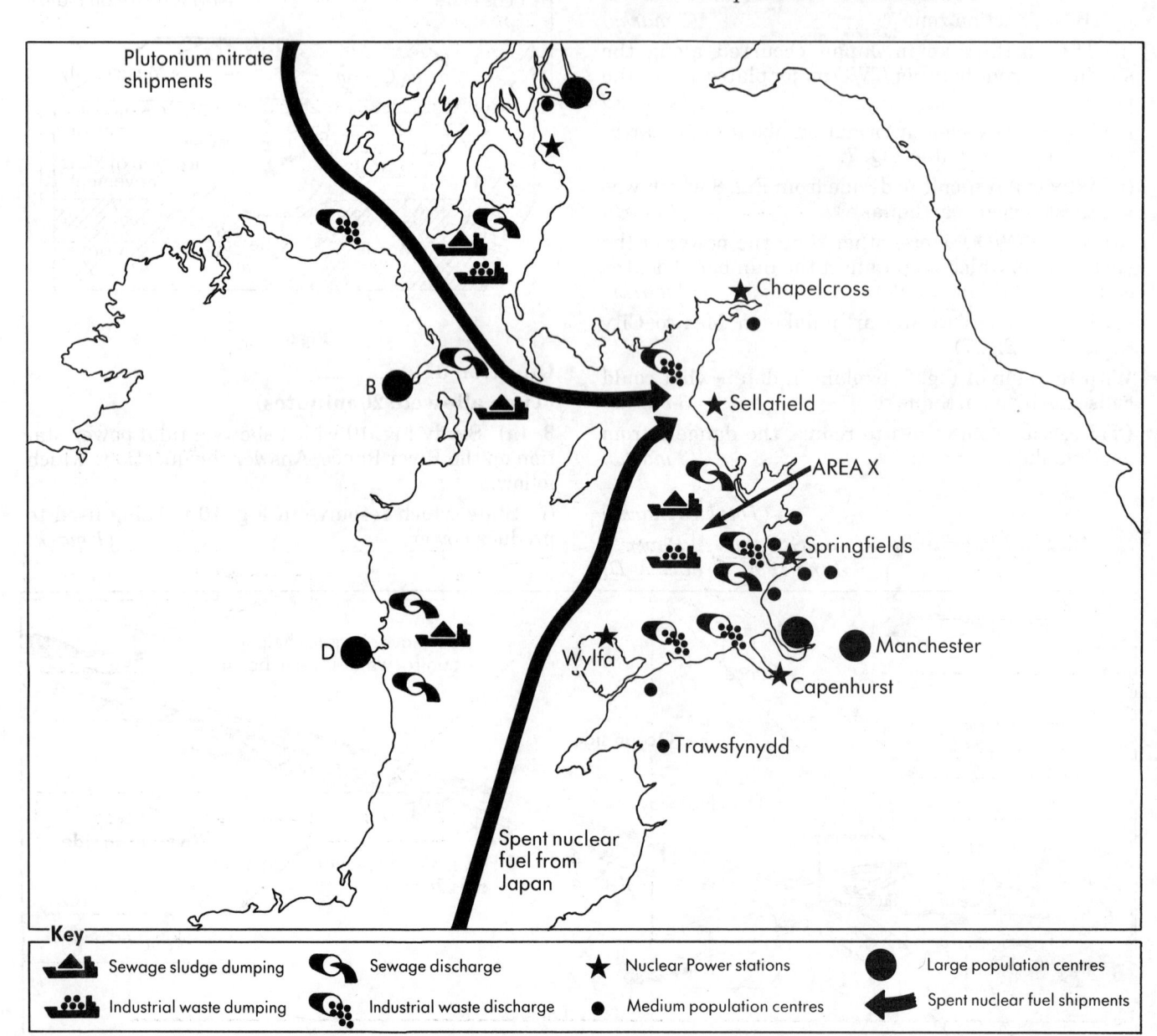

Fig. 12

(i) Using your atlas if you wish name the cities B, D and G on Fig. 12. *(3 marks)*

(ii) State two types of pollution shown on Fig. 12 *(2 marks)*

(iii) State fully one reason why Area X experiences so much pollution. *(3 marks)*

(iv) State fully one argument which could be used by someone who disapproves of the activities shown on Fig. 12. *(3 marks)*

(Total 30 marks)

(Northern Ireland Schools Examinations and Assessment Council, Paper 1, November, 1990, Grades C–G)

Question 4

(Time allowed: 12 minutes)

4 Fig. 13 shows average statistics for farms in Manitoba (Canadian Prairies) and Denmark.

	Manitoba	Denmark
Average farm size	259 hectares	26 hectares
Average farm income	£165 per hectare	£925 per hectare

Fig. 13

(a) on Fig 14 draw and label a bar to represent the average farm income in Denmark. *(1 mark)*

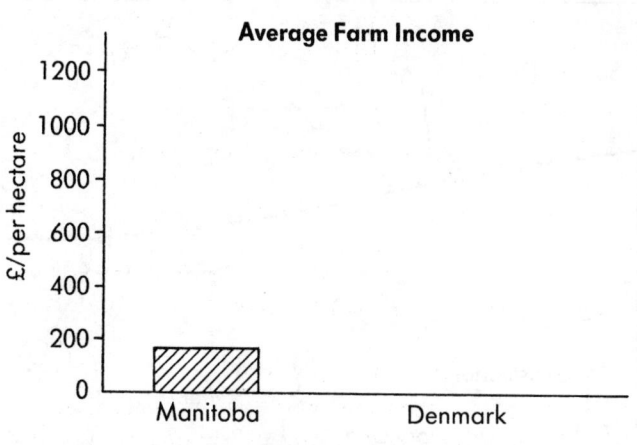

Fig. 14

(b) Give two reasons why farms in Denmark have a higher average income per hectare than farms in Manitoba. *(2 marks)*

(c) Give reasons to explain why Manitoba is suited to cereal farming. *(2 marks)*

Fig. 15 is a diagram showing inputs and outputs on a Danish co-operative dairy farm.

(a) On Fig. 15 complete the boxes to name the two missing products. *(1 mark)*

(b) Why is skimmed milk returned to the farm? *(1 mark)*

(c) What is meant by the term 'co-operative farming'? *(1 mark)*

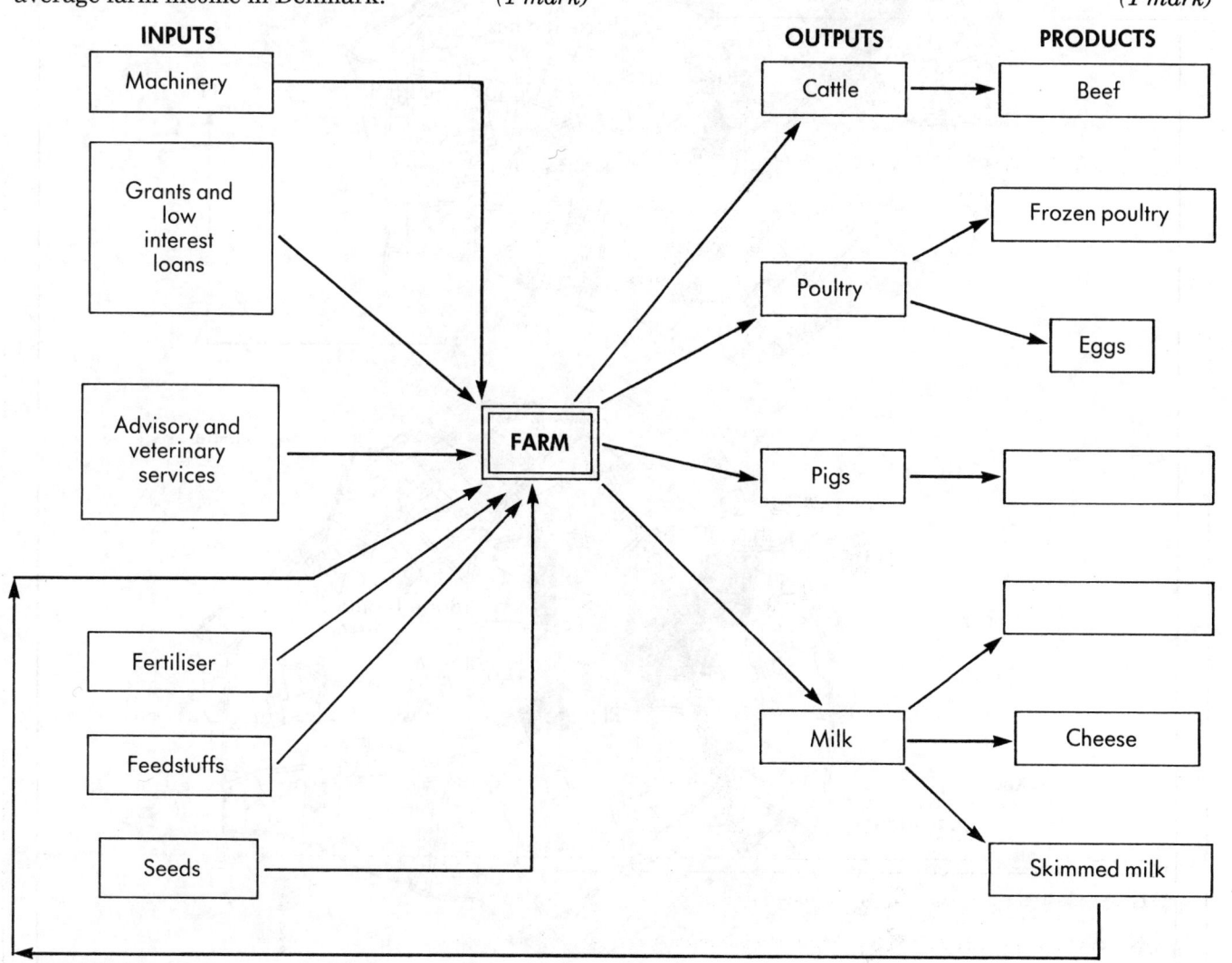

Fig. 15

144 *Practice in answering questions*

Key (Fig. 16):
- ⇢ Expanding Sahara Desert
- ▒ Desert front
- ⊘ Pockets of desertification
- Ⓝ Nomadic pastoralists
- Ⓕ Farmers
- ---- International boundaries

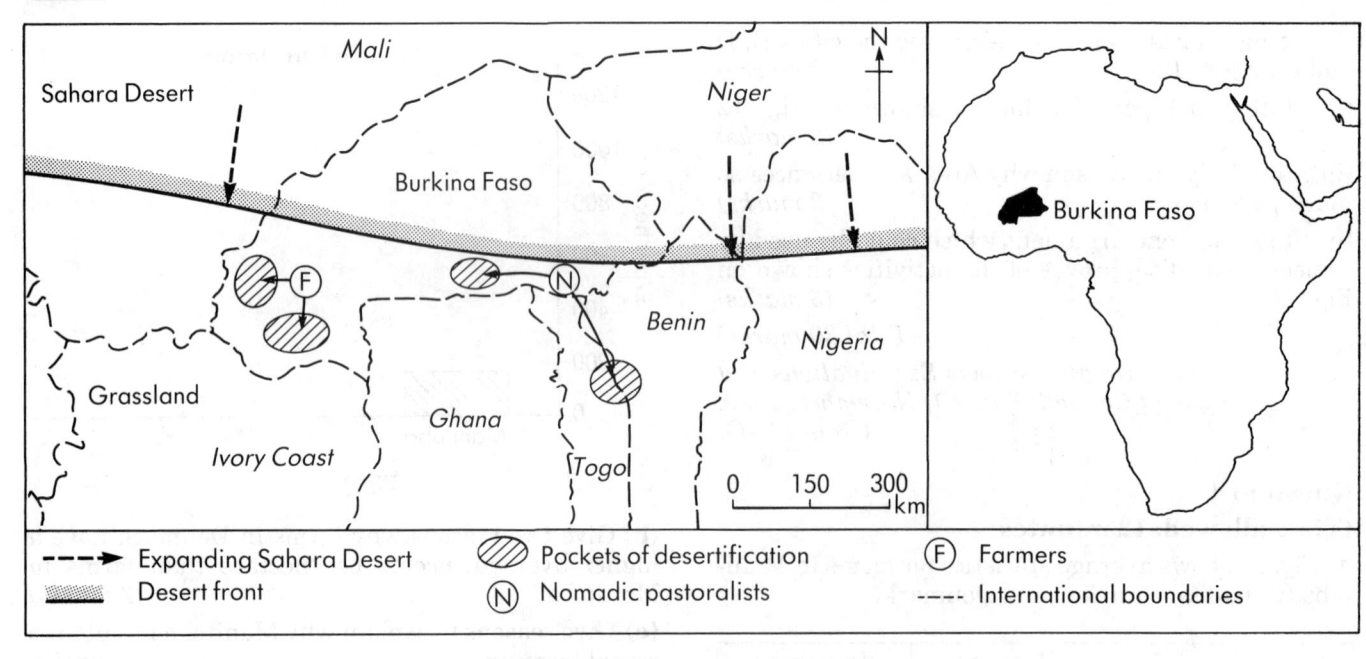

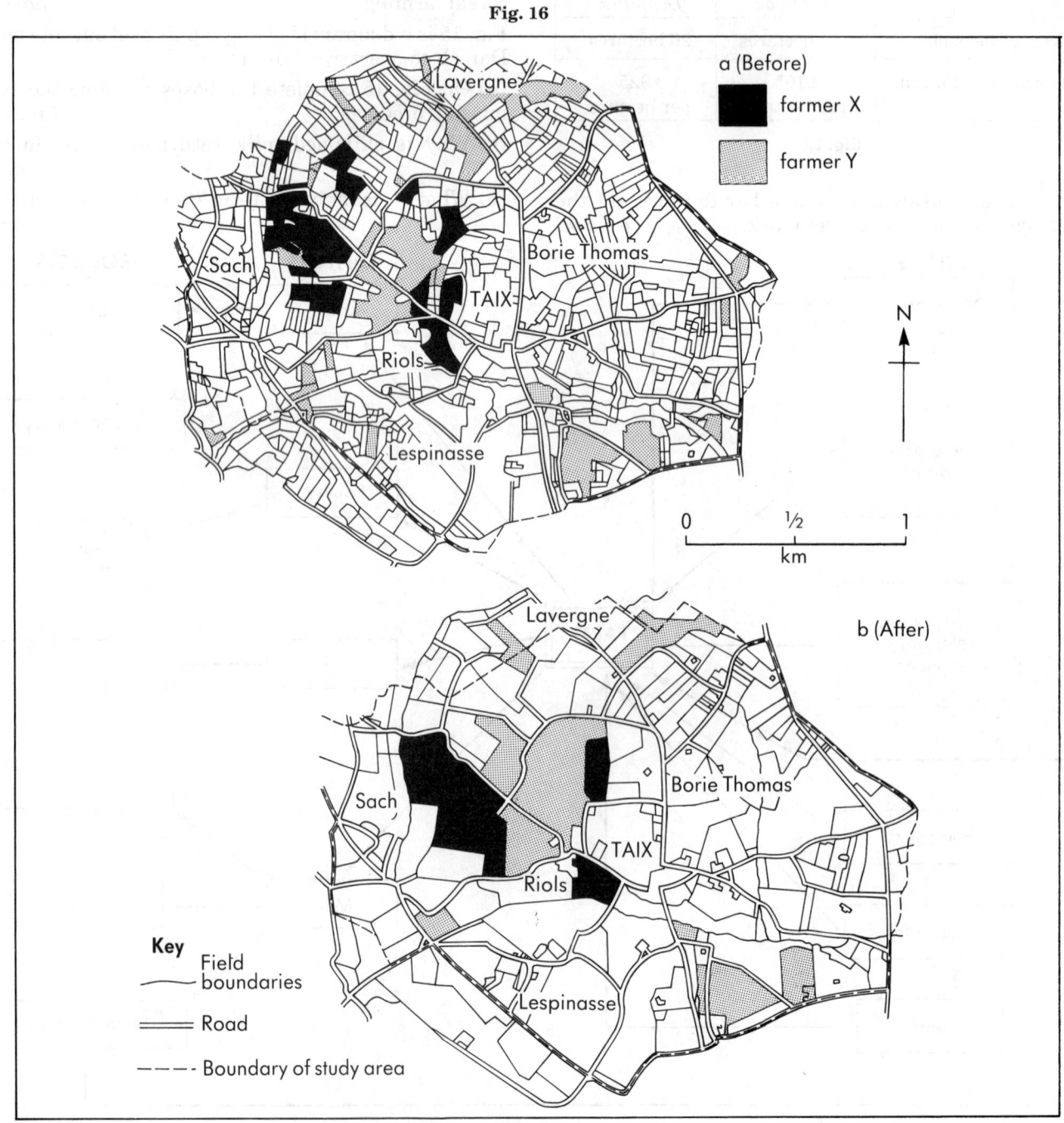

Fig. 16

a (Before)
- ■ farmer X
- ▒ farmer Y

Key (Fig. 17):
- Field boundaries
- Road
- ---- Boundary of study area

b (After)

Fig. 17

Practice in answering questions 145

In the past twenty years new varieties of crops have been developed for the Third World which give higher yields and which have helped create 'The Green Revolution'.

Describe the advantages and disadvantages of growing these higher yielding varieties. *(4 marks)*

(Total 12 marks)

(London East Anglian Group, Syllabus D, Paper 1, June 1991, common paper)

Question 5
(Time allowed: 35 minutes)

5 (a) Study Fig. 16 which shows the expanding desert in Burkina Faso, W. Africa. Answer the questions which follow.

(i) The activities of both nomadic pastoralists and farmers can result in desertification. Explain how each may have contributed to the spread of desert-like conditions in this area. *(6 marks)*

(ii) State and explain any two other factors which contribute to the problem of desertification worldwide. *(6 marks)*

(iii) In areas subject to desertification, state how the way of life of people may be affected. *(4 marks)*

(b) Study Fig. 17 which shows an agricultural area in France before and after attempts to improve agricultural output by land reorganization. Answer the questions which follow.

(i) State the main differences in the area after the reorganization took place. *(5 marks)*

(ii) Describe the advantages of schemes such as this to farmers. *(5 marks)*

(iii) State why some users of the countryside might object to reorganization schemes such as this. *(6 marks)*

(c) For a named example of either subsistence or commercial farming, state how the farmers' land use decisions are influenced by environmental and human factors. *(8 marks)*

(Total 40 marks)

(Northern Ireland Schools Examinations and Assessment Council, Paper 3, June 1991, Grades A and B)

Question 6
(Time allowed: 35 minutes)

6 (a) Study the field sketches, Fig. 18. They show the same farm in 1949 and 1989.

(i) Using the information in the field sketches, complete the following table. *(6 marks)*

	Changes which have taken place between 1949 and 1989
Woodland and trees	
Field boundaries	Many hedges hae disappeared. Some have been replaced by wire fences.
Fields	
Water features (marsh, pond, stream)	
Crops	
Footpath	
Wildlife habitats	

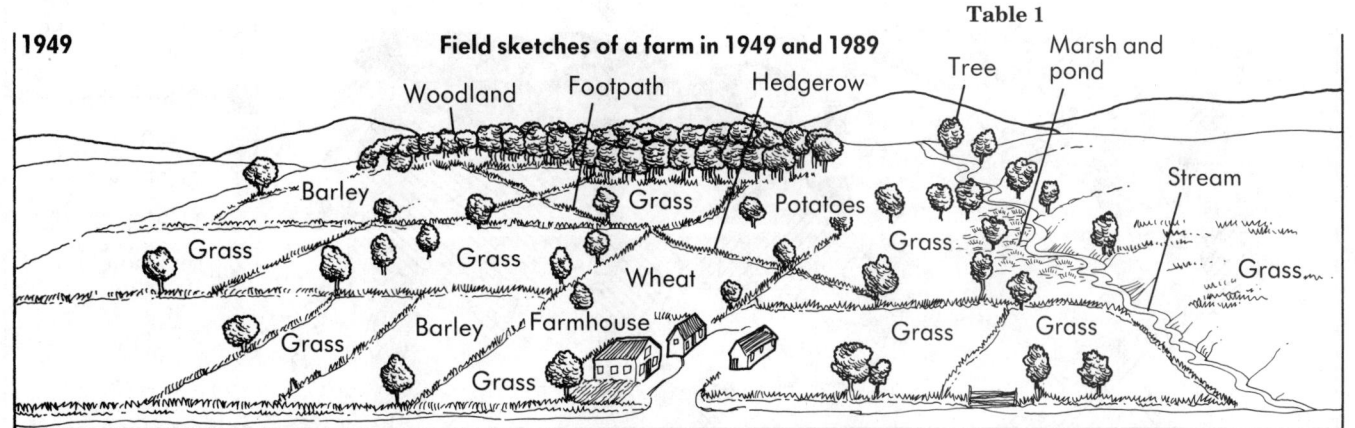

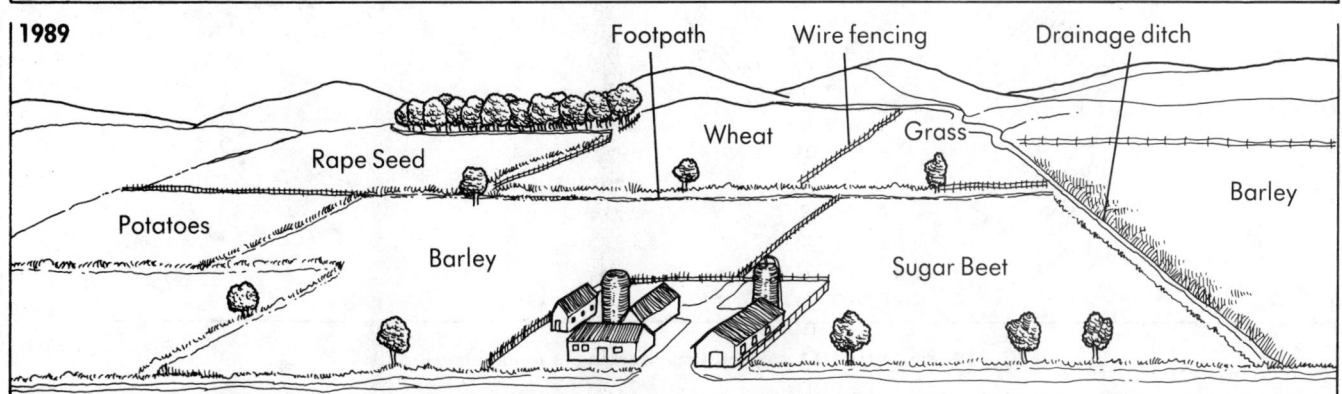

Table 1

Field sketches of a farm in 1949 and 1989

Fig. 18

(ii) Give THREE reasons which might explain why the farmer has removed hedgerows and trees from his farm. *(6 marks)*

(iii) What effect may hedgerow removal have had on the soil? *(2 marks)*

(iv) Give TWO reasons which might explain the removal of the pond and the digging of a ditch. *(4 marks)*

(v) Which of the two views of the farm do you prefer? Say why. *(2 marks)*

(b)

Group of Animals	Farm in 1949	Farm in 1989
	Number of species	*Number of species*
Mammals	19	6
Birds	34	9
Butterflies	19	8
Fish	9	0
Dragonflies	9	0
Gastropods (snails)	23	6

Table 2

Study Table 2. It shows changes in wildlife on the farm between 1949 and 1989.

(i) Describe the changes in wildlife on the farm between 1949 and 1989. *(2 marks)*

(ii) Apart from the removal of their habitats, give one other reason to account for the changes in wildlife described in (b) (i). *(2 marks)*

(iii) How might the farmer defend himself/herself against the charge of destroying the landscape and the wildlife of the countryside? *(3 marks)*

(c) (i) Describe the main features of a NAMED ecosystem you have studied.

Named ecosystem *(1 mark)*
Description *(4 marks)*

(ii) Show how the ecosystem has been changed and the effects this has had. *(4 marks)*

(Total 36 marks)

(Midland Examining Group, Syllabus E, Paper 2, June 1990, stepped question)

Question 7

(Time allowed 30 minutes)

7 (a) Fig. 19 shows employment in manufacturing throughout the world.

Suggest reasons for differences in the contribution made by manufacturing in the employment structure of various world areas. *(4 marks)*

(b) High technology industries have grown in recent years in the area between London and Bristol shown on Fig. 20.

(i) Why are high technology industries described as 'footloose'? Explain how this influences their location. *(3 marks)*

(ii) Account for the attraction of the area shown for the

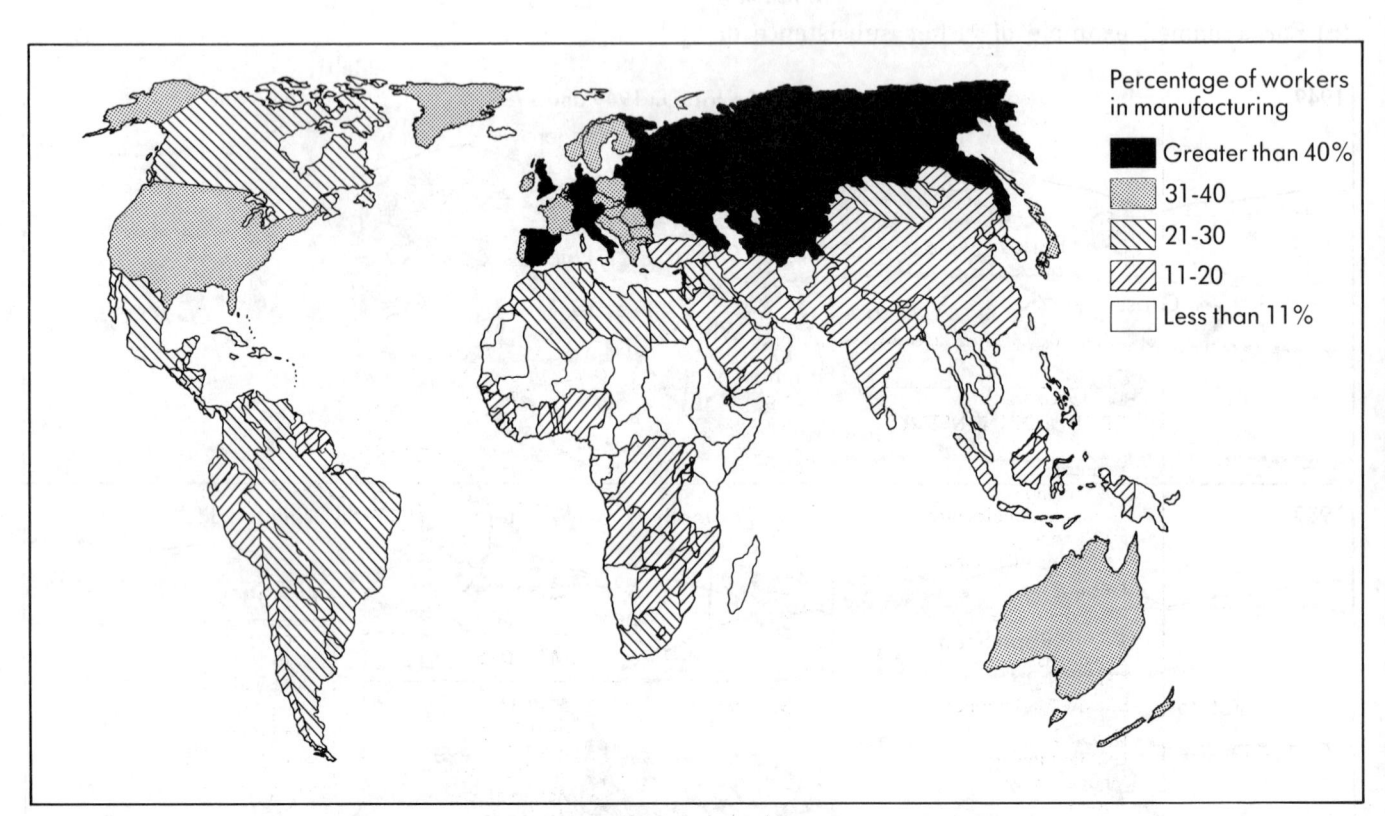

Fig. 19 Percentage of total workforce working in manufacturing 1984

Practice in answering questions 147

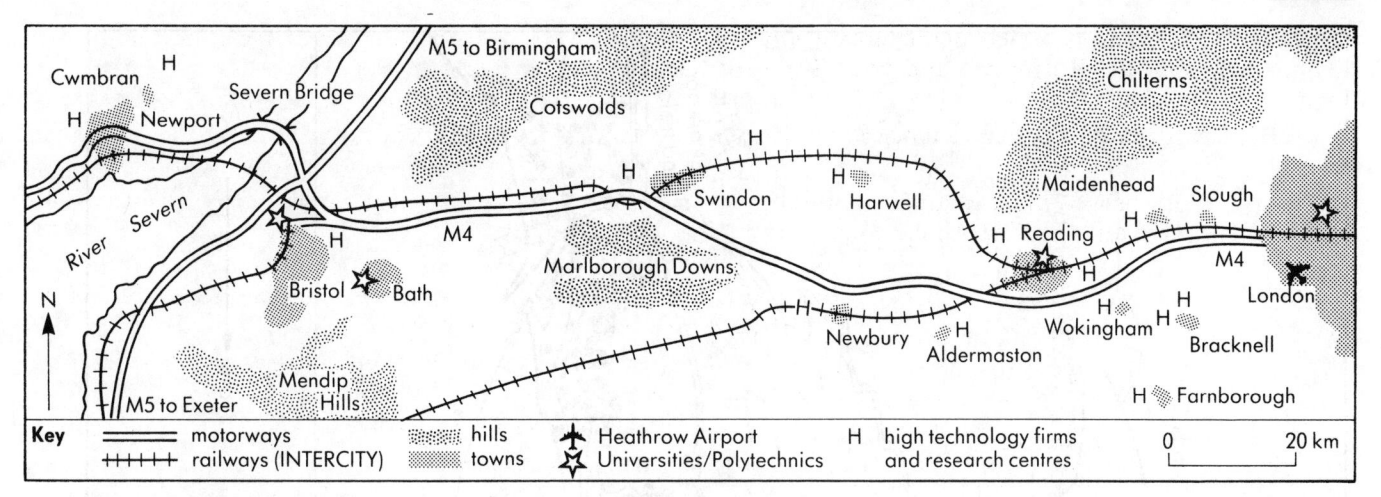

Fig. 20

location of high technology industries. *(5 marks)*

(iii) Modern industrial developments, including high technology industries, are often located in rural areas, small market towns and New Towns, rather than in large established industrial areas. Give arguments for and against this new trend in industrial location.
(6 marks)

(c) Study Fig. 21.

(i) Write down A,B,C as a list to represent the areas shown and state which of the industrial groups 1,2 or 3 you would expect to be located in each of these areas.
(1 mark)

(ii) Explain your choice of locations in (c) (i).
6 marks)

(Total 25 marks)
(Midland Examining Group, Syllabus B, Paper 2, June 1990, Grades A–E.)

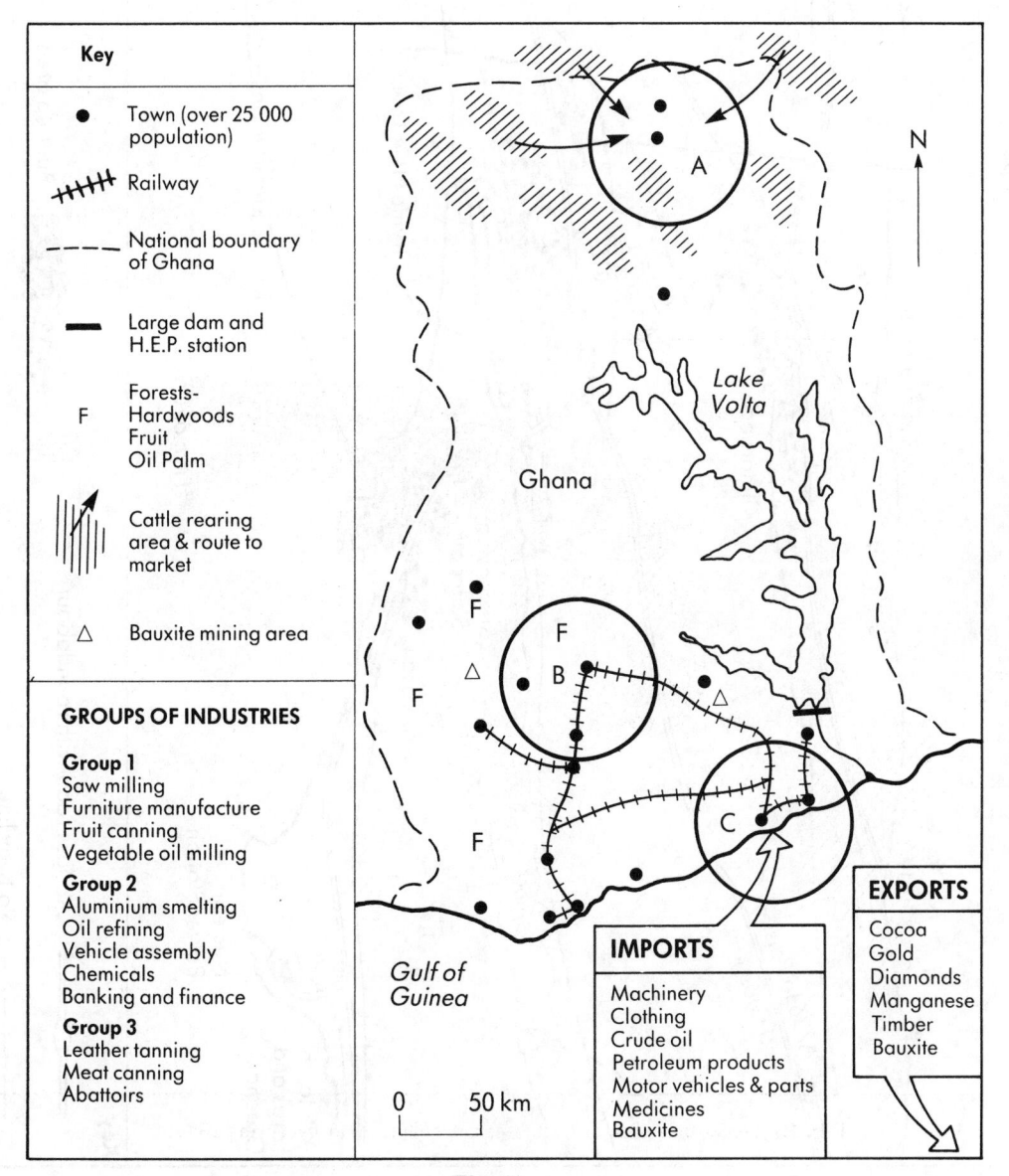

Fig. 21

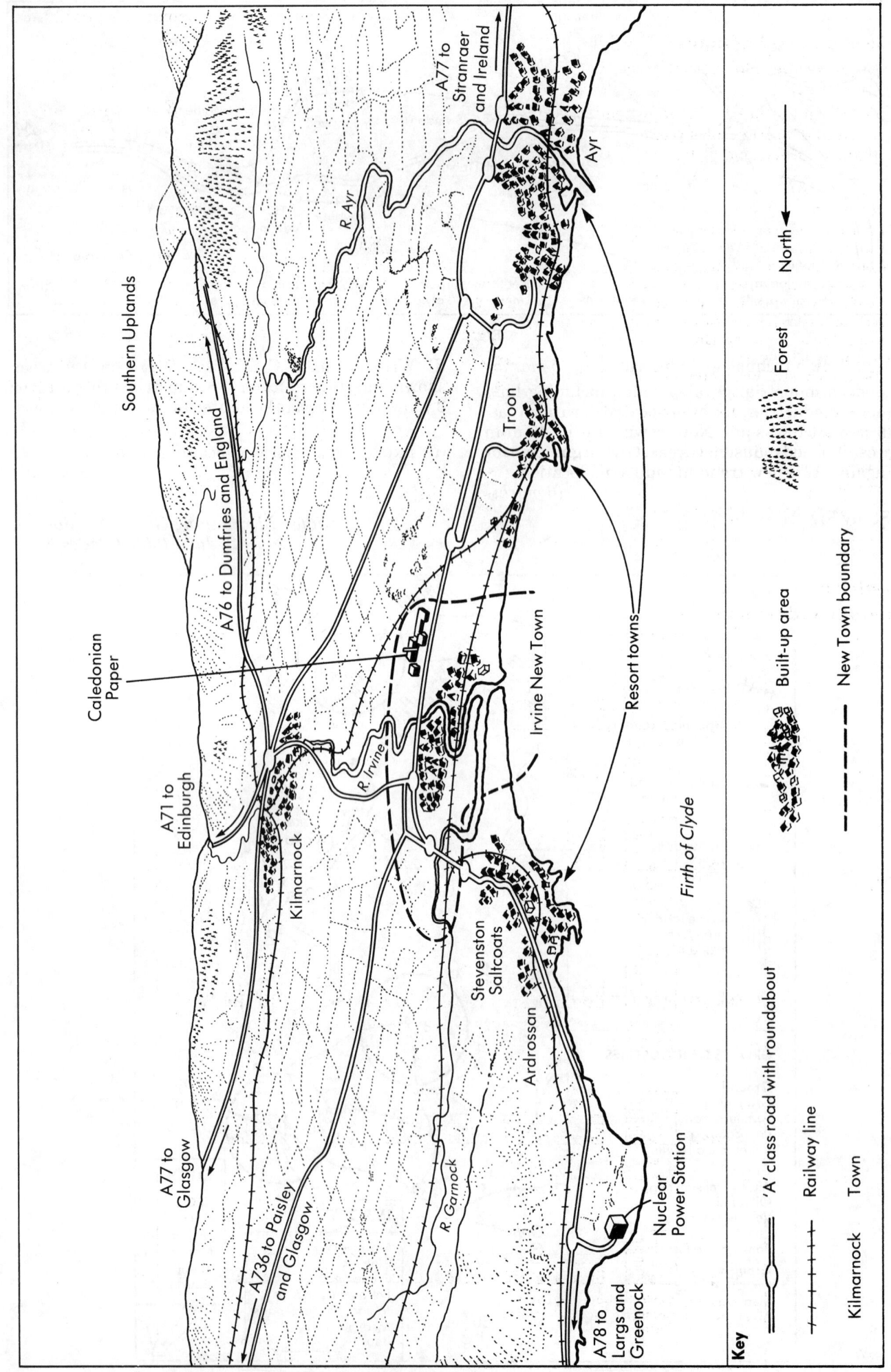

Fig. 22 A landscape sketch of the location of Caledonian Paper in Irvine, Ayrshire

Question 8
(Time allowed: 17 minutes.)

8 Look at all the information given in Figs. 22 and 23.

(a) Do you think that the Meadowhead site in Irvine was a suitable location for a paper mill?
Explain your decision fully. *(6 marks)*

(b) Describe the social and economic benefits that a large investment such as this might bring to an area.
(4 marks)
(Total 10 marks)
(Scottish Examination Board, Standard Grade, Credit Level, May, 1991)

The giant mill-building at Meadowhead marks the culmination of years of negotiations, but the price was very high.

Initially, all negotiations for the new paper-mill were conducted through Locate In Scotland. Caledonian were looking for a 30–40 hectare site, preferably with rail access.

There followed a further period of 2 years before the final decision was made. Issues which had to be resolved included availability of water and electricity, labour supply and the suitability of the site to carry such a large structure.

Adapted from The Irvine Times

"One of the advantages of placing a new mill on a 'greenfield' site is the freedom to choose the best location. Several towns and cities fitted the bill but, in the end, Irvine was chosen.

One of the modern aspects so important to Caledonian is the pool of staff educated and trained for high-tech manufacturing industry. When we first became interested in Scotland, we dealt with Locate In Scotland, and when we decided to locate in Irvine, we talked to the Irvine Development Corporation."

A management spokesman

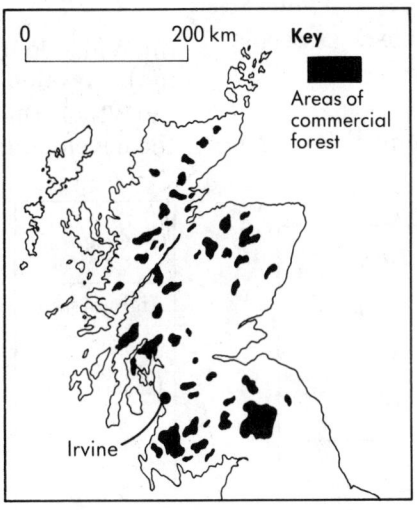

Fig. 23

Question 9
(Time allowed: 15 minutes)

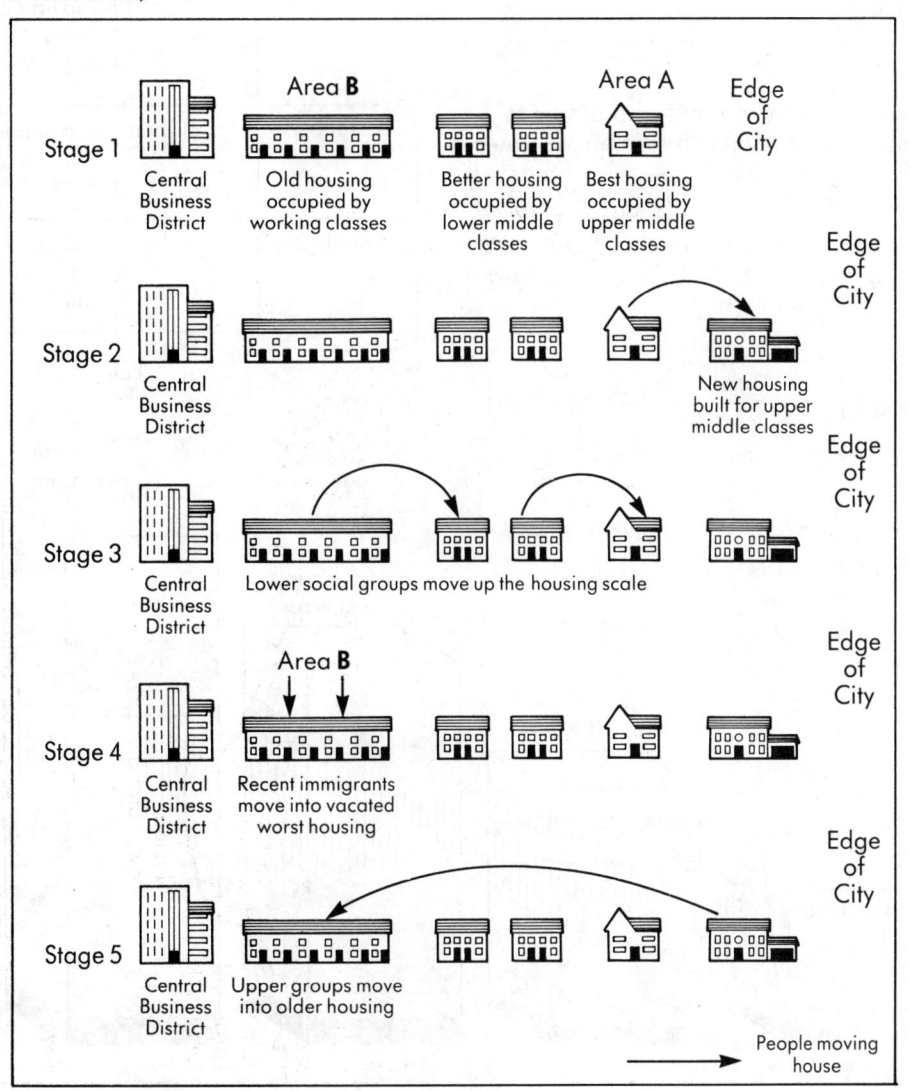

Fig. 24

9 (a) Study Fig. 24 which shows changes in population movements in a developed world city.

(i) Suggest two ways in which the houses in area A are likely to be better than those in area B in stage 1.

(ii) Explain why lower social groups are able to move to better housing in stage 3. *(3 marks)*

(b) (i) Explain what the term 'immigrant' means.

(ii) Suggest two reasons why recent immigrants move to the house in area B in stage 4. *(3 marks)*

(c) In stage 5, yuppies and upper middle class people move into an old inner city area.

(i) Explain the term 'yuppies'.

(ii) This movement will change the inner city area. What is this change called?

	Tick
Commercialisation	
Counter-urbanisation	
Gentrification	
Redevelopment	
Suburbanisation	

(iii) Suggest two reasons why yuppies and upper middle class people may be attracted to live in an old inner city area. *(4 marks)*

(Total 10 marks)
(London East Anglian Group, Syllabus B, Paper 1, June 1991, Common paper)

Question 10
(Time allowed: 30 minutes)

10 Population

(a) Study the graph Fig. 25, showing world population.

(i) What is the estimate for the world's population in the year 2000? *(1 mark)*

(ii) What term is used to describe a population count? *(1 mark)*

(iii) Which FOUR of the areas shown on the graph are in the developing world? *(2 marks)*

(iv) Why is the population increasing more rapidly in the developing world? *(6 marks)*

Origin	Numbers	Desinations	Reasons
Afghanistan	5.9 million	Iran and Pakistan	Civil War
Israel	2.5 million	Occupied Territories (e.g. Gaza Strip), Jordan and Kuwait	Palestinians resettled after Israeli occupation
Vietnam	1.2 million	Hong Kong, Japan, China and other S.E. Asian countries	Political and economic factors
Ethiopia	1.1 million	Sudan and Somalia	Drought and civil war
Mozambique	1.0 million	Zimbabwe, South Africa and Malawi	Civil war

Table 3

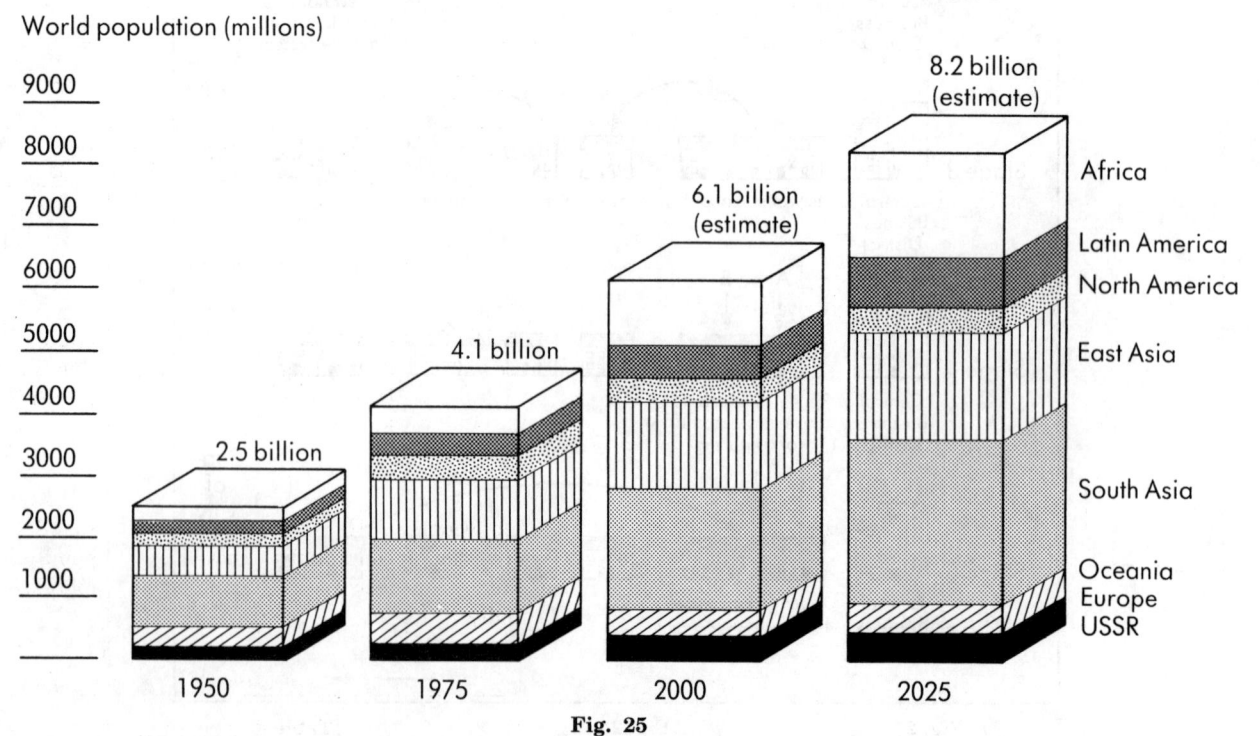

World population (millions)

Fig. 25

Practice in answering questions **151**

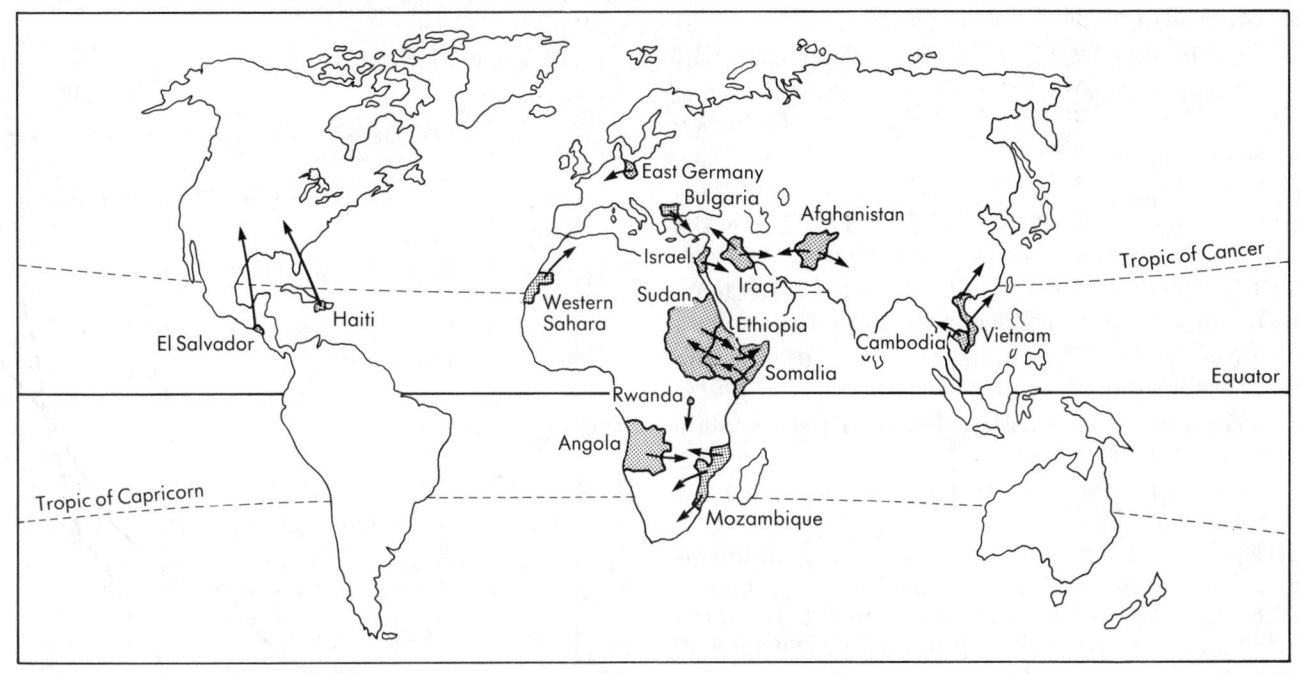

Fig. 26

(b) Study Table 3, which shows details of the five largest migrations of refugees during the late 1980s.

(i) What is a 'refugee'? *(2 marks)*

(ii) Use Table 3 to state the main cause of people becoming refugees. *(1 mark)*

(iii) What are the political and economic factors which may have caused people to migrate as refugees?
(4 marks)

(c) Study the world map, Fig. 26, showing the major refugee migrations during the 1980s.

(i) Comment on the pattern of refugee migrations as shown on Fig. 26. *(4 marks)*

(ii) Suggest why the governments of some countries are reluctant to receive refugees and other migrants.
(4 marks)

(Total 25 marks)

(Southern Examining Group, Syllabus A2, Paper 2, June 1991, Grades A–G)

Question 11
(Time allowed: 22 minutes)

11(a) Study Fig. 27 which shows the Demographic Transition model.

In Table 4 are descriptions of the four stages shown in the Demographic Transition model. They are not in the correct order.

(i) Complete the table:

STAGE A on the diagram is described in Box 4
STAGE B on the diagram is described in Box __
STAGE C on the diagram is described in Box __
STAGE D on the diagram is described in Box __
(3 marks)

(ii) Complete the line on Fig. 27 for the total population.
(2 marks)

(iii) Mark on Fig. 27 an X to show when the population

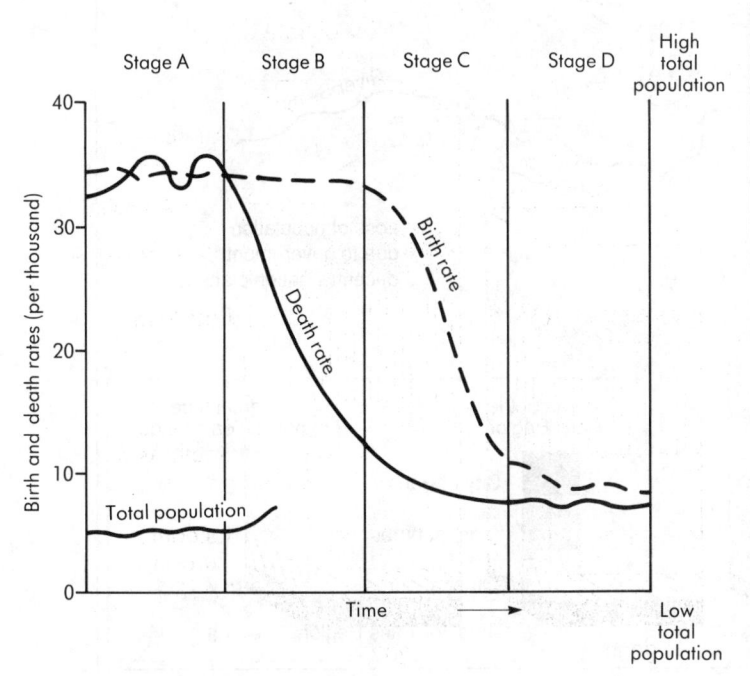

Fig. 27

Box 1	Box 2	Box 3	Box 4
Falling Birth Rate	Low, fluctuating Birth Rate	High Birth Rate	High, fluctuating Birth Rate
Low Death Rate	Low, fluctuating Death Rate	Falling Death Rate	High, fluctuating Death Rate
Population increasing quite rapidly	Little population increase	Rapidly increasing population	Little population increase

Table 4

Practice in answering questions

was decreasing.

(iv) At which stage, A, B, C or D, is the population of the UK?

(v) At which stage, A, B, C or D, is the population of India? *(3 marks)*

(b) Study Fig. 28.

Paris and Calcutta are both cities with more than a million people. Describe and briefly explain how the growth rates of the two cities have differed. *(4 marks)*

(c) Fig. 29 shows some aspects of the Paris Regional Plan and population change in the Paris Region.

(i) Describe the main movement of population within the Paris Region. *(1 mark)*

(ii) People move into the Paris Region. Briefly explain why. *(2 marks)*

(iii) What is the main reason for people moving away from the Paris Region? *(1 mark)*

(d) The growth of Paris has caused many problems such as overcrowding, traffic congestion and lack of space for office and industrial development. The Paris Regional Plan was drawn up to try to solve some of these problems.

(i) Describe the Plan and explain how it aims to solve the problems. *(7 marks)*

(ii) How effective do you think the Paris Regional Plan has been? Give reasons to support your answer. *(3 marks)*

(Total 26 marks)

(Northern Examining Association, Syllabus B, Paper 2, June, 1990, Stepped question)

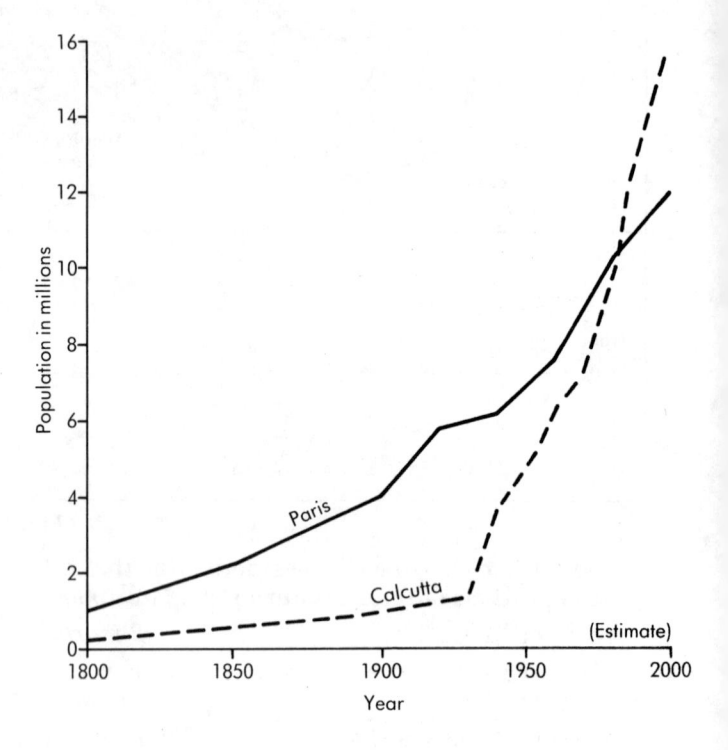

Fig. 28 Population growth in the Paris Region and Calcutta

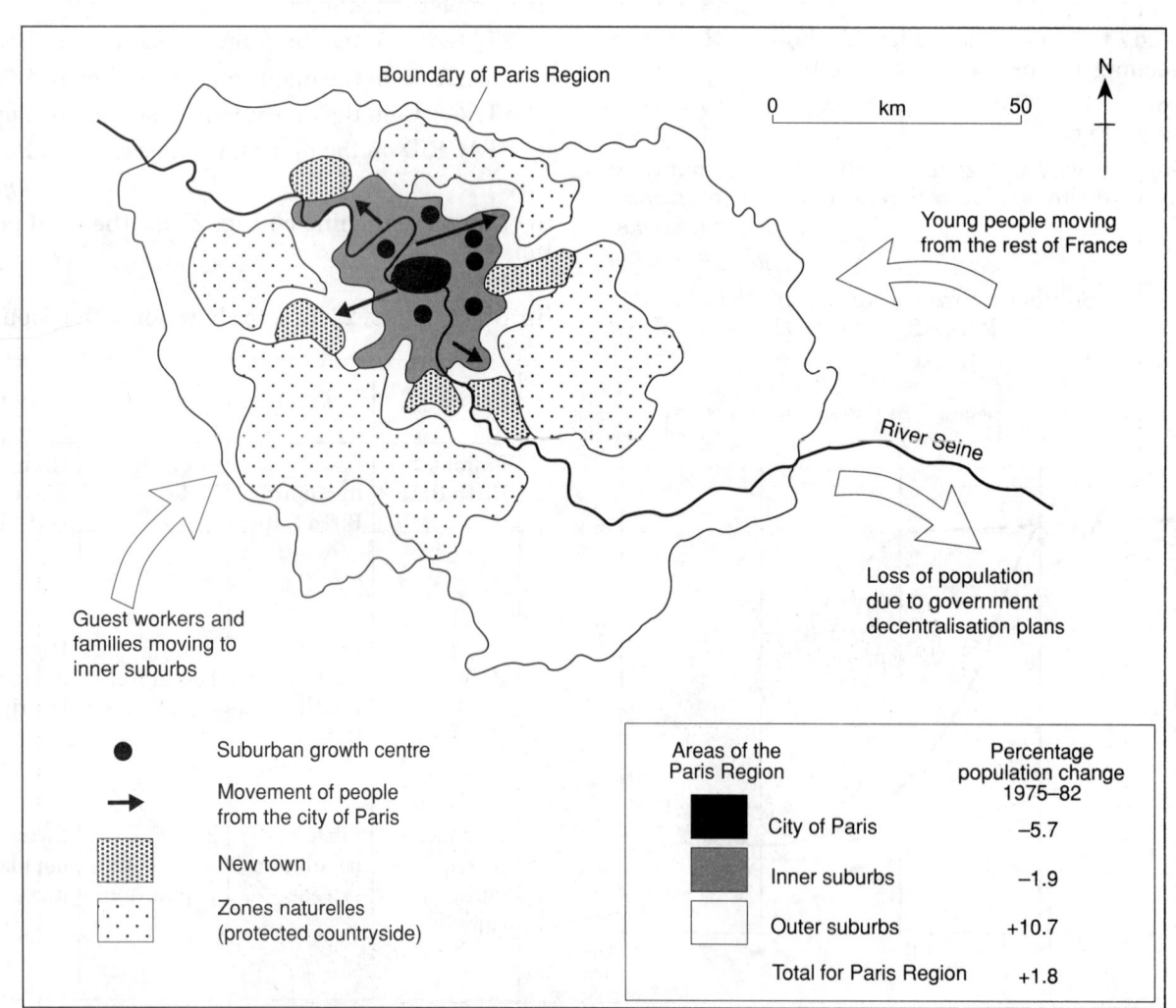

Fig. 29

Areas of the Paris Region	Percentage population change 1975–82
City of Paris	−5.7
Inner suburbs	−1.9
Outer suburbs	+10.7
Total for Paris Region	+1.8

Question 12
(Time allowed: 26 minutes)

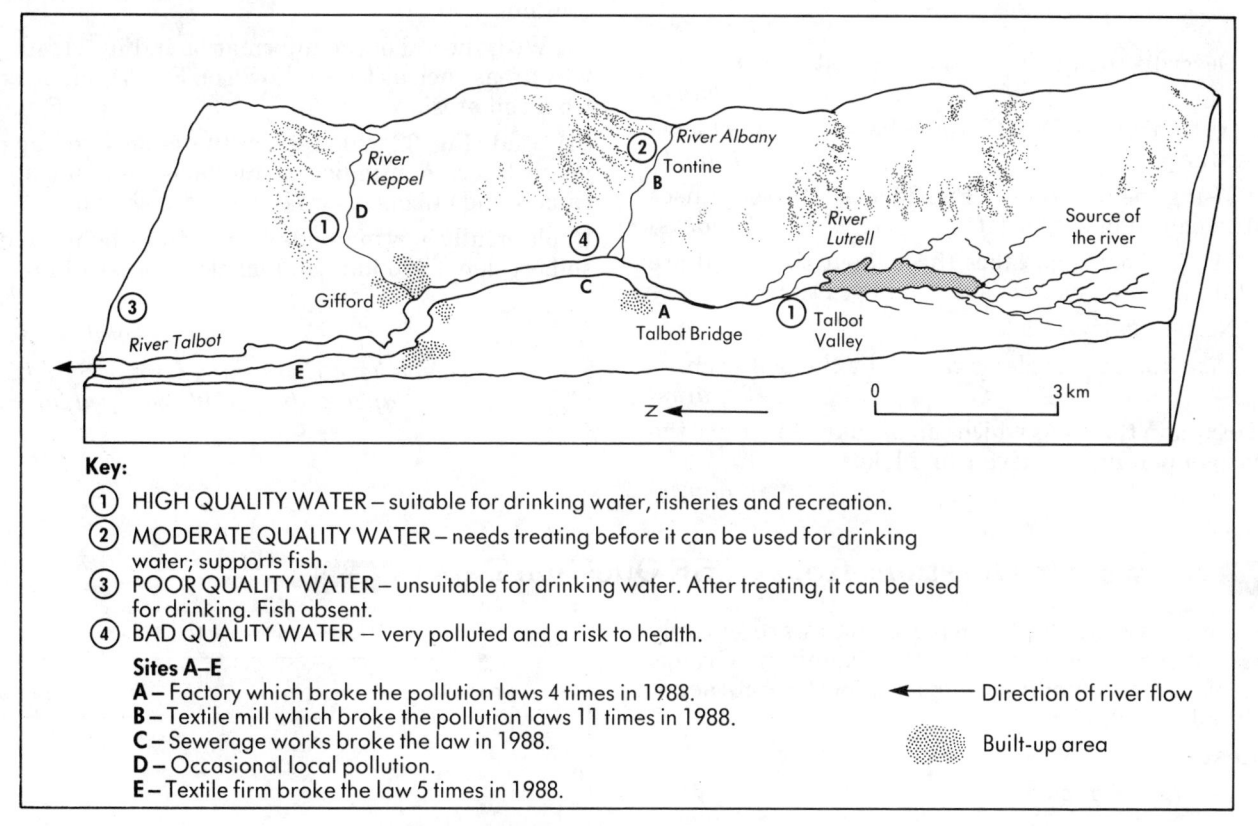

Key:
- ① HIGH QUALITY WATER – suitable for drinking water, fisheries and recreation.
- ② MODERATE QUALITY WATER – needs treating before it can be used for drinking water; supports fish.
- ③ POOR QUALITY WATER – unsuitable for drinking water. After treating, it can be used for drinking. Fish absent.
- ④ BAD QUALITY WATER – very polluted and a risk to health.

Sites A–E
- A – Factory which broke the pollution laws 4 times in 1988.
- B – Textile mill which broke the pollution laws 11 times in 1988.
- C – Sewerage works broke the law in 1988.
- D – Occasional local pollution.
- E – Textile firm broke the law 5 times in 1988.

Fig. 30 The River Talbot – pollution levels

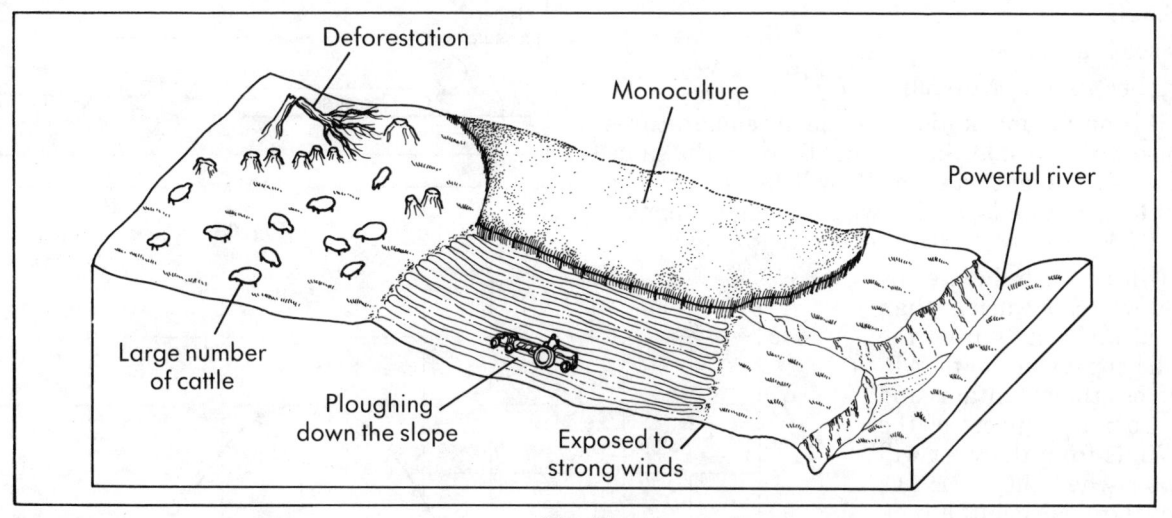

Fig. 31

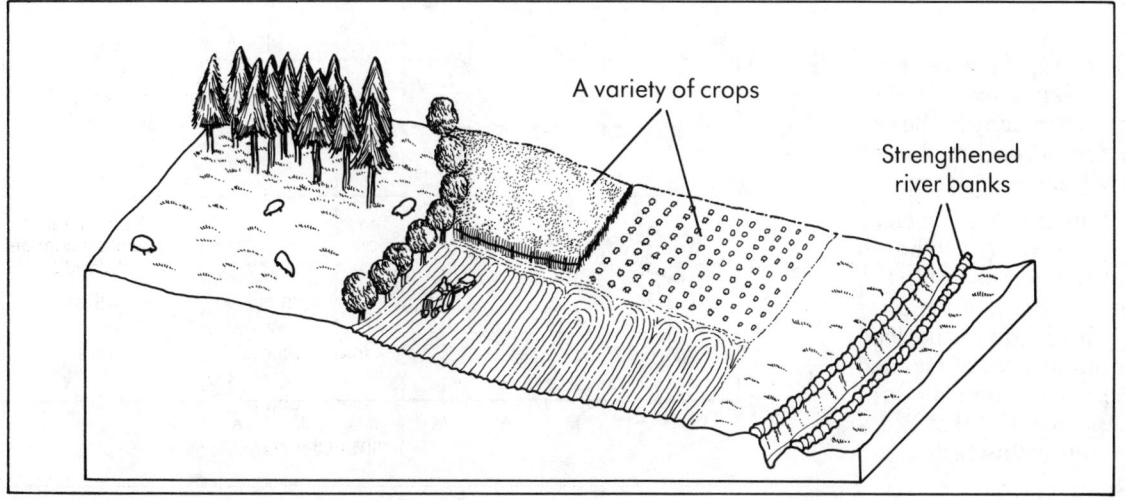

Fig. 32

(a) Study Fig. 30 which shows a river system in Western Europe.

(i) Name two rivers which flow into the River Talbot.
(2 marks)

(ii) Describe the quality of the water at site D.
(1 mark)

(b) (i) Which site, A,B,C,D or E, has the greatest level of water pollution? *(1 mark)*

(ii) Using the evidence in Fig. 30, describe the causes of the pollution at this site. *(3 marks)*

(c) Many rivers and lakes throughout the world are polluted. For a river or lake you have studied:

(i) Name the river or lake.

(ii) Describe the problems caused by the pollution.
(3 marks)

(iii) Explain the steps which can be taken to reduce the levels of pollution in rivers and lakes.
(6 marks)

(d) In trying to increase food production, farmers may misuse the land and cause soil erosion.

Study Fig. 31 which shows some of the causes of soil erosion.

(i) With the aid of the information in Fig. 31, suggest why areas such as those shown on Fig. 31 might suffer from soil erosion. *(6 marks)*

(ii) Study Fig. 32 which shows the same landscape ten years later. A number of methods of reducing the causes and effects of soil erosion are shown.

Explain fully how methods such as these help to reduce soil erosion. (You may add labels or notes to Fig. 32).
(6 marks)

(Total 28 marks)

(Northern Examining Group, Syllabus C, Paper 2, June 1990, Stepped question)

Answers to Questions from GCSE Question Papers

Please note that the following answers are entirely those of the authors and that the Examining Groups accept no responsibility whatsoever for the accuracy or method of working.

Question 1

1 (a) (i) thermometer

(ii) In a Stevenson screen

(iii) 13.5 °C

(b) (i) see Fig. 2A

(ii) October 10.5 °C; November 6.7 °C

(c) (i) B is an upland station and mean temperatures decrease with altitude. Since A and B are on the same latitude, the upland station, B, will be cooler. The normal temperature lapse rate with altitude is approximately 0.56 °C for every 100 metres of ascent.

(ii) In winter A is influenced by the sea which is warmer than the land and winds from the sea will keep A warmer than B. C is across the mountains and away from the effects of the sea. Winds from the west will be cooler when they reach C, making the mean monthly temperatures lower than at A.

(iii) C

(d) (i) The map shows an area of high pressure over Wales. There are few clouds in the sky and the tempereature during the day will be very warm.

(ii) Diagram B shows a clear sky in February. Heat radiated by the land surface is lost in the atmosphere and the land temperature drops. In diagram A the cloud covers limits the loss of radiated heat. The clouds form a warm atmospheric 'blanket' that keeps the land temperature higher.

(e) (i) See Fig. 6A

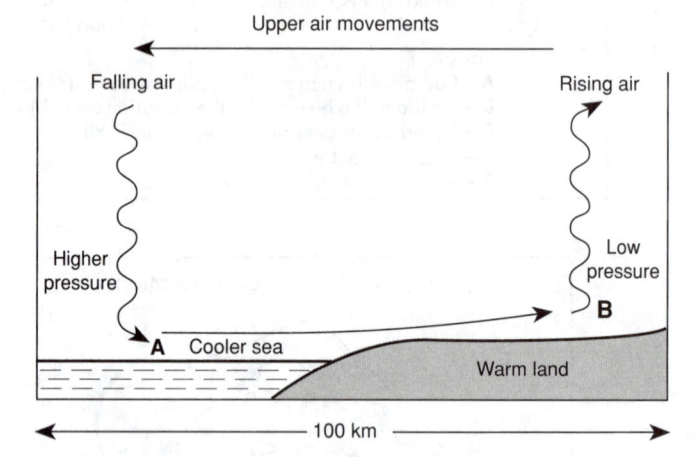

Fig. 6A

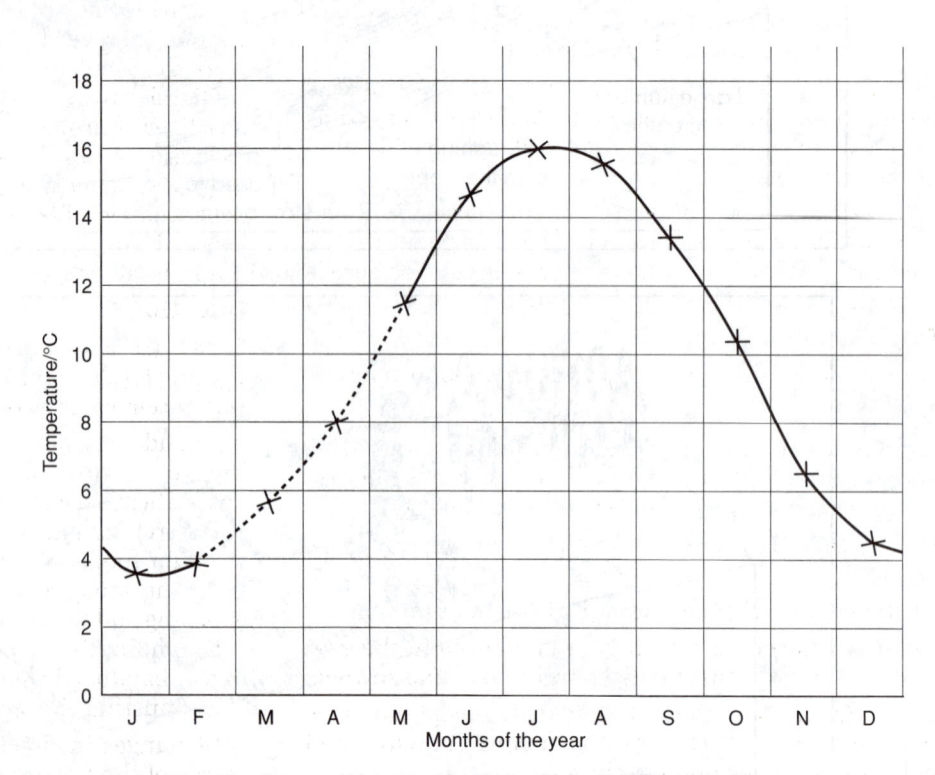

Fig. 2A

(ii) As the land warms the air rises forming an area of low pressure. The air then drifts out to sea. It becomes cooler and denser and sinks creating high pressure. At sea level the air from the high pressure blows towards the low pressure over the land. This causes a sea breeze blowing inland.

Question 2

(a) (i) A One of the large rigid segments into which the crust of the earth is divided.

B The area where one plate (oceanic) is being overridden by another plate (either oceanic or continental) and pushed down into the mantle.

(ii) Pacific plate; Eurasian plate

(b) (i) Whether to judge 'seriousness' by the power of the earthquake (American is then the most serious), or by the deaths caused (Tangshan is the most serious).

(ii) Density of population of affected area.

Level of technology; medicine and relief services available.

(c) The North American plate, which is a continental plate, is moving towards the Cocos (oceanic) plate, which is also moving on a collision course. The North American plate overrides the Cocos plate forcing it down into the mantle. The movement of the plates against one another causes enormous pressures. These pressures build up until the rocks tear apart at the weakest point which is the focus of the earthquake.

(d) Establish a scientific early warning system to monitor earth movements.

Design buildings, bridges and roads to withstand tremors of all but the most severe earthquakes.

Provide safe shelters where people can go when an earthquake occurs because there are usually secondary shocks.

Question 3

3 (a) (i) water

(ii) The drawbridge is raised and the ships pass through the navigation lock.

(iii) Six moveable gates are used to control water level; the navigation lock also plays a part.

(iv) The river flows into the sea and tides move up and down stream in uncontrolled ways. This energy has now been harnessed using modern technology to generate electricity.

(v) Natural sources of energy have been utilised and as a result fossil fuels are not needed to generate the electricity. Water is a renewable resource and there is no pollution from burning fossil fuels.

(b) (i) Timber

(ii) Oil – 30 years; Gas – 40 years; Coal – 350 years

(iii) Oil

(iv) Reduce the amount used, by finding alternative sources of energy. Develop the use of renewable resources such as water power and solar energy.

(c) (i) City B – Belfast; City D – Dublin; City G – Glasgow

(ii) Sewage discharge; industrial waste dumping.

(iii) It is adjacent to a well-populated area to the east and is used to dump and discharge waste and sewage.

(iv) Polluting the coastal areas seriously damages marine ecology, threatens the fishing industry and pollutes estuaries and beaches.

Question 4

4 (a)

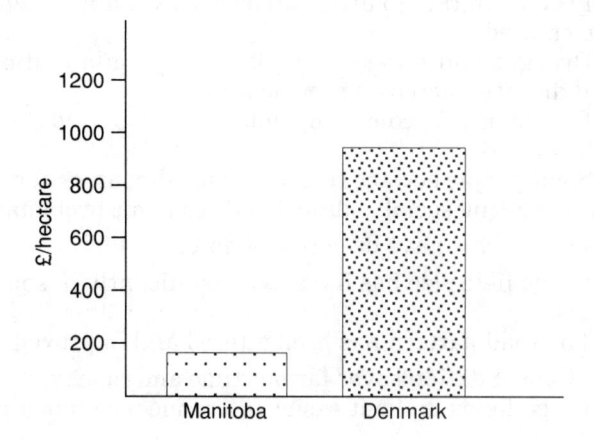

Fig. 14A

(b) Danish farming is more intensive;

Denmark specialises in high value farm products – pork, bacon etc.

(c) Approximately 500 mm rainfall a year with a Spring maximum. Moisture is available when the cereals are growing.

Hot, sunny summers – 21 °C in July with a growing season extending from mid-April until September.

(a) Pork; butter.

(b) To be used as food for the pigs.

(c) Voluntary groupings of farmers to achieve the advantages of bulk buying of raw materials; shared machinery; marketing power and standardised quality.

Advantages – Heavier yields of rice and other cereals adding to the food supply of the country. Increase in farm incomes and rural standards of living, for some people. Increased demand for fertilizers has created work for people in fertilizer factories.

Disadvantages – Poor farmers cannot afford fertilizers. Farmers need to be trained to use modern irrigation techniques. When yields are high prices drop and farmers are no better off. Poor yields creat debt, the rich become richer while the poor become poorer. Using large amounts of fertilizers can result in rivers becoming polluted.

Question 5

5 (a) (i) Nomadic pastoralists may have overstocked grazing lands so that they became overgrazed and the vegetation cover was destroyed.

Abandoning old pastures for new without attempting to restore or revive plant life. Pockets of desertification can result.

Destroying part of the vegetation cover by cutting wood for fuel and shelter.

Farmers may remove vegetation cover to grow crops, exposing soil to erosion.

Extending farmland into marginal areas which have to be abandoned when rainfall is insufficient

Exhausting the fertility of the soil by monoculture.

(ii) Changes in climate causing the migration southwards of the Sahara desert

Overpopulation of marginal farmlands, the land cannot support the number of people.

(iii) Traditional ways of life have to be adapted or abandoned.

People migrate to urban areas where shanty towns are created.

Drought and hunger are followed by malnutrition and disease, increasing the death rate.

People my become dependent on aid and lose self-reliance.

Some people become refugees in neighbouring countries creating social, political and economic problems.

(b) (i) Farms have been consolidated.

Average field size has increased significantly in some parts.

The road pattern has been altered and improved.

(ii) Consolidation saves farmer time and money.

Large fields make it easier to use modern machinery.

Improved road system makes distribution and collection of produce faster and cheaper.

A more efficient farm layout can reduce labour costs and the numbers employed on the farms.

(iii) Changes in the field pattern destroy the traditional landscape.

Modernisation may cause unemployment.

Some families may have further to travel to work and traditional farming methods are abandoned.

(c) I have chosen hill farming in Wales as an example of commercial farming.

Land use decisions will be affected by environmental and human factors as follows.

The relief and climate make farmers limit types of production to basic crops, grass and fodder crops.

Relief and quality of soil make farmers adopt an extensive grazing pattern making use in the summer months of high moorland pastures. Farming is therefore mixed, some arable plus fodder crops and cereals where land is suitable. Cattle and sheep grazing is important.

Climatic considerations determine that there is a carefully balanced rhythm of activity and land use throughout the year.

Local markets will influence land use. In the past there was a need for pit props in the coal mines which led to the growth of conifer plantations on hill land. Subsidies, grants and quotas which enable farming to continue despite the marginal conditions of the hill lands.

Tradition and cultural factors (e.g. the Welsh language), together with family ownership of the land.

The growth of tourism has provided opportunities for alternative incomes.

The new jobs created in nearby small towns by the Welsh Development Agency may lead to the abandonment of marginal farms.

Car ownership and better roads have improved distribution of farm products such as milk and may provide additional job opportunities for members of the farmer's family.

Question 6

6 (a) (i) Spaces on table should be completed as follows.

Woodland and trees – Woodland reduced; trees removed from river banks; trees in field boundaries largely removed.

Fields – Fields have been consolidated to make larger, regular shaped fields. Total field area has also been increased.

Water features – Stream has been straightened to form a drainage ditch. Marsh and pond area has been drained.

Crops – Overall arable area has been increased. Less grass, new crops introduced, e.g. rape and sugar beet. Potatoes and wheat areas larger.

Footpath – Realigned around edges of new fields.

Wildlife habitat – Significantly reduced e.g. woodland, marsh, pond and hedgerows.

(ii) To increase the amount of cultivated land.

To create large consolidated fields in which large quantities of a single crop can be grown.

To make it easier to use large, modern machinery.

(iii) Increased the danger of soil erosion (removal) by wind and water. Reduced the soil moisture retaining capacity.

(iv) The pond is an obsolete feature. Horses and other animals can be provided with piped water – if animals are still on the farm.

Improves drainage and straightens field boundaries for easier working.

(v) The 1949 landscape. The grass, field hedge and tree landscape has become to be regarded as 'typical' of England and gives the countryside its distinctive character.

(b) (i) All species have been reduced; fish and dragonflies have disappeared completely. Proportionally the butterflies have been least affected.

(ii) Increased use of chemicals to control pests, weeds and diseases.

(iii) Farming is a business. To survive in a difficult economic climate he cannot afford to be sentimental and must adopt the most efficient and profitable methods.

Over history the landscape has changed dramatically. What we see now is the result of enclosures of large open fields mainly during the 18th and 19th centuries.

(c) (i) Ecosystem – Heathland

Heathland is characterised by an absence of trees, tall bushes and shrubs are also scarce. The main ground cover is heather and bracken. Below this dominant layer there is a range of creeping plants - grasses, sedges, ferns and lichens.

The vegetation has developed on an acid podsol soil from which minerals have been leached to give the soil a white colour.

Heathland provides shelter and food for invertebrates such as heather beetles, caterpillars and millipedes. Decaying vegetation attracts ants and beetles.

Fires may occur on heathland naturally when the heather and bracken are very dry. Fresh young shoots appear in the ashes and the plant succession quickly re-establishes itself. Trees, living creatures and shrubs may be destroyed in these fires.

Heathland is an amenity for nearby towns, for walking, picnics and pony riding.

(ii) The most dramatic changes are the result of controlled periodic burning, usually in a 12–15 year cycle. As parts of a heath are burned at different times, the heath as a whole is in different stages of regeneration. Human activity is concentrated in the mature areas which are accessible for road traffic.

Human use of heathland causes environmental degradation. Vegetation is damaged, pathways destroyed and litter may cause unwanted fires. Intensive use by people from nearby towns can cause extensive damage, especially from unofficial car parking or cross-country motor-cycling.

Intensive use by humans has driven wild animals such as deer into less accessible areas and sheep grazing is limited to a few select and protected centres.

Question 7

7 **(a)** Levels of economic development vary from country to country and the least developed countries are characterised by low levels of manufacturing industry. Political factors may have helped the development of manufacturing in some countries, for example the CIS, previously the USSR, gave a high priority, under the Communists regime, to industrial development. Some countries, particularly those of the developing world are essentially producers of food or industrial raw materials for export. As a result manufacturing is less important, for example southern Africa.

In developed countries, technology allows a high productive capacity with a relatively small labour force. In these countries, such as the USA, a higher percentage of the workforce is employed in service industries.

(b) (i) Footloose industries are industries not tied to the local availability of raw materials so there is a free choice of location. Footloose industries tend to be market orientated.

(ii) Nearness to London, a major market; access to motorways, railways and international airports; nearness to universities and polytechnics which have research centres and produce a highly educated workforce; attractive rural or semi-rural areas for the workforce to live in.

(iii) For: Industries are located away from congested city centres.

Factories can be laid out efficiently on new greenfield sites.

Sites near motorways cut labour and transport costs because traffic flow is relatively unhindered.

New job opportunities and high wages brought to rural areas where unemployment and low wages are common.

Key workers and management can be attracted by the work environment and being able to live in rural towns and villages.

Against: Rural areas are being over-developed and small market towns clogged by industrial traffic.

Cities are being deprived of population and job opportunities.

Traditional way of life in rural areas is being changed by influential newcomers.

In some regions the existing motorway network has reached saturation point.

(c) (i) A industrial group 3

B industrial group 1

C industrial group 2

(ii) A Group 2. Area A is dominated by cattle rearing and a long way from other raw materials or cheap power. Industries are food processing and tanning of hides.

B Group 1. Area B is a hardwood forest area with fruit and oil palm production. It is not close to cheap power supplies or a port so the industries are based on local products.

C Group 3. Area C has industries dependent on imports and local power. The importance of the import/export trade has also made banking and finance important. The advantages of the location of C are the port facilities and hydro-electric power from the dam on Lake Volta.

Question 8

8 **(a)** Yes. A large greenfield site was available.

It is not far from large commercial forest areas which could provide the softwood timber needed to make paper.

Irvine New Town and other nearby towns could provide the labour force.

The River Irvine provides an essential supply of water, one of the major raw materials required by the industry.

Electric power was available.

Coastal towns could provide amenities and attractive housing for key workers.

(b) The plant brought a modern high technology industry into a region characterised by traditional industries.

It provided new employment opportunities to replace the declining traditional industries.

It offered high skill training and high wages to local people.

It provided a significant addition to the economic base of Irvine and its region.

It brought additional money and spending power into the area.

Question 9

9 **(a)** (i) Rooms are larger and there is more living space in area A.

Houses in area A are likely to have more modern facilities.

(ii) As upper classes move to new houses other groups move to better housing that has been vacated - this is called succession.

(b) (i) A settler that has moved into a country or region from another country or region.

(ii) Recent immigrants tend to be at the bottom of the 'pecking order' and initially have access to the worst housing.

Earlier immigrants from their own country or region may be housed there already so recent immigrants join their own ethnic or religious communities.

(c) (i) Young upwardly mobile workers employed in modern high income jobs which allow them to have a high standard of living.

(ii) Gentrification

(iii) Old, but well-built properties are relatively cheap and can be modernised to create fashionable homes of character.

Urban re-development in an old inner city area may create pockets of expensive new housing near to city centre banks, offices and other places where yuppies and upper middle class people work.

Question 10

10 **(a)** (i) 6.1 billion

(ii) Population census

(iii) South Asia; Latin America; Africa; East Asia.

(iv) A high birth rate is accompanied by a declining death rate as modern medicine limits infant mortality and enables people to live longer. In some regions greater prosperity combines with religious beliefs whic oppose birth control. In South America most people are Roman Catholic, a religion opposed to birth control. Cultural factors, such as the status of having a large family, particularly many sons, has encouraged large families. In the developing world a very high proportion of the total population is of child-bearing age so there are high fertility rates.

(b) (i) A person who escapes to a foreign country to avoid war, or political or religious persecution.

(ii) Civil war

(iii) Political factors – Opponents of the government may flee to avoid execution or imprisonment.

Minorities may be expelled e.g.'ethnic cleansing', Yugoslavia.

A wish to practice their own religious beliefs (Pilgrim Fathers).

New laws that persecute or limit the freedom of minority groups.

Economic factors – Natural disasters make it impossible to make a living e.g. drought.

High levels of unemployment and low standards of living at home.

Better job opportunities in other countries, opportunity to make good in a new land.

(c) (i) Most of the movements are from developing countries where there has been political repression and civil war.

Migrations are to neighbouring countries rather than to countries a long way away.

Most movements are land-based, not involving a sea journey.

Most movements are to countries with a higher standard of living or where work is available.

(ii) Countries cannot afford to house and support refugees.

Refugees can cause social unrest if they seem to be getting preferential treatment.

Fear that ideas brought in by the refugees may spread, e.g. political extremists from East Germany.

May add to the social and political divisions already existing in the country.

May worsen employment prospects for the indigenous population.

Question 11

11 **(a)** (i) Stage B –3; Stage C – 1; Stage D – 2.

(ii) (iii)

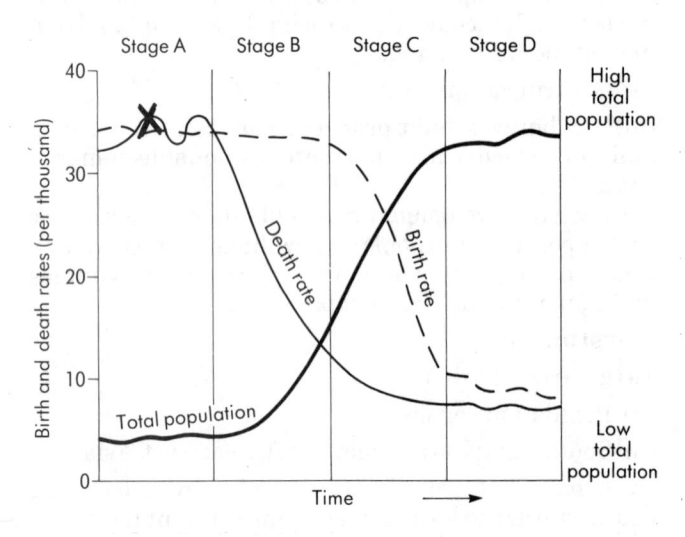

Fig. 27A

(iv) Stage D

(v) Stage B

(b) The population of Calcutta grew fairly steadily until about 1930, since when there has been a dramatic increase with no signs of this very rapid growth coming to an end.

Paris has also had a continuous growth but at more moderate rates. the 'plateau' of low growth from about 1920-1935 was probably the effect of the first World War in which large numbers of males were killed. The rate of growth in recent years shows a slowing down after rapid increases in the 1960s and 1970s.

(c) (i) Movement away from the city to the inner and outer suburbs.

(ii) The capital is a magnet to young people.

The Paris Region offers a wider range of job opportunities than the rest of the country.

Guest workers are attracted to the Paris Region.

(iii) Government decentralisation plans.

(d) (i) The regional plan has been designed to reduce congestion in Paris itself. Five new towns have been built on the edges of the city and suburban growth centres have been identified in the inner suburbs. Outward growth has been controlled by the establishment of zones naturelles.

The new towns and suburban growth centres provide new housing, shopping and industrial locations outside the city. This aims to reduce overcrowding in central Paris and also means that some industrial and commercial traffic need not go into the centre. Since more jobs are available on the outskirts of Paris, journeys to work in the central area are reduced and this will cut down traffic congestion.

New housing and jobs in the outskirts attract migrants who would otherwise have made for Paris itself.

(ii) The population of the city dropped in the period 1975–1982 which should ease overcrowding. Although the population of the entire region increased by 1.8 per cent, growth was concentrated mainly in the outer suburbs that include the new towns. Population redistribution has been achieved. There is no information on changes in the location of industries and jobs, or of changes in traffic flows. So it is difficult to come to an overall conclusion.

Question 12

12 **(a)** (i) River Lutrell; River Keppel

(ii) High quality water, suitable for drinking, fish and recreation.

(b) (i) E – cumulative effect of all pollution in the system at this point.

(ii) E is the site nearest the river mouth. Although there were only five local incidents at E in 1988, water from all the incidents recorded at A,B,C and D flow through E. So E has been affected by the breaking of the pollution laws by the factory at A, by the textile mills at B and E, and pollution by the sewage works at C. Additionally there has been unspecified pollution at D.

(c) (i) River Orwell, Suffolk.

(ii) Pollution of mussel beds.

Wildlife habitats (fish and birds) destroyed.

Water made unfit for bathing.

Unsightly shoreline and beaches for sailors and holidaymakers.

(iii) Research into alternative means of dispersing waste products and potential pollutants may produce other ways of dealing with the problem.

Effluent and waste that has to be discharged into rivers and lakes may be processed to reduce the amount of pollution caused.

Legal requirements need to be established to ensure process of waste is maintained at high levels of efficiency to avoid accidents.

Enforce legal controls on the amounts and range of discharges permitted.

Seek means to avoid occasional local pollution.

Set up monitoring procedures to ensure that regulations are obeyed.

(d) (i) Overgrazing pastures can result in the destruction of the vegetation cover which exposes the soil to erosion.

Deforestation means that the vegetation does not intercept heavy rainfall. Rain splash removes the topsoil and this may cause sheetwash and sheet erosion.

Monoculture means that the same nutrients are used in the soil year after year. This can lead to soil exhaustion and the abandonment of the farmland.

The uncultivated, exposed land is open to erosion.

Ploughing loosens the topsoil. Ploughing down the slope encourages the movement of topsoil downhill and provides channels down which heavy rain can run, washing away the ridges between the drills and removing soil.

Exposed ploughed land may also be eroded by strong winds that carry the topsoil away.

A powerful river, as it deepens its channel, undercuts its banks which then collapse, so the edges of the cultivated land recede. Eroded soil deposited in the river channel is removed by transportation so the process of erosion continues.

(ii) The planting of trees has helped to 'fix' the soil. Heavy rains are intercepted by the trees so the ground is protected from sheet erosion.

The number of grazing animals has been reduced so there is less danger of the vegetation cover being destroyed and the topsoil is not exposed to erosion.

Contour ploughing does not encourage the downhill movement of soil. Rainwater is trapped in the drills and absorbed into the soil.

A variety of crops means that the soil fertility can be maintained and there is less likelihood of cultivated land being abandoned or exposed to erosion. Wind erosion is reduced by the vegetation cover

Strengthened river banks mean that the land close to the river has been stabilised and will not be washed into the river.

9 COURSEWORK AND FIELDWORK

In the national criteria laid down for the GCSE Geography examination, it was established that a school-based component should account for at least 20 per cent of the marks in all Mode 1 examinations. This has given practical work and field work a new importance in the examination. In fact fieldwork is a compulsory element in every syllabus.

In this section, therefore, three main themes have been highlighted:

1 New terminology, which you will find in the examination syllabuses and which you will hear your teachers use.

2 Answers to questions you may wish to ask about this portion of the examination.

3 Ideas on how to organize your work and on what will make a good study.

TERMINOLOGY

Different Examination Groups have devised different forms of examination within the national criteria set down for GCSE geography. Here are some of the most common terms in use. Your Examining Group will use one or more of these terms, but not all of them.

1 Practical work

Practical work is seen as an approach to learning which allows students to be *actively* involved in learning. Practical work may take various forms, e.g. fieldwork outside the classroom or school; classroom-based projects; classroom-based simulated fieldwork. In practical work, students will apply the skills, techniques and ideas which are included in the examination syllabus.

The Scottish Certificate of Education Standard Grade is one of the examinations with a practical element.

2 Coursework

The Midland Examining Group requires the production of work based on one or two field studies, to satisfy the requirements of its Syllabus B. The coursework has to include work based on first-hand and personal field investigations. The coursework is a record of the student's personal study, but the information may be collected by groups of hole classes.

Under the examining regulations of the Northern Examining Association Syllabus D, however, there are three coursework units plus one/two planned enquiries.

These two examples show you how 'coursework' can mean very different things with different Examination Groups and even in different syllabuses of the same Group; so you must be certain of what exact examination requirements are that you will have to meet. In all coursework, however, the examiners will be looking for evidence of your knowledge and understanding of the material included in your syllabus and evidence of your ability to use geographical skills.

3 Enquiry-based practical unit

This is a label used by the Southern Examining Group, Syllabus B, to describe a unit designed to allow pupils to undertake a geographical enquiry on *either* a new area of study, *or* on one or more of the four modules contained in the syllabus.

In this unit, work can be done as a class investigation, a group study or by individual candidates.

4 Investigational Study

The Northern Ireland School Examination and Assessment Council examinations include an investigation in which students are expected to:

(a) design, organize and carry out a geographical enquiry;

(b) use basic geographical techniques to collect, represent and interpret information;

(c) communicate their findings effectively.

The investigational study may be done either by individuals or by groups.

5 Individual study

This is a study which is based upon first-hand individual work. The work may be done in the home area or elsewhere. The study has to be submitted as part of the examination.

The individual study has to be:

(a) appropriate to the candidate's level of ability;

(b) related to the key ideas and issues listed in the syllabus;

(c) related to the assessment objective of the syllabus.

6 Geographical enquiry

Candidates may be expected to submit one long, or two or three shorter pieces of work, which must include field work in at least one component. The enquiry may be planned by the teacher and carried out by a group, with individuals in the group having particular tasks. It could, however, be an investigation of a problem decided upon by the candidate and carried out individually.

7 Decision-making exercises

This is practical work which forms part of the assessment programme. The DME (decision-making exercise) is based upon a range of material which is given to the students before the exercise is held, so that they can familiarize themselves with the information. The actual question(s) is/are not given to the students until the exercise starts. The question(s) will require the student to analyse and evaluate the data provided. This data will be related to a particular part of the syllabus.

SOME KEY QUESTIONS

1 Do I have to do practical and/or field work?

The type and importance of the study you are expected to make varies from one Examination Group to another. Whichever Examination Group the school uses, however, the Geography examination at GCSE level and the Scottish Certificate of Education, Standard Grade examination require some kind of practical study to be undertaken by candidates. This applies whether you are entered for the examination through a school or a college.

The National Criteria for Geography emphasize the importance of investigations in the field. In the National Criteria this aim is stated:

'to develop a range of skills through practical work, including investigations in the field...'

All Examination Groups insist that field work forms an important part of the work in Geography.

2 Why do I have to do practical work or an investigation in Geography?

There are three main reasons:

(a) To enable you to show your ability to:
   (i) design, organize and carry out a geographical enquiry;
   (ii) use basic geographical techniques for obtaining, observing, recording, analysing, classifying and interpreting data;
   (iii) communicate information.

(b) To allow you to demonstrate a variety of geographical skills, including basic ones such as using equipment correctly; choosing and using particular techniques such as field sketching (see the following examples); careful observation and the recording of data. The best candidates will be able to show their mastery of higher-order skills such as the ability to analyse, synthesize and evaluate the information collected.

(c) Fieldwork is an essential part of the work of the geographer. In doing fieldwork with their classes, teachers try to achieve the following objectives:

Attitudinal and aesthetic objectives

To arouse students' curiosity.
To develop favourable attitudes towards learning.
To provoke students to ask questions and identify problems.
To sharpen students' perception and appreciation of changing geographical landscapes.
To give students the experience of the pleasure of discovery.
To enjoy the study of geography and acquire a deeper interest in the subject.

Knowledge objectives

To develop better understandings of the nature of things discussed in the classroom and in books.
To enable students to observe and think, and acquire knowledge.
To understand the relationships between physical features and human activities.
To associate the different phenomena which together comprise the geography of an area.
To develop an awareness of problems relating to human occupance of the land.

Skill objectives

To develop an understanding of geographical modes of inquiry.
To distinguish between necessary and extraneous information.
To orient a map in the field.
To relate real features to map symbols.
To develop skills in data collection, recording and analysis.

From the list above you can see that there are three main goals:

(i) to help you enjoy your work, to become more curious about the world and to be more aware of how it is changing;
(ii) to help you increase your geographical knowledge;
(iii) to teach you those skills which are used by Geographers and which will be useful to you long after you have left school or college.

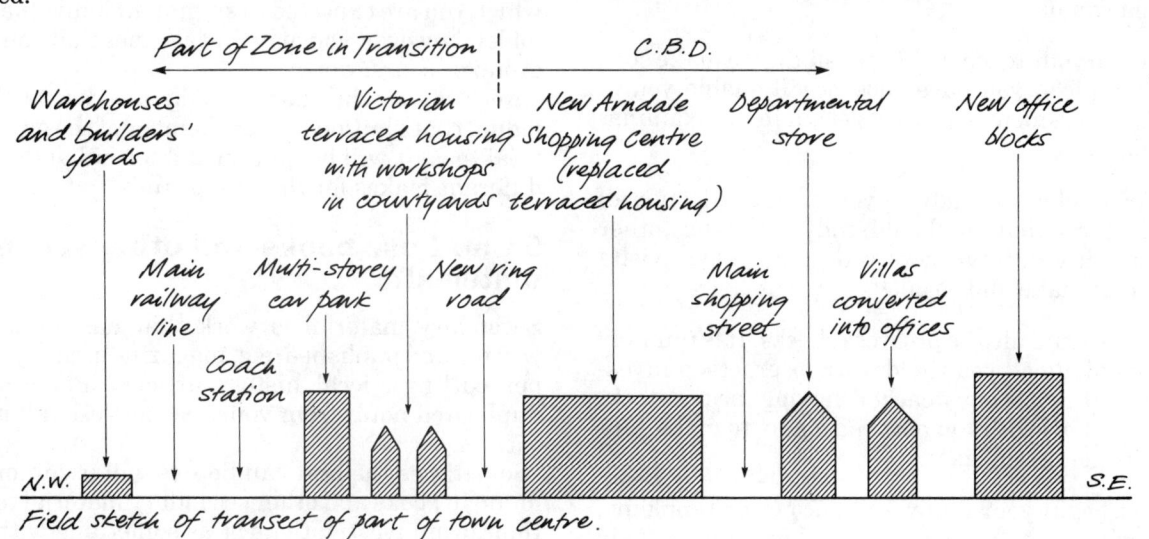

Field sketch of transect of part of town centre.

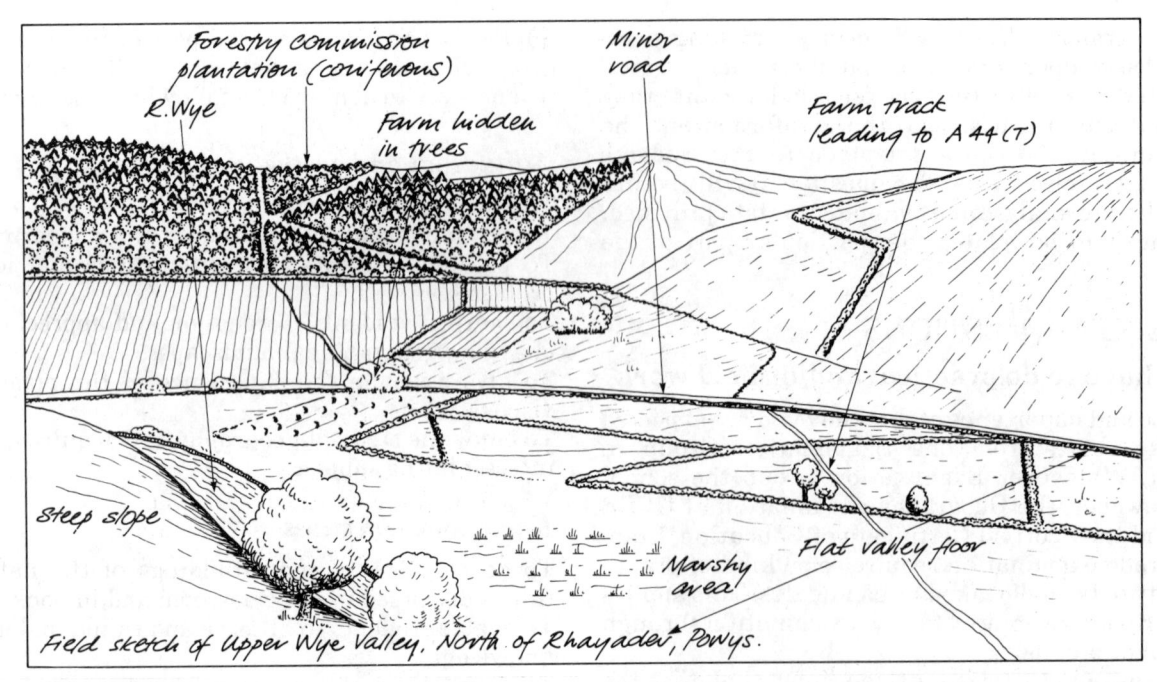

Field sketch of Upper Wye Valley, North of Rhayader, Powys.

Labels on sketch: R. Wye; Forestry commission plantation (coniferous); Farm hidden in trees; Minor road; Farm track leading to A 44 (T); Steep slope; Marshy area; Flat valley floor.

3 How much help can I expect from my teacher(s)?

The Examination Groups recognize that you will need help from your teacher. Some people will need more help than others. To make sure that everyone is marked fairly, the Examination Group will ask your teacher to tell them how much help you received.

For example, The Southern Examining Group asks teachers to record all assistance given on the reverse of the candidates assessment sheet.

In general, you can expect your teacher to help you most at the beginning of your study but to help you less as the work proceeds. So what can you expect?

(a) The teacher must help you first of all by making certain that you know exactly what is required of you in the examination. This will vary according to the Examination Group and according to the syllabus you are following, so it is vital that you know *exactly* what you have to do.

(b) Your teacher will help you choose your topic(s) by discussing the possibilities of the different ideas you may have. It is your teacher's duty to ensure that you choose a topic that enables you to show what you know, how well you understand your work in Geography, and what you can do.

(c) It is also your teacher's responsibility to make sure that the topic(s) you have chosen will enable you to meet the assessment objectives set out in the examination syllabus.

(d) Your teacher will advise you on the selection of course material that you should study—statistics, other relevant sources, interviews you might make, visits you need to make and so on.

(e) There should also be progress checks. It is unlikely that you will do all your field work or practical investigation without your teacher having brief 'stock-taking' sessions with you now and again, to make sure that all is going well.

(f) If you begin your study and encounter problems, your teacher may fell that you need extra help. This help will probably consist of talking about the problems and the relevance of some of the work you had intended to do. If this does happen, the teacher will keep a record of the extra help you have been given so that your work can be assessed fairly when it is finished.

(g) Your teacher will *not* normally help with:

(i) data refining and presentation—except perhaps to give help with the choice of techniques you might use to present your material, e.g. maps, sketches, photographs, charts, statistical methods;

(ii) the analysis and interpretation of your data;

(iii) formulating your conclusions;

(iv) the actual writing up of the work.

4 Do I have to work on my own?

This will vary with the nature of the coursework or investigation, but in most cases the simple answer is, no! Geography examiners know that practical work and field work is often carried out as a group activity. If work is done in this way, your teacher will have to identify clearly the contribution that *you* made to the work of the group. If you are sitting an examination in which you are expected to submit an individual course folder, however, you may find at times that you do little group or coursework.

Since the teacher has to make a record of the individual contribution of each member of the group to the total task, it will be quite usual for individuals to get different makes for the group study.

5 Can I use books and other secondary material?

Secondary material is work that has already been written and published, e.g. magazine articles, newspaper cuttings, local history articles. Photocopied or duplicated notes from your teacher also fall into this category.

Sometimes the best candidates will *use* information found in books and other secondary material to extend their own investigations or as something with which they can compare their own findings. The candidates who will get the lowest marks are those who copy out pages of lesson notes, or from books. Your teacher will need to be sure that in your investigation you do not depend too much upon textbooks and lesson notes. If you do use such material, it is important that you acknowledge where it came from.

6 What happens if someone cheats?

Your teacher will warn you that you must not use unfair practices in preparing your practical work or investigation. So even if a student gets an expert in Geography to do his/her work, it is very likely that the teacher who knows them well will suspect that it is not their own work.

In that case the teacher will:
(a) not sign the certification for the work, which is an official part of the examination procedure;
(b) report the matter to the Examination Group.
This may then disqualify the student from taking the Geography examination.

7 How will my study be marked?

All the Examination Groups have carefully worked out the criteria by which practical work and investigations will be marked.

Here are the kinds of considerations which will be taken into account:

(a) The practical work or fieldwork itself

(i) Did you choose suitable techniques and skills to investigate your study?
(ii) How well did you use those techniques and skills?
(iii) How sound is the data (information) you collected?
(iv) Did you organize your work properly?
(v) Did you show initiative in collecting data?
(vi) Did you get on with your study and finish the task?

(b) The written report

(i) Did you place your investigation into a broader geographical setting, eg. did you relate your own farm study to the regional and national patterns of farming?
(ii) Did you choose suitable methods for analysing your data?
(iii) How well did you analyse the information you collected?
(iv) How well did you interpret the results you obtained?
(v) How good are your maps and diagrams?
(vi) Were your maps and diagrams relevant to your study?
(vii) Does your argument seem convincing?
(viii) How sound are your conclusions?
(ix) Is your report well presented?—pages numbered, a contents page, a bibliography (a list of books etc. that you read).
(x) Did you have enough 'stickability' to complete the report?

You may find it useful to use this as a checklist while you are doing your study.

HOW CAN I WRITE A GOOD STUDY?

Choose a topic which involves
either *considering an argument* with points to be made for and against, e.g. the argument for a planned local by-pass;
or *investigation of a problem*, e.g. why a local shopping centre seems to be in decline;
or *testing an assertion*, e.g. that all rivers flow slower the further they are from their source.

You must be quite clear about the purpose of your study, so you must define your objectives precisely. The more specific you are in stating your objectives, the easier it will be to focus upon the key questions or problems you should investigate.

The following chart shows a general approach which all GCSE Groups should find satisfactory. If you follow the steps shown in the diagram, you should produce a systematic and well-structured study.

1. IDENTIFY AN ISSUE OR PROBLEM ⟶ What questions are important to me? Do I do it on my own or as part of a group?

2. FORMULATE A THEORY ⟶ What theory can I formulate which could explain the questions I wish to ask? Does my teacher think this will be a worthwhile investigation?

3. COLLECTING DATA ⟶ What information do I need to collect? How can I best collect it? What range of skills/techniques will I use? Are my ideas practical in terms of the time I have to do it? What special arrangements do I have to make? e.g. interviewing a farmer. Does my teacher approve of the plan I have?

4. RECORDING DATA ⟶ Where can I get information about techniques I could use to record data? How will I store the results I obtain in the field to use in my final report? Have I used a variety of techniques? Has my teacher suggested others? Are my maps, diagrams etc. relevant to the study and not just decorative?

5. ANALYSING DATA ⟶ How will I present my results?

6. GENERALIZATIONS AND CONCLUSIONS → Have I achieved a good balance between writing, diagrammatic representation, maps in the presentation of my argument?
If I worked in a group, can I point out my individual contribution?
Have I explored the key questions I identified? What evidence have I now got which would lead me to: (a) reject the theory in 2; (b) accept the theory in 2? What major conclusions should I make in my report?

7. WRITE MY REPORT

You can see that in the early stages you need to discuss your ideas with your teacher to make sure that you are on the right lines.

Don't think of your study as a separate part of the course. In the National Criteria to which your Examination Group had to conform when setting up your syllabus, it is stated that field work 'should always be an integral part of the course.' A good study will show close links with the rest of your work in Geography. The skills you have learned in class can be applied to your practical work, the knowledge you have been taught should be used in the development of your argument in the study.

One other aspect of the work is also important in this respect. All GCSE syllabuses aim to develop an appreciation of the part played by *values and attitudes* of people or groups in different situations. In the past, Geography teachers tried to appear to be neutral when dealing with controversial matters. In order to understand the character of places, however, we need to probe the feelings, motives and priorities of the people involved. For example, a planning issue can raise much emotion and there can be conflicts of values between those who place a high priority on profits and efficiency and others who want to maintain what they see as the quality of the environment.

You should show awareness of these matters in your study.

In summary:

1 choose a well-defined manageable problem or a question or hypothesis to be explored;

2 collect your data by first-hand observation; through field work and other sources such as old maps;

3 analyse your data carefully and present the data accurately;

4 write a conclusion which is based upon the evidence you found and in which you evaluate the question or hypothesis with which you started.

PRESENTATION OF YOUR STUDY

Some Examining Groups say little about this, but that does not mean that it is not important. The Southern Examining Group, however, tells candidates exactly what they expect, and this is a useful guide whichever your own Examining Group. Here are the points made:

1 All sketches, diagrams, maps and graphs included in the study should be referred to in the written text of your study;

2 Maps should be clearly labelled to show title, compass direction, key and scale;

3 Bulky items, e.g. town guides, should be kept to a minimum and usually should be included in an Appendix;

4 Your teacher will give you precise guidance on what information to include on the cover sheet of your study and the size of the folder in which the work is to be presented, but all should contain;

— a table of contents
— a statement of the aim of the study
— methods used to collect data
— the data and findings
— analysis and interpretation of data
— conclusion
— bibliography (if needed)
— appendix (if needed).

Above all, make sure that your practical work and investigations meet the requirements of the Examination Group for the syllabus you are studying. Your teacher should check this with you, so ask him/her if you have any doubts.

10 THE EXAMINATION

The day before

Do not attempt any revision on the evening before the examination. If you must revise, spend part of the morning or afternoon just looking through your notes or text books. On no account spend the hours immediately prior to the examination on last-minute revision. Such revision is seldom remembered and can make you mentally exhausted or confused before you have had an opportunity to write an answer paper. Spend this time before the examination checking your pencils, pens and other materials which you will require during the examination. Always have a spare pen and pencil available, but do not clutter your desk with unnecessary coloured pencils (four colours are usually sufficient) or a wide range of technical drawing equipment. Your teacher will advise you what you can take into the examination with you, but here is a suggested list:

Two HB pencils, pen, rubber, ruler, four coloured pencils (brown, green, red, blue), compass and a protractor. A spare pencil and pen in a pocket are also useful.

There are three golden rules which you should follow while taking the examination. They are:

1 Read the whole paper carefully and if you have a choice, spend a little time deciding which questions you can answer best.

2 Time yourself carefully throughout the examination.

3 Leave sufficient time at the end to read your answers.

Read the paper carefully

Some Examination Groups provide additional time which can only be used for reading the questions. This is very valuable time because the questions will probably have many parts to them and it is easy to choose a question mistakenly because you have only read the first part and know you can answer that part.

Having read all the questions, go back and mark with a tick those you intend to answer. Be sure you have read the rubric at the beginning of the paper and know exactly how many questions you must answer. No marks are given for additional answers and you will waste marks if you answer fewer questions than you are asked for.

Always answer the question you feel you know most about first, and leave to last the one you are least happy with. Do not panic if you can only answer the number required. No one will know that you could not select more than were requested.

You may find that there is one small part of a question you have selected which you cannot answer. If this should happen, do not be over-concerned. The part you cannot answer may be worth only one or two marks.

Time yourself

Before the examination you should have practised writing answers to a strict time limit. It is absolutely essential in the examination to keep very closely to the time allocation for each question. Where a map question is part of a written paper, it is very easy to spend a long time on a map, leaving very little time for the other questions. The tendency is to leave too little time for the final questions on the paper. This will lose marks, as each question will have a number of marks allocated. Try to work out before the examination how many minutes you should spend on each question, allowing at least five minutes at the end of the examination for reading what you have written. If you find you are spending too long on a question, for example, you have spent 40 minutes on a question which should only take 30 minutes, stop writing, leave some space to complete your answer if there is time and go straight on to the next question.

If you complete a question in much less than the time allotted, start the next question but return to the first again at the end of the paper and add any second thoughts. Make sure you answer all the questions you are required to answer. Do not spend too long on any one answer—you will not make up marks if you have insufficient time to complete the final questions.

Leave time at the end

It is always worth reading through what you have written in the last five or ten minutes of the examination. Mistakes you may have made can be corrected and new facts added. Maps and diagrams can be improved by adding more detail or additional names. These amendments in the final minutes of the examination can add valuable marks to the total.

Finally, it must be emphasized that examinations are invigilated very strictly and any attempt at cheating can easily be spotted and can only result in failure for the people concerned.

One way in which many examiners eliminate any possibility of cheating is to forbid candidates to take paper of any kind into the examination room. Even if this rule does not apply to you, in your own interest it is worthwhile observing it.

Examination myths

A number of myths have grown up about examinations, possibly because secrecy must surround the marking process to ensure that no one is especially favoured or disadvantaged. Let us destroy some of these myths.

Myth no. 1 Whatever the results, a certain percentage of the candidates must fail.

Since the GCSE examination is intended to record what candidates have achieved, groups of grades are described in positive terms and state what the candidate must achieve to obtain these grades. This means that if you reach the required criteria you cannot fail.

Myth no. 2 Examiners are out to trick candidates.

Questions are never set deliberately to catch you out. The team of examiners responsible for approving the question paper wants to give candidates a fair opportunity to show their merits and this can only be done by asking straightforward questions. It is true that some candidates do not always understand a question or are suspicious because of the way a question has been worded. The analysis of question styles earlier in this section should have helped you to appreciate the variety of questions which can be asked and how they should be answered.

Myth no. 3 Your marks for a whole paper will be lowered if you write a silly answer to one of the questions.

This is quite untrue. Each answer is marked on its own merits and no attention is paid to the way other questions have been answered. In our experience candidates very rarely write three sensible answers and one which is nonsense. A silly answer is usually followed by others equally worthless.

Myth no. 4 The marks you are given depend on which examiner marks your paper.

A number of the GCSE questions require short answers which are objective, in that the answer given is either right or wrong, for example, 'Give TWO ways in which an area of lakes and forests may be affected by acid rain.'

Two marks are awarded, and the examiner should have little difficulty in deciding whether the answers given are worth one mark each.

Many question sections, however, require longer answers, which make them more subjective. Examination Groups are fully aware that examiners left to their own devices are likely to mark very differently from one another. Every effort is made, therefore, to standardize the marking. There are various ways in which this is done. In many cases the examiners meet after the paper has been taken and before the marking begins, so that they can identify problems and agree a common marking scheme in considerable detail. During the marking period, samples of the examiners' work are checked, with the result that a number of scripts are marked by more than one examiner. This system of checking and standardization also applies to course work.

Because course work will be marked by your own teachers, they will attend courses explaining how the work is to be marked. A detailed marking scheme will be drawn up and approved, and after the examination has taken place a sample of the papers will be moderated. That is, they will be re-marked by an assessor from another school who may decide, in some cases, that different marks should be awarded.

Myth no. 5 Marks are deducted for mistakes.

Examiners ignore irrelevant and inaccurate facts and only award marks for correct information. They cannot deduct marks for obvious mistakes.
Here is an example:
'Name a new town in Britain and give reasons why new towns have been developed.'
It would be possible to score marks for giving the correct answers why new towns have been developed, even though the example provided of a new town was wrong, eg. Glasgow.
Only correct information receives marks; incorrect facts are ignored.

This section has tried to remove any lingering anxieties which you may have had about the geography examination. It is doubtful, however, whether anyone who enters an examination room feels totally self-confident, but careful planning and thorough revision can help to make the experience a very rewarding one when the results are published.

Myth no. 6 There is no appeal system

An appeal system is operated by all the Examining Groups. In Scotland, for example, schools have an automatic right to appeal against an award. If a candidate fails or gets a lower grade than expected and the school has good evidence that the candidate should have done better, an appeal against the result can be made and evidence submitted by the school to support their opinion.

Examining Groups will normally charge a fee for rechecking a candidate's marks and providing a written report on the examination papers. If the assessment is at fault, a reassessment will be made and the grade amended.

SKILLS

Many of the skills you must understand and be able to use for the GCSE examination are connected with the interpretation of visual material such as maps, diagrams and statistics. Sections 1–5 of this book contain an extensive variety of these illustrations with further examples in other sections. To help you revise the different stimuli used, examples have been listed below, together with their figure or table references. Check each type carefully and make certain you understand what the illustration shows, since similar material will form the basis of question stimuli in the examination.

Maps	*Figs.*
OS map extracts	Inside back cover.
Town plans	2.12B.
Weather maps	1.3B.
Sketch maps	1.6B, C; 2.1; 2.3B; 2.5B 2.8B; 2.10A; 2.15B; 2.16B; 2.17A; 7.3.
Distribution maps	1.10A; 2.4A; 2.5A; 2.8A; 2.11; 2.14B; 2.15E; 2.16A; 2.18A; 2.19; 2.20B; 3.1; 3.2A, B; 3.3A, B; 3.4B, C, D, E; 3.5B, C; 3.6; 3.7A; 3.8C; 3.9A, B; 3.10; 3.11; 3.12; 3.13; 3.15; 4.1A; 4.3A, B; 4.4A; 4.5A; 4.6B; 4.7; 4.9B; 4.10C; 4.11; 5.3A, B; 5.4B; 5.6; 5.10.
Choropleth map	2.11
Flow maps	3.7B.

Diagrams |
--- | ---
Pie graphs | 3.3C; 3.8A; 4.6A.
Line graphs | 5.1; 6.2A; 6.4A; 6.5B.
Bar charts | 3.5A; 3.7B; 3.8B; 6.3B.
Population pyramids | 2.18B.
Diagrams | 1.4E; 1.7B, C, D; 2.2; 2.6B; 4.4C; 4.5B; 4.15A; 5.2; 5.4A; 5.8A, C.
Block diagrams | 1.4A, B, C, D; 1.5B. 1.10B, E; 5.6; 5.8B
Flow diagrams | 2.14A; 3.7A; 4.1B; 4.2B; 5.9.
Network diagrams | 2.9A, B; 2.14C.
Cross-sections | 1.3A; 1.6D; 1.8A, B; 1.9A; 1.10C; 3.4A.
Models | 2.10B; 2.12A; 2.13A, B; 2.14D; 4.5C; 4.8; 4.9A.

Photographs |
--- | ---
Ground photographs | 1.7A; 1.9B; 2.19B; 2.20; 3.9C; 3.14; 4.6C; 4.12B; 4.13A, B; 4.15.
Oblique aerial photographs | 1.1A; 1.5A; 1.6A; 2.15A.

Other material |
--- | ---
Cartoons | 2.15D.
Newspaper articles and extracts | 7.6.

Statistical data |
--- | ---
Statistical tables | 3.8A; 5.1.

GLOSSARY

Accessibility The degree to which a location is being reached or is 'get-at-able'.
Acid Rain Rainfall with pH values of less than 5.6. The acidity is caused by sulphur and nitrogen gases which have combined with water vapour to form weak sulphuric and nitric acids.
Administrative centre A settlement that is responsible for the control of its region. It may be the capital city or an important local town.
Age/Sex pyramid A type of bar graph that illustrates the structure of a population. It is made up of horizontal bars representing different age categories, which are placed on either side of a central vertical axis.
Air mass A mass of air, with similar properties of temperature and moisture covering a large area of the earth's surface and bounded by fronts. (See *Front*).
Alluvial plain Level land bordering a river on which alluvium (fine material carried by the river) is deposited, e.g. plain of the R. Ganges.
Altitude The vertical distance above mean sea level, usually measured in metres or feet. It can also mean the distance above the horizon of the sun or stars.
Anticline A fold of rock strata forming an arch. (See *Syncline*).
Anticyclone A region of high atmospheric pressure. (See *Cyclone*).
Aquifer A porous, tilted layer of rock between impermeable layers which allows water to travel distances underground, e.g. central Australia.
Arable land Land which is ploughed and used for growing crops.
Area of Outstanding Natural Beauty (AONB) In the UK an area of land that has special landscape value which is considered worthy of protection. AONBs are the responsibility of local planning authorities, who have powers to preserve and enhance the natural beauty of the area.
Arête A knife-edge mountain ridge, often formed by the erosion of two adjoining cirques, e.g. Striding Edge in the Lake District.
Arid region An area with low rainfall where the conditions are desert or semi-desert, e.g. Painted Desert of Arizona.
Atmospheric pressure The weight of a column of air at a particular point. At sea level, pressure equals about 1000 millibars, which represents a force of 1000 dynes acting on one square centimetre. Above sea level, the column of air is shorter and the pressure is lower. Atmospheric pressure is increased when air is descending. (See *Anticyclone* and *Millibar*).
Backwash The flow of sea water back down a beach towards the sea. (See *Swash*).
Barchan A crescent-shaped sand dune, with the horns of the crescent pointing down wind, e.g. desert areas of Turkestan.
Barometer The instrument used for measuring atmospheric pressure. (See *Atmospheric pressure*).
Basin irrigation A means of providing water for cultivation that involves the flooding of basin-like hollows surrounded by earth banks.

Bergschrund The gap or crevasse left round the upper rim of the ice within a cirque as the ice moves downwards.
Boulder clay The rocks and finely-ground rock flour carried down by a glacier and left as a deposit when the ice melts, e.g. soils of East Anglia.
Break of bulk point The location at which a cargo is transferred from one form of transport to another. At this point, transport costs will increase because of the extra handling incurred.
Built-up area That part of the landscape which is covered by houses and other buildings.
Calcareous Containing a considerable proportion of calcium carbonate, e.g. calcareous soils of the North Downs.
Campos The tropical grasslands or savanna of Brazil, located south of the Amazon Basin.
Capital 1 A town or city that is the chief town of a country, province or state and which contains the seat of government. 2 In economics, the stock of money and goods used for promoting and conducting a business. Capital is one of the factors of production, together with land, labour and business expertise.
Cash crops Crops which are produced for sale and not for consumption locally, e.g. coffee.
Central Business District (CBD) The commercial, social and cultural core of a city, where the chief shops and offices are concentrated. It is also the focus of the urban transport network and is often the area of maximum traffic congestion. It is the area of higher land values, so buildings are concentrated and are built to maximum heights.
Central goods Those goods, services and functions that tend to be grouped together in urban centres or central places.
Central place An accessible location from which goods and services are provided for the surrounding area.
Central Place Theory The theory that there is a pattern in the number of towns, cities and villages (central places) and in the ways in which the central places provide goods and services for their surrounding areas (hinterlands).
Chemical weathering (See *Weathering*).
Cirque, Corrie An armchair-like hollow with steep sides and rear walls formed through erosion by ice and snow and found in regions which are, or have been, glaciated. Sometimes the hollow is filled by a lake, e.g. corries in Snowdonia.
Climate The average weather conditions of a place or region throughout the seasons.
Cloud A mass of small water droplets or ice crystals formed by the condensation of water vapour in the atmosphere.
Cold front The boundary line between a mass of advancing cold air and a mass of warm air which the cold air pushes under. (See *Warm front*).
Common Agricultural Policy (CAP) The policy drawn up among the member countries of the EC to ensure a fair standard of living for farmers and farm

workers and the availability of farm products at reasonable prices.

Commuter A person who travels a considerable distance regularly (usually daily) to and from work.

Concentric model of urban land use A model describing the arrangement of functional zones within a city.

Condensation The conversion of a vapour into a liquid. Clouds are formed by the condensation of water vapour in cold air above the earth's surface.

Confluence The point at which two streams join together, e.g. confluence of the Red River and Mississippi.

Coniferous forest A forest of mainly cone-bearing trees which have needleshaped leaves. Such trees are usually evergreen, e.g. Sitka Spruce.

Conservation The protection of the natural environment and its resources for the future. It also includes the protection of some man-made environments, such as old buildings and historic sites.

Continental climate The climate experienced in the interiors of the large continents, especially in North America, Eastern Europe and Central Asia.

Continental shelf A gently-sloping shelf forming the sea bed bordering the continents. It is normally less than 100 fathoms in depth and eventually the sea bed drops steeply to the ocean depths.

Contour A line drawn on a map to join all places at the same height above sea level.

Conurbation An extensive area of streets, houses and other buildings formed by the joining up of several neighbouring and formerly separate towns, e.g. West Midland conurbation

Convectional rainfall Rain caused by the heating of surface layers of air which then rise and cool until condensation takes place and rain falls. Convectional rainfall frequently occurs over land on hot afternoons in the tropics. The rain takes the form of heavy thunderstorms which quickly disperse in the evening.

Core region The area where economic activity is at its greatest, for example the Glasgow-Edinburgh section of the central Lowlands of Scotland. (See *Peripheral region*).

Corrasion The wearing away of rock by material that is being transported, e.g. by ice, rivers, wind or waves. The most common form of corrasion is produced by a river and its load.

Correlation A statistical technique that determines the extent to which a relationship exists between two variables.

Corrosion The wearing away of rocks by chemical action, e.g. the solution of chalk in river water.

Crater The funnel-shaped hollow in the cone of a volcano, through which the molten rock and other materials find their way to the surface. Extinct volcanoes leave craters which may be filled with water or which form large basins, e.g. Ngorongoro Crater in Tanzania.

Crevasse A deep vertical crack in a glacier.

Cyclone A region of low pressure, sometimes called a depression. It also means a violent storm which occurs in the tropics. (See *Anticyclone*).

Datum level The level which is used as the basis for measuring altitudes and depths of the sea.

Deciduous forest A forest consisting mainly of trees which lose their leaves at some time of the year.

Deforestation The removal of the tree cover of an area by felling or burning.

Delta The area of alluvium formed at the mouth of a river where the material is not removed by tides or currents, e.g. Nile Delta.

Density of population The average number of people living in a particular area, e.g. 500 per sq. kilometre.

Denudation The wearing away of the land by various forms of erosion.

Depopulation The decline or reduction of population in a geographical area.

Depression (See *Cyclone*).

Desert An almost barren area where the precipitation is so low that very little or no vegetation can grow, e.g. Kalahari desert.

Desire line The straight line (shortest distance) between the point of origin of a trip and the destination.

Development area In the UK an area where economic growth is encouraged by grants and subsidies to industries which set up factories there.

Dry farming A method of farming in areas of limited rainfall where the land is treated in various ways to conserve the moisture it contains, so that crops can be grown. Dry farming does not involve the use of irrigation, e.g. western states of the USA.

Dry valley A valley in which there is normally no stream. Dry valleys occur in the chalk downlands of southern and eastern England.

Dune A mound or ridge of sand formed by the wind, either near the sea or in a desert, e.g. dunes of Death Valley, California (desert), coast south of Blackpool, Lancashire (onshore winds).

Dust bowl An area of man-made desert caused by over-grazing, deforestation or the ploughing-up of unsuitable land. The term is usually applied to areas of central and western USA such as Oklahoma, where there was severe wind erosion in the 1930s and where strict conservation measures have been introduced in recent years.

Ecology The scientific study of the relationship of a plant or animal to its natural environment.

Ecosystem A community of plants and animals sharing a particular environment. Ecosystems can be at different scales, for example on a world scale the rainforest is an ecosystem. A pond is a small-scale ecosystem. Ecosystems have inputs of oxygen, nutrients, water, heat and carbon dioxide. The output is organic matter such as leaves.

Effluent The waste products from a factory or industrial site. Effluent is often discharged into rivers or the sea.

Entrepôt A place which acts as an intermediary centre for trade between two or more foreign centres, receiving goods from one part of the world for onward transmission to another part of the world, e.g. Rotterdam, Hong Kong.

Epicentre The point on the earth's surface immediately above the origin of an earthquake. (See *Seismic Focus*).

Erosion The wearing away of the earth's surface by various natural agents, particularly wind, water and ice.

Estuary The mouth of a river, which is kept clear of alluvium by tides. It is usually funnel-shaped and suitable as a harbour, e.g. Mersey Estuary.

Evaporation The process whereby a liquid turns into a gas. Water vapour in the atmosphere is the result of evaporation from the earth's surface and transpiration — the release of water vapour by plants.

Expanded town A town where planned growth was

undertaken under the Town Development Act (1952). Expanded towns relieved overpopulation and congestion in the big cities.

Fahrenheit scale The temperature scale used in some parts of the world, e.g. the USA. The freezing point of water is set at 32 ° and its boiling point at 212 °F.

Flood plain The plain bordering a river which has been formed from river deposits, e.g. flood plain of the River Thames. (See *Alluvial Plain*.)

Fold mountains Mountains which have resulted from folding of the earth's crust, e.g. the Alps.

Food chain The links by which energy is passed from one form of living organism to another. For example, green plants provide food for herbivores which are eaten by carnivores. Different food chains are often linked to form a food web.

Footloose industry An industry which is not tied to a particular location by raw materials, energy or labour requirements. Hi-tech industries are footloose, since they use easily transported components and electricity as the form of power.

Fragmentation The process by which farmland is divided up into small scattered units, so that one owner may have several fields in small parcels in different parts of a locality.

Front The line separating cold and warm air masses. (See *Cold Front* and *Warm Front*).

Functional zone An area that is dominated by a particular function in a town or city, e.g. a residential or industrial zone.

Gap town A town situated on a gap between hills, usually where a river has cut through the hills. Gap towns are often important route centres, e.g. Dorking, south of London.

Geyser A hot spring which at intervals throws a jet of hot water and steam into the air. Geysers occur in volcanic regions, e.g. Old Faithful in Yellowstone National Park, USA.

Glacier A mass of ice which moves slowly down a valley or across the earth's surface until it melts or breaks up in the sea as icebergs, e.g. Rhone Glacier in Switzerland.

Gorge A deep, steep-sided valley, e.g. Cheddar Gorge. The American word *canyon* has a similar meaning, e.g. Grand Canyon.

Green belt A belt of land around a town, city or conurbation where there are severe restrictions on new buildings. The restrictions are imposed to preserve the open character of the countryside, e.g. London's Green Belt.

'Green Heart' The name given to the rural area in the Netherlands, which is almost surrounded by the Randstad. The region consists of farmland and woodland.

Greenhouse effect The effect of certain gases in the atmosphere in trapping the sun's heat. Increases in the quantities of these gases result in higher temperatures on earth — global warming.

Gross Domestic Product (GDP) The total value of goods and services produced by a country over a period of time, usually a year.

Gross National Product (GNP) The gross domestic product plus the income obtained from investments abroad, less income earned in a country by foreigners.

Guest workers (gastarbeiter) Workers from other countries who are attracted to a country by higher employment and wages than they can obtain in their own country.

Gully A channel cut by rainwater. Gullies are usually long, narrow and not very deep. They are often formed on hillsides by water erosion.

Habitat The natural environment of a plant or animal, e.g. the natural habitat for orchids is the tropical rain forest.

Hanging valley A tributary valley which enters the main valley high above the valley floor. Streams flowing down the tributary valley form a waterfall or rapids at the point of entry, e.g. Bridal Falls in the Yosemite Valley, California.

Head of navigation The farthest point up a river that can be reached by ocean-going ships.

Heavy industry The production of goods which are heavy and normally bulky when compared with other industries, e.g. iron and steel, shipbuilding and the manufacture of railway rolling stock.

Hinterland The land behind a seaport which provides most of the exports of the port and takes most of the imports, e.g. the hinterland of Rotterdam stretches to Switzerland.

Humus The decaying or decayed remains of animal and vegetable matter in the soil.

Hydraulic action The process by which flowing water impounds and compresses air pockets. This pressure may break down the rock.

Hydrological cycle (See *Water cycle*).

Ice ages Periods in the past when the polar ice-sheets extended much further towards the Equator than at present. Ice-sheets and glaciers covered large areas of land and sea.

Igneous rock Rock that has been solidified from molten magma, e.g. basalt and granite.

Impervious rock Rock which does not allow water to pass through it easily, e.g. clay.

Industrial inertia The tendency for firms and industries to remain in a location after the causes which determined the original location have disappeared or are no longer significant, e.g. the manufacture of cutlery at Sheffield.

Infrastructure The roads, piped water supply, communications and other services which are essential for the development of a complex society. Infrastructures reach their most advanced form in highly-developed countries such as the United States. They are less developed in countries of the developing world such as Bangladesh.

Intensive cultivation Methods of cultivation in which large amounts of capital and/or labour are applied per unit of land.

Irrigation The man-made distribution of water on the land to allow crops to grow in areas where there is insufficient rainfall for cultivation, e.g. Central Valley of California.

Isobar A line on a map joining places with the same atmospheric pressure.

Isohyet A line on a map joining places having the same amount of rainfall over a certain period.

Isotherm A line on a map joining places having the same temperature, either at one time or over a certain period of time.

Karst A limestone region with most drainage underground, making the surface dry and barren, e.g. Dinaric alps of Yugoslavia.

Lagoon A shallow stretch of water, either partly or completely separated from the sea by a narrow strip of land or coral reef.

Latifundia system A system of farming in which the land is divided into large estates for extensive farming, e.g. cereal cultivation. The estates are owned by landlords and worked by landless labourers.

Lava Molten rock, sometimes called magma, which flows from a volcano or zone of crustal weakness. When it hardens, it forms a black rock, e.g. King Arthur's Seat, Edinburgh.

Levée The raised bank of a river formed during flooding, when alluvium is deposited.

Ley farming The planting of grass on arable land to form a pasture.

Llanos The tropical grasslands or savanna north of the Amazon Basin.

Loess A layer of fine silt or dust which has been deposited by the wind. If forms a very fertile soil in parts of central China and western Europe. In Benelux and France it is known as *limon*.

Longshore drift The movement of material such as sand and shingle along a beach as the result of waves breaking at an oblique angle upon the shore. The movement along the English Channel is from west to east, because the prevailing winds are from the southwest.

Mangrove swamps A swampy area on the coast or near a river mouth in tropical areas, covered by mangrove trees. Long roots hold the trees in the mud and also help to collect fresh deposits, which allow the mangrove swamp to enlarge itself, e.g. parts of the Nigerian coast.

Manufacturing industry Industry that processes materials or assembles components to produce finished goods or components, e.g. the car industry.

Maritime climate A climate influenced by the sea, giving a low range of temperatures between summer and winter. The sea cools the land in summer and warms it in winter, e.g. Devon and Cornwall.

Marginal land Land that is only sufficiently fertile to yield a return that just covers the costs of production.

Meander A bend or loop in the course of a river as it crosses flat land, e.g. lower Mississippi.

Mechanical weathering (See *Weathering*).

Migration The movement of individuals or groups from one place of residence to another. The movement can be within a country — internal, or to another country — international.

Millibar A unit of pressure equal to one-thousandth of a bar. Isobars are usually drawn at intervals of four millibars, e.g. 1000, 1004, 1008, etc.

Mixed farming The combination in one farm or district of both pastoral and arable farming.

Monsoon The type of wind system found mainly in the tropics, where there is a reversal of direction from season to season, e.g. the south-west monsoon which brings rain to India, Bangladesh and Pakistan in summer.

Moraine The rock material brought down by a glacier and deposited when the glacier melts providing morainic deposits such as terminal moraine, e.g. Cromer Ridge in Norfolk.

Multiple nuclei model A model of urban land use based upon the assumption that urban functional regions develop through the integration of a number of separate nuclei.

National Park A region preserved in a natural state, partly to provide recreational areas for people to enjoy and partly to conserve the area because of its scientific and historical importance, e.g. Peak District National Park.

Natural vegetation Vegetation that has developed in an environment untouched by man and which therefore closely corresponds to the prevailing conditions of climate and soil.

Network Interconnected lines of communication which form a net-like pattern, e.g. the motorway network of the UK.

New town A planned urban settlement built to provide homes and work, so as to relieve the congestion which exists in the large cities.

Nomadism The practice of roving from place to place which is still carried on by some groups, such as the Bedouin, in search of pastures for their livestock and for trade. Nomadism is a declining way of life; many nomads now live in settlements.

Nucleated settlement A form of rural settlement in which farms and other buildings are clustered together, especially around a central feature such as a church.

Oasis A fertile area in a desert where water is found, e.g. Kharga Oasis in Egypt.

Occlusion The joining of a warm front and a cold front in a low pressure area to make an occluded front.

Outport A port which, because it is nearer the sea than its parent port, is more accessible to large vessels, e.g. Cuxhaven is the outport for Hamburg.

Overpopulation An excess of population in an area in relation to the available resources and skills needed for further development.

Pampas The grasslands lying inland around the River Plate estuary in South America.

Pastoral farming The practice of rearing and breeding animals which feed on grass, e.g. sheep and cattle.

Perennial irrigation Irrigation methods that provide water for agriculture all through the year.

Peripheral region A region which is remote from the centre of economic activity (the core). Peripheral regions are on the edge of regions and some way from the main centre of activity, e.g. Brittany is a peripheral region within France. (See *Core Region*).

Permeable rock A rock which allows water to soak through it, e.g. sandstone.

pH scale A measure of the alkalinity or acidity in a soil or liquid. 0 is completely acid and 14 highly alkaline. pH 7 is neutral (the pH value of pure water).

Plantation An estate, usually in tropical or subtropical regions, devoted to the large-scale production of one or more cash crops, such as bananas or sugar-cane.

Plateau An extensive, mainly level area of high land, e.g. the Deccan Plateau of India.

Plates The large rigid segments into which the earth's crust is divided. Six major plates are recognized which 'float'. Plates may collide by converging and form a destructive plate margin. Diverging plates form a constructive plate margin, with new material welling up from below.

Pollution The fouling of the environment by humans, making it harmful for living organisms. Pollution can also reduce the amenity value by creating eyesores, such as rusty vehicles abandoned in the Australian outback.

Prairies The gently undulating, generally treeless, plains of North America. Once grasslands, the Prairies are now the grain growing areas of the continent.

Precipitation Water in any form which falls to earth. It therefore includes sleet, snow, hail and dew as well as rain.

Prevailing wind The most common wind experienced in a locality, e.g. westerly winds in Great Britain.

Primary energy Energy which is derived directly from a fuel such as coal. By contrast, electricity is a secondary form of energy, since it is produced from primary materials.

Primate city The largest city in a country or region. It is the centre of political affairs, trade, economic and social activity.

Push-pull factors A model of migration. The 'push' factors encourage people to leave a particular area; 'pull' factors are the economic and social attractions (real and imagined) offered by the location to which people move.

Rain shadow An area with a relatively light rainfall, when compared with neighbouring areas, because it is sheltered from the prevailing rain-bearing winds by high land, e.g. the Midlands are in the rain shadow of the Welsh Mountains.

Randstad Literally 'ring city', it is the urban region which forms a horseshoe shape in the Netherlands and includes Haarlem, Amsterdam and Utrecht in the north, with The Hague and Rotterdam in the south.

Range of a good The maximum distance people will travel to purchase a good or obtain a service offered by a central place.

Raw materials Materials used for manufacturing into saleable commodities, e.g. flour (already partially manufactured), iron, cotton.

Renewable resource A resource, such as timber which comes from trees, which can be replaced by replanting. Non-renewable resources include fossil fuels and minerals, of which there are limited supplies and which, in time, will become exhausted.

Ridge of high pressure A long and relatively narrow area of high pressure giving anticyclonic weather for a limited time before it moves away.

Rift valley A valley caused by the sinking of land between two roughly parallel faults, e.g. Great Rift Valley of East Africa.

Rotation of crops The planting of crops over a period of time on the same land in a particular order, e.g. wheat, potatoes, barley, grass.

Run-off The amount of rainfall which reaches the streams. Some flows over the surface and is known as surface run off. Some sinks into the ground and appears elsewhere as springs, this is called throughflow.

Scatter diagram A diagram using data plotted on a graph to show the amount of correlation between two sets of statistical data.

Scrub Low-growing shrubs and short trees found in areas of low rainfall or poor soils, e.g. some hill areas in Mediterranean countries where the scrub is known as *maquis*.

Sector model A model based on the principle that the structure of an urban area is determined by the location of routes radiating out from the city centre.

Sedimentary rock Rock formed in layers that have been deposited, in many cases as sediments under water, e.g. sandstone, limestone.

Seismic focus The place of origin of an earthquake in the earth's crust. (See *Epicentre*).

Selva The equatorial rainforest of the Amazon Basin.

Service centre A place that provides goods and services for the surrounding area.

Service industry An industry that provides a facility or service instead of manufactured goods, e.g. banking and tourism.

Shanty town (squatter settlement) An unplanned settlement built illegally on land in or on the edge of a city. Shanty towns are found mainly in areas of the Third World, in which city populations are growing rapidly.

Shifting cultivation Sometimes known as 'bush fallowing' or 'slash and burn'. A form of primitive agriculture practised in the tropics (e.g. New Guinea) in which a piece of forest is cleared, the trees and shrubs burnt and crops planted in the ashes. After a few years the soil is exhausted, erosion may have stripped away the fertile soil and so the plot is abandoned, allowing poor secondary forest to develop. The farmer moves his home and the procedure is then repeated elsewhere.

Silt A deposit of fine material laid down in a river or lake.

Sink hole or Swallow hole A saucer-shaped hollow in a limestone region which has been formed by water dissolving the rock, allowing water to flow down to underground streams.

Slum A deteriorating urban area, usually part of an inner city, characterized by poverty, overcrowding and dilapidated housing.

Smog A fog laden with smoke and other pollutants, usually found in industrial or densely populated urban areas, e.g. Los Angeles.

Snow line The lower limit of snow on a mountain. In summer the snow line will move up the mountain side, in winter it will be lower down.

Soil erosion The wearing away of top soil, mainly as a result of wind and rain action.

Sphere of influence The area surrounding a town, within which the town has major social and economic influence.

Squatter settlement (See *Shanty Town*).

Steppes The level, generally treeless plains of Eurasia, used, like the Prairies, for grain production.

Subsistence farming The type of farming in which the produce is used mainly by the farmer and his family and little is therefore sold, e.g. as practised by primitive groups in Malaysia.

Swallow hole (See *Sink Hole*).

Swash The forward movement of sea water up a beach after a wave has broken. (See *Backwash*).

Syncline A trough or inverted arch in rock strata. (See *Anticline*).

Taiga The coniferous forest zone of the northern CIS and Europe.

Terrace cultivation Terraces are steps cut on the slopes of hills, edged by mud walls to make platforms of flat, cultivable land which can be irrigated if necessary, e.g. the island of Bali.

Third World Another name for the less-developed countries of Africa, Asia and Central and South America.

Tor A body of rock standing up above a hill or undulating land surface. Granite tors are found on Dartmoor.

Tourism The industry which provides accommodation and other facilities for people travelling for pleasure.

Toxic chemicals Chemicals that are poisonous, such as sulphates and the soluble salts of copper, zinc and lead.

Transhumance The practice of moving herds between different regions to benefit from the best grasslands at different times of the year, e.g. as practised in the Alps with movement to the summer pastures in the mountains and then back to the valleys in the winter.

Transpiration The loss of water vapour from plants. Water drawn upwards from the roots passes out from minute pores (stomata) into the atmosphere.

Tsunami A sea wave generated by an underwater earthquake. The waves can travel across the oceans for considerable distances, reaching heights of tens of metres in shallow water. They can cause considerable danger to shipping and coastal regions.

Tundra The almost treeless plains of northern Canada, Alaska and Eurasia found mainly within the Arctic Circle and consisting of patches of lichens, bushes and some dwarf trees.

Urban field (See *Sphere of Influence*).

Urban renewal The regeneration of urban areas, especially inner city areas. It is designed to keep people and jobs in the inner city areas and to improve living conditions by replacing out-of-date housing.

Wadi A dry, usually steep-sided river valley in desert areas which can suddenly fill with water after a storm.

Warm front The boundary line between a mass of warm air and cooler air over which it rises. (See *Cold front*).

Warm sector The region of warmer air lying between the cold and warm fronts of a low pressure system.

Water (or hydrological) cycle The circulation of water from the oceans, rivers and lakes by evaporation into the atmosphere, where it condenses and falls as rain, so enabling the cycle to continue.

Water table The level under the ground which is saturated with water. This level will drop during dry weather and varies with the nature of the rocks.

Weathering The disintegration of rocks as a result of exposure to the atmosphere. Weathering is either mechanical (frost-thaw etc.) or chemical (by solution and chemical change).

Wind rose A diagram showing the proportion of winds blowing from different parts of the compass at a certain place over a period of time.

Zone in transition A zone on the edge of the CBD of mixed land use. Industry, commerce and poor housing are mixed together and are changing as business and other activities move outwards from the CBD.

INDEX

Africa
  hunger in 114–5
  Sahel 89
agriculture *see* farming
aid
  against soil erosion 118
  to developing areas 109–11
air photographs
  interpretation of 3, 9–10, 136
air pollution 121–2
Amazonia
  development of 96–8

Brazil
  development in 96–8
British Isles
  climate 20
  energy resources 24–7
  farming 20–4, 54
  industry 27–34, 50–3, 54
  National Parks 56–8
  population 38–40
  ports 36–8, 51–2
  self-test exercise 126–7
  tourism 54, 56–60
  urban geography 40–50

CAP (= Common Agricultural Policy) 62–3
central place theory 46–7
chalk 15–16
china clay 16–17
Christaller 46–7
cities *see* urban geography
climate
  British 20
  factors affecting 20
  monsoon 89–91
  savanna 88–9
  tropical 92
coastlines 11–13
  deposition 11–12
  erosion 12
  types of 12–13
communication patterns
  on maps 1
compass directions 1
conservation
  in National Parks 56–8, 116–7
  of resources 113–4
  of soil 117–20
coursework for GCSE examination vii, 160–4
crofting 54
cross-sections 1

Denmark
  farming 65
depopulation, rural 40, 54–5, 57, 81, 82–3, 105
deposition
  by glaciers 9–10
  by rivers 8
  by the sea 11–12
  by wind 14
deserts

desertification 89
scenery 13–15
developing countries 85–111
  aid to 109–11
  characteristics of 85–8
  industrialization in 101–3
  monsoon lands 89–92
  savannas 88–9
  self-test exercise 128–9
  transport networks 99–101
  tropical rain forests 92–8
  urbanization 104–8
development gap 85
development plans
  multi-purpose schemes 103–4, 118–21
  S. Italy 80–1
development problems
  flood control 118–9
  general 85–8
  industrialization 101–2
  population growth 112–3
  savannas 89–91
  soil erosion 117–8
  S. Italy 80–1
  tourist industry 83–4, 109
  transport 99–101
  tropical rain forests 92–8
  urbanization 104–8
diagrams
  types used in examination 167
diseases 87–8, 115
drainage basins 8–9

earthquakes 18–19
EC (= European Community)
  agricultural policy 62–4
energy
  and pollution 123
  consumption, W. Europe 68
  consumption, world 113
  resources
    Britain 24–5
    France 68–70
    W. Germany 72
  sources 24–5, 113
erosion
  glaciers 9
  rivers 7–8
  sea 12
  soil 117–9
  water 14, 117–8
  wind 13–14, 118
Europe, Western
  energy 68–70
  farming 62–5
  industry 70–5
  land reclamation 66–8
  population 61–2
  self-test exercise 127–8
examination
  boards xv
  general introduction to vii–xiv

174

popular myths   162–3
revision for   viii–ix
skills needed   164
syllabuses   vii
examination questions   132–8
answering practice   vii, 139–159
direct and indirect   137
multi-part   134
objective tests   134
Ordnance Survey   134–5
skills needed   167
structured   133–4
expanded towns
in Britain   40–2
extrusions   18

farm size
in W. Europe   63
farming
Britain   20–4, 54
Denmark   65
Green Revolution   98–9
India   91–2
monsoon areas   89–92
pollution from   122–3
tropics   93–9
W. Europe   62–65, 80, 83
fieldwork for GCSE examination   vii, 160–4
fjords   13, 82
flood control   118–9
forests
tropical   92–8, 113
fragmentation
in W. Europe   63–4
France
energy resources   68–70
fronts   4–6

Germany, West
energy resources   72
gastarbeiter   73–4
industrial regions   73
GCSE examination *see* examination
glaciation   9–11
highland   9
lowland   9–10
GNP (= Gross National Product)   85
gorges   8, 15
granite   16–17
Green Revolution   98–9
growth poles
in S. Italy   81

hierarchy of streams   8–9
high pressure systems   5
holiday industry *see* tourism
hunger
Africa   114–5
world   86–8
hydrological cycle   7–11

immigration   40
India
farming   91–2
multi-purpose development   103–4
industrial location
centralization   33–4
decentralization   33, 34

factors affecting   27–9, 32–4, 71
inertia   71–2, 72
industrial regions
heavy industrial triangle   70–2
in W. Germany   73
London basin   50–2
M4 corridor   32
North-east England   31–2
S. Wales   52–3
industrialization
in developing areas   101–3
industries
coal   52–3, 70–1
declining   31, 53, 71
footloose   72
growing   32
iron and steel   29–31, 52, 70–1
manufacturing   29–31, 50–1
pollution from   123
service   33, 74–5
tourism   11, 13, 54, 56–60, 81–4
infrastructure   52–3, 81
intrusions   18
irrigation   90–1, 103–4, 119–21
Italy, S.
development   80–1
farming   64

labour supply
in W. Germany   73–4
land reclamation
in the Netherlands   66–8
land use conflicts
general   115–7
National Parks   57–8, 116–7
Randstad   80
latifundia   64
less-developed countries *see* developing countries
life expectancy   88
limestone   15–16
low pressure systems   4–6

Malaysia
forest products   95–6
map interpretation   164
landscape types   7–19
OS 1:50 000   1–3
OS 1:25 000   3
self-test exercise   125–6
techniques   1–3
weather maps   4–5
maps
sketch   2, 135
Ordnance Survey   1–3, 134–5
topological   35
types used in examination   164
weather   4–5, 135
Mediterranean region
tourism   83–4
migration   39–40, 81, 104–8
models
industrialization   101–2
push-pull   40, 105
transport network evolution   99–101
underdevelopment   85–6
urban   42–4
monsoon   89–91
multi-purpose development schemes   103–4

Index

National Parks 56–8, 116–7
natural resources 113–4
Netherlands
   land reclamation 66–8
   planning problems 80
networks
   transport 35–6, 99–101
   waterways, in W. Europe 75–7
newspaper material 137
new towns
   in Britain 40–2
Norway
   rural depopulation 82–3

oil industry
   North Sea 25–7
Ordnance Survey maps 1–3, 134–5

Parks, National, Country and Forest 56–8, 116–7
photographs 3, 9–10, 136–7
plantation agriculture 94–6
plates, crustal 17–19
pollution
   air 106–8, 121–2
   water 9, 83, 122–3
population
   change 39–40, 54–5, 62, 81, 82, 105
   density 61–2
   distribution 38–9, 62
   growth, world 112–3
ports 36–8, 77–8
   in developing areas 99–101
poverty, world 86–8
push-pull model 40

rainfall
   acid 121–2
   in deserts 14
   types 6
resources
   conservation of 113–4
   natural 113–4
Rhine valley
   waterway 76–7
rice-growing 91–2
rivers 7–9

savanna lands 88–92
self-tests 125–131
   British Isles 126–7
   developing world 128–9
   environmental issues 129–30
   map work 125–6
   social issues 129–30
   W. Europe 127–8
shanty towns 105–8
shifting cultivation 93–4
sketch maps 2, 135
smog 6, 122
soil erosion 117–9
spheres of influence, urban 44–6
Sri Lanka
   food exports from 91–2
steel industry 29–31, 103–4
Switzerland
   service industries 74–5

systems
   definition of 20
   farm 21–2
   farming 20–1
   hydrological 7–9

Tanzania
   tourist industry 109
Third World *see* developing countries
tors 16
tourism 59–60
   and National Parks 56–8
   coastal 13
   glaciated highlands 11, 54
   Italy 81
   Mediterranean area 83–4
   Norway 82–3
   savanna 89
   Tanzania 108–9
trade
   and developing world 94–6, 99–102
traffic
   in cities 48–9, 123–4
transport networks 35–6
   in Norway 82
   in W. Europe 75–7
   waterways
transport of material
   by rivers 8
tropical rainforests 92–8
tsunamis 19

underdevelopment model 85–6
urban geography 40–50
   central place theory 46–7
   expanded towns 40–2
   green belts 49–50
   land use change 44
   land use models 42–4
   new towns 40–2
   planning 47
   pollution from sewage 123
   renewal 47–9, 79, 80
   rural-urban fringe 49–50, 80
   traffic problems 48–9, 123–4
   urban fields 44–6
   urban problems 47–9, 79, 80
   urbanization 104–8

vegetation
   forests 113
   savanna 88–9
   tropical rain forest 92–3
vulcanicity 18

water circulation system 7–9
waterways
   in W. Europe 75–7
weather 4–7
   maps 4–5
   station 6
   symbols 4
weathering, chemical 15, 16
West Germany *see* Germany, West
Western Europe *see* Europe, Western